SLEIGHT OF MOUTH
VOLUME II
How Words Change Worlds

Robert B. Dilts

Design: Keith Sarver, Gerardo Gomez
and Antonio Meza

Illustrations: Antonio Meza

Dilts Strategy Group

P. O. Box 67448

Scotts Valley CA 95067

USA

Phone: (831) 438-8314

E-Mail. info@diltstrategygroup.com

Homepage: http://www.diltstrategygroup.com

Copyright © 2023 by Robert Dilts and Dilts Strategy Group. All rights reserved. This book or parts thereof may not be reproduced in any form without written permission of the Publisher.

Library of Congress Control Number: 2023923290

I.S.B.N. 978-1-947629-48-6

Table of Contents

Dedication — XII
Acknowledgments — XIII
Preface — XV

  The Fabric of Reality — XV
    David Hume's Three Fundamental Assumptions — XV
    The Foundations of Illusion — XVII
  Francis Bacon's Four "Idols" of Civilization — XVIII
    The Idols of the Tribe — XVIII
    The Idols of the Den — XXI
    The Idols of the Market Place — XXIII
    The Idols of the Theater — XXVII
  Words Create Worlds — XXVIII

1- Introduction and Background — 1

Levels of Change — 2
Beliefs — 4
Beliefs and the Nervous System — 5
The Power of Beliefs — 6
Beliefs and Subjective Experience — 7
Limiting Beliefs — 9
"Groundless" Reality — 10
Thought Viruses — 12
The Structure of Belief — 13
Applying Sleight of Mouth — 16

2 - Principles of Sleight of Mouth — 17

Energy Follows Attention — 18
Words Direct Attention — 18
Language Frames and "Reframes" our Experience — 19
Outcome Frame Versus Problem Frame — 19
The Power of the Outcome Frame — 21

Table of Contents

Holons and Holarchies	22
Languaging Levels of Change	24
Filtering Negative Identity Judgments	26
Balancing Ego and Soul	26
Resonance	27
Resonance and Persuasion	28
Rapport	29
Pacing and Leading	29
Second Position	31
Summary	32
3 - Skills of Sleight of Mouth	**33**
Persuasion	34
CRASH versus COACH States	35
Moving from CRASH to COACH	36
Developing Emotional Intelligence	36
Taking Meta Position	39
Engaging Multiple Intelligences	40
Summary: Basic Steps for Using Sleight of Mouth to Transform a Limiting Belief	42
4 - Intent	**43**
Limiting Beliefs Frequently Assume Negative Intent	46
"Towards" Versus "Away From" Intentions	47
The Principle of Positive Intention	49
Applying the Sleight of Mouth Pattern of Intent	49
Flipping Intentions from "Away From" to "Toward"	51
Skillfully Using the Pattern	52
An Example of Applying the Sleight of Mouth Pattern of Intent	54
Reflections on the Example	56

Table of Contents

5 - Redefine   57
One-word Reframing   59
Proper Naming   61
Applying the Sleight of Mouth Pattern of Redefine   62
Creative Uses of the Sleight of Mouth Pattern of Redefine   66
Redefining as a Mindset   68

6 - Consequence   71
Identifying Consequences Involves a Particular Mindset   73
Chains of Consequences   73
Evaluating Chains of Consequences   75
Leveraging Positive Consequences   76
Applying the Sleight of Mouth Pattern of Consequence   78
Exploring Different Levels of Consequences   80
Reflections on the Case   82

7 - Another Outcome   85
The Connection between Outcomes and Intentions   87
Strategies for Exploring Other Relevant Outcomes   88
Shifting from Problem Frame to Outcome Frame   89
Meta Outcomes   89
Applying the Sleight of Mouth Pattern of Intention   90
Summary and Reflections   94

8 - Chunk Down   95
Examples of Applying Chunk Down   97
George Washington and the Cherry Tree – A Retelling   99
Applying the Sleight of Mouth Pattern of Chunk Down   102
Reflections on Chunking Down   108

Table of Contents

9 - Chunk Up — 109

The Danger of Overgeneralizing — 112
Applying the Sleight of Mouth Pattern of Chunk Up — 113
Creatively Applying the Sleight of Mouth Pattern of Chunk Up — 120
Reflections on Chunking Up — 121

10 - Analogy — 123

Chunking Laterally and "Abductive" Thinking — 126
Applying the Sleight of Mouth Pattern of Analogy — 130
Examples of the Sleight of Mouth Pattern of Analogy — 131
The Creative Use of Analogy — 137

11 - Counter Example — 139

Adding Nuance and Flexibility to a Generalization through Counter Examples — 141
Challenging the Validity of a Generalization with Counter Examples — 142
Eliciting Resources by Identifying Counter Examples — 144
Applying the Sleight of Mouth Pattern of Counter Example Using Questions — 144
Applying the Sleight of Mouth Pattern of Counter Example Using Statements — 147
Reflections on Counter Examples — 150

12 - Hierarchy of Criteria — 151

Dynamics and Dilemmas of Hierarchies of Criteria — 153
A Hierarchy of Criteria Creates a Consistent Path to Action — 156
Applying the Sleight of Mouth Pattern of Hierarchy of Criteria — 158
A Creative Example of Using the Sleight of Mouth Pattern of Hierarchy of Criteria — 162
Reflections on Hierarchy of Criteria — 164

Table of Contents

13 - Apply to Self — 165

Testing the Validity of a Generalization with the Sleight of Mouth Pattern of Apply to Self — 169
Applying the Sleight of Mouth Pattern of Apply to Self — 171
Reflections on Apply to Self — 176
Leveraging a Belief to Change Itself — 176
Reflections on the Example — 178

14 - Change Frame Size — 179

The Relationship between Changing Frame Size and Chunking — 182
Frames can be Created by Establishing Reference Points — 183
Changing Frame Size Shifts the Context in which Something is Perceived — 183
Applying the Sleight of Mouth Pattern of Change Frame Size — 184
A Creative Example of Applying the Sleight of Mouth Pattern of Changing Frame Size — 190

15 - Model of the World — 193

Applying the Sleight of Mouth Pattern of Model of the World — 196
A Creative Example of Applying the Sleight of Mouth Pattern of Model of the World — 199

16 - Reality Strategy — 201

Reality Strategies and Confirmation Bias — 204
Applying the Sleight of Mouth Pattern of Reality Strategy — 205
A Creative Application of Reality Strategy — 210
Reflections on Reality Strategies — 211

Table ot Contents

17 - Meta Frame — 213

The Difference between Meta Frame, Apply to Self and Change Frame Size — 216
A Meta Frame Determines How a Particular Experience is Perceived, Interpreted, and Evaluated — 217
Applying the Sleight of Mouth Pattern of Meta Frame — 218
A Creative Example of Meta Framing — 222
Reflections on Meta Frames — 224

18 - Strategies for Using Sleight of Mouth — 225

Chains of Meaning — 226
Chains of Causes — 228
Comparisons — 231
Polya Patterns — 211
Polya's Patterns of Plausible Inference — 231
  1. Meta Pattern: Probability — 232
  2. Verification of a Consequence — 233
  3. Verification of a Contingency — 234
  4. Inference from Analogy — 234
  5. Disprove the Converse — 235
  6. Comparison with Random — 235
Using Polya Patterns to Introduce Doubt — 235
Polya Pattern Worksheet — 237

Table of Contents

19 - Examples of Applying Sleight of Mouth 239

Sleight of Mouth and "The Socratic Method"
 - Unpacking Beliefs and Assumptions 240

Reflections on Socrates' Dialogue with Polemarchus and the
 Socratic Method 250

Applying Socrates' Sleight of Mouth Strategy 253

Sleight of Mouth and Transforming "Thought Viruses" 259

Abraham Lincoln's Use of Sleight of Mouth to Invalidate
 Pro-Slavery Theology 260

Reflections on Lincoln's Sleight of Mouth Strategy 263

William Shakespeare's Mark Antony – Using Sleight of Mouth to
 Flip Perceptions of Reality 266

Reflections on Mark Antony's Sleight of Mouth Strategy 274

Summary of Mark Antony's Sleight of Mouth Strategy 276

Applying Mark Antony's Sleight of Mouth Strategy to
 Flip Perceptions of Reality 279

William Shakespeare's *Henry V* – The Power of "Outframing"
 with Sleight of Mouth to Inspire Fervent Motivation 285

Reflections on Henry's St. Crispian's Day Speech 289

Dwight Eisenhower's D-Day Message to his Troops on June 6, 1944
 – Pre-Framing a Deeper Connection to Create Confidence 292

Reflections on Eisenhower's D-Day Message 296

Gandhi on Passive Resistance and the "Soul Force"
 – Connecting Beyond Individual Identity 301

Reflections on Gandhi's Sleight of Mouth Strategy 307

Sleight of Mouth and Strategies of Genius 311

Review and Examples of Some Key Strategies for Using
 Sleight of Mouth 316

Table of Contents

20 · Conclusion — 319
Detecting Thought Viruses — 320
Strategies of Genius Promote a Useful Mindset for Ecologically Applying Sleight of Mouth — 324
Oprah Winfrey: Sleight of Mouth and the Power of Purpose — 326
- The Path — 327
- The Seeds — 327
- The Roots — 238
- The Road — 328
- The Climb — 330

Overview of Oprah Winfrey's Use of Sleight of Mouth — 332
Final Reflections — 334

Afterword — 336

Appendix: Biographies of Key Sleight of Mouth Models — 337

References and Bibliography — 341

About the Author — 343

Dedication

.This book is dedicated to all of those through the decades who have shared with me the mission to explore and apply the power and magic of language in order to help create a world to which people want to belong.

Acknowledgments

I would like to acknowledge:

Antonio Meza for his innovative illustrations, which help to bring the principles underlying the Sleight of Mouth patterns to life with both artistry and humor.

Keith Sarver and Gerardo Gomez for their contribution to the design and layout of these pages.

Doug O'Brien for his passion for the subject and for his valuable input as I was preparing material for this book.

My brother Michael Dilts who sparked my interest in language and has been an ongoing support to me on my personal and professional journey,.

Preface

It has been almost 25 years since the publication of the first volume of *Sleight of Mouth*. Much has changed in the world since then, including an explosion of new technologies and the birth of new generations (X, Y, Z, etc.). And yet, the way in which people build beliefs and use language to influence one another has remained essentially the same.

I have been planning and collecting material for a *Sleight of Mouth Volume 2* for more than two decades. I felt compelled to complete this volume at this time because it seems to me that we live more and more in a world where Sleight of Mouth necessarily forms the basis for people's decisions and actions. In the late 1990's the Internet and social media were not nearly the force in shaping people's opinions that they are today. Access to news and other information was much more limited. Today, we are bombarded with automated messages and "spam," fake news, conspiracy theories and extreme views of all types. As a result, the level of political rhetoric and social divisiveness has greatly increased in the past decades. The power of language to shape our world, for better of for worse, is stronger than ever.

Sleight of Mouth is about the power and the "magic" of language and, as always, there is both white magic and black magic. Magic of all types also has a structure; and that is what this book is about.

The Fabric of Reality

Of course, words themselves are "surface structures" that both reflect and influence deeper cognitive structures through which we create, update and change our inner maps and models of the world. In this preface, I want to present some of the key principles and patterns (the epistemology) that govern those deeper structures and that determine the effectiveness of the Sleight of Mouth patterns and interventions that I will be describing in the coming chapters.

David Hume's Three Fundamental Assumptions

We unavoidably build our maps of reality based on beliefs and assumptions. Even "science" is based on deeply held assumptions and beliefs that we make about our perceptions and measurements. Enlightenment era philosopher David Hume identified three of the fundamental assumptions through which we build our models of the external world.

1. The present and future will behave like the past.

2. We can observe cause and effect.

3. We can reason from effects that we perceive to the causes that produce those effects.

While these may seem to be irrefutable and common sense, they are still assumptions not facts, and can lead to fallacies and errors. In many areas of our lives, for instance, the present and future do not always necessarily behave like the past. Contexts and conditions evolve and transform. In the external physical world, things like technological advances, climate change and other global forces create conditions such that the same behavior no longer produces the same result it used to. On an individual level, as we age, learn and grow, our present and future responses to the same situation can diverge significantly from those of the past. It is important to keep in mind, as we build our maps of the world, that it is indeed an assumption that present and future will behave like the past, and that the past is not necessarily the best predictor of the future.

Similarly, Hume pointed out that we cannot directly observe *cause and effect*. All we can actually "observe" is *contiguity* – i.e., that something happens and that something else follows. We "infer" that the first thing has *caused* the second thing. He uses the example of a white billiard ball striking a red billiard ball. We see the white one hit the red one and the red one moves. We infer that the white one has "caused" the red one to move and that, if we see the white ball strike the red ball again, the same thing will happen. This makes sense, but it is not always accurate. For instance, if we substitute a hollow white ball that is the same size as the first one and send it at the same angle and speed at the red one, the white ball is more likely to bounce off the red one as opposed to causing the red one to move.

The deeper cause-effect principle, then, becomes about energy transfer. Transfer of energy related to mass is what "causes" the movement. And we cannot directly observe this transfer of energy, only its consequences.

The situation becomes more complex when dealing objects that have "collateral energy" (i.e., their own internal source of energy). The illustration of this, given by systems theorist Gregory Bateson, is that if you kick a soccer ball with a certain force in a certain direction, you can with some accuracy predict where it will end up. If you kick a dog with the same force and in the same direction, there is no way you can accurately determine where and how far the dog will go before it stops.

We observe a person say something to another person and that person begins to cry. We infer that the first person's words have "caused" the other to cry. Yet, in different circumstances, the same words spoken by the same person could lead to the other person laughing or becoming angry. What *causes* the reaction in the other person is something deeper that we cannot directly observe.

As Hume also maintained, observing a particular effect does not necessarily presuppose a certain cause. Seeing a dog running, for instance, does not necessarily mean that someone kicked it. There could be many other reasons. Similarly, seeing a dent in a car does not necessarily mean that the driver has been reckless. A person's cough or sneeze may not necessarily be caused by illness.

The Foundations of Illusion

Much of the time, we unconsciously operate from the types of assumptions that Hume has identified. When we do not question such assumptions, they can become the basis for fallacies and illusions. For example, we see the sharp edge of a knife touch a person's skin and then we see a red liquid emerging from where the knife has touched. We immediately infer that the knife has cut the skin and caused it to bleed. But there are other possibilities. These are precisely the types of inferences that magicians use to create illusions.

We see a woman getting into a long wooden box with holes at either end. We see her head emerge from the hole at the top of the box and her feet extending out of the hole at the bottom of the box. The magician saws the box into two pieces such that the woman's head is coming out of one piece and the feet out of the other. Aghast, we infer that the woman has been sawed in half like the box. Yet, the magician then puts the two pieces of the box back together, opens the lid and the woman emerges healthy and whole. The magician has leveraged our assumptions about cause and effect to create an illusion.

Similarly, we perceive a particular effect and assume that it must have been produced by a corresponding cause. We watch a witchdoctor pulling a mass of bloody tissue from the body of a person sick with cancer. We infer that the witchdoctor's hand must have somehow entered the person's body and removed the cancerous tumors. Later, we may discover that the "bloody tissues" are actually chicken guts that have been "hidden up the witchdoctor's sleeve."

The types of assumptions that create these illusions are precisely those that are both utilized and examined in the applications of Sleight of Mouth. In fact, around the time I was first formulating the various Sleight of Mouth patterns I learned to do a number of card tricks and several other types of "sleight of hand" illusions, like making a coin "disappear" and then "reappear." All of these tricks involve leveraging the types of assumptions that Hume described.

In addition to the ones identified by Hume, there are some other, generally unconscious, assumptions about reality and the relationship between "map" and "territory" that are at the foundation of the effective use of Sleight of Mouth. These are best summarized by Francis Bacon's four "idols" of civilization.

Francis Bacon's Four "Idols" of the Mind

In his classic work *Novum Organum* (1620), English essayist, lawyer, statesman, and philosopher, Francis Bacon identified another set of typically unquestioned assumptions that we make while building our maps of the world. He termed these assumptions "idols," implying that they were like objects of worship; accepted and adored, often blindly or excessively. Bacon organized these sets of assumptions into four successive levels, each of which built upon the previous level, using the metaphors of *the tribe, the cave, the marketplace* and *the theater*.

The Idols of the Tribe

Bacon's first group of "idols" were what he called the "idols of the tribe." As he described it:

> *The idols of the tribe are inherent in human nature and the very tribe or race of man; for man's sense is falsely asserted to be the standard of things; on the contrary, all the perceptions both of the senses and the mind bear reference to man and not to the universe, and the human mind resembles those uneven mirrors which impart their own properties to different objects, from which rays are emitted and distort and disfigure them.*

The idols of the tribe relate to the fact that, as human beings, we can never know reality directly. We have to experience reality through our sensory filters, and those filters are limited. We can only make maps of the reality around us through the information that we receive through our senses and through how we connect that information to our own personal memories and other experiences. Our sensory organs are filters in that they have a limited capacity to pick up information. A bee looking at this page would perceive it very differently than we do because the whole sensory organization of the bee's eyes are different.

The Universe is a massive bundle of energy and information, a quantum stew of vibration, particles, and waves. The way we experience this bundle of energy is through the filters of our senses and nervous systems. Our perception of the world begins as what psychology pioneer William James called a "humming-buzzing confusion" that we organize based on the structure of our own filtering mechanisms.

As human beings, we perceive about one billionth of the stimuli that occur around us. Possessing a unique nervous system is one way reality is filtered. Different species of animals, having different sensory modalities, experience reality in extraordinarily different ways. A honey bee sees reality through the lens of 20,000 separate eye-cell clusters. Each one responds either to a very specific wavelength of light or to certain chemicals floating in the air. As a result, the picture of the world processed by a bee's nervous system is inconceivable to us. A porpoise's brain is almost as large as a human one, but 80 percent is devoted to processing sound. Hearing to a porpoise is a kind of sonar, like a bat's, that brings back three-dimensional images closer to sight than sounds. A porpoise can hear how large a shark is and in what direction it is moving. A bat can hear which way an insect is buzzing through the air. And to see the world as a chameleon, whose right and left eyes rotate independently in their sockets, would be an adventure through a whole new reality even if the territory being explored was exactly the same.

Thus, we perceive only a portion of the world determined by our neurological and genetic limitations. Even our sense of touch is influenced by the distribution, location and type of nerves in the receiving surfaces. The fact that we can't see the molecules of a chair moving does not mean that they are not moving. We just do not have the apparatus to notice.

At the same time, our perceptual filters are what allow us to experience the universe in a unique and special way. Without the limitation of the eyes to experience a certain frequency of light, viewing a sunset or a rainbow would be impossible. Without the filter of our eardrums, the sweet sound of music would be impossible to hear. Filters are designed to take in useful information and leave out what we do not need.

English writer and philosopher Aldous Huxley referred to our brains as a great "reducing valve" preventing us from being overwhelmed by the potentially massive amounts of information present in the universe around us. Our perceptual abilities are what Huxley called "the doors of perception." It is easy for us to forget that the order and the structure that we perceive in the world is as much a reflection of our own nervous system and perceptual assumptions as it is information about "external reality." Consider the case of the pygmy who had never been outside of the forest canopy. He had never experienced seeing the horizon. His nervous system was built to register the relationship between the size of an object and its relative distance, but he had never before been in an environment in which he directly experienced that relationship. When the pygmy was brought out of the forest and shown the vast plains of the savanna, objects that were far away looked tiny to him. When buffalo appeared on the horizon, he asked, "What kind of bugs are those?" When he was told that they were buffalo he said, "You're lying."

We succumb to "the idol of the tribe" when we forget that our perceptions of the world are not the world, even what we consider to be the most immediate and concrete perceptions. Movies and animation, for instance, are based on fooling our perceptions. We see movement where there is none. A "moving picture" is not really moving, rather it is a number of individual still images. When there are enough images presented quickly enough, our eyes are no longer able to distinguish and register the separate pictures. So we think we "see" movement. Our entire perceptual world is based upon such illusions of the senses.

In a very real way, all reality is "virtual reality."

The "idols of the tribe" come from our belief that our perceptions are, in fact, accurate mirrors of reality, rather than "uneven mirrors which impart their own properties to different objects." As a result of this belief, we tend to ascribe more regularity to the world than is really there; a regularity that is produced by our own nervous systems. World renowned physicist Albert Einstein went so far to maintain, "Physical concepts are free creations of the human mind, and are not, however it may seem, determined by the external world." As he pointed out, "Time and space are not conditions in which we live, but modes by which we think." He claimed, "Time does not exist – we invented it. Time is what the clock says. The distinction between the past, present and future is only a stubbornly persistent illusion." Einstein even asserted, "Concerning matter, we have been all wrong. What we have called matter is energy, whose vibration has been so lowered as to be perceptible to the senses. Matter is spirit reduced to point of visibility. There is no matter."

According to Bacon, the "idol of the tribe" also creates "blind spots" and biases in which we think our way of perceiving is more "real" than others. There is a revealing story told about the groundbreaking artist Picasso in which he was riding on a train. The passenger sitting next to him, upon discovering who he was, told Picasso that, while he knew Picasso was famous, he had to admit that he really didn't appreciate Picasso's art. When Picasso asked why, the passenger replied that he liked realistic art that looked just like reality. Picasso asked the man what he meant by looking "just like" reality. Annoyed by the ridiculousness of Picasso's question, the passenger reached into his pocket and pulled out a photograph of his wife saying, "I mean like this. This picture looks exactly like my wife." With a twinkle in his eye Picasso said incredulously, "My but she's awfully small and flat!"

Our cognitive and perceptual filters reject some distortions but are oblivious to others. The idol of the tribe is clearly the deepest and most influential of all the idols. Until we are able to fully realize and understand that our perceptions are not in fact accurate "mirrors of reality," we won't even have the hope of recognizing and transcending the other idols.

The Idols of the Den/Cave

Bacon called the second type of idol "the idols of the den" or "the idols of the cave."

> *The idols of the den are those of each individual; for everybody (in addition to the errors common to the race of man) has his own individual den or cavern, which intercepts and corrupts the light of nature, either from his own peculiar and singular disposition, or from his education and intercourse with others, or from his reading, and the authority acquired by those whom he reverences and admires, or from the different impressions produced on the mind, as it happens to be preoccupied and predisposed, or equable and tranquil, and the like; so that the spirit of man (according to its several dispositions), is variable, confused, and, as it were, actuated by chance.*

The "idols of the den" result from generalizing one's own limited experience of the world and projecting it onto the rest of the world. It is easy for people to forget that their own personal experiences, education and culture are not shared by everyone else. Not everyone thinks the way we do, shares the same cultural background, or has learned what we have learned.

Our individual personal experiences and our unique personal history are filters which influence our perceptions of the world, and the way we choose to experience the world. Each of us has a personal history of our interaction with the living and non-living world around us. We build internal models and maps based upon our life experiences, many of which are unique to us. We each develop unique interests, habits, likes, dislikes, and rules of behavior. The actions and responses we choose to make at any given moment will reflect the learning we have acquired as a result of previous personal experiences.

A camera records an event by taking in light signals and filtering them into a literal image. Our filters are much more complex than that of a camera – we "perceive," which means that we add meaning to every signal coming our way. It does not matter to a camera if a bus is painted yellow, but when we see it, we infer that it is likely a school bus, children could be aboard and certain precautions must be taken. Perception is the first and most important step in turning the raw data of the universe into reality. Seeing the world is far from the passive act it appears to be, for when we look at something, we see it colored by our own set of unique experiences. If I am looking at a sunset and feel depressed, my mood seeps into the sunset, making the whole appearance of the scenery sad. If I am joyful, the same sunset reflects my joy back to me. This fusing of "me" and things "out there" is what makes the lens of perception magical. The "state" we are in is a major filter to how the world is represented to us. Just by listening, looking, smelling, tasting, and feeling, I can turn *the* world into *my* world.

As an example, there was a man who was growing older and becoming bald. The wispy thin hair on top of his head sometimes distressed the once-dashing young paramour. When he was in his late sixties, he resigned to wearing a wig. To try to cheer him up, the man's son invited him to a party where many distinguished guests would be present. The company was sparkling, and the older man seemed greatly impressed. "Weren't all those people fascinating?" the younger man asked his father. "Remarkable," the older gent replied, "and did you see how much hair they all had?"

All of us see the world just this subjectively. When we walk into a room, we see what is important to us, screening out what is indifferent. We give significance and meaning to our experience based on our own personal history. Psychoanalysis founder Freud's notion of "transference," in which we project onto authority figures the characteristics of our parents or significant others, is a good example of the idol of the den.

Cultural filters, which we begin to learn from birth, influence where we place our attention, how we describe the world, the patterns and relationships we learn, and what our culture/subculture emphasizes. In today's world of social media and increasingly virtual reality, this idol is greatly exaggerated by so called "filter bubbles" or "algorithmic editing," which display to individuals only information they have shown interest in and are likely to agree with, while excluding other views.

The idol of the den arises when we begin to think, "All intelligent people think and act like me/us." "My/Our values and ways of doing things are the 'right' ones. Our interpretations are better than theirs." The idols of the den cast their shadow when we begin to make judgments about people who are different from us, rather than embrace diversity and learn from it.

The Idol of the Marketplace

According to Bacon, a third type of idol emerges from the interaction of human beings with one another, rather than their interaction with nature.

> *There are also idols formed by the reciprocal intercourse and society of man with man, which we call idols of the market, from the commerce and association of men with each other; for men converse by means of language, but words are formed at the will of the generality, and there arises from a bad and unapt formation of words a wonderful obstruction to the mind. Nor can the definitions and explanations with which learned men are wont to guard and protect themselves in some instances afford a complete remedy; words still manifestly force the understanding, throw everything into confusion, and lead mankind into vain and innumerable controversies and fallacies.*

The idol of the marketplace relates to our assumptions about our verbal communication with others and is, in many ways, at the core of Sleight of Mouth. Language is a fundamental way that we make maps and descriptions of our experience and communicate that experience to others. According to Bacon, the idol of the marketplace emerges as a result of two fundamental assumptions we make with respect to language.

1) Words refer to real entities, and

2) People share the same interpretation of words

The belief that words refer to real entities is probably one of the most pervasive "idols" of humankind. Bacon's comment that "words are formed at the will of the generality" implies that the idols of the marketplace are most related to the filtering mechanism of generalization. A major problem with words is that they become "detached from the original experience" to which they refer and become isolated from the context in which they were established. As psychologist and researcher Julian Jaynes poignantly pointed out:

> *Because in our brief lives we catch so little of the vastness of history, we tend too much to think of language as being solid as a dictionary, with a granite-like permanence, rather than as the rampant sea of metaphor which it is.*

Anthropologist and early NLP influence Gregory Bateson liked to say that "the name is not the thing named." When we use words to describe experience, not only are the words themselves not the experience, but the experiences these words are describing may not actually be in the "real world."

Language is what is known in NLP as "secondary experience." It is a map of our perceptual and personal maps. In their book *The Structure of Magic*, NLP founders Bandler and Grinder asserted that language itself is a type of "meta model." It is a way that we make and share models of our perceptual and personal experiences. As such, language is a "map of a map" more than it is a "map of the territory." As Albert Einstein pointed out:

> *The first step towards language was to link acoustically or otherwise commutable signs to sense-impressions. Most likely all sociable animals have arrived at this primitive kind of communication – at least to a certain degree. . . In [this] early stage the words may correspond directly to impressions. At a later stage this direct connection is lost insofar as some words convey relations to perceptions only if used in connection with other words (for instance such words as: "is", "or," "thing"). Then word-groups rather than single words refer to perceptions. When language becomes thus partially independent from the background of impressions a greater inner coherence is gained.*
>
> *Only at this further development where frequent use is made of so-called abstract concepts, language becomes an instrument of reasoning in the true sense of the word... But it is also this development which turns language into a dangerous source of error and deception.*

What Einstein is claiming is that it is only when language becomes sufficiently disassociated (or generalized) from the sensory experience that it was initially designed to represent, can it become a tool for reasoning and creative thinking as opposed to a mere descriptive device. For instance, the sentence, "The man rode the horse," fits the grammatical rules of English and will most likely correspond to specific memories and impressions that most of us have had of observing a person on a horse. Sentences like, "The horse rode the man," or "The man rode the light beam," however, fit grammatical rules but require one to use creative imagination in order to "make sense" out of them. They stimulate us to go beyond the limits of our memory.

But language is a double edged sword – one edge allows us to create new models independent of the sensory content of our life experiences and to give a greater coherence and order to our experiences, but the other edge severs the all important connection between our conceptual maps and the sensory experience they are intended to organize. This leads to what Bacon referred to as a "wonderful obstruction to the mind." Wonderful in its ability to stimulate creativity, but obstructing in its tendency to "throw everything into confusion, and lead mankind into vain and innumerable controversies and fallacies."

In *The Structure of Magic Vol. I* Bandler and Grinder echo Bacon and Einstein's attitudes and concerns about the use of language when they write:

> *The most pervasive paradox of the human condition which we see is that the processes which allow us to survive, grow, change, and experience joy are the same processes which allow us to maintain an impoverished model of the world – our ability to manipulate symbols, that is, to create models. So the processes which allow us to accomplish the most extraordinary and unique human activities are the same processes which block our further growth if we commit the error of mistaking the model of the world for reality.*

It is the assumption that people share the same interpretation of words that creates many communication problems. There are many variations in the ways that people give meaning to the same words. If someone says, "Yesterday I had an accident," people will believe they "understand" what that person is saying. But what exactly was the "accident." The person may have stumbled down the stairs, tripped into somebody, cut a finger, been in an automobile accident, or even had a bowel movement. One can make sense out of a phrase such as that in many different ways. We "understand" the verbalization, "I had an accident," but we may each have different representations. To give new twist to an old saying, "A word is worth a thousand pictures."

This is because words are developed according to the placement of attention. For example, an Eskimo's number of words for snow are much more varied than that of an English speaker. [Contrast this with the extensive number of words Americans have for "money."] From this perspective, as Julian Jaynes points out, "language is an organ of perception, not simply a means of communication."

The idol of the marketplace comes, again, from confusing the map and the territory—from confusing "the name with the thing named"—and assuming that everyone else is using the same "name" for the same "thing." We listen to somebody say they "had an accident," or they are "in trouble" and we make sense of it for ourselves without really knowing the other person's representation for it. When we forget that not everyone shares the same representations for words, we fall prey to the idol of the market, and our chances of misunderstanding and miscommunication become dramatically increased.

The Idols of the Theater

Bacon's final class of idols were the "idols of the theater."

> *Lastly, there are idols which have crept into men's minds from the various dogmas of peculiar systems of philosophy, and also from the perverted rules of demonstration, and these we denominate idols of the theater: for we regard all the systems of philosophy hitherto received or imagined, as so many plays brought out and performed, creating fictitious and theatrical worlds. Nor do we speak only of the present systems, or of the philosophy and sects of the ancients, since numerous other plays of a similar nature can be still composed and made to agree with each other, the causes of the most opposite errors being generally the same. Nor, again, do we allude merely to general systems, but also to many elements and axioms of sciences which have become inveterate by tradition, implicit credence, and neglect.*

Bacon's "idols of the theater" refer to institutionalized ideas about reality, such as philosophical systems, political ideologies, social norms, religious dogmas and even scientific conventions. They relate to the fact that our perceptions are also filtered through social constraints such as traditions, rules and other social patterns. These are passed on through families, social groups, societies, and cultures just as readily as genetic factors. These filters result from being members of a social system and they include our cultural biases, our accepted ways of perceiving, and all socially agreed upon fictions.

Like the idols of the marketplace, the idols of the theater arise largely as a result of the interactions between humans and the creation of a consensual reality. These realities include definitions of gender differences and roles, sanity, acceptability, social significance, etc. The value of such social filters is that they help us to create and maintain a sense of stability, connectedness, safety and community. We feel that we share a common bond and identity with others by sharing the same filters. Through our social, political and religious beliefs, we have a sense of continuity over time. We feel connected to our forebearers and part of a group.

Yet, in many ways, it is the idols of the theater that change most through history. We reflect on the religious, social and political beliefs and biases of our ancestors or of other cultures and we find them strange and even laughable. In doing so, we ourselves can fall victim to the idols of the theater. The idols of the theater are a result of thinking, "Our religion or political system is the correct one." Or, "Their religion and political views are strange, wrong and even dangerous." In challenging the old idols, we often unknowingly set up new ones in their place.

While the idols of the theater can in some ways seem the most "entertaining" of Bacon's idols, they can also be the most deadly and pernicious. Wars, religious persecution and genocide are primarily the result of the idols of the theater. The "idols" of the theater manifest in the form of racism, cultism, prejudice, intolerance, and "witch hunts" directed towards those who do not fit with accepted conventions or who object to their assigned "role" in the "play."

The creation and performance of a play is a means of "nominalizing" experience. It captures a constantly transforming organic process and packages it as an event. The idols of the theater are even further disassociated from the territory than the other idols, because they are necessarily based on the other idols. Without language (the idol of the marketplace) there could be no theater. Without personal experience and education (the idol of the cave) there could be no language. Without our ability to create mental maps of the world (the idol of the tribe) there would be no culture or education.

One of the problems with nominalizing experiences is that they are perceived as no longer subject to feedback, change or growth. When a political, social, religious or scientific system becomes nominalized and fixed, it has fallen prey to the idol of the theater.

Words Create Worlds

Like Hume's assumptions, Bacon's "idols" are still very much part of our modern reality, and in some ways even more exaggerated by the Internet, social media and other "technological advances." As I will show in the coming chapters, Sleight of Mouth patterns and interventions can either leverage or challenge these assumptions and "idols" to achieve various types of outcomes.

In the Conclusion to the first volume of Sleight of Mouth I wrote:

> *In many respects, what this book presents is just the beginning of the potential applications of the Sleight of Mouth patterns. The Sleight of Mouth patterns form a powerful system of language patterns which can be applied to produce deep and far reaching changes. These patterns have been used throughout human history as the primary means for stimulating and directing social change and for evolving our collective models of the world. The next volume of Sleight of Mouth, for instance, will examine how historical figures (such as Socrates, Jesus, Lincoln, Gandhi, Einstein, and others) have applied Sleight of Mouth patterns to shape the religious, scientific, political and philosophical systems which form our modern world. It will explore how these individuals sought to address and "outframe" the thought viruses behind racism, violence, economic and political oppression, etc.*
>
> *Volume II of Sleight of Mouth will also define fundamental strategies for using groups and sequences of Sleight of Mouth patterns, and explore the structure of the belief or "convincer" strategies by which we form and assess belief systems (such as George Polya's patterns of "plausible inference").*

This is what I will do in the coming chapters. To accomplish this, I have organized the book into several sections.

1. I will begin by going over the background, principles and skills relating to the use of Sleight of Mouth.

2. I will then review each of the fourteen Sleight of Mouth patterns, providing the following for each of them:

    a. A definition of the pattern

    b. A core question that establishes the mindset associated with that pattern

    c. Examples of the pattern from well-known historical figures

    d. A joke or humorous anecdote that illustrates the pattern

    e. An example of how hypnotherapy pioneer Milton Erickson applied the pattern with his psychiatric patients

3. Next, I will present a number of strategies for applying the Sleight of Mouth patterns, emphasizing mathematician George Polya's Patterns of Plausible Inference.

4. Following that, I will then provide a number of examples from history illustrating how groups of Sleight of Mouth patterns have been applied in order to:

    - Unpack belief statements and examine assumptions
    - Challenge and transform limiting beliefs and thought viruses
    - Flip perceptions of reality
    - Inspire fervent motivation
    - Create confidence
    - Connect to something beyond individual identity

5. I will conclude by showing how various *patterns of genius* can be combined with the Sleight of Mouth patterns to engage the power of purpose.

    Throughout the book, I will also identify "red flags" that indicate potentially limiting beliefs and "thought viruses."

    Fundamental to the applications of Sleight of Mouth is the notion that words can create worlds. It is my wish that, through the deeper understanding of language and belief provided by this book, that we can learn to use words to ultimately create a world to which people want to belong.

    Robert Dilts
    Paris, France
    November, 2023

Chapter 1

Introduction and Background

Introduction and Background

Levels of Change

There is a very insightful quote, attributed to the Chinese philosopher Lao Tzu, that goes:

> Watch your thoughts, they become words.
> Watch your words, they become actions.
> Watch your actions, they become habits.
> Watch your habits, they become your character.
> Watch your character, it becomes your destiny.

A key implication of this quotation is that directing or changing our destiny begins with our thoughts and words. *Sleight of Mouth* is about how our thoughts and words can shape our actions, habits, character and ultimately our destiny.

The process of change is influenced by different levels of factors that can be organized into several distinct categories. The **environment** level involves the specific external conditions which we must respond to or utilize through our actions or behavior. **Behaviors** without any inner map, plan or strategy to guide them, however, are simply "knee-jerk" reflexes or reactions to the environment. At the level of **capability** we develop particular skills and strategies (i.e., *thoughts*) that enable us to select, alter and adapt our behaviors, given our goals and environmental conditions. At the level of **beliefs and values** we give meaning to our environment, behaviors and capabilities. Our beliefs and values determine our motivations and goals, and thus direct, encourage or inhibit the development or application of particular capabilities, plans or strategies (i.e., our *habits*). The level of **identity** consolidates and integrates collections of behaviors, capabilities, beliefs and values into a unified sense of self (our **character**). The level of **purpose** relates to the fact that our identity is part of a larger system that reaches beyond ourselves as individuals to our family, community, culture and ultimately our planet. Our participation in this bigger system is what ultimately determines our *destiny*. We can represent these levels as a type of pyramid with the following structure.

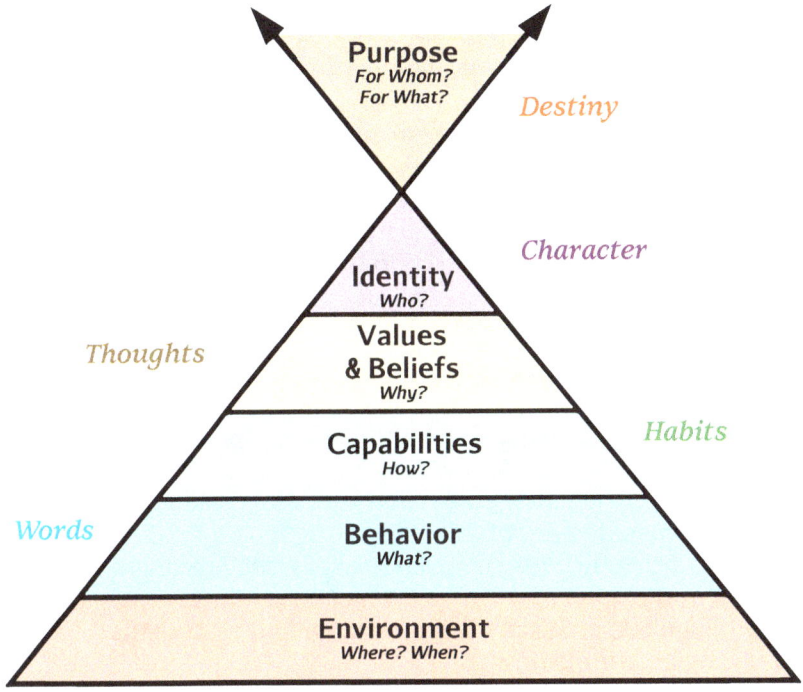

Levels of Change Pyramid

* *Environmental* factors determine the external opportunities or constraints to which a person has to respond. Answer to the questions **where?** and **when?**

* *Behavior* is made up of the specific actions or reactions made within the environment. Answer to the question **what?**

* *Capabilities* guide and give direction to behavioral actions through mental maps, plans or strategies. Answer to the question **how?**

* *Beliefs* and values provide the reinforcement (motivation and permission) that selects supports and directs the development or application of particular capabilities. Answer to the question **why?**

* *Identity* integrates belief and value systems into sense of role and self. Answer to the question **who?**

* *Purpose* comes from our place in the larger systems of which we are a part. Answer to the question **for whom** and **for what?**

As the diagram illustrates, Lao Tzu's reported quote presents an interesting parallel into the Levels of Change pyramid. *Actions* are our behaviors. *Habits* are built from capabilities and beliefs. *Character* is shaped by and integrates those habits into our identity. *Destiny* is the way our character becomes expressed in the larger systems that determine our purpose. Repeated behaviors form capabilities; capabilities reinforce certain beliefs; beliefs fashion the expression of identity; and identity determines purpose.

The process of change can also go from the top of the pyramid downwards, and often does. Shifts in our sense of purpose and identity create a reprioritization of our values and reevaluation of beliefs. Updated beliefs and values bring different capabilities into the foreground and push others into the background. This brings about a resulting change in behavior.

From the perspective of NLP and Sleight of Mouth, all of these levels can be influenced by, and expressed through, particular structures of thoughts and words. In fact, all of these levels are forms of "neurolinguistic programs." Thus, changing our thoughts and words can truly shape our destiny.

Beliefs

Sleight of Mouth patterns can be fundamentally characterized as "verbal reframes" which influence beliefs, and the mental maps from which beliefs have been formed. Beliefs play a powerful and important role in the Levels of Change pyramid. They are what connect our purpose and identity to our capabilities, our actions and our environment. Forming or shifting beliefs can have a dramatic affect both up and down the pyramid.

In fact, the term "Sleight of Mouth" is drawn from *Sleight of hand*, a type of magic done by card magicians. This form of magic is characterized by the experience, "now you see it, now you don't." A person may place an ace of spades at the top of the deck, for example, but, when the magician picks up the card, it has "transformed" into a queen of hearts or a Joker. The verbal patterns of Sleight of Mouth can produce a similar sort of "magical" quality by creating fundamental shifts in perception and the assumptions upon which particular perceptions are based.

Beliefs and the Nervous System

The thoughts and words that make up beliefs are created and processed by the nervous system. Thus, they can also alter and shape the way the nervous system functions. Core beliefs will involve the nervous system much more deeply than superficial thoughts (see *Sleight of Mouth I,* pp. 111-112).

Neurologically, beliefs are associated with the limbic system and hypothalamus in the midbrain. The limbic system has been linked to both emotion and long-term memory. While the limbic system is a more "primitive" structure than the cortex of the brain in many ways, it serves to integrate information from the cortex and to regulate the autonomic nervous system (which controls basic body functions such as heart rate, body temperature, pupil dilation, etc.). Because they are produced by deeper structures of the brain, beliefs produce changes in the fundamental physiological functions in the body and are responsible for many of our unconscious responses. In fact, one of the ways that we know that we really believe something is because it triggers physiological reactions; it makes our "heart pound," our "blood boil," or our "skin tingle" (all effects that we cannot typically produce consciously). This is how a polygraph device is able to detect whether or not a person is "lying." People show a different physical reaction when they believe what they are saying than when they are "just saying" it as a behavior (like an actor might recite a line), or when they are being untruthful or incongruent.

Experientially, there are three physiological centers typically associated with belief: the head, the heart and the gut.

1. The head is the center for reason and for planning.

2. The heart is more about passion, connection and compassion.

3. The gut tends to be more about our inner world, including intuition and often evaluation.

There are neurological reasons for this. For instance, it makes sense that reason and planning would be in the head because all of the so-called distance receptors are up in the head—the eyes, the ears, the nose and the mouth. Everything that connects us to the outer world tends to be up in the head. Neuroscientists are also continually learning more and more about all of the sophisticated networks of nerves around the heart and also the networks of nerves around the belly—what they call the "enteric nervous system." While the head links us to the outer world, the belly is more attuned to our inner world. The heart is in between the head and the gut. Thus, the heart tends to reflect the connection between our inner world and the outer world.

For thoughts and words to have power, they need to engage one or more of these key physiological centers.

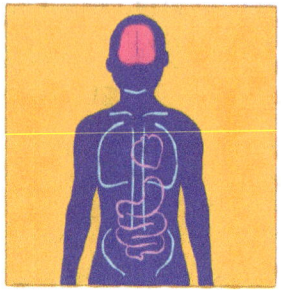 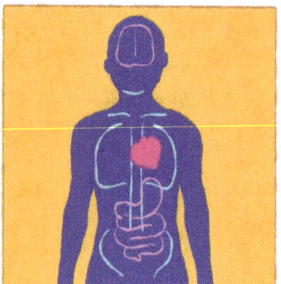 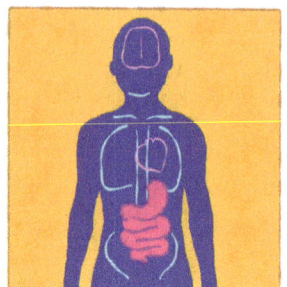

Head, Heart and Gut are the Three Main Physiological Centers Associated with Belief

The Power of Beliefs

It is the intimate connection between beliefs and deeper physiological functions that also creates the possibility for them to have such a powerful influence in the area of health and healing (as in the case of the placebo effect). Beliefs tend to have a self-organizing or "self-fulfilling" effect on our behavior at many levels, focusing attention in one area and filtering it out of others. A person who deeply believes he or she has an incurable illness will begin to organize his or her life and actions around that belief, making many subtle and often unconscious decisions, which reflect that belief. A person who deeply believes that his or her illness will be cured will make quite different decisions. And because expectations generated by our beliefs affect our deeper neurology, they can also produce dramatic physiological effects. This is illustrated by the example of the woman who adopted a baby, and because she believed that "mothers" were supposed to provide milk for their babies, actually began to lactate and produced enough milk to breast feed her adopted child!

The potential impact of beliefs on health was shown in a study of 100 cancer "survivors" (patients who had reversed their symptoms for over 10 years) who were interviewed about what they had done to achieve success. The interviews showed that no single treatment method stood out as being more effective than any other. Some had taken the standard medical treatment of chemotherapy and/or radiation, some had used a nutritional approach, others had followed a spiritual path, while others concentrated on a psychological approach. The only thing that was characteristic of the entire group was that they all believed that the approach they took would work for them. This reflects a process that is undoubtedly similar to the placebo effect.

The power of beliefs with respect to learning was demonstrated in an enlightening study in which a group of children who were tested to have average intelligence was divided at random into two equal groups. One of the groups was assigned to a teacher who was told that the children were "gifted." The other group was given to a teacher who was told that the children were "slow learners." A year later the two groups were retested for intelligence. Not surprisingly, the majority of the group that was arbitrarily identified as "gifted" scored higher than they had previously, while the majority of the group that was labeled "slow" scored lower! The teacher's beliefs about the students effected their ability to learn.

Another good example of the power of beliefs to both limit us and empower us is that of the 'four minute mile'. Before May 6, 1954, it was believed that four minutes was an unbreakable barrier to the speed with which a human being could run a mile. In the nine years prior to the historic day in which Roger Bannister broke the four-minute ceiling, no runners had even come close. Within six weeks after Bannister's feat, the Australian runner John Lundy lowered the record by another second. Within the next nine years nearly two hundred people had broken the once seemingly impenetrable barrier.

These examples demonstrate that our beliefs can influence or even determine our degree of health, intelligence and performance of all types.

Beliefs and Subjective Experience

There are a number of dimensions of our subjective experience that are influenced by our beliefs, and which are also involved in forming and sustaining our beliefs.

- Our **sensory experience** is what provides the raw materials from which we construct our maps of the world. Beliefs are typically generalizations drawn from the data of our past and present experience, and can be updated and corrected by new experience. As a generalization about our experience, beliefs necessarily delete and distort aspects of the experiences that they have been developed to represent. This gives beliefs the potential to limit us as easily as empower us.

- **Values** are what give our beliefs and experience meaning. They are the higher-level motivations which the belief has been established to support or reflect. Beliefs connect values to our experiences through statements of "cause-effect" and "equivalence."

- **Expectations** relate to the anticipated future consequences produced by beliefs. One of the most important functions of beliefs is to prepare us for the future by making predictions about what is likely to happen. The connection between language and imagination is part of what creates the self-fulfilling property of beliefs and gives them the power to shape our realities.

- Our **internal states** act as both filters upon our experience and the impetus for our actions. Our internal states are often the container or foundation supporting a particular belief or generalization, and determine the emotional energy invested in sustaining the belief.

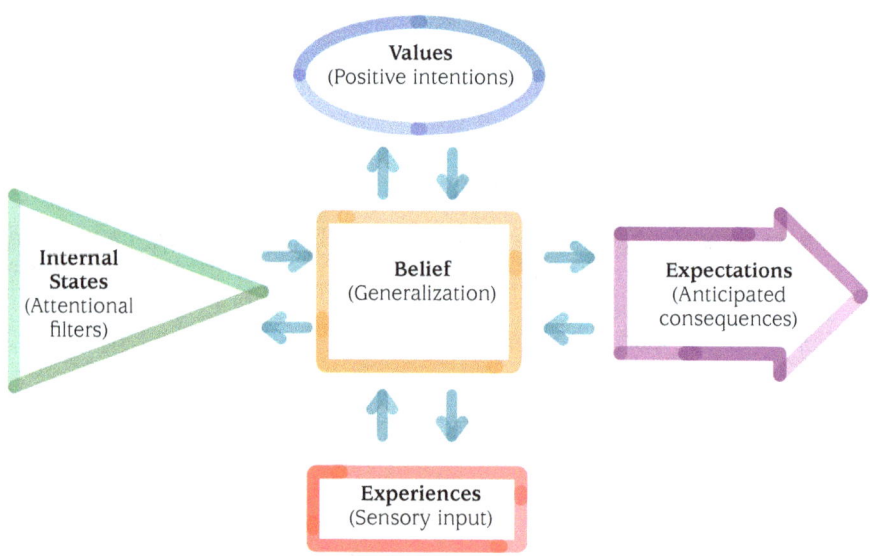

Our beliefs are generalizations which link together experiences, values, internal states, and expectations

Beliefs both create and reflect particular constellations of these four dimensions of our subjective experience. This is what I call the "Meta Structure" of beliefs (see *Sleight of Mouth I*, pp. 206-210.). Consider the example mentioned earlier of the person who deeply believes that his or her illness can be cured. The belief, "I can be cured," might link together key values associated with health—such as "accountability" and "self care"—with an internal state of "confidence," and the expectation that, "I will get better and better." These provide the motivation and impetus for the person to comply with his or her treatment, take good care of him/herself and focus on signs of improvement. Any indications of improvement reinforce the generalization "I can be cured" as well as the state of confidence, the expectation of improvement and the values of accountability and self-care. They form a type of "virtuous circle."

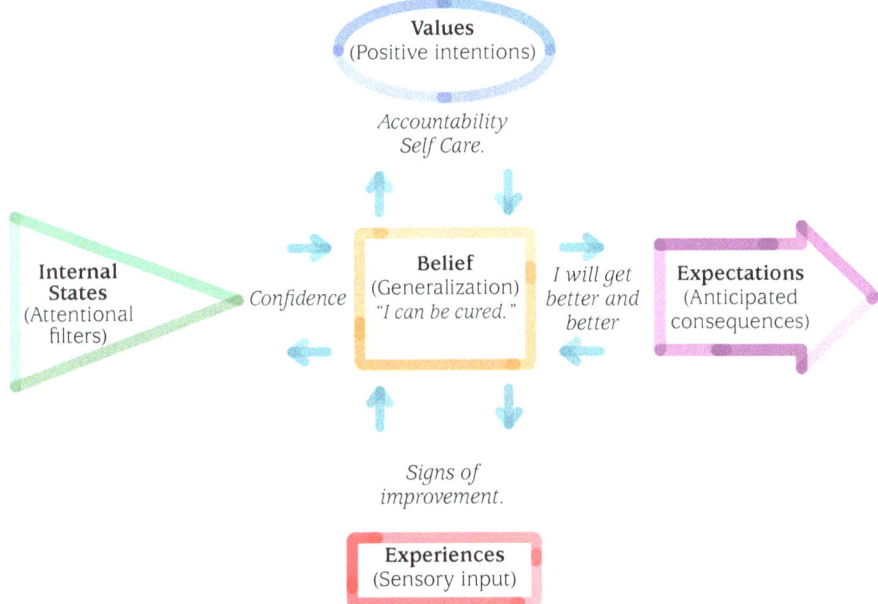

Beliefs both create and reflect particular constellations of the four experiential dimensions

Limiting Beliefs

A belief like "I have an incurable illness" will most likely develop a completely different constellation. Instead of an inner state of confidence, it is likely to produce apathy and the expectation that "I will get worse and worse." Rather than signs of improvement, the person is likely to focus on any indication that the illness is progressing. Values such as "avoiding disappointment" may emerge, making the person less likely to do or try things that might help. Instead of a virtuous circle, this constellation can produce a downward spiral.

To use the Sleight of Mouth patterns effectively, it is important to keep all of these dimensions of subjective experience in mind. In order for a belief to truly be updated and sustained, there will need to be some shift in each of these elements. Certain Sleight of Mouth patterns will influence some of these dimensions more than others; e.g., values versus expectations. Creating a shift in one of these facets of subjective experience can make it easier for others to adjust as well.

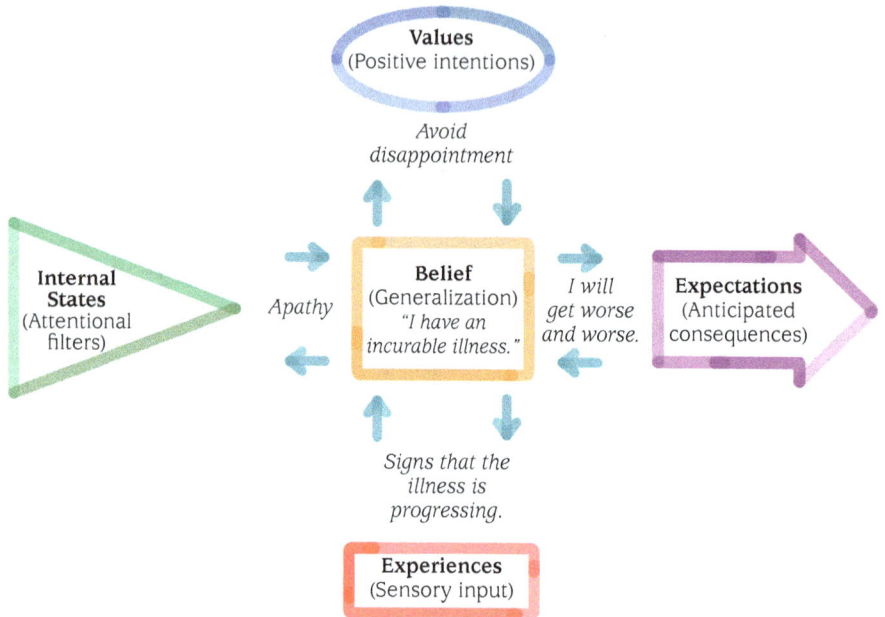

Beliefs both create and reflect particular constellations of the four experiential dimensions

Limiting beliefs can become more difficult to change when they are separated from the experiences, values, internal states and expectations with which they are linked. When this happens, the belief can become perceived as some type of disassociated "truth" about reality. This leads people to begin to view the belief as "the territory" rather than a particular "map," whose purpose is to help us effectively navigate our way through some portion of our experiential territory. This situation can become even further exaggerated when the limiting belief is not even one that we have formed from our own experiences, but which we have picked up from others.

"Groundless" Reality

It is an inescapable part of our human condition that we cannot derive our maps of reality completely from our ongoing sensory experience. There are many fundamental aspects of reality that are not directly perceivable through our five senses. We cannot directly see, for instance, that our planet is a globe. We infer that through observations of other planets and hypothesize that our planet is spherical. This creates expectations that we can then verify through other direct observations.

Unlike other animals, much of our reality is constructed from information (thoughts and words) that is not a part of our immediate sensory environment. This creates a great potential for creativity and flexibility, but also and equal potential for distortion and confusion. Belief in "God" and many other religious and political beliefs, for example, are not founded upon or verified by direct, measurable observation. The validations and proofs come from our inner subjective experience and the type of cognitive mechanisms that form the foundation of the Sleight of Mouth patterns.

We begin building much or our belief system when we are children, before we have had a lot of life experience to draw from. Instead, we rely on the experience, expectations and values of others. That is, we build beliefs on second hand experience. This has both advantages and disadvantages. It accelerates our ability to learn through the experience others, but it can also proliferate or exaggerate distortions, biases and outdated information. It can be important to have ways of recognizing and updating beliefs based on new experiences and changing conditions.

In today's world of social media, Photoshop, virtual reality, fake news, and the Metaverse, we are increasingly called upon to navigate territories that are neither tangible nor concrete. We must build and evaluate beliefs that cannot be connected to direct observation. This creates what is known as "groundless reality," which means a reality based on consensus alone.

Consider the surprising number of people who still vehemently argue that the world is flat. The main proof is that you cannot see the curvature through direct observation. Even when standing on the tallest mountain the horizon looks level, not curved. They argue that the photographs taken from space are "doctored" and a "hoax." They say that NASA (the U.S. space agency) even admits that those photographs are composites; that NASA is part of a conspiracy. They maintain that "NASA is a tool of the government and the people working there rely on their budgets, so they need to keep that money rolling in, which is why they keep churning out material that suggests the world is round." This type of language is the realm of Sleight of Mouth. And more than any other time in history, Sleight of Mouth is shaping people's belief systems. This is why it is crucial to be familiar with the patterns and have ways of evaluating whether they are being used in a useful and helpful manner or in a potentially harmful way.

It is important to keep in mind that, from the perspective of Sleight of Mouth, all beliefs are simply that; they are beliefs. They are part of the way we build our maps or models of the world. They are not the territory. They are not the actual world. The purpose of beliefs is to help us to navigate this territory. Therefore, any belief, no matter how far fetched or irrational it may seem, can be helpful or harmful. Even the same belief can be helpful in some contexts and not in others.

One of the goals of this book is to provide ways of being able to know when a Sleight of Mouth pattern is being used helpfully or potentially harmfully. The harmful use of Sleight of Mouth can create a type of limiting belief that I call a "thought virus."

Thought Viruses

In essence, a *thought virus* is a limiting belief that has become disconnected from the surrounding "meta structure" that provides the context and purpose of the belief, and determines its "ecology." (See *Sleight of Mouth I* pp. 211-220.) Unlike a typical limiting belief, which can be potentially updated or corrected as a result of natural changes in various aspects of our subjective experience, thought viruses are frequently based on other generalizations or beliefs (which are often other limiting beliefs). When this happens, the thought virus becomes its own self-validating "reality" instead of serving a larger ecology.

In other words, thought viruses are self-reinforcing limiting or damaging beliefs (to ourselves or others) built as a result of other people's thoughts, words and beliefs, rather than on our own personal subjective experience of the "territory." They are maps of maps and therefore not naturally corrected or adjusted by new experience. Many thought viruses are also unconscious.

Such thought viruses can "infect" one's mind and nervous system just as a physical virus can infect the body or a computer virus can infect a computer system leading to confusion and malfunctions. Just as the programming of a computer, or a whole system of computers, can be damaged by a "computer virus," our nervous systems may be capable of being "infected" and damaged by thought viruses.

Biologically, a virus is actually a little piece of genetic material. Our genetic code is our body's physical program. A virus is an incomplete chunk of programming. It enters into the cells of its "host," who, if not immune to the virus, unwittingly makes "a home" for it and even helps to reproduce and make more of the virus.

A computer virus is parallel to a biological virus in that it is not a whole and complete program. It has no "knowledge" of where it belongs in the computer, of which memory locations are safe or open for it; it has no notion of the computer's ecology. It has no perception of its identity with respect to the rest of the computer's programming. Its primary purpose is simply to keep reproducing itself and making more of itself. Because it does not recognize or respect the boundaries of other programs and data in the computer, it writes over them indiscriminately, wiping them out and replacing them with itself. This causes the computer to malfunction and make serious errors.

A thought virus is similar to these other types of viruses. It's not a complete, coherent idea that fits in with and organically supports a person's larger identity and purpose in a healthy way. It is a particular thought or belief that can create confusion or conflict. Limiting beliefs and thought viruses must be dealt with similarly to how the body deals with a physical virus or a computer deals with a computer virus – by recognizing the virus, becoming "immune" to it and not giving it a place in the system.

It is important to remember that a virus—biological, computer or mental—has no real intelligence or intention of its own with respect to the system it is in. A belief statement, for instance, is just a set of words, until it is given "life" through the values, internal states, expectations and experiences we connect to those words. Similarly, a biological virus is only harmful if the body allows it in and confuses the virus with itself. Infection by a virus is not mechanical and inevitable.

A computer "anti-virus" program, for instance, recognizes the virus code based on its structure and removes it. Similarly, in immunizing itself to a virus, the body's immune system becomes better at recognizing and clearly sorting out the different patterns in the genetic codes of viruses. It checks the virus' structure more thoroughly and deeply.

We can do the same type of thing with our own neuro-linguistic programming. One of the goals of this book is to provide ways to examine beliefs, detect those which are potentially harmful, and "reprogram" them to be more helpful. That is the positive use of Sleight of Mouth. In order to do that, it is necessary to take a closer look at the structure of those programs.

The Structure of Belief

Beliefs are typically expressed in the form of either a "complex equivalence" or "cause-effect" relating to an important value or criterion. Values are expressed by words such as "success," "safety," "love," "integrity," etc. These types of words are meaningful but can be notoriously vague. To gain practical meaning, values must be connected to experiences through beliefs. A typical belief statement links a particular value to some other part of our experience. The belief statement, "Success requires hard work," for instance, links the value "success" to a class of activity ("hard work"). The statement, "Success is mainly a matter of luck," connects the same value to a different class of activity. Depending upon which of these beliefs a person had, he or she would most likely adopt a different approach to attempting to reach success.

Complex equivalences are linguistic statements which imply "equivalences" between different aspects of our experience ("A = B," or "A means B"). This type of language pattern is typically used to make definitions of values and establish evidences for whether or not values have been met or violated. To say that "A resting heart rate of 60 beats per minute is healthy," or "Having a lot of money means you are successful," are examples of complex equivalences reflecting beliefs.

Cause-effect statements (characterized by words such as "cause," "make," "force," "leads to," "results in," etc.) link values causally to other aspects of our experience. Such linguistic structures are used to define the causes and consequences of particular values. Benjamin Franklin's classic adage, "Early to bed and early to rise *makes* a man healthy, wealthy and wise," is an assertion of causal factors leading to the achievement of certain values. The saying that "power corrupts" or "love heals" are statements relating to the consequences of values related to experiences.

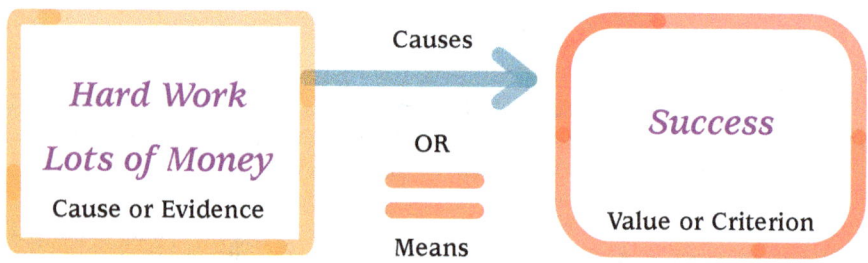

Beliefs are typically expressed in the form of either a complex equivalence or cause-effect

In the model of Sleight of Mouth, a complete "belief statement" must contain either a complex equivalence or cause-effect assertion. A verbalization such as, "People don't care about me," for instance, is not yet a full "belief statement." It is a generalization related to the value of "caring"; but does not yet reveal the beliefs associated with the generalization. To get the *beliefs* related to this generalization, one would need to ask questions like, "*How do you know* that people don't care about you?" "What *makes* people not care about you?" "What are the *consequences* of people not caring about you?" or "What does it *mean* that people don't care about you?"

Belief statements can also be elicited through "connective" words, such as "because," "whenever," "if," "after," "therefore," etc.—i.e., "People don't care about me *because*…" "People don't care about me *if*…" "People don't care about me, *therefore*…"

In the coming chapters of this book, we will use the following group of common types of limiting as examples to illustrate how to apply the various Sleight of Mouth patterns. (The example related to learning

Sleight of Mouth might of particular relevance to some readers.) As you can see, they all fit the fundamental belief structure identified earlier.

Some common types of limiting belief statements to be used as examples in this book.

Applying Sleight of Mouth

Sleight of Mouth patterns can be viewed as verbal operations that shift or reframe the various elements and linkages which make up the complex equivalences and cause-effects that form beliefs and belief statements. These patterns may be used to confirm or reinforce a belief, introduce doubt, sway opinions or incite action. When used properly to help change a limiting belief their goal is to create flexibility by:

- Adding a new or different legitimate perspective
- Expanding an existing perspective
- Seeing an old perspective from a new or different point of view

The purpose of Sleight of Mouth is not to attack or humiliate someone for having a limiting belief; rather, it is to help the person widen and enrich his or her map of the world in order to become "open to doubt" the limiting belief and "open to believe" something more empowering.

As I mentioned in *Sleight of Mouth I*, the patterns were initially identified by modeling well known people who had positively influenced the world or the course of history in some way through language – people like Aristotle, Plato's Socrates, Jesus, William Shakespeare, Abraham Lincoln, Sigmund Freud, Mohandes Gandhi, Martin Luther King Jr. and Milton H. Erickson (one of my own teachers and mentors). I have included brief biographies of some of the key models for Sleight of Mouth in Appendix A. I have also examined the language patterns of people who influenced the world in more negative ways (such as Adolf Hitler, conspiracy theorists and purveyors of "fake news") in order to understand and define how the patterns may be misused as well.

In the coming pages, I will be referencing examples from this modeling process as well in order to illustrate the patterns, show how they can be used and demonstrate their potential power.

Chapter 2
Principles of Sleight of Mouth

Principles of Sleight of Mouth

In order to understand and apply the Sleight of Mouth patterns effectively it is important to be aware of some basic principles that guide the ecological and successful use of the Sleight of Mouth patterns.

Energy Follows Attention

A primary principle for effectively using Sleight of Mouth is that "energy flows where attention goes." That is, energy follows attention. If I put my attention on writing (or reading) these words, that is primarily what my energy will be devoted to. If I shift my attention to what I want to write in the next chapter, my energy will follow that focus. If I bring my attention to looking for spelling or grammar mistakes in what I have already written, that will be the focus of my energy.

Attention can be very tightly focused or loosely focused. I can put my attention on the details of specific words or on big picture dreams and ideas. I can direct my attention to the past or the future, to myself or to others, to concrete objects or to open space. These will all influence the quality and level of energy that I engage.

Words Direct Attention – The Paradox of Negation

Language (both verbal and non-verbal) is one of the key ways that we direct attention. If I write or say, "Notice the letters in this sentence," your attention will likely (at least for a time) be drawn to the letters I am using to write these sentence. If I write or say, "There is a lot of white space on this page," your attention will most likely be drawn to that. Questions, of course, also direct attention, such as, "How many words are in this sentence?"

One interesting paradox of language is the use of negation. For instance, if I say, "*Don't* notice the letters in this paragraph," it is likely that your attention will actually be brought to the letters I am using to write the sentence. Similarly, if I write or say, "*Ignore* the white space on this page," you are likely to actually do the opposite and suddenly become aware of it. In this way, language can sometimes create a paradoxical affect. Something that sounds positive can create a negative affect (and vice versa). For example, saying, "Never doubt yourself," can actually bring up self-doubt.

The formulation of a particular belief statement determines where attention and (thus) energy will be directed. Shifting attention and energy is one of the main purposes of the various Sleight of Mouth patterns. This is the essence of "reframing."

Language Frames and "Reframes" our Experience

Words not only represent our experience, but frequently they "frame" our experience. Language frames our experience by bringing certain aspects of it into the foreground of our attention and leaving others in the background. *Frames* greatly influence the way that specific experiences and events are interpreted and responded to because of how they serve to "punctuate" those experiences and direct attention. A painful memory, for example, may loom as an all-consuming event when perceived within the short-term frame of the five minutes surrounding the event. That same painful experience may seem almost trivial when perceived against the background of one's lifetime. Looked at with the past in the foreground, a traumatic experience can seem like an unhealed wound. Viewed with the present and future foregrounded, it can be a life changing learning experience.

Reframing involves using language to shift our perception of an event in a way that brings potential resources, choices and possibilities into the foreground.

Outcome Frame Versus Problem Frame

One of the most important frames applied in the effective use of Sleight of Mouth is the "outcome frame." The basic emphasis of the *outcome frame* is on establishing and maintaining focus and attention on a goal or desired state. Establishing an outcome frame involves keeping a particular goal or desired state in the foreground, even when addressing obstacles and challenges.

An outcome frame stands in contrast with a "problem frame." A *problem frame* places the emphasis on "what is wrong" or what is "not wanted," as opposed to what is desired or "wanted." A problem frame leads to a focus on what is wrong or not working. In contrast, an outcome frame leads to a focus on desired outcomes and effects, and the resources required to attain them. Thus, an Outcome Frame involves staying solution focused and oriented toward positive possibilities in the future. A problem frame fixates on what is not working, why it won't work and whose fault it is.

Problem Frame	*Outcome Frame*

• What is to be avoided?	• What do you want?
• Why is it a problem?	• How can you get it?
• What caused it?	• What resources are available?
• Whose fault is it?	

A belief is stated in a "problem frame" is one of the first and most important indicators that it is likely to be or become a limiting belief or thought virus.

A key goal of Sleight of Mouth would be to "reframe" such a belief statement to bring the desired outcome into the foreground. From the perspective of Sleight of Mouth, all "problems" presuppose desired outcomes. If someone says, "My problem is that I am afraid of failure," it can be assumed that there is an implied goal to "Be confident that I am going to succeed." Similarly, if there is a problem such as "No matter what I do I will never get enough," it can be assumed that the outcome is to "Produce what I want and need through my actions."

People often unintentionally and unconsciously state their outcomes negatively, such as: "I want to avoid embarrassment," "I want to quit smoking," "I want to get rid of this obstacle," etc. Doing so places the focus of attention back onto the problem, and, paradoxically, reinforces it. Thinking, "I want to not be so afraid," actually carries the suggestion "be afraid" as part of the thought itself. Shifting to an outcome frame would involve considering, "What *do* you want?" or "If you were not so afraid, what would you be experiencing instead?"

The Power of the Outcome Frame

Martin Luther King, Jr.'s famous "I Have a Dream" speech is powerful example of the application of the outcome frame to create change.

> *I say to you today, my friends, that in spite of difficulties and frustrations of the moment I still have a dream. It is a dream deeply rooted in the American dream.*
>
> *I have a dream that one day this nation will rise up and live out the true meaning of its creed, "We hold these truths to be self-evident; that all men are created equal."*
>
> *I have a dream that one day on the red hills of Georgia the sons of former slaves and sons of former slave-owners will be able to sit down together at the table of brotherhood.*
>
> *I have a dream that one day even the state of Mississippi, a desert state sweltering with the heat of injustice and oppression, will be transformed into an oasis of freedom and justice.*
>
> *I have a dream that my four little children will one day live in a nation where they will not be judged by the color of their skin but by the content of their character.*

While King clearly names the "difficulties and frustrations" of injustice and oppression, he continually brings attention strongly back to the desired state of equality, brotherhood, freedom and justice. It is a powerful type of framing and reframing, and launched a significant social movement. In his speech, King goes on to say that, with that focus, "we will be able to work together, to pray together, to struggle together, to go to jail together, to stand up for freedom together, knowing that we will be free one day."

This illustrates the power of an outcome frame. Attention and energy are not taken up and absorbed by the obstacles and problems. It puts the difficulties that emerge in perspective and makes it worth the challenges struggles.

It is important to point out that King's language incorporates some other patterns that we will be exploring later on in this book – notably the use of analogies, such as "the table of brotherhood," "a desert state sweltering with the heat of injustice" and "an oasis of freedom." As we will see, this choice of words potentially activates the nervous system and evokes experiences far beyond the literal train of thought that King is presenting.

It is also significant that the outcome King is emphasizing is at the level of purpose. It is about the listener's place in the larger system of which they are a part – establishing *for whom* and *for what* attention and energy will be directed. It is notable that, at the end of the speech King says:

> *When we let freedom ring, when we let it ring from every village and every hamlet, from every state and every city, we will be able to speed up that day when all of God's children, black men and white men, Jews and Gentiles, Protestants and Catholics, will be able to join hands and sing in the words of the old Negro spiritual, "Free at last! Free at last! Thank God almighty, we are free at last!"*

Another important indicator that distinguishes between empowering beliefs and potentially limiting beliefs is the degree of inclusion and exclusion implied by the beliefs. King talks about "all of God's children." Hitler, on the other hand, only included "the Aryan race." Listening for divisive "us versus them" language is and important part of Sleight of Mouth "thought virus" detection.

Holons and Holarchies

This brings up another important principle of the effective use of Sleigh of Mouth related to the notions of "holons" and "holarchies." The term *holon* refers to entities that are in themselves whole while simultaneously being part of larger wholes and made up of smaller wholes. As human beings, for example, we are whole and independent individuals in and of ourselves. At the same time, we are also part of successively bigger systems that include but also transcend us. We are also made up of smaller wholes. Specifically, we are made up of whole atoms (which themselves are made of subatomic particles), that make up whole molecules, that combine to create whole cells, which join together to make whole organs and a whole interconnected nervous system from which our whole body is formed. We, in turn, are part of progressively larger wholes: a family, a professional community, the whole system of living creatures on this planet and ultimately the whole universe. This creates a type of *holarchy* made up of the different levels of wholes. Such holarchies also apply to our psychological make up as much as our physical reality.

An important principle of applying Sleight of Mouth is that any belief that focuses on benefiting one part of the holarchy to which we belong at the expense of another will be inherently problematic. Limiting beliefs and thought viruses tend to, either knowingly or unwittingly, exclude or even attempt to get rid of or destroy crucial parts of the holarchies to which they refer. This creates predictable and unavoidable problems. Learning to listen for and detect this type of language is an essential skill for the appropriate and ecological application of Sleight of Mouth.

We are part of progressively larger wholes: a family, a professional community, the whole system of living creatures on this planet and ultimately the whole universe.

Languaging Levels of Change

Even though, as we established in the previous chapter, Sleight of Mouth patterns operate at the level of belief, those beliefs can be about any other level. We can have beliefs about our environment, behavior, capabilities, identity or purpose. We can even have beliefs about beliefs. Beliefs about identity can be particularly impactful.

When reflecting on or formulating a particular belief statement, it is important to recognize the types of words that are likely to bring attention, and thus energy, to a particular level of change.

- Identity is associated with language like: "I am a...", "He/She is a...". "You are a..." or "They are..."
- Belief level language is often in the form of statements of judgments, rules, and cause effect, e.g., "if... then..." "you should..." "we have to..."
- The level of capabilities is indicated by word such as "know," "how," "I am able." "think," etc.
- Behavioral levels language refers to specific behaviors and observable actions, e.g., "do," "act," "walk," "say," etc.
- Language at the environmental level refers to specific observable features or details in one's external context, e.g., "white paper," "high walls," "large room," etc.

Consider the following groups of belief statements and how each one direct attention to different levels of change:

- Identity: *"You are a stupid/learning disabled person."*
- Belief: *"If you cannot spell well you cannot do well in school."*
- Capability: *"You are not very good at spelling."*
- Behavior: *"You did poorly on this particular test."*
- Environment: *"The noise in the room makes it difficult to take tests."*
- Identity: *"I am a healthy person."*
- Belief: *"If I am healthy I can help others."*
- Capability: *"I know how to influence my health."*
- Behavior: *"I take actions to improve my health regularly."*
- Environment: *"The medicine helped me to heal."*

It is important to add that language reflecting purpose and identity is often symbolic or metaphoric, e.g., "I am like a lighthouse," "He is a bitter person," "She is like the sunshine," etc. Paradoxically, people actually reveal less about themselves and their purpose by giving accurate sensory based descriptions than they do by speaking in symbols and analogies. For example, if I describe myself as a "Caucasian male who is wearing a black leather jacket, sitting in a wooden chair, typing at a lap top computer with recently trimmed finger nails, etc." I have revealed very little about "me" or my purpose. If, on the other hand, I describes myself as, "like a pioneer that likes to explore new territory and blaze trails for others to follow," I have made a description that is not "literally" accurate, but has said a lot more about who I am and what "makes me tick."

Attention can also be brought to different levels of change through non-verbal "meta messages." For example, consider the difference in the implications of the following messages:

> "***You*** *should not be doing that here.*"
> "*You* ***should not*** *be doing that here.*"
> "*You should not* ***be doing*** *that here.*"
> "*You should not be doing* ***that*** *here.*"
> "*You should not be doing that* ***here***.*"

The words in the sentences are exactly the same but, based on the placement of the italicized words (or voice inflection if spoken), the message takes on different implications relating to a particular level of emphasis: *You* (identity) *should not* (beliefs/values) *be doing* (capability) *that* (behavior) *here* (environment). These types of meta messages determine at which level the message is received and interpreted. For example, if an authority figure says, "***You*** weren't respecting the rules," this is much more likely to be taken as an identity message. If the same person says, "You weren't **respecting the rules**," then he or she is not emphasizing the individual identity so much as the level of behavior.

Filtering Negative Identity Judgments

Negative identity judgments, about oneself or others, are another major source and indicator of limiting beliefs and thought viruses. Such judgments are often the result of interpreting particular behaviors, or the lack of ability to produce certain behavioral results, as a statement about character or identity. Shifting a negative identity judgment to an outcome frame or back to a statement about a person's behavior or capabilities can greatly reduce the impact it has mentally and emotionally.

As an example, a person struggling with a serious illness might develop the identity belief "I am a victim." Notice that the statement is formulated in a problem frame and at an identity level. A helpful reframe could be to say, "It is important to get support so you can meet your symptoms with all of your resources." This shifts attention back to an outcome frame and moves it to levels of behavior and capability. This can help the person to shift his or her relationship to the illness, open up to other possibilities, and to view himself or herself as a participant in the healing process.

A similar type of reframe could be done with a statement like "I am a failure." A response could be, "I guess you have more to learn in order to master all of the elements necessary for success." Again, this puts the limiting identity level judgment back into a more proactive and solvable framework.

Balancing Ego and Soul

Our identity and sense of purpose can be viewed as being composed of two complementary aspects: what we could call our "ego" and our "soul." Our *ego* relates to the fact that we are a unique and separate whole in and of ourselves. Thus, our ego is oriented towards things like personal safety and security, approval, control, achievement and self-benefit. At the identity level, ego relates to our social roles and who we feel we should be or need to be in order to achieve those things. At the level of purpose our ego is oriented toward survival, recognition and our personal ambitions

Our *soul* relates to the complementary fact that we are simultaneously part of a larger holarchy. Our soul can be considered as the unique life force, essence, or energy that we come into the world with that is expressed outwardly to the holon we are part of. Thus, our soul is more focused on motivations such as service, contribution, connection, care and cooperation. At the identity level, soul relates to our mission and the unique gifts that we bring into the world. At the level of purpose,

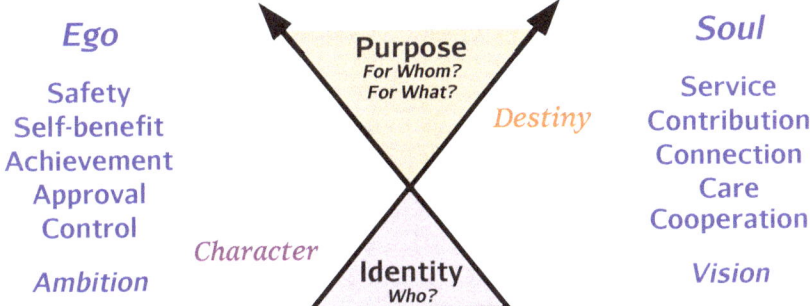

our soul is oriented toward our vision of what we want to create in the world through us but that is beyond us, as in Martin Luther King's "I Have a Dream" speech.

Supporting the balance between ego and soul is another crucial principle for the effective and ecological use of Sleight of Mouth. Some beliefs will emphasize ego at the sacrifice of the soul, creating isolation and narcissism. Others demean or even vilify the ego, leading to lack of self-care and burnout. It is important to realize that neither ego inflation nor deflation is sustainable or productive. Maintaining a healthy and dynamic balance between ego and soul, and identifying beliefs that threaten that, is key to applying the Sleight of Mouth patterns properly.

Resonance

As I pointed out in the previous chapter, beliefs are "neurolinguistic programs." Language is a key part of belief, but it is the "neuro" that gives the words their power. The effectiveness and success of any Sleight of Mouth intervention will depend upon the degree of resonance it produces in the nervous system – especially in the three belief centers of head, heart and gut. You can say what you think is the most creative and clever thing, but if it produces no resonance in the listener (or in yourself) it will be "just words."

Derived from the Latin *resonantia*, meaning "echo" or literally "re-sound," *resonance* refers to a type of mutual influence between systems or objects that are specially attuned to one another. For example, if one has two guitars that are similarly tuned and plucks a string on one of the guitars, the corresponding string on the other guitar will begin to vibrate without being physically touched. The same kind of resonance can occur between corresponding notes on a piano, tuning forks, etc. It can even occur between different instruments.

I have a video that I like to show about resonance in which different types of horns are blown near an open piano, such that you can see and hear the piano strings. Blowing a horn produces a sound that causes different piano strings to vibrate. Even after the sound created by the horn stops, you can hear the resonance in the piano strings. There is no direct physical contact between the horn and the piano, other than the vibrations carried in the air.

This is good analogy to what I mean by resonance with respect to Sleight of Mouth. The words that we use are like the different horns. Our nervous system is like the piano strings. Different words will produce resonance with different strings. Some produce greater resonance with more strings. Others create little to no resonance. We feel the impact of some words only in the head for instance. Others will touch our heart or gut, or give us "goose bumps" on our skin.

Resonance and Persuasion

The great Greek philosopher Aristotle identified three basic means of persuasion:

1. the appeal to reason (*logos*),

2. the appeal to emotion (*pathos*)

3. the appeal of the speaker's character (*ethos*).

From the perspective if Sleight of Mouth, "reason" (or "logos") would be at the level of *mental capability*; "pathos" or emotion is generally at the level of *values*; and "character" is at the level of *identity*. All three levels are important for the effective use of Sleight of Mouth. Resonance at the identity level becomes especially significant when there is little actual information or data available to support a particular belief. As Aristotle points out:

> *Persuasion is achieved by the speaker's personal character when the speech is so spoken as to make us think the speaker credible. We believe good people more fully and more readily than others: this is true generally whatever the question is, and absolutely true where exact certainty is impossible and opinions are divided.*

When we use Sleight of Mouth patterns, our goal is to be persuasive as opposed to combative, which produces dissonance. Psychologically, the term resonance is used to refer to "the complex of internal body processes that occur in emotional states such as rapport or empathy." Thus, the degree of resonance a person will experience with respect to our spoken words will likely increase when we have good rapport with that person. Rapport is a way of strengthening what Aristotle called "ethos."

Rapport

People generally experience more rapport with people who share similar feelings and ideas. Incorporating key words commonly used by a particular individual is a way of creating a sense of similarity and thus enhancing rapport. Mirroring their non-verbal communication can also greatly enhance their experience of rapport, because they will perceive you as being "like them". Some ways to non-verbally pace or mirror people include putting yourself into a similar body posture, using similar intonation patterns and expressions, etc.

When people interact and begin to naturally establish rapport with one another, frequently there is a matching of certain behaviors that starts to occur. They will begin to sit in a similar posture, speak at a similar rate and in a similar tone, and even take on similar gestures. This is a process called "pacing" in NLP.

Pacing and Leading

Pacing is the process of observing and feeding back key verbal and non-verbal cues from another person, in order to strengthen resonance and rapport. It involves having the flexibility to pick up and incorporate other people's vocabulary and behavior into one's own vocabulary and actions.

For instance, one way to develop rapport is by listening to the kinds of language patterns a person uses and then doing a type of "active listening" by matching some of their words. So if somebody says, "I *feel* that we need to go more deeply into this," you might say, "Yes, I understand that you have a *feeling* that we need to explore this." In addition to matching key words, you can match voice tone and tempo, and physical posture.

Leading involves the attempt to get another person to change, add to or enrich his or her thoughts or behaviors. We lead by suggesting other words, ideas or actions. We can also lead by shifting our own actions.

The basic idea of *pacing and leading* is to incrementally introduce somebody to changes in their behavior or world view by first matching and acknowledging, and then widening their model of the world. For instance, when people are being introduced to something new, it is best to start with something familiar and then move to something new. Pacing before leading is a very important principle for the persuasive use of Sleight of Mouth.

A good example of the power of pacing before leading comes from a sales seminar for a telemarketing group. There was one customer that no one had been able to sell to. It turned out this person talked very s...l...o...w...l...y. However, he was the president of a big company that could become a very important customer. People would call him and say, "Hello, sir, I know you're a very busy man, if I could just take a minute of your time," speaking at about twice his tempo.

But that isn't the way that person thinks, or listens. As a way to improve his communication skills, a member of the group was instructed to call this man up and say, "Hello... (very slowly) ... I'm from xxx company... and I'd really like to have some time... to talk with you.... when you really have some time... to think about our products... I know it's really important for you... to take your time and think about things... Could you tell me when we could call...." and so on. Instead of saying, "I'll only take a minute," the group member was to say, "When could I call you back when you would have enough time to think about this comfortably and thoroughly?" The company president felt so comfortable with the approach that he scheduled a meeting, and the telemarketing group ended up getting the account.

As this example illustrates, one of the most important outcomes of pacing is the establishment of rapport. When people know you can think as they do and can take their world view into account, they are much less resistant to new ideas.

For example, once during a presentation on communication skills I was giving, a man stood up and said, "All this stuff you are saying about communication seems too easy. I'm in the REAL WORLD. These theories are only for seminars. I just don't *feel* that it will work with MY clients." So I said, "You certainly have a legitimate concern. Why don't you come up and be a demonstration subject? You pretend that you're one of your difficult clients in the real world, and we'll try to *get a hold* of how this might put you more *in touch* with them."

So he came up and started "role playing." The first thing I did was to subtly put myself into a similar body posture. He said, "Well, I'm a busy man. I have to see a hundred people like you every day. Most of them are full of crap and end up wasting my time. Let's hurry up and get through this." As I responded to him I began to match my speech to the man's breathing, and said, "It sounds to me... like you want someone... you *feel* you can trust... Someone who cares.... about what you need... and will support you...Think of somebody you have really trusted... in your life... and how you *felt*... That's the kind of relationship... I'd like to develop with you." I continued pacing his breathing, and finally after about three minutes of this the man stopped me and said, "You know, I was going to try to be as resistant as I could, but right now I'd buy anything from you."

This example demonstrates the value of using simple but subtle non-verbal cues to help establish rapport and to pace and lead another person's state so that they are more open to receiving your messages.

When used properly, Sleight of Mouth is a sophisticated form of pacing and leading. The patterns of verbal reframing are clearly an attempt to lead someone to a new or different point of view, but they also need to pace some part of that person's experience in order to be effective. It also helps when we are able to simultaneously pace a person through some non-verbal means as well.

Second Position

Resonance, rapport and pacing are greatly facilitated and enhanced when we can get inside the other person's mind and experience and put ourselves in their "shoes." This is what is known as "second position" in NLP. ("First position" is our own point of view.) Taking *second position* involves stepping into another person's point of view within a particular situation or interaction. From second position, you see, hear and feel what the interaction is like from the other person's perspective; i.e.. to "be in his or her skin," "walk a mile in his or her shoes," "sit on the other side of the desk," etc.

You can take second position on different levels through a series of thought experiments. You can imagine being in the other person's environment. You can imagine behaving and acting the way they do. You can practice thinking the way they think. Especially important for Sleight of Mouth, you can try on their beliefs and values to experience what that is like. You can even explore what it would be like to be that person and have their sense of purpose.

The value of second position when using the Sleight of Mouth patterns is that it gives you deeper insight into the person and sharpens your intuition about which Sleight of Mouth patterns would be most effective. It also helps to ensure the ecological use of the patterns by creating greater understanding and empathy.

Summary

When using the Sleight of Mouth patterns, it is important to keep in mind all of these principles:

- *Energy Follows Attention*
- *Words Direct Attention – The Paradox of Negation*
- *Language Frames and "Reframes" Our Experience – Outcome Frame Versus Problem Frame*
- *Holons and Holarchies*
- *Languaging Levels of Change*
- *Filtering Negative Identity Judgments*
- *Balancing Ego and Soul*
- *Creating Resonance*
- *Promoting Rapport*
- *Pacing and Leading*
- *Putting Yourself into Second Position*

They will greatly enhance the positive impact you are able to achieve and more easily appeal to emotion (pathos) and character (ethos) as well as reason (logos). I will be referring back to them throughout the book and give more insight and examples as to how they support the applications of Sleight of Mouth to produce positive and ecological change.

Chapter 3

Skills of Sleight of Mouth

Skills of Sleight of Mouth

Just like a card magician performing sleight of hand is applying key skills, the effective use of Sleight of Mouth requires skillfulness. The patterns of Sleight of Mouth can be likened to particular card tricks. Performing the card trick effectively requires manual dexterity but also skillful interaction with the audience. Similarly, Sleight of Mouth requires verbal dexterity combined with other interactive and interpersonal abilities. This chapter will go over some important skills that support the principles presented in the previous chapter and which are necessary to apply the Sleight of Mouth patterns effectively and ecologically.

Persuasion

As I pointed out earlier, Sleight of Mouth is intended to be used as a form of persuasion. The term *persuasion* comes from the Latin *persuadere*, which is derived from *per* (meaning "thoroughly") and *suadere* (meaning "to advise or urge"). Thus, "persuasion" literally means to "thoroughly advise.. The modern usage of the word has come to mean, "to move by argument, entreaty, or expostulation to a belief, position, or course of action" (Webster). Put simply, persuasion is essentially the attempt to use language (and non-verbal communication) to influence the thoughts and actions of others by appealing to their values, beliefs, and motivations.

Effective persuasion is a result of a combination of skills requiring:

1. Intellectual and Emotional intelligence

2. Personal and Relational Skills

3. Verbal and Non-Verbal Communication

In this chapter, I will cover a number of these skills and their relevance to the application of Sleight of Mouth,

CRASH Versus COACH States

Internal state is a key part of the "Meta Structure" of belief and is one of the most important influences on how we form and express beliefs. Limiting beliefs invariably create difficult feelings that can plunge us into unhelpful survival strategies such as attack, escape or rigidity (fight, flight, freeze). When this happens, we are likely to collapse into a stuck internal state that can be summarized by the letters in the word CRASH:

Contraction

Reactivity

Analysis Paralysis

Separation

Hostility, Hurting and Hating

When we are in a CRASH state, our filters are shut down. We are in a state of "neuromuscular lock." Nothing works and it is easy to feel frustrated, defensive, helpless, and trapped. When people are in a CRASH state, what they think makes no difference, what they say makes no difference, and what they do makes no difference. Limiting beliefs and thought viruses create CRASH states and CRASH states lock limiting beliefs and thought viruses into place.

In order to transform limiting beliefs, it is important to cultivate qualities such as flexibility and stability, balance, connection and the ability to self-reflect. These qualities are characterized by what is called the COACH state:

Centered

Open

Attending with Awareness

Connected

Holding, Honoring and Hospitable

This involves being centered in yourself, especially in the "gut" (your belly center); open to new information, ideas and possibilities, especially open in the heart; attentive to what is going on within and around you with awareness and mindfulness, particularly in the head; connected to all of your intelligences and inner resources, head, heart and gut; and holding whatever is happening from a mindset of creativity, curiosity and respect (hospitality).

One of our primary ways of supporting others to transform limiting beliefs is to ground ourselves in our COACH state and support others to do the same. When we can do so, we create a field of resources between ourselves and others that simultaneously brings out the best of each other. We refer to this special relationship and the rapport it produces as the COACH Container. Creating a strong and rich *COACH Container* is essential for the effective and ecological use of Sleight of Mouth.

Moving from CRASH to COACH

A vitally important skill for the effective use of Sleight of Mouth is the ability to recognize CRASH states in ourselves and others and to have ways to help ourselves and others move from a CRASH state to a COACH state.

COACH and CRASH states are not "all or nothing" phenomena. There are many degrees of expression of each state. Some can be quite subtle. The various dimensions of CRASH – contraction, reactivity, analysis paralysis, separation and hostility – can occur separately or together. The same is true for the qualities of their COACH state. To develop more skill at recognizing different degrees of CRASH or COACH, it can be helpful to imagine a zero to ten scale, where zero is a strong CRASH state and ten is a robust COACH state. For Sleight of Mouth to work most effectively a person needs to be at least at a level seven or more on that scale. Becoming a "magician" with Sleight of Mouth involves learning to recognize the cues in yourself and others that reflect where you are and they are on that scale.

If you detect that you or the person are starting to show signs of CRASH it will be important and useful to make adjustments that bring you back into a COACH state. Some simple tactics to remember are: "slow down, pause, breathe, center." *Slowing down* your breath, your thoughts, your tempo of voice, etc., helps to bring more awareness. *Pausing* and taking a moment of silence and stillness allows you to reconnect to your inner resources. *Breathing* is simple way of promoting the opening and expanding of attention. *Centering* brings you back to calm and solid place in yourself. You can encourage these same actions in others as well if you notice that they are slipping into a CRASH state.

Developing Emotional Intelligence

A solid COACH state is the foundation for emotional intelligence. *Emotional intelligence* involves the ability to interact successfully with emotions by recognizing them, understanding their function, and responding resourcefully to them. Being able to intelligently respond to the difficult feelings brought up by limiting beliefs is another core skill of Sleight of Mouth.

The primary areas involved in applying emotional intelligence are: (1) dealing with uncomfortable emotional states and (2) stimulating or eliciting resourceful emotional states. Emotional reactions are typically considered to be the "juice" which brings energy into a particular situation or interaction. Emotional responses themselves, however, can be perceived as either "positive" or "negative." Positive emotions are associated with motivation and enthusiasm. Negative emotions are associated with problems and limitations.

Usually, though, emotions themselves are not the problem. It is the behavior produced by the emotion, and the effects of that behavior on others, that determines whether a particular emotion is a problem or a resource. Emotions are a type of energy whose purpose to stimulate us into action in some way. Any emotion held in a CRASH state is probably going to produce problematic reactions. The same emotion held in a COACH state will fulfill its function in a more appropriate way.

Dealing with "negative" emotions in an emotionally intelligent way involves:

(a) staying in a COACH state while experiencing the emotion,

(b) seeking and understanding the function that the emotion is intended to serve, and

(c) bringing inner resources that help to add more behavioral alternatives, given the function of the emotion and the specific context related to the emotional response.

Knowing how to deal with "negative emotions" is an indispensable skill for using the Sleight of Mouth techniques.

The function of "fear," for instance, is usually "protection." The function of "anger" may be motivation to "act," or "set boundaries." Once the function has been understood, appropriate choices of behavior can be explored and connected with the function of the emotion. Rather than behaviorally responding with violence when angry, for example, a person can develop other choices which satisfy the intention of the anger: i.e., talking about his or her feelings, taking a walk, focusing on a project, etc.

The basic competences needed for emotional intelligence are:

1. *Recognizing* the presence of a particular emotional state.

2. *Acknowledging* the presence of that state without judgment.

3. *Holding* the emotional state in an environment of "equanimity" and curiosity (COACH state).

4. *Understanding* the emotional state and its function.

5. *Resourcing* the emotional state by connecting it to other complementary emotions and states.

6. *Transforming* or refining the expression of the emotional state to be more harmonious and productive with respect to its function.

7. *Integrating* the emotional state as a contributing part of a larger system.

These same skills can be applied to the limiting belief itself and are a form of pacing before leading.

To apply Sleight of Mouth effectively, it is important to pace and lead limiting beliefs and the emotions that accompany them. Thus, a first step before trying to change anything is to welcome and understand those beliefs and emotions. Otherwise, Sleight of Mouth ends up being a type of manipulation or debate. To help remember the competences of emotional intelligence when meeting a limiting belief, I find it useful to say to myself, or even say out loud the following statements that I learned from my mentor Milton H. Erickson, M.D., who will figure prominently throughout this book.

1. *That's interesting.*

2. *I'm sure that makes sense.*

3. *Something needs to be held, heard, or healed.*

4. *Welcome.*

I find that these simple statements can do a lot to set the tone of an interaction and remind me of the principles and skills I have been presenting.

Taking Meta Position

In the previous chapter I mentioned the importance of being able to take a "second position" with others in order to better understand them and create resonance and rapport. There is another perceptual position that is important for the effective use of Sleight of Mouth known as "meta position." The term *meta* is a Greek word meaning "over," "between" or "above." In English, it is also often used to mean "about." A "meta model," for example, is a model *about* other models. "Metacognition" is the awareness of one's own cognitive processes, i.e., cognition *about* cognition. "Meta messages" are messages *about* other messages, which provide frames or context markers that influence the meaning of those messages.

Taking a *meta position* is a key skill for being able to reflect thoughtfully upon particular situations and interactions. With respect to an interaction, meta position involves disassociating from that interaction and observing it as though you were a witness to it and not a participant. A card magician, for instance, needs to do this to anticipate the responses of the audience to what the magician is doing and saying, and to react accordingly. The same is true for using Sleight of Mouth. The ability to take meta position also allows you to get some distance from the interaction itself and not become stuck in or myopic with respect to your own perspective. That psychological distance can also help you to stay in a COACH state in emotionally challenging situations.

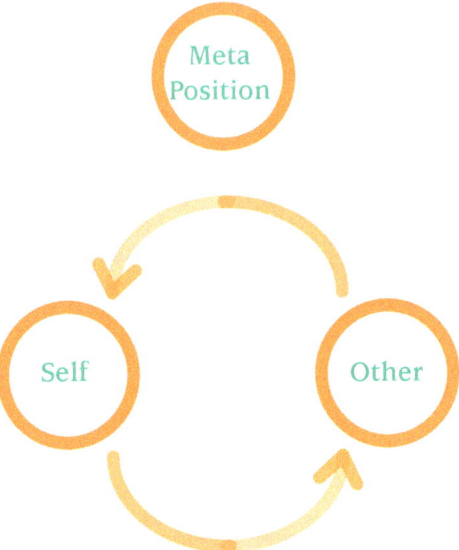

Meta position involves reflecting on an interaction between yourself
and another as if you were an observer.

In conflict situations, for example, achieving a "meta position" is essential for a successful resolution. A meta position would be a position "above and between" the two in conflict, which includes and acknowledges both conflicting perspectives, but creates something new. The new perspective either synthesizes the conflicting positions or allows them to co-exist in harmony. The function of a conflict mediator, for instance, is to be in an official "meta position" to the parties in conflict.

With respect to reflecting on oneself, the ability to take a meta position involves introspectively understanding one's own thoughts and actions. It is a type of self-monitoring position. Taking a meta position with respect to oneself would involve asking questions such as, "How am I thinking and feeling right now?" "Do I feel, look and sound congruent with respect to what I am doing?" "What internal state do I want to be in, and how do I want to think about what is going on?"

Engaging Multiple Intelligences

While Sleight of Mouth is naturally focused on words, using it successfully requires more than words. Words themselves only gain meaning through their connection to other parts of our experience. To apply Sleight of Mouth effectively, it is important to engage *multiple intelligences*. The basic principle of multiple intelligences is that, *the more ways you have to understand something, the more you understand it*. If you only have a verbal way to express or understanding something, you are very limited. If, however, in addition you have a metaphorical way, a somatic way and a visual way, you can express it more creatively and understand it more completely.

To apply Sleight of Mouth, it is important to engage multiple intelligences.

Visual images, for instance, are more effective than words for bringing out the interrelationships between the key elements of change. Verbal representations come more from the "left-brain" and focus more on objects and sequencing while visual representations are generated by the "right-brain" and emphasize patterns and relationships. Incorporating color into the images can also bring out a whole different level of nuance with respect to feelings.

It has been said that "a picture is worth a thousand words," but a word can also create a thousand pictures depending on how it used. Even though we are using words, we may be working to paint a picture in the mind's eye. Sleight of Mouth creates change by engaging memory, emotion, and imagination.

One of the other essential areas of intelligence necessary to promote change is the intelligence of the body; what is called "somatic intelligence." This shows up as a type of body language. Many of the things we say, we can also show with our body as a type of "somatic model." Let's say that a person talks about being "stuck in a state of inertia." I could say, "Show that inertia with your body. What is a movement or gesture that characterizes what is going on?" I might then say, "Now, show the desired state with your body. What would be different?" This often brings greater insight into what is going on than a lot of verbalization.

Being able to move between words and other forms of representation can be extremely important when practicing Sleight of Mouth. In fact, when I am using Sleight of Mouth, my focus is rarely just on the words themselves, but rather on the inner experience and desired state that I am seeking to create through the words. Different Sleight of Mouth patterns will naturally engage different intelligences. Keeping my focus on the deeper experiential meaning I want to convey helps me to intuitively select and formulate an appropriate Sleight of Mouth intervention.

Ultimately, Sleight of Mouth patterns are much more than simply verbal formulas, they are a *mindset* and an application of certain perceptual principles. As I present the patterns in the coming pages, I will also be commenting how to apply the principles and skills I have presented in these opening chapters. As we shall see in some of the illustrations and examples I will present in the coming chapters, Sleight of Mouth does not always take the form of a verbal retort to another verbal statement. It can take the form of a fairly complex interaction over time.

Summary: Basic Steps for Using Sleight of Mouth to Transform a Limiting Belief

Putting together the sequence of principles and skills I have described in the previous chapters; we can map out a fundamental set of steps for effectively applying Sleight of Mouth to transform a limiting belief.

1. **Start in COACH State**. Make sure you and whomever you are interacting with is in a COACH state at a level of at least seven on a scale of zero to ten.

2. **Establish the Desired State** (in words, body language and an image, if possible). Explore the question, "What do you want to experience, do or create more of?" (e.g., express myself calmly and clearly; Have a feeling of security and abundance.) This will establish the outcome frame to continually return to.

3. **Identify the Inner Barrier** by exploring, "What stops you from achieving your desired state?" (A simple formula is, "I want to do X, but Y happens instead.")

4. **Bring awareness to the inner barrier and find the belief that is creating it** – "What feelings, images, words and body language are associated with the barrier?" (e.g., *"If I speak, people will laugh at me;"* *"No matter what I do, I will never get enough."*)

5. *"Taste the poison"* – "What type of inner response (CRASH) does that limiting belief create?"

6. **Find the positive function of the belief** – "What does having this belief and accompanying response do for you?"

7. **Create a *"belief bridge"*** – "What other belief honors the function of belief barrier, but connects to you to a larger perspective and to more of your inner resources? What are the 'magic words' that transform the barrier and awaken deeper resources?" (e.g., *"I am an adult now, and I can learn;"* *"I will always rise from the ashes."*)

8. *"Taste the medicine"* – "What type of inner response does that new belief create in you when you say the words (and engage the other representations associated with it)?"

The main purpose of the Sleight of Mouth patterns is to achieve step seven – creating a "belief bridge." Without the other steps, however, step seven can be a bit like rolling the dice in a "crap shoot." The linguistic patterns of Sleight of Mouth can be used either reflexively or skillfully. Applying the principles and skills of Sleight of Mouth that I have presented in the previous chapters will help you to identify potential limiting beliefs and thought viruses, reframe them, and hopefully create a better, healthier, more whole, creative, and productive life for yourself and others, and a more functional and ecological world for future generations. That is my wish and my intention for this book.

Chapter 4
Intent

Intent

*I*ntent is the first Sleight of Mouth pattern. It involves directing attention to the purpose or intention behind a belief rather than focus on the content of the belief itself (see *Sleight of Mouth I*, pp. 48-49). Intent is the cornerstone of all the other Sleight of Mouth patterns, as it addresses the underlying motivation *behind* the belief and its contents. This is why the Sleight of Mouth symbol for Intent is an arrow pointing behind the belief statement.

The word "intent" is derived from the Latin *intendre*, which literally means "to stretch out" or "extend." An *intention* is typically defined as "the purpose, end or aim toward which thoughts are directed"; or "an anticipated outcome that guides your planned actions." It is also used to mean "a determination to act in a certain way." A person with the intent "to help," for instance, may not know exactly what he or she is going to do or will need to do, but is ready and willing to engage in any number of specific actions which may satisfy that general intention. The intent to "bring positive energy" or to "stay focused" can have many different specific expressions given the circumstances. The same would be true for the intent to "hurt" or to "punish." From this perspective, an intention is a type of filter that directs our attention and brings certain capabilities and actions into the foreground.

Our intentions direct our thoughts, behaviors, and decisions, and indicate what we want or hope to accomplish through some cognitive or physical activity. They are the internal source of thoughts, words, and actions. Some crimes, for instance, require proof of intent to be considered "criminal." For some religious groups, the mere intent of some action is considered the basis for a "sin," if even the action does not take place.

In one of the most poignant scenes from the New Testament, Jesus is being put to death through the horrible means of crucifixion. According to Luke (23:34), Jesus says, "*Father forgive them for they know not what they do."* The implication of this is that, even though what his executioners are doing is terrible, he believes that they are not acting from an evil intention and deserve forgiveness rather than punishment.

As this example shows, the interpretation of words and actions are typically based on the intentions of their speakers or actors. This is particularly important with respect to verbal language since words can be vague and ambiguous. Every form of language is subject to deletion, distortion, and generalization. In the United States, for example, politicians and lawmakers attempt to interpret the *U.S. Constitution* based on the "intentions" of the nation's founders. Correctly identifying the intention is necessary to interpret the message or meaning of a particular verbal or behavioral expression.

The impact of intention is humorously illustrated in the following joke.

> *Two Irish-Catholic plumbers are out repairing a pipe at a building across from a notorious house of prostitution. After a while, they notice one of the town doctors walking by. The doctor stops briefly, looks both ways, and then quickly dashes into the house of ill repute. The two plumbers shake their heads at one another. The senior plumber says, "It's hard to believe that the doctor would do such a thing. He has a wife and kids." A little while later, the Protestant minister comes walking down the street. Like the doctor, the minister stops, looks both ways, and then darts into the brothel. Again, the senior plumber shakes his head in disgust. "I can't believe the minister could be such a hypocrite; preaching against lust at the church and then doing something like this." Some more time passes, and along comes the Rabbi, who, just like the others, pauses, looks both ways, and then dashes into house of sin. "What's the world coming to," bemoans the plumber. "At least we Catholics still have some moral character." Just about this time the Catholic priest comes by, repeating the same pattern as the others. After looking both ways, the priest slips into the house of prostitution. With a look of admiration, the older plumber says, "Boy, somebody must awfully be sick in there in order for the good Father to be willing to go into a place like that."*

The older plumber's "Sleight of Mouth" here, of course, is that the priest has a different intent than the others. Therefore, what he is doing is not reprehensible, in contrast to them.

Limiting Beliefs Frequently Assume Negative Intent

Our beliefs about others are frequently founded on assumptions about their intentions. Limiting beliefs about others generally assume some type of *negative intention* on their part. Such beliefs can quickly spiral into divisiveness, aggression and even violence. This is especially true when negative intentions are ascribed to *anonymous "others"*. Many conspiracy theories, for instance, are built on the assumption of a vast powerful network, such as a government or secret society, that has negative or ill intentions – e.g., to try to fool, control or eliminate people. This, of course, is what Adolf Hitler did in his book *Mein Kampf* when he railed against the negative intention of "the Jew" to "destroy the racial foundations of the people he has set out to subjugate." Hitler wrote:

> *With satanic joy in his face, the black-haired Jewish youth lurks in wait for the unsuspecting girl whom he defiles with his blood, thus stealing her from her people. With every means he tries to destroy the racial foundations of the people he has set out to subjugate. Just as he himself systematically ruins women and girls, he does not shrink back from pulling down the blood barriers for others, even on a large scale. It was and it is Jews who bring the Negroes into the Rhineland, always with the same secret thought and clear aim of ruining the hated white race by the necessarily resulting bastardization, throwing it down from its cultural and political height, and himself rising to be its master.*

It is particularly significant that Hitler places this negative intention at the level of *identity* and *purpose*, as it elevates the intensity of reactivity. Like all Sleight of Mouth patterns, *Intent* can be used in either a helpful and productive or a divisive and damaging way. The assumption of negative intentions is one of the "red flags" to pay attention to with respect to Sleight of Mouth, as it usually means that the other patterns are likely to be used reactively or defensively as well. This is especially important when it is combined with the process of "othering" – i.e., creating binary distinctions at the identity level. Examples of this would include terms like: Jews, Negroes, Whites, Capitalists, Communists, Conservatives, Liberals, Socialists, Americans, Russians, Germans, Chinese, etc.; any type of anonymous, collective "other."

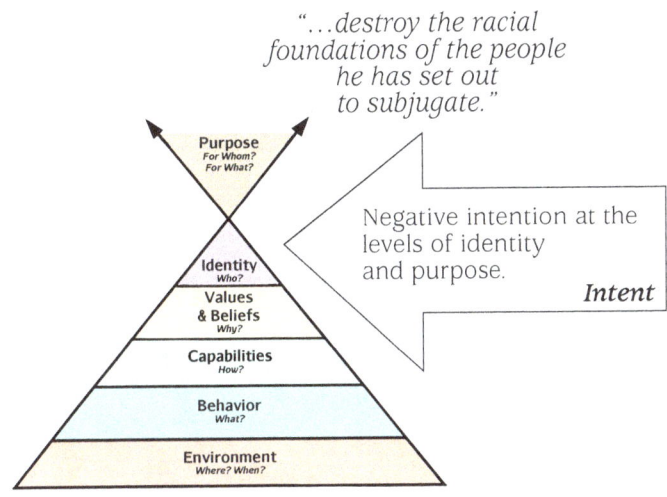

"Towards" Versus "Away From" Intentions

Another key distinction with respect to intentions is whether they are directed "towards" or "away from" something, e.g., "toward safety" or "away from danger." *Away from* intentions often create paradoxes by focusing attention and energy on what is *not* wanted rather than on what is wanted. If we do not know what we want to go toward, we can "jump out of the frying pan and into the fire," which could be a potentially worse situation.

"Away from" intentions tend to emerge from CRASH states. Likewise, CRASH states can also be created by "away from" intentions. The desire to avoid, stop or get away from something can easily lead to contraction, reactivity, analysis paralysis, separation, and hostility. Those qualities, in turn, can stimulate the desire or need to avoid, stop, or get away from something.

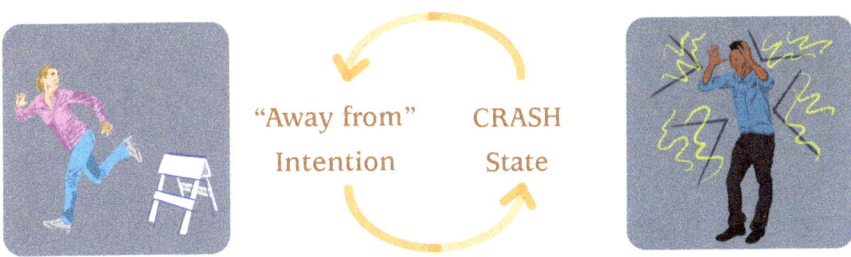

Sleight of Mouth 47

When combined with the assumption of the negative intent of "others" at the identity level, "away from" intentions can easily precipitate violence and even war. Hermann Goering (the second most powerful man in Nazi Germany behind Adolf Hitler), maintained at the Nuremberg trials in 1946 (from *Nuremberg Diary* by G. M. Gilbert) that:

> *Of course, the people don't want war... That is understood. But... it's always a simple matter to drag the people along whether it's a democracy, a fascist dictatorship, a parliament, or a communist dictatorship. Voice or no voice, the people can always be brought to the bidding of the leaders. That is easy. All you have to do is tell them they are being attacked and denounce the pacifists for lack of patriotism and exposing the country to danger. It works the same in any country.*

Goering's chilling remarks show how powerful the Sleight of Mouth pattern of *Intent* can be when misused. Telling people that "they are being attacked" and denouncing dissenters "for lack of patriotism and exposing the country to danger" creates a perception of negative intention and the need to move "away from," which fosters a sense of insecurity and jeopardy from both without (those external "others" who are attacking you) and within (those internal "others" exposing you to danger). The result is to trigger the fundamental survival strategies associated with CRASH state of "fight, flight or freeze." Thus, this combination of "negatively intended anonymous others" with "away from" motivation constitutes another fundamental red flag to the potentially manipulative and unecological use of Sleight of Mouth.

Conversely to this, establishing a COACH state tends to produce a "toward" intention, and vice versa.

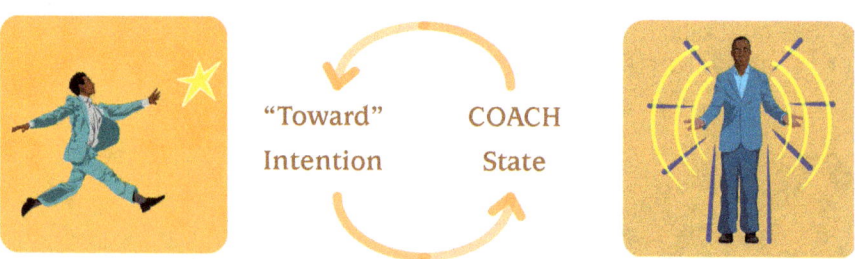

Therefore, the effective and ecological use of Sleight of Mouth always emphasizes a positive intention stated in a "towards" expression.

The Principle of Positive Intention

The principle of positive intention essentially states that: At some level, our feelings, thoughts, and behavior have been developed to serve some positive intent or purpose, even if the feelings, thoughts, and behaviors themselves are problematic or harmful. For instance, the positive intention behind aggressive behavior is often "protection." The positive intention or purpose behind fear is usually "safety." The positive purpose behind anger can be to "maintain boundaries." Hatred may have the positive purpose of "motivating" a person to take action. The belief, "If I try X, I will fail," could be motivated and sustained by the intention to prevent disappointment.

Intentions are invariably related to *values* (e.g., safety, honesty, control, growth, connection, achievement, etc.) and provide the underlying motivation for particular feelings, thoughts, and actions. Intentions at one level are sometimes derivatives of other deeper intentions. The intention to "attack someone," for example, may come from the deeper intention to "protect oneself." Similarly, the intention to "punish someone," may come from the deeper intention to "teach them something."

Any attempt to strengthen, question or transform a belief, and the associated response, needs to take into account the positive intention the belief and corresponding behavior was developed to serve. If a new possibility or other perspective does not resonate with the intention that spawned the belief and is holding it in place, it is likely to be rejected or viewed with suspicion. This is why *Intent* is the first Sleight of Mouth pattern. Finding a resonant positive intention is going to make the rest of the conversation or intervention much easier and more impactful.

Applying the Sleight of Mouth Pattern of Intent

The effective use of any of the Sleight of Mouth patterns does not come from applying an abstract verbal formula. Finding the right words comes from taking on a particular mindset associated with the particular Sleight of Mouth pattern. The mindset for *Intent*, for instance, is directed toward the questions: *What is the positive purpose or intention of this belief? What does having this belief (and related responses) do positively for the person who is expressing it?*

Reflecting on the limiting belief statements we have established previously, here are some possible examples of applying the pattern of Intent.

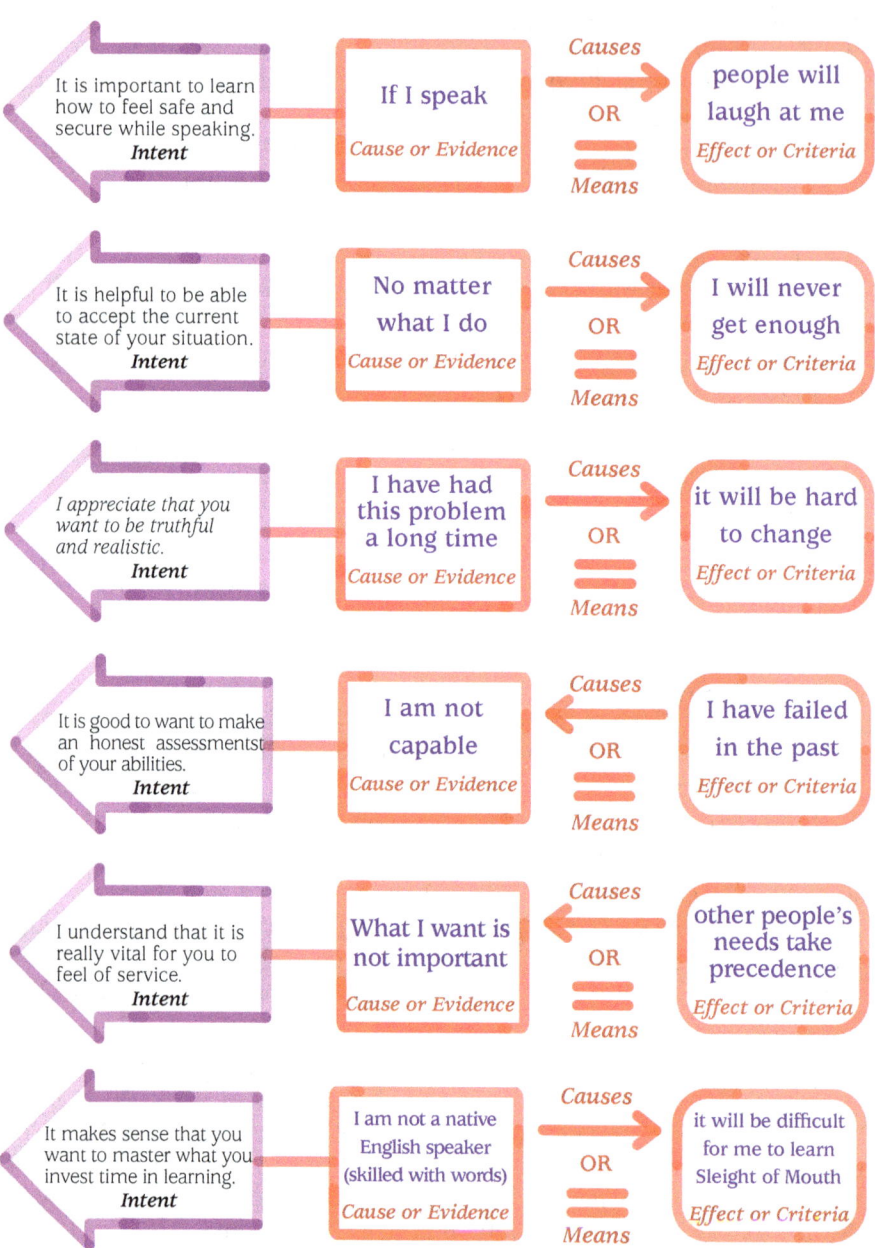

Of course, key to the effectiveness of any of these statements is the degree of resonance they produce with the person holding the belief. This is where skills such as rapport and second position are particularly important.

Flipping Intentions from "Away From" to "Toward"

It is important to note that all these statements involve the "toward" formulation of the intent. The persons making these limiting belief statements would probably not have initially identified these as their intentions. They would mostly likely begin with an "away from" version of the intent, such as:

1. If I speak people will laugh at me. → *Avoid humiliation.*
2. No matter what I do I will never get enough. → *Avoid disappointment.*
3. I have had this problem a long time, so it will be hard to change. → *Avoid struggle.*
4. I am not capable because I have failed in the past. → *Avoid frustration.*
5. What I want is not important because other people's needs take precedence. → *Avoid rejection.*
6. Because I am not a native English speaker (skilled with words) it will be difficult for me to learn Sleight of Mouth. → *Avoid unnecessary effort.*

Holding the positive intention mindset, we need to *flip* the "away from" formulation to a "toward" expression by asking the question (either to ourselves or the other person), "If you could avoid/stop/get rid of X, what would that get for you instead?" In our examples, this shift produced the following reframes:

1. *Avoid humiliation.* → Feel safe and secure while speaking.
2. *Avoid disappointment.* → Accept the current state of the situation.
3. *Avoid struggle.* → Be truthful and realistic.
4. *Avoid frustration.* → Honest assessment of abilities.
5. *Avoid rejection.* → Feel of service.
6. *Avoid unnecessary effort.* → Master what you invest time in learning.

This type of "flipping" of attention and orientation is one of the reasons I use the analogy to sleight of hand to describe these patterns. Applying the skills of sleight of hand, a two of clubs can suddenly turn into an ace of diamonds. Flipping an intention from "away from" to "toward" can produce a similar sort of affect.

These various reframes, of course, are not intended to be the conclusion of an argument but rather the beginning of a more productive conversation. Once a positive intention is identified, other ways to fulfill it can be explored and discussed.

Skillfully Using the Pattern

When applying the pattern of Intent, or any of the Sleight of Mouth patterns, it is important to watch out for any types of CRASH that may be present (in yourself or the other person) and consistently maintain an outcome frame. As I pointed out earlier, CRASH states tend to bring out the "away from" version of the intention. Trying to use Sleight of Mouth while someone is in a CRASH state usually just takes you in circles or even makes things worse. Staying in your own COACH state and maintaining an attitude of genuine interest and curiosity is crucial to the effective and ecological use of Sleight of Mouth.

As an example, when my son Drew was about six years old and his younger sister Julia was four, they got into a physical altercation in which my son, who was bigger, was clearly being the aggressor. I separated them and, rather than punishing him, I asked my son what his intention was in hitting his sister. Of course, he looked at me like I was a complete idiot and responded, "I want to hurt her." Needless to say, this does not sound at all like a positive intention. It was also clearly coming from a full-on CRASH state.

I had him take a few deep breaths and then said, "Okay, I get that. What will it do for you to hurt her?" "I will get back at her," came the reply. "And what does it do for you to get back at her?" I went on, in a voice that was curious, not accusatory. "Then I am getting even with her for what she did to me. She took one of my things and wouldn't give it back," he explained. "And what does it do for *you* to get even with *her*?" I asked. "Well, then it's fair," he responded.

"Ah, so what you really want is *fairness*," I said. "As your father I will do everything in my power to keep you from hitting your little sister. You are bigger than her and that isn't fair. But I will also do everything in my power to help you get a fair solution here. Let's explore how you can use your words instead of your fists to get a fair result." This led to a simple coaching session in which he was able to express to his sister, "What I feel" and "What I want," instead of using physical aggression. The reminder to "use your words" was practically a mantra in our household from then on, sometimes preceded by a "time out," if there was the presence of too much ongoing CRASH. (As a side note, it might be interesting to know that my son grew up to become a diplomat.)

As this example illustrates, a seemingly negative intention (to hurt someone) can actually come from a positive intention (fairness). This positive intention, however, became distorted through the filters of a CRASH state. Reducing the CRASH state and continuing to explore the intention behind the original intention were important to reach a successful conclusion.

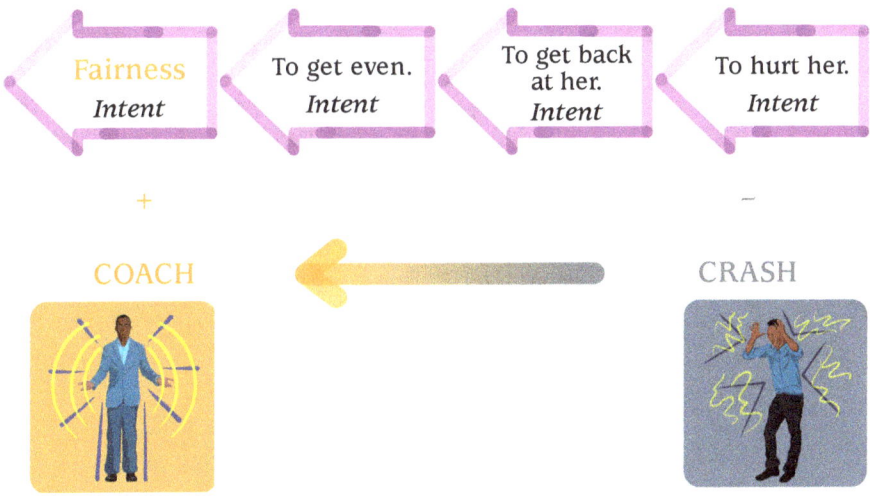

When confronted with what appears to be a negative intention, it is helpful to ask the question, "What does that do for you?" Asking this question several times typically leads to successively deeper and more positive expressions of the intention. For example, let's say that a person has an intention of "punishing someone else." The intention of "punishment" might be "to teach them a lesson." The intention of "teaching them a lesson" might be to "change their behavior." The intention of "changing their behavior" might be to "make me feel more safe." The intention of "feeling more safe" might be "the freedom to be myself"; and so on. The expression of the intention shifts from a focus on stopping or changing the external behavior of others to expressing more of one's own potential at an identity level. This, in turn, can become the new focus of attention and energy.

Defining the positive intention of a particular belief or behavior opens up the possibility of finding more options, which achieve the same intention but in a different and more appropriate manner. New paths and strategies can be explored, which are just as effective in reaching the intention, but avoid other problems and challenges.

An Example of Applying the Sleight of Mouth Pattern of Intent

A focus on the positive intention behind thoughts and behaviors was a major foundation for Milton Erickson's work as a psychiatrist and healer. He sometimes went so far as to claim that "the symptom is the solution." By that he meant that symptoms are frequently an attempt to bring some type of balance or wholeness into a person's life but were coming out in a distorted (CRASH) expression.

A good example of Erickson's emphasis on intention is presented in his *Collected Papers* (Vol. VI, pp. 124-129) in which he describes how he treated a very religious woman with three children who:

> *During the course of listening to a sermon one Sunday... had become horribly distressed to find herself unaccountably impelled to utter a variety of obscenities, particularly vulgarisms concerning body functions and sexual activity, all being ascribed to Jesus. She fought the overpowering vocal impulses desperately along with compelling desires to grimace, to gesticulate, and to posture.*

The woman, being quite distraught went home and locked herself in her room, where the symptoms continued into the next day completely out of control. Her husband, who knew Erickson, desperately called him to their house to see if he could use hypnosis to take away the symptoms. Erickson, who always viewed any symptoms as having a positive intention, took an unusual approach. As he describes it:

> *All appropriate and fitting hypnotic suggestions were offered in the proper sequence and progression that the author's experience had disclosed to be most reasonably effective. However, those suggestions were embellished, interlarded, couched, and elaborated with obscenities, vulgarities, and profanities that far exceeded the worse she had uttered.*

> *She was utterly appalled, horrified, and what was most important, completely silenced with a rigid fixation of her attention upon the author and the hypnotic suggestions being offered to her in such a peculiar emphatic fashion.*

Erickson then acknowledged to the woman that he was doing the same thing that she was doing (even worse), but with one major difference. He was doing it intentionally. Erickson then brought the woman's attention to the intent behind her own words and behaviors by suggesting that she was to continue her symptomatic behavior in a "satisfying" but "better" manner. He explained:

> *[S]ince her manifestations would occur in either the presence or absence of others, her symptomatology could be entirely adequate if she alone knew of it. Thus, her utterances need not be so loud, since she could hear even the softest whispers as well as the loudest shouts. Additionally, the posturing could also be minimal, since she could be aware of it and any associated thoughts, however minimal the postural movements were.*

Clearly, Erickson was directing the woman's focus to the intent behind her words and behaviors rather than to the content of her utterances and actions. For those words and behaviors to become "satisfying" but "better," they would need to fulfill the intention behind them. In fact, Erickson instructed the woman to practice many different variations of the symptoms. He also suggested that "weekly, biweekly, or even less frequently she would go into the garage, get into her car, close the door, turn on the car radio full volume, and 'let loose with everything'."

Erickson reports that the woman was able to practice and incorporate the new patterns of behavior well enough that for the most part she could get through the day without a manifestation of the symptoms, periodically going into the garage to "get it out of her system," first at weekly intervals and then monthly intervals, until she was finally symptom free. Seven years later Erickson saw the woman on a different matter. Still free of those symptoms, she *"reminisced with amusement about her previous condition"* and demonstrated to Erickson that she could even voluntarily speak the vulgarities and make the movements without any distress or loss of control.

Reflections on the Example

This example illustrates how creatively Sleight of Mouth patterns can be used when you have internalized the mindset associated with them. In reflecting on Erickson's unusual and innovative approach, it is important to note that he had to first interrupt the woman's ongoing "CRASH-Away From" cycle, which was spiraling out of control. Given Erickson's role as a hypnotherapist, and his propensity to engage people's "creative unconscious" rather than their conscious cognitive processes, he did not get any explicit statements of the woman's belief or intentions. However, the fact that the symptoms emerged in church and that she was "horribly distressed" about them, makes it is easy to assume that she probably thought that they were "bad" or "sinful," that there was no positive intention behind them, and that she might be "crazy" or "possessed."

By mirroring (and exaggerating) her words and behavior back to her from a COACH state, not only did Erickson shock the woman out of her CRASH state, but simultaneously created a powerful dilemma. A respected psychiatrist was able to say and do the same things she was doing and was clearly not bad, out of control, crazy or possessed. This shifted the attention from the words and behaviors themselves to the intention behind them. What is their source and what is their intended purpose? By having the woman continue her symptomatic behavior in a "satisfying" but "better" manner, Erickson also shifted from an "away from" problem frame to a "toward" outcome frame.

In such cases, it was not Erickson's style to inquire what the woman discovered about the intentions or "associated thoughts" that accompanied the words and behaviors. Given that the woman was clearly religious, it is likely that she had judgments about certain thoughts and feelings that she had tried to repress, and which consequently erupted out in a CRASH induced form. As a result, she had never had any coaching on how to how identify the purpose of those thoughts and feelings and how to express them in an appropriate way that fulfilled their ultimate intention (as I did with my son). This is what Erickson was able to accomplish through the skillful use of the Sleight of Mouth pattern (and mindset) of *Intent*. In this way, the symptoms were indeed transformed into the solution.

Chapter 5

Redefine

Redefine

The second Sleight of Mouth pattern of *Redefine* involves substituting new words for those used in the belief statement that mean something similar but have different implications (see *Sleight of Mouth I*, pp. 49-51). In its simplest form, *Redefine* involves restating the belief using different vocabulary that reduces any potential CRASH associated with the belief and gives more positive choices regarding the belief and it's contents. This can be done with either or both parts of the belief statement.

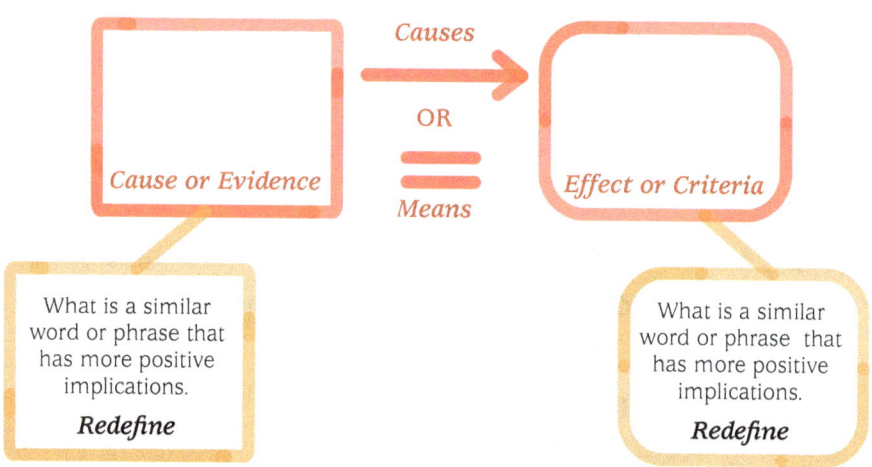

Redefining is fundamentally a form of renaming or relabeling. The names we give things influence their meaning to us. Studies made on the relationship between language and health (Rodin, 1986), for instance, indicate that there is a connection between physical health, sense of control and "symptom labeling." That is, a patient's sense of control affected the way he or she experienced and labeled bodily sensations as symptoms relevant to health or illness, and vice versa. People who have less of a sense of control are more apt to label a physical sensation as a "symptom" of illness. Likewise the label given a particular physical sensation will affect the degree of control a person feels about it. For example, a person with a stomachache can either say, "My stomach hurts" (a bodily sensation), "I have indigestion" (an indication of a problem) or "I am getting the flue" (a symptom of a more serious illness). This type of labeling determines a great deal about how the person approaches dealing with his or her situation.

A classic example of Redefining is to substitute the word "discomfort" for "pain." To say, "You might experience some *pain* with this procedure" is likely to create more anticipatory anxiety and CRASH than to say, "You might experience some *discomfort* with this procedure." In fact, the term "discomfort" actually names the desired state (comfort) as an essential part of the experience, which serves as a type of positive embedded suggestion.

One-word Reframing

In the first volume of *Sleight of Mouth*, I presented the notion of "one-word reframing" (pp. 52-54). This involves taking a word expressing a particular idea or concept and finding another word for that idea or concept that puts either a more positive or negative slant on it. Words like "rally," "gathering," "protest," "riot" or "mob," for instance, could all be used to describe the same event, each giving a more positive, neutral or negative spin on it. The following anecdote is a good illustration of how Redefining and one-word reframing can create a dramatic shift in perception.

> *Hesitantly, a young woman approached her lover.*
>
> *"We've been together for a while now," she said finally.*
>
> *"I know," said the young man.*
>
> *"There are some things that I want to ask you that are very important for me to know," she said. "Will you promise to answer me completely honestly?"*
>
> *"I promise," said the young man.*
>
> *"Do you think I am pretty?" she asked.*
>
> *The young man paused for a moment. "No," he finally replied.*
>
> *"Do you want to be with me forever?"*
>
> *"No" again came the reply.*
>
> *"Do you love me?" she inquired.*
>
> *Considering his promise, the young man shook his head and said, "No."*
>
> *"If I left, would you cry?" she wondered.*
>
> *Again, the young man answered, "No."*

> With a heavy heart, the young woman turned to leave. But before she could go, the young man gently took her arm and turned her toward him.
>
> "I don't think you are pretty," he said. "I think you are beautiful. I don't want to be with you forever. I need to be with you forever. I do not just love you. I adore you. And if you left, I would not cry. If you left, I would die."

The young man Redefines "pretty" to "beautiful," "want" to "need," "love" to "adore" and "cry" to "die." This, of course, shifts the whole meaning of his initial responses. It can also be the case that what seems to be a relatively subtle difference can have major implications, as is humorously shown in the one-word reframing at the end of the following joke.

> A salesman dies suddenly and finds himself at the entrance to heaven. He is greeted by Saint Peter who informs him that he gets to choose whether he wants to spend the rest of eternity in heaven or in hell. Being a savvy salesman, he asks, "Well, can I look around a little before I choose?" "Sure," replies Saint Peter. The salesman takes a tour around heaven and sees people sitting quietly in prayer, strumming harps and singing hymns. Frankly, it strikes him as pretty boring. When gets down to hell, however, he sees people sitting on the beach under the sun. Each man is accompanied by a beautiful woman, and is drinking from a bottle of champagne. Impressed, the salesman returns to Saint Peter and says, "I've made my decision, I'll take hell." As Saint Peter accompanies him back to hell, the man is surprised to find that the sun on the beach seems much hotter, and has turned into a searing fire. The women have lost their beauty and look like old hags, and the champagne tastes like vinegar. "Hey, wait a minute, protests the salesman, why is this so different than it was when I was down here before?" "Well, then you were a prospect," replies Saint Peter. "Now you're a customer."

The terms "prospect" and "customer" might appear to be similar and in some contexts may even be used interchangeably. A customer could be the same thing as a prospect. The subtle but significant difference is brought out by the exaggerated situation portrayed in the joke.

The Heinz food and beverage company used the pattern of *Redefine* in a creative way to transform the perception of one of its main products. Heinz Tomato Ketchup was notoriously slow pouring, which was considered a problem by some customers and a fault by some competitors. Heinz marketers, however, cleverly redefined the "slow-pouring" qualities of the ketchup as "too thick and rich to run" and thus a sign of better quality than their competitors. The product is still one of the top selling brands of ketchup in the world today.

Proper Naming

My colleague Stephen Gilligan and I use a form of Redefining in our coaching work that we call "proper naming." A "proper" name is one that brings out the best in people, presupposes resources and, at the same time, tells the truth of the situation. Proper naming is especially important for identity level statements. For example, if a client says, "I am an imposter," we might respond, "I understand that a part of you wants to act more authentically." This illustrates a basic principle for using *Redefine* effectively, which is, when possible, restating something in an outcome frame ("act more authentically") rather than a problem frame (being "an imposter"). It also restates the issue as an intention from "a part" of the person (which is more accurate, since some other part of them is clearly making the judgment). Finally, it shifts attention to the level of behavior (acting authentically) rather than an assertion of truth about the person's deeper identity.

Similarly, if someone says, "I am not good enough," we might reflect it back as, "I understand that there are some crucial areas in your life in which you believe you can improve." Again, the issue is restated in an outcome frame ("improve" versus "not good enough") and the focus is shifted from a defect of identity ("I am not good enough") to the level of environment ("some crucial areas") and belief about capability ("believe you can improve"). In this sense, proper naming is a type of Redefining whose purpose is to help people to view their experiences in a way that awakens a wider perspective and puts them in touch with potential resources and solutions.

This is no doubt the positive intention of "political correctness." There is less negativity and stigma associated with a term like "intellectually challenged" than "mental retardation." Similarly, the term "cognitively impaired" is less charged than "suffering from dementia." As always, key to the effectiveness of any *Redefine* is the degree of resonance it produces with the receiver. Complaints about political correctness stem from it superficializing or masking the actual issues or that it is an attempt to deny or distort the truth to avoid being offensive (an "away from" motivation). That is why "proper naming" needs to presuppose resources *and* still tell the truth of the situation.

Applying the Sleight of Mouth Pattern of Redefine

Conversationally, *Redefine* is often effectively used as a type of active listening, in which you are reflecting back and paraphrasing your understanding of what the other person is saying they believe. In this way, it is not intended to be a confrontation but rather an attempt at understanding and clarity. The following are examples of how we might apply the pattern of *Redefine* to the six example limiting beliefs we have been working with.

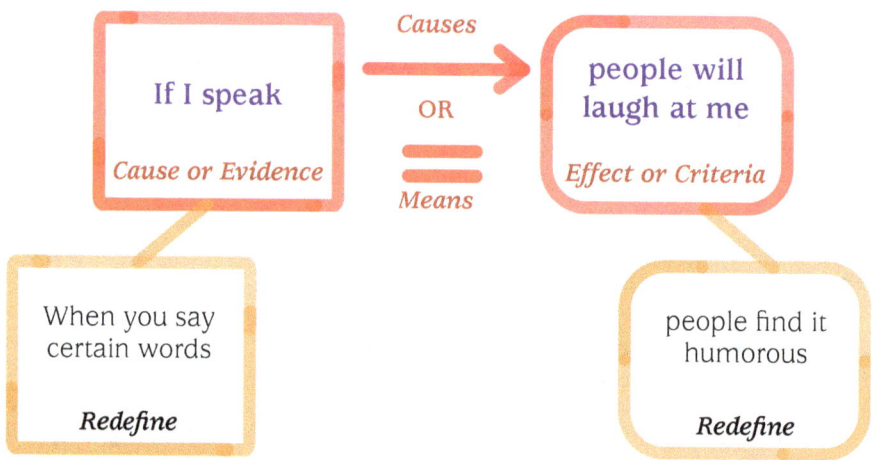

In this example, "speak" has been redefined as "saying certain words," which subtly makes the point that probably not everything the person says triggers laughter. "People will laugh at me" has been redefined as "people find it humorous." "Me" has been switched to "it," which shifts the reaction from an identity level to a behavior level. Similarly, "find it humorous" assumes a different intent than "laugh at," which can be considered a type of rejection.

Again, the purpose of such a use of Sleight of Mouth is not to attempt to conclude an argument but rather to reduce the level of CRASH accompanying the belief and begin a more productive exploration. In this case, it could lead to a discussion about which types of words were said and how they were said; and what was it that people found humorous about them.

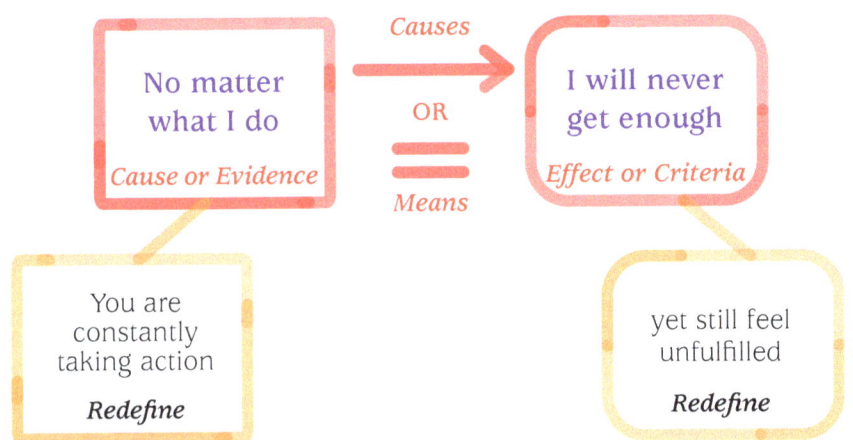

Here "no matter what I do" has been redefined as "you are constantly taking action." This shifts the situation from being about an unsolvable problem ("no matter what I do") to an attempted proactive solution ("constantly taking action"). "I will never get enough" has been redefined as "yet still feel unfulfilled," which moves the focus from an expected future ("will never") to the present and the past ("yet still"). It also introduces the notion of "feeling unfulfilled" in place of "never getting enough." The implication is that the judgment of "never getting enough" is based on a feeling, which is something within the person that can be examined and possibly changed, as opposed to some type of external karmic reality. Further, similar to using the term "discomfort" instead of "pain," the word "unfulfilled" actually contains a reference to the desired outcome of "fulfillment."

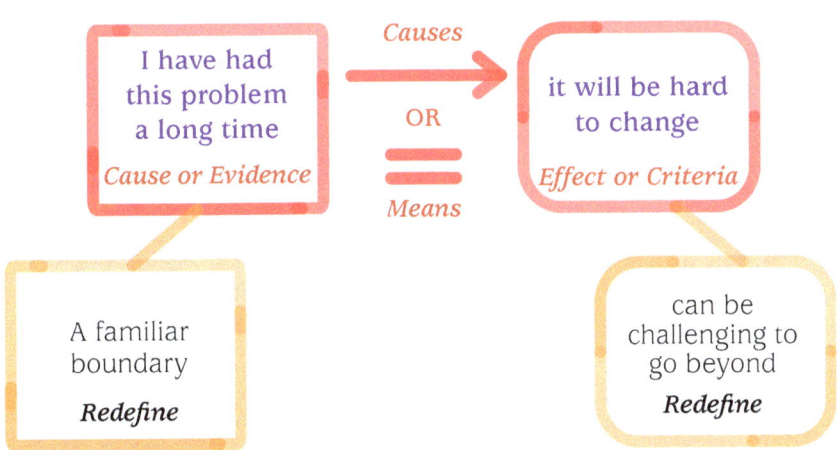

Sleight of Mouth 63

For this example, "having the problem for a long time" has been redefined as being "a familiar boundary." The introduction of the notion of "familiarity" brings up different set of associations, some which could be positive. The term "boundary" redefines "problem" as a type of obstacle that can be moved (or moved beyond) as opposed to something that is part of the person's make up.

In the second part of the statement, "will be" has been redefined as "can be," which shifts it from something that is definite to being merely a possibility. "Hard" has been redefined as "challenging," which has a more positive and proactive implication. "Go beyond" has been substituted for "change," shifting to more of an outcome frame and opening the possibility that success is less about altering the boundary or problem itself and more about the person's ability to transcend it.

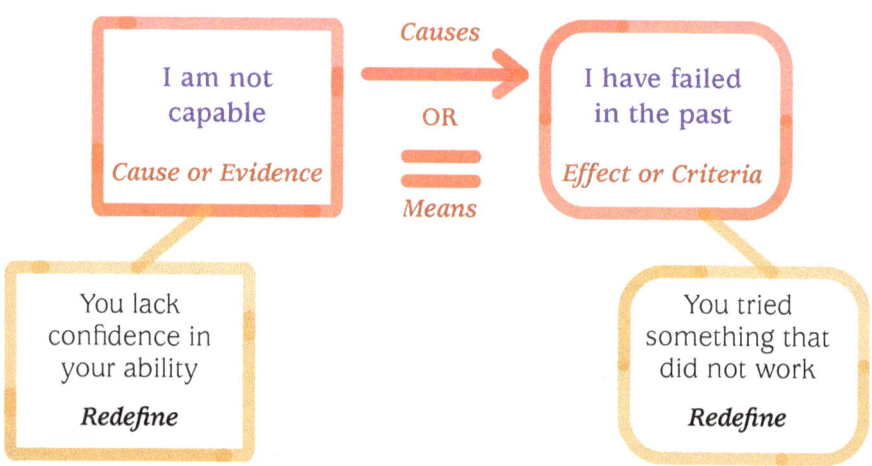

In this instance, "am not capable" is *Redefined* as "lack of confidence in your ability," shifting the issue from being an identity attribute to one of self-confidence. "Failed in the past" is relabeled as "tried something that did not work," the implication being that there are other things to try and that it is still possible to find and do "something that works." This puts the issue of capability back into an ongoing process related to the present and future rather than function of the past.

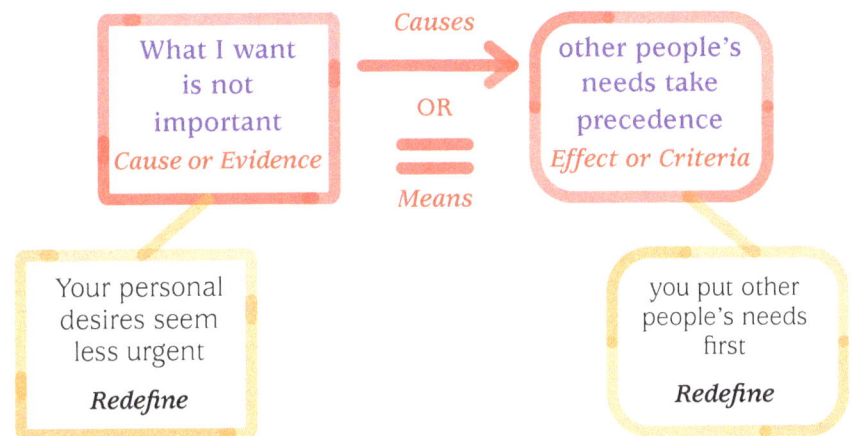

In this scenario, "What I want is not important" has been shifted to "Your personal desires seem less urgent." The word "is" has been *Redefined* as "seem," which indicates that it a matter of perception instead of reality. "Urgent" has been used in place of "important," making the issue more one related to timing than individual value on an identity level. "What I want" has been redefined as "your personal desires." This subtly narrows the scope of the issue from an all-inclusive category ("what I want" – which could mean *everything* I want) to a subset that has more than one possibility ("personal desires").

Importantly, in the second part of the statement, "putting other people's needs first" has been substituted for "other people's needs take precedence." This makes the issue more about the belief-holder's choices and priorities than a statement about his or her value as a person. The implication is that it is possible to reprioritize and make different choices.

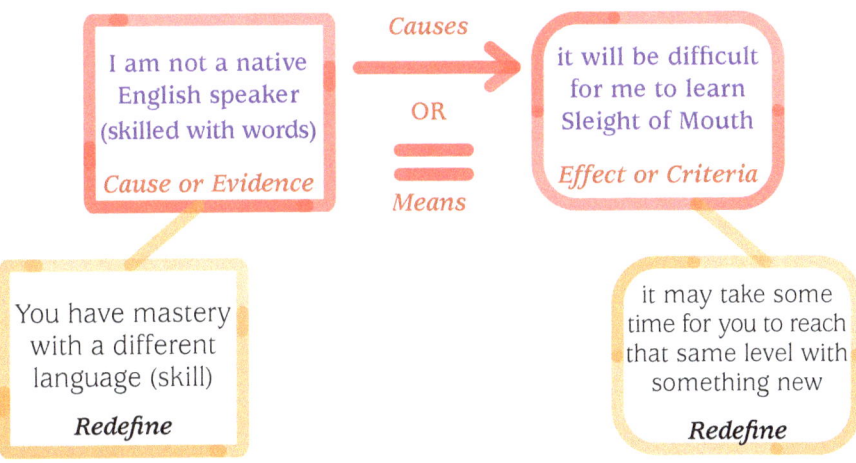

In this last example, not being "a native English speaker" (or skilled with words) is redefined as having "mastery with a different language" (or skill). This brings in the presupposition that the belief-holder is capable of mastery, which is naturally connected to his or her resources. It also brings attention to what he or she is capable of rather than what he or she "is not."

In the second part of the statement, "It will be difficult for me to learn Sleight of Mouth" is replaced by "it may take tome time for you to reach that same level with something new." The substitution of "may" for "will be," implies that what follows is a possibility, not necessarily a fact. "Difficult for me to learn" has been redefined as "take some time to reach that same level (of mastery)." The implication here is that "learning" is not "all or nothing." There is a wide range between beginner and master and that path of acquisition is not all equally easy or difficult. The presupposition is that the belief-holder can achieve the same level of mastery as she or he has with another language (or skill) that he or she has already mastered; it is just a matter of time.

Finally, "Sleight of Mouth" has been redefined as "something new." Once again, the implication is that Sleight of Mouth is not a single "thing." It is composed of many parts, some of which will be new to the belief-holder, but not necessary all of it. Thus, parts of it may already be familiar or easy to learn.

Of course, all of the examples above are just one possible way of Redefining the various belief statements. There is a limitless variety of other possibilities. Which ones will be more effective for a particular person will depend on the level of resonance, rapport, delivery, etc. Hopefully, however, these examples will give you a foundation in the principles and purposes of Redefining.

Creative Uses of the Sleight of Mouth Pattern of Redefine

As with all Sleight of Mouth patterns, Redefining is a function of a mindset focusing on finding another way to name or talk about a potentially limiting belief that reduces any CRASH associated with it and opens up other possibilities. This mindset primarily focuses on the question: *What is another word (or phrase) for one of the words (or phrases) used in the belief statement that means something similar but has more positive implications?* There are other uses for Redefining as well. For instance, it can also be applied to bring in a new or different perspective on order to get people to re-evaluate or reconsider a particular belief.

As an example, in *Mathew 15:11*, Jesus is quoted as saying, "*Not that which goeth into the mouth defileth the man; but that which cometh out of the mouth, this defileth a man.*" Jesus' *Redefine* makes reference to the hypocritical behavior of some people who strictly follow rules, such as dietary restrictions ("that which goeth *into* the mouth"), yet verbally inflate themselves and disparage others ("that which cometh *out* of the mouth"). A key implication is that what "defiles" someone is not on the level of environment (what they put in their mouths) but rather on the level of their expressed thoughts and beliefs (what comes out of their mouths).

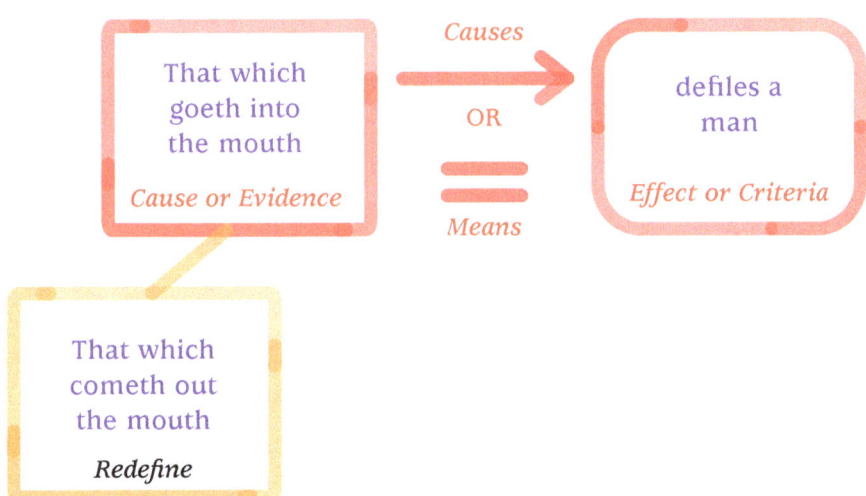

Abraham Lincoln applied a somewhat similar tactic in a speech he gave challenging pro-slavery theology. White people who were supposedly Christian with Christian values argued that it was okay to enslave black people because they were "inferior" to white people and could be treated differently. Like Jesus in the previous example, Lincoln used *Redefine* to highlight the inconsistency of that belief system.

> *Suppose it is true, that the Negro is inferior to the white, in the gifts of nature; is it not the exact reverse justice that the white should, for that reason, take from the Negro, any part of the little which has been given him? "Give to him that is needy" is the Christian rule of charity; but "Take from him that is needy" is the rule of slavery.*

Lincoln redefines the notion of "inferiority" as having been "given little" and thus being "needy." He then redefines "slavery" as "taking something away from" somebody. The two put together, "take from the needy," suddenly stands out as being clearly opposed to the "Christian rule of charity."

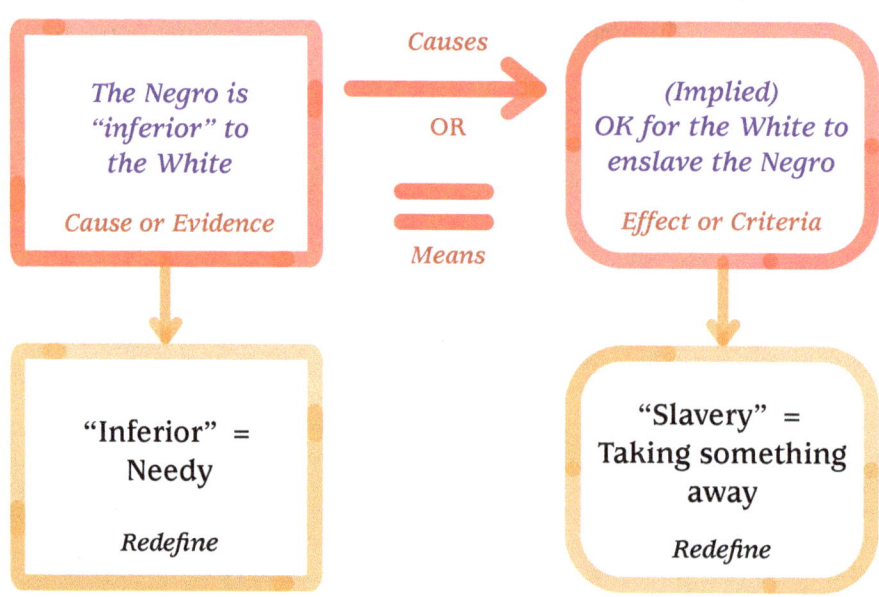

Redefining as a Mindset

As we have pointed out, Sleight of Mouth patterns can be even more effective when combined with multiple intelligences. Milton Erickson creatively used this approach to apply the pattern of Redefine with a young woman who had developed an "awful inferiority complex" about her looks. She had been in an automobile accident in her early teens that had left her with a small scar on the right side of her mouth. She felt the scar was "disgusting" and had developed a habit of hiding the scar from anyone's sight, continually covering the right side of her face with her hand. Although right-handed, she had learned to eat with her left hand so she could keep her face hidden with her right hand. She could not drive a car because that would leave her face uncovered. She would only go out on dates at night and then only walk on the right side of the boy she was dating so that they would not see the scar.

Erickson discovered that the young woman liked to draw and gave her the assignment to investigate and learn everything she could about "beauty marks" and "beauty patches" that some women used. She was then to make a number of sketches showing various beauty marks and their locations on women's faces. He also had her make a self-portrait of her own face. When they compared all of the drawings at their next meeting, she was surprised and shocked to discover that her scar looked exactly like some beauty marks. This completely shifted her perception of her scar as something that should be considered "disgusting" to something that could actually enhance the beauty of her face. As a result of this redefinition, Erickson reports that she "rapidly freed herself of the habit of covering her mouth and lost her feeling of inferiority."

Erickson's engagement of the young woman's interest in drawing helped to increase the resonance of redefining the "scar" as a possible "beauty mark." His intervention demonstrates that Redefining does not always necessarily need to be done in a direct verbal statement. When it is taken on as a mindset it can have many creative applications.

Chapter 6
Consequence

Consequence

Beliefs have consequences. Some consequences are intended; others are not. Some are positive; others are problematic. Even beliefs that sound positive can produce problematic effects. A belief like, "I am a capable person so I don't need help," for example, can produce problems if taken to an extreme. There are times when it is useful and necessary to ask for help. Sometimes beliefs produce a surprising secondary effect. A belief like, "The only way to get what I want is to focus on what is in my own best interest," can lead to enhanced cooperation with others, if the person thinks, "I will get my needs met better if I cooperate with others rather than fight with them. So, helping others is in my own interest."

In fact, more than the content of the belief, the consequence of holding a particular belief is another important indicator of whether it is likely to be a limiting belief or thought virus. Thus, the Sleight of Mouth pattern of *Consequence* involves directing attention to an effect (positive or negative) of the belief statement, or the generalization defined by the belief.

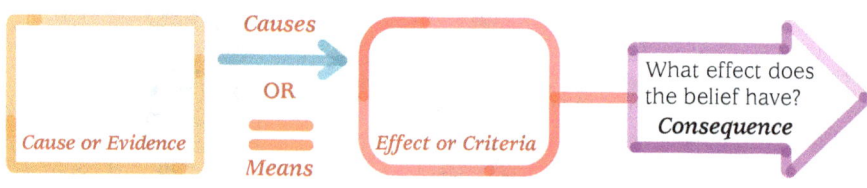

We naturally expect particular beliefs to be connected with certain consequences. Consider the joke about the surgeon who has just completed a complex and risky procedure. When asked if the operation was successful, the surgeon replies, "Oh yes, the operation was very successful. The patient died, but the operation was perfect."

Of course, we naturally expect that a "successful" operation would produce a positive result for the patient as opposed to simply a flawless procedure. Different interpretations of beliefs lead to different consequences, which is why it can be important to be clear about them.

Identifying Consequences Involves a Particular Mindset

Applying the pattern of *Consequence* involves taking on a particular mindset. An humorous example of this mindset is illustrated in the following anecdote.

> *Father O'Mally answers his phone.*
>
> *A voice asks, "Hello, is this Father O'Mally?"*
>
> *He replies, "It is."*
>
> *"This is the IRS (the government tax agency). Can you help us?"*
>
> *"If possible."*
>
> *"Do you know a Pat McCormick?"*
>
> *"I do."*
>
> *"Is he a member of your congregation?"*
>
> *"He is."*
>
> *"Did he donate $10,000 to your church?"*
>
> *"He will."*

The implication of this exchange is that Mr. McCormick has declared to the tax authorities that he has given Father O'Mally's church $10,000 and is taking it as a write-off on his taxes. Given that it is a fairly large amount, the IRS representative is checking with Father O'Mally to verify that Mr. McCormick has indeed made the donation. There are naturally negative consequences for Mr. McCormick if he has lied. Of course, there are positive consequences for Father O'Mally's church to receive the donation. Father O'Mally's response that "He will" indicates that Mr. McCormick has not actually made the donation but that Father O'Mally realizes that he has an opportunity. If Father O'Mally says, "No," Mr. McCormick gets in trouble and the church still doesn't get the money. However, Father O'Mally knows that, as a Consequence of his declaration, Mr. McCormick will certainly now donate the money to avoid getting into trouble.

Chains of Consequences

Consequences often follow from other consequences to form a type of chain. Chains of Consequences can also be used effectively in Sleight of Mouth, as is illustrated in the following fictional interaction between a man and a police officer who has pulled him over for speeding.

Officer: *May I see your driver's license?*

Driver: *I don't have one. I it was suspended when I got my 5th DUI (driving under the influence violation).*

Officer: *May I see the owner's card for this vehicle?*

Driver: *It's not my car. I stole it.*

Officer: *The car is stolen?*

Driver: *That's right. But come to think of it, I think I saw the owner's card in the glove box when I was putting my gun in there.*

Officer: *There's a gun in the glove box?*

Driver: *Yes sir. That's where I put it after I shot and killed the woman who owns this car and stuffed her in the trunk.*

Officer: *There's a BODY in the TRUNK?!?!?*

Driver: *Yes, sir.*

[Hearing this, the officer immediately called his Captain. The car was quickly surrounded by police vehicles, and the Captain approached the driver to handle the tense situation.]

Captain: *Sir, can I see your license?*

Driver: *Sure. Here it is.*

[It was valid.]

Captain: *Who's car is this?*

Driver: *It's mine, officer. Here's the owner's card.*

[The driver owned the car.]

Captain: *Could you slowly open your glove box so I can see if there's a gun in it?*

Driver: *Yes, sir, but there's no gun in it.*

[Sure enough, there was nothing in the glove box.]

Captain: *Would you mind opening your trunk? I was told you said there's a body in it.*

Driver: *No problem.*

[The trunk is opened and there is no body.]

Captain: *I don't understand it. The officer who stopped you said you told him you didn't have a license, stole the car, had a gun in the glove box, and that there was a dead body in the trunk.*

Driver: *Yeah, and I'll bet that liar told you I was speeding, too.*

The driver in this ridiculous story intentionally creates a chain of Consequences to try to discredit the officer who has pulled him over for speeding. The driver makes a series of statements that have more and more serious implications. The Consequences are so serious in fact that the officer calls in his superior to help deal with the seemingly perilous situation. The officer has presumably informed his or her captain of all the statements, which are then one-by-one shown to be false by the driver. The ultimate Consequence, asserted by the driver, is that everything the officer has said about the driver is not true, including the claim that he was speeding.

Another example of chains of Consequences is Albert Einstein's claim:

> *If relativity is proved right the Germans will call me a German, the Swiss will call me a Swiss citizen, and the French will call me a great scientist.*
>
> *If relativity is proved wrong the French will call me a Swiss, the Swiss will call me a German, and the Germans will call me a Jew.*

Evaluating Chains of Consequences

When we hold any belief too strongly and try to force the facts or our behavior to fit that belief, it can have problematic ramifications, as is humorously illustrated in the following joke.

> *A man goes to a clothing store to pick up a new suit that is being tailored for him. When the man puts on the pants, however, one leg is shorter than the other. The man starts to complain, but the tailor counters, "The suit is just fine. Lean over to your left a bit and no one will notice." The same thing happens with the coat. The sleeves are of different lengths and the collar is not shaped correctly. The tailor tells the man, "If you'd just lift your shoulder a bit and tilt your head back it will be just fine." The fitting session goes on and, after many such adjustments, the man's body is so contorted, he can barely walk. When he leaves, he limps out of the store, looking like Quasimodo (the Hunchback of Notre Dame).*
>
> *Just as the man is walking out the door of the shop, two people are walking by on the other side of the street. "Gosh, look at that guy over there," says one person to the other, "The poor fellow must be horribly deformed." "Perhaps so," replies the companion, "But I want to find out who his tailor is. That suit fits him perfectly."*

Some beliefs are like the suit that the man is wearing; they fit perfectly, if we contort ourselves to match them. If you believe that the world is flat and the photos of it being a sphere are a government perpetuated hoax, for instance, there are numerous consequences. How do you explain the movement of the sun and the phases of the moon. Some "flat-earthers" contend that the sun and moon are still there, but they're much closer and have their own separate light sources. Others believe that the planets and the stars are just projections on a huge dome. Thus, the moon landing had to be faked because you can't get past the dome. Some even say that proves the conspiracy theory that the U.S. government killed President Kennedy because he wanted to go to the Moon, and it would have exposed the hoax.

Such a string of confirming consequences might make sense within a particular group of beliefs but begins to necessitate "contortions" in other parts of our belief systems and requires putting a lot of blame on anonymous "others." If we maintain a COACH state and an outcome frame and apply some of the principles presented so far in the book, upholding such a belief system ends up feeling like the man trying to fit himself into the poorly tailored suit.

Leveraging Positive Consequences

Beliefs, of course, can also have powerfully positive effects. I have spoken previously about the potential impact of beliefs when it comes to health and healing. An interesting example of the Sleight of Mouth pattern of consequence with respect to healing is presented in *Matthew* (9:27-31):

> *And when Jesus departed thence, two blind men followed him, crying, and saying, Thou son of David, have mercy on us. And when he was come into the house, the blind men came to him: and Jesus saith unto them, Believe ye that I am able to do this? They said unto him, Yea, Lord. Then touched he their eyes, saying, According to your faith be it unto you. And their eyes were opened...*

Jesus' comment, "According to your faith be it unto you," is a good example of connecting a positive consequence to a belief. The assertion of this consequence appears to have been a main part of Jesus's impact and teachings. According to *Mark* (9:23), Jesus went so far as to assert, "If you can believe, all things are possible to him who believes."

Speaking of Jesus, there is a fascinating case involving the use of Consequence in the work of Milton Erickson (*Uncommon Therapy*, p. 28). Erickson was on the staff at a psychiatric hospital where there was a young patient who called himself Jesus. He paraded about as the Messiah, wore a sheet draped around him, and attempted to impose Christianity on people. One day Erickson approached him on the hospital grounds and said, "I understand you have had experience as a carpenter." Since Jesus was supposedly a carpenter's son and would have worked in his youth as a carpenter, the patient could only reply that he had. Erickson went on to ask him if he was interested in serving Mankind. Of course, that would be a consequence of being Jesus as well. The young man had to agree. Erickson then mentioned that the Psychology Laboratory needed some bookcases built and used the two consequences as leverage to involve the young man in a project to build them. This gave the young man something productive to do that brought more grounded relationships as well appreciation from others. According to Erickson, the patient eventually became a productive handyman for the Psychology Laboratory.

This is a classic example of the application of the Sleight of Mouth pattern of Consequence. A limiting belief can be reframed and leveraged by finding potentially positive consequences.

Applying the Sleight of Mouth Pattern of Consequence

As is illustrated by the Erickson case of the person who believed he was Jesus, the mindset behind the Sleight of Mouth pattern of Consequence involves exploring, *what is an effect of the belief, or the relationship defined by the belief that can be leveraged for something productive? Is there any positive benefit or by-product of this belief?*

It is important to keep in mind that a "by-product" is different than an "intention." *By-products*, even if they are positive, are frequently not consciously intended. They happen as an after-effect or ramification of some action or condition. While positive by-products may reinforce a particular action or condition, they can also be used to lead it in a different direction.

Reflecting on the limiting belief statements we have been using in the previous chapters, the following are some possible examples of applying the pattern of Consequence.

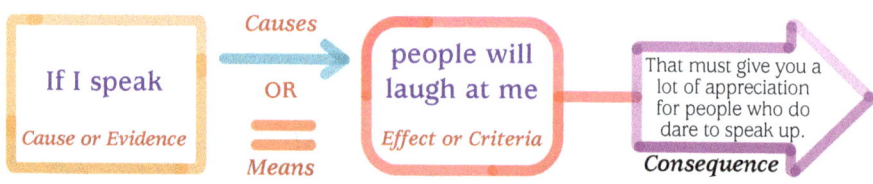

This example suggests that a Consequence of the belief "If I speak people will laugh at me" could be having greater "appreciation for people who do dare to speak up." Pointing that out shifts attention from the fear of being laughed at to the possibility of "daring to speak up." It also implies that the person holding the belief is not alone in such a fear, as there are others who have also potentially been laughed at for what they have said, yet still find the courage to express themselves verbally.

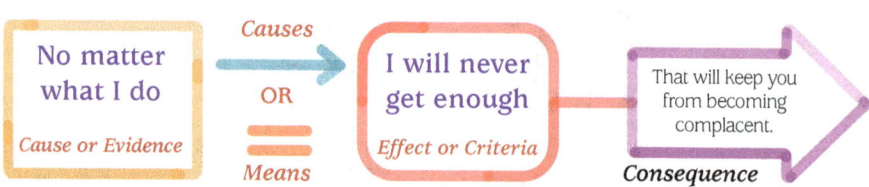

This statement proposes that a positive Consequence of the belief "no matter what I do I will never get enough" could be to prevent the person from becoming smug and uncritically self-satisfied with themselves or their achievements. Thus, it could serve the belief holder by supporting the person to remain active and motivated to keep trying.

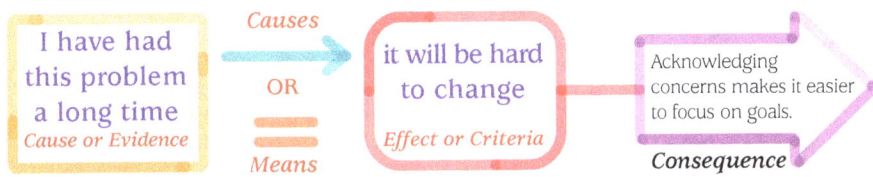

The purpose of suggesting the Consequence that "acknowledging concerns makes it easier to focus on goals" is to shift attention from a problem frame to an outcome frame. The implication is that, by declaring the issue expressed in the belief statement, it no longer needs to be the focus of attention and energy. Instead, concentration can be put on what the belief holder actually wants as opposed to what the person is trying to get rid of.

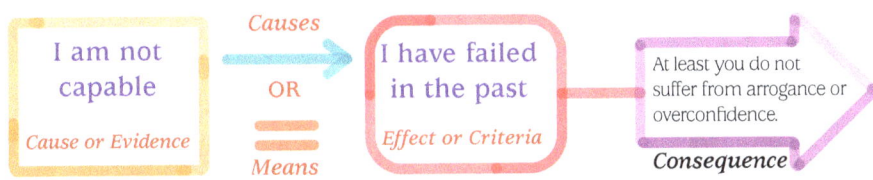

Asserting the Consequence that the belief "I am not capable because I have failed in the past" prevents the belief holder from being "arrogant or overconfident" suggests that it could have the positive result of helping the person maintain a healthy ego by keeping the person from becoming pompous or conceited. Another implication is that beliefs about one's own capability can be a function of personal bias (arrogance, overconfidence). Of course, this bias can go both ways, either inflating or deflating one's self-perception. Thus, the wording of the Consequence subtly begs the question of whether the belief holder might be being overly self-critical.

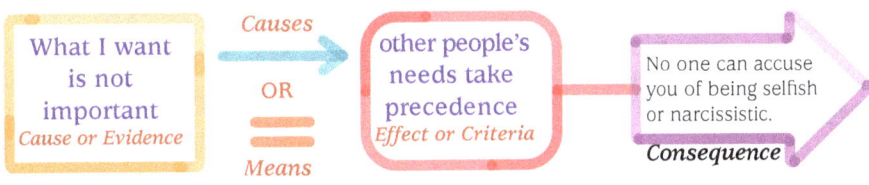

Similar to the previous example, the Consequence that "no one can accuse you of being selfish or narcissistic" for letting "other people's needs take precedence," suggests that the belief is serving to keep the person's ego in check. In this case, however, the wording of the Consequence moves the issue to the identity level (i.e., "*being* selfish or narcissistic" versus "*suffering from* arrogance or overconfidence"). Again, implying that such self-judgments are influenced by identity level traits also brings up the possibility that the opposite could also be an influence, i.e.: being self-deprecating and without healthy boundaries.

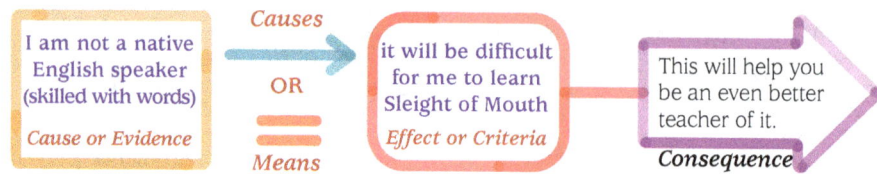

The proposed Consequence that potential difficulties learning Sleight of Mouth will make the person "an even better teacher of it" suggests an intimate connection between learning and teaching. The implication is that, because the person will deeply understand the challenges of learning the processes and patterns of Sleight of Mouth, he or she will know how to help others to better navigate those challenges. Oftentimes, people who learn something quickly and easily have a lot of pre-existing unconscious competence. Because it comes so naturally to them, they don't necessarily make as good of a teacher as someone who has had to struggle a bit and consciously figure out the necessary links and connections. Like several the other examples in this section, the wording of the Consequence also shifts attention from the belief holder's concern with his or her own personal challenges (ego) in learning to a focus on supporting others in their learning process (soul).

It is hopefully obvious that none of the suggested Consequences in this section are intended to belittle the limiting belief or to secure some type of agreement from the belief holder. Rather, their purpose is to introduce other perspectives and shift attention to stimulate deeper reflection on the belief and belief statement that could lead to new insights or other possibilities.

Exploring Different Levels of Consequences

As these examples illustrate, consequences can occur at different levels: environment, behavior, capabilities, values, identity, or purpose. Some beliefs may produce a problematic consequence at one level and a positive consequence at another level, or vice versa. In fact, this points to another important "virus detection" process: checking the consequences of a particular belief at different levels. What seems positive or harmless at one level may create problems at another level.

The belief that the world is flat, for instance, may seem trivial or silly on a behavioral level. For most people, that particular belief would not affect how they conduct their daily behavior; how they get to work, make their meals, manage their finances, etc. The consequences it can lead to at the level of identity and purpose however – i.e., it is a government hoax perpetrated to fool people and take their money and can lead to murder if someone threatens to expose it – can have a much darker affect. Similarly, Hitler's tirade against "the Jews" might have initially appeared to be just another incident of intolerance with respect to religious beliefs. Yet, when taken to the level of identity and purpose, it led the extermination of millions of people.

Conversely, a belief that wreaks havoc at the lower levels (environment, behavior, and capabilities) may be linked to more positive consequences at the level of identity and purpose that can lead to a helpful transformation. An intriguing example is provided by Milton Erickson (*Phoenix*, pp. 44-46) in which he describes his work with a young man who had quite a different belief system than that of a flat-earther. Erickson recounts:

> *I received a telephone call from a young man who told me, "I'm working on a ship as a seaman and I'm awfully afraid I'm going to go into orbit." I told him I thought it would be inadvisable to continue working on board that ship. So, he got a job working in a mine. And he found that even if he were a mile deep into the Earth, he was still obsessed with the fear of going into orbit.*

The young man saw some other psychiatrists who recommended hospitalization and electro-shock therapy to treat his delusion. The man decided to come to Phoenix to work with Erickson, who tried several unsuccessful interventions, such as having the young man "count his steps as he walked along the street and to memorize the street names" as a distraction. According to Erickson:

> *That, "I'm going to go into orbit, I'm going to go into orbit," obsessed him... interfered with him. He couldn't get very much sleep because he was afraid he was going to go into orbit. And I finally realized I couldn't do anything for him except settle down with him and explain to him, "Now apparently it is your destiny to go into orbit. Now astronauts go into orbit... they come back to earth again. And as long as you are going to go into orbit why not get it OVER with?" So, I had him take salt pills and a canteen of water and I had him walk about fourteen hours a day along the tops of mountains around here, and he had to come in at 10:30 at night to report that he had not yet gone into orbit. But he slept well, as you would walking around on mountain tops with a canteen of water and walking for about fourteen hours a day. And finally, he began to get just a little bit dubious about going into orbit.*

Erickson reports that, eventually, the young man's sister from California called and asked if her brother could come to her place to do some odd jobs for her. Erickson told the young man he could go because his sister lived near mountains, and he would always be able to hike up to the mountains with his canteen if he felt as if he were going to go into orbit. Several months later, the young man came back to visit Erickson and told him he now realized that the fear of going into orbit was a crazy delusional idea and thanked Erickson for saving him from the state mental hospital and electro-shock treatment. According to Erickson, the man went on to get a job, later married a woman with a child, and was happy being a husband and a father.

Reflections on the Case

In addition to the brilliant use of Consequence, this case illustrates a few principles we have presented so far in this book. The young man's statement, "I'm awfully afraid I'm going to go into orbit," is a clear indictor of a type of "away from – CRASH cycle" that I described earlier. The "away from" creates more CRASH and the CRASH creates more "away from."

Erickson's first attempted interventions at the levels of environment, behavior, and capabilities (working in a mine, having the man count his steps and memorize street names) seem reasonable, but they all still assume a problem frame and direct attention toward avoiding or getting rid of the belief and the CRASH state it is producing. The resistance this produces can have the paradoxical effect of reinforcing the cycle.

Erickson's ultimately successful application of Consequence shifted attention to the levels of purpose and identity. Erickson tells the young man that apparently it is his "destiny to go into orbit." Erikson also invokes the identity of "astronauts" who go into orbit and "come back to Earth again." This then leads to the consequence *"as long as you are going to go into orbit why not get it OVER with?"* That, in turn, shifts the situation from avoidance to an outcome frame. And it then follows that walking along the tops of mountains should make transition to orbit happen even more quickly since the young man will be closer to the sky.

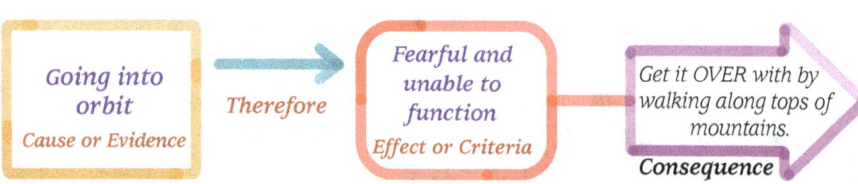

Shifting from an *away from* motivation to going *towards* "getting it over with" means the young man no longer has to fight against the belief. In fact, he is now completely and congruently aligned with it. This undoubtedly starts to reduce some of the CRASH associated with the belief. Sleeping well after the long walks also lessens the propensity for CRASH. Walking for hours in a COACH state along the tops of mountains affords a lot of opportunity for self-reflection and reassessment, even if it is not conscious. It is not surprising that the young man, through the feedback of his own direct experience, begins to "come back to earth again," becomes dubious about his limiting belief and develops a new relationship with himself, his identity, and his purpose.

There is another instructive example from Erickson that illustrates the sometimes-paradoxical nature of Consequences. Erickson grew up on a farm and tells the story of how, one day, his father was trying get a large calf into the barn. He had a rope around the calf's neck and was pulling with all his might while the resistant calf pulled in the other direction. Erickson's father asked the young Milton to help him. Instead of joining his father to pull on the rope, Erickson walked behind the calf and started pulling forcefully on its tail. This caused the calf to start pulling "away from" Milton, which, of course, meant that the calf ended up going "toward" his father and was thus easily led into the barn.

This is why I say that Sleight of Mouth patterns are more about "mindset" than specific verbal formulations. Erickson's actions with the calf were a "somatic" Sleight of Mouth. The calf is like a person with a limiting belief. Trying to change or control the person and their belief is like the father struggling to pull the calf into the barn. Sleight of Mouth patterns, such as that of Consequence, are like Erickson going behind the calf and pulling on its tail. By seemingly joining with the belief, we can skillfully redirect the attention and energy associated with it.

Chapter 7

Another Outcome

Another Outcome

An *outcome* is the result of some action or condition. Some outcomes are desirable and intended. Others are unwanted or unexpected. When taking action, outcomes (desired or undesired) are generally the key focus of our attention and energy. They are the center point around which we organize our thoughts and behavior. Thus, shifting an outcome can bring about a major change in the way we are thinking and acting. This is the main purpose of the Sleight of Mouth pattern of Another Outcome. *Another Outcome* essentially involves switching attention to a related but different result than that addressed or implied by a particular belief statement.

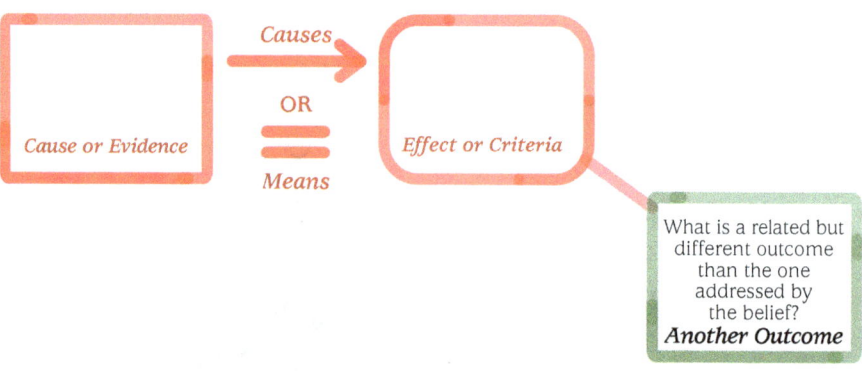

On the surface, this pattern has similarities to both Intent and Consequence, but it engages a fundamentally different mindset. It is more directly related to the content of the belief; especially the "effect" of a cause-effect statement. *Consequences* are essentially the by-product of a particular action or condition. *Outcomes* are the result of expectations and typically indicate an anticipated result of an action or condition that is either desired or to be avoided. As I pointed out earlier, *intentions* are generally more related to values. Thus, a particular intent may be expressed through a number of possible actions and outcomes. So, there is a close relationship between intentions and outcomes, but they are not the same.

The Connection between Outcomes and Intentions

A humorous illustration of the connection between intent and outcome, but also their difference, is provided by Mark Twain in his *Notebooks*. He quips about an alleged shooting incident, "At bottom I did not believe I had touched that man. The law of probabilities decreed me guiltless of his blood for in all my small experience with guns I had never hit anything I had tried to hit, and I knew I had done my best to hit him." The implication is that his intent to hit the person was a guarantee that he would **not** achieve the outcome of actually hitting him.

As expressions of intentions, though, shifting an outcome can have a "backwards" influence on interpreting intentions. A good example of this comes in the first few lines of Mark Antony's famous speech in William Shakespeare's play *Julius Caesar*. Speaking to a potentially hostile crowd after Caesar has been killed for allegedly trying to become a dictator, Antony (an acknowledged friend of Caesar) begins his oratory by stating, "I have come to *bury* Caesar not to *praise* him." Burying and praising are behavioral outcomes that are expressions of differing intentions. The intention behind praise would be to express approval or admiration for someone. The intent behind burying would be more about putting them to rest. Antony uses this distinction between the two outcomes to successfully reduce suspicions about what he is about to say.

Another illustration of how shifting an outcome can produce or reflect a shift in intent is provided by the following joke.

> *A little boy strides through his backyard, a baseball cap on his head, and toting his ball and bat. "I'm the greatest baseball player in the world," he says proudly. Then he tosses the ball in the air, swings with all his might and misses. He picks up the ball again, throws it into the air, saying to himself, "I'm the greatest baseball player ever!" He swings mightily at the ball again, and again he misses. He pauses a moment to examine the bat and ball carefully. Then once again he throws the ball into the air repeating, "I'm the greatest baseball player who ever lived." He swings the bat hard once more and again misses the ball. "Wow!" he exclaims. "What a fantastic pitcher I am!"*

Is the outcome for the batter to hit the ball or to miss the ball? It could be either, depending upon which is more relevant for your point of view. In baseball, the batter wants to hit the ball. The pitcher, on the other hand, wants to throw the ball in such a way that batter misses the ball. Being a "baseball player" includes both. The boy in this case is potentially in the position of both batter and pitcher. We assume he is tossing the ball to himself with the intention to hit it. Being "the greatest baseball player in the world" would mean he should hit the ball soundly every time. So, the outcome initially seems at odds with the belief about himself that he keeps repeating. However, given the outcome of missing three times (a strikeout), the boy can reinterpret his intention to be that of a pitcher. In that case, the outcome is a success and thus serves to validate his belief.

A classic example of Another Outcome comes from John F. Kennedy's 1961 presidential inaugural address, in which he states, "Ask not what your country can do for you – ask what you can do for your country." This request is clearly a shift from an outcome and intention related to ego (what your country can to do for *you*) to one related more to soul (what you can do for *your country*). The purpose was to bring awareness to a set of issues related to the larger holon (your country) to which citizens belonged and the possible contributions that they could make to the progress of that bigger system, which would benefit them and many others as well.

Not all outcomes are desired. Many beliefs, especially limiting beliefs, are built and directed toward avoiding negative outcomes. Sometimes drawing attention to an even more negative outcome can be used to create a shift in focus of attention and intention. For example, *Matthew* (10:28) quotes Jesus as saying, "Fear not them which kill the body, but are not able to kill the soul; but rather fear him which is able to destroy both soul and body in hell." The death of the body would be the ultimate outcome to avoid for most people. Jesus' purpose in making such a statement is clearly to lead attention to an outcome worse than that in order to create a shift of attention to something he believes is deeper and more purposeful (and potentially brings more balance between ego and soul).

Strategies for Exploring Other Relevant Outcomes

The mindset associated Another Outcome is to create a switch in focus from one outcome to a different outcome that shifts attention and energy to a more useful or productive direction. It explores, *"What other related outcome could be more useful and productive than the one stated or implied by the belief?"* For this to be effective, there has to be some degree of pacing and leading. If the outcome being introduced has no connection with the belief, it will be easily rejected or resisted. If the positive intention of a particular belief has already been established, the search can focus on an outcome that is more relevant, appropriate, or productive with respect to that positive intention. There are two other fundamental strategies that can be applied to help identify other potential outcomes.

Shifting from Problem Frame to Outcome Frame

Since most limiting beliefs are likely stated in an *away from* form (problem frame), a more useful outcome can be found by refocusing on what to go *towards* instead (outcome frame). A classic example is that of a man who came to Milton Erickson because of phantom limb pain. He had fallen off a roof and injured his arm so badly that it had to be amputated. He suffered pain in the vanished limb for months and found no relief in various kinds of treatment. Finally, he traveled to Phoenix to be visit Erickson. Though skeptical because of the past failures to treat his symptoms, the man wanted to see if Erickson could "use hypnosis to take the pain away." Instead, Erickson said to him, "I think anyone who has suffered as much phantom limb pain as you have, deserves at least as much phantom limb pleasure," and made that the initial focus of their hypnotic work. Through this approach, the man was ultimately able to make good progress with respect to the relief of his symptoms.

Erickson's statement brilliantly shifts the outcome from an *away from* problem frame (getting rid of the phantom limb pain) to a *toward* outcome frame (experiencing at least as much pleasure as the pain the man has endured). It creates a major shift in how attention and energy is focused. Like the young man who believed he was going to "go into orbit" in the previous section, trying to suppress or get rid of a symptom can paradoxically bring even more attention and energy to it and can become a "CRASH–Away From" loop. Proposing to create "phantom limb pleasure" introduces the possibility that if you can experience pain, you can then equally experience pleasure. Rather than numbing out, it also brings out the potential for something more positive to come from the loss of the arm by making it a possible source of pleasure as opposed to only trauma.

Meta Outcomes

Another strategy to find other possible outcomes involves exploring what are called "meta outcomes" in NLP. A *meta outcome* is the "outcome of an outcome." Exploring meta outcomes involves considering the questions, "What will be the result of achieving that outcome?" or "What else are you attempting to achieve by reaching that outcome?"

As an example, let's say a person has the outcome of "winning the lottery." The chances of actually attaining such an outcome may be small, setting the person up for disappointment. The "meta outcome" of this outcome, however, may be discovered by asking, "What do you want to achieve by winning the lottery? The answer might be something like, "Then I'll have a lot money, and won't have to worry about paying my bills." If you ask again, "And what would be the result of having a lot of money and not having to worry about paying your bills?", you might get the answer, "Then my life would be easier and more stress free." Thus, the deeper meta outcome of "winning the lottery" is to have "an easier, more stress-free life." Winning the lottery is only one means to achieve this meta outcome. There are many other strategies and outcomes (such as practicing stress management techniques, making sound investments, learning effective financial planning and money management skills, etc.) that can also help to reach the same meta outcome; and which may be more easily achievable. Knowing about meta outcomes and pursuing them does not require giving up on the initially stated outcome ("winning the lottery") but can add more options that make it much more likely that the meta outcome will ultimately be attained.

Meta outcomes are, of course, linked to intentions. Identifying meta outcomes can thus shift intentions and their focus. In fact, exploring the anticipated outcome of an outcome typically leads to a successively higher-level focus. For example, let's say that a person has an outcome of "punishing someone else." The meta outcome of "punishment" might be "to teach them a lesson." The meta outcome of "teaching them a lesson" might be to "change their behavior.. The meta outcome of "changing their behavior" might be to "make a more secure and harmonious relationship." The meta outcome of "making a more secure and harmonious relationship" might be "to grow and evolve together." The chain of outcomes (and associated intentions) naturally moves from *away from* to *towards* and from the level of behavior to identity and purpose.

Applying the Sleight of Mouth Pattern of Intention

Like all the Sleight of Mouth Patterns, identifying Another Outcome can be done by asking the relevant questions, like the meta outcome question. You can also apply the mindset and introduce the results conversationally, as in the example of Erickson with the man who was suffering from phantom limb pain. One way to do that is to simply say something like, "Perhaps the real/ultimate goal is not to X (the outcome addressed or implied by the belief) but rather to Y (the more productive outcome)." Or, "Maybe the issue is not so much about X as it is about Y."

The following are examples of how the pattern of Another Outcome could be applied to the group of limiting beliefs we have explored in the previous sections.

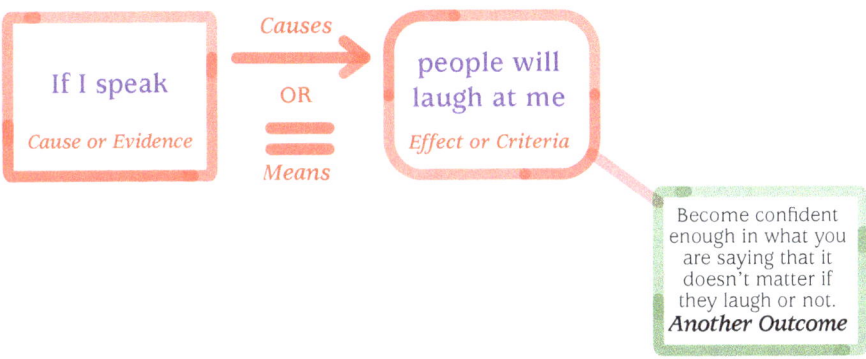

Here, the focus has been shifted from avoiding the external behavior of others "laughing at me" to going toward the outcome of developing the capability within oneself of having "enough confidence in what I am saying."

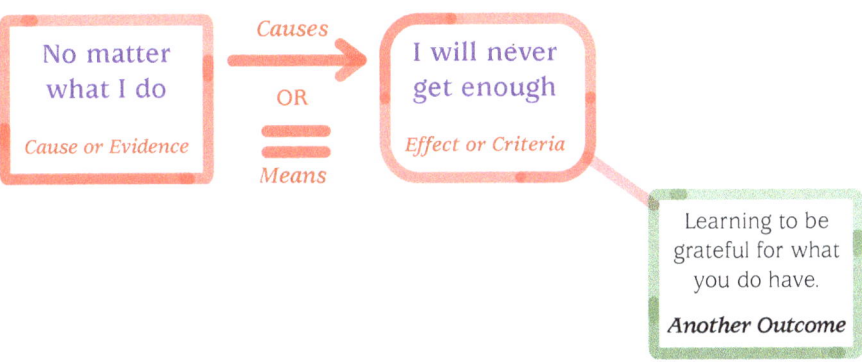

In this example, the focus is again shifted from a problem frame at the level of behavior (doing) and environment (getting) to an outcome frame at the level of capability (learning to be grateful). This serves the purpose of helping the person be more internally referenced and less dependent on external conditions for their sense of fulfillment. The notion of gratitude also shifts attention from what is missing to appreciation for what one does have, including things that were not obtained through one's actions.

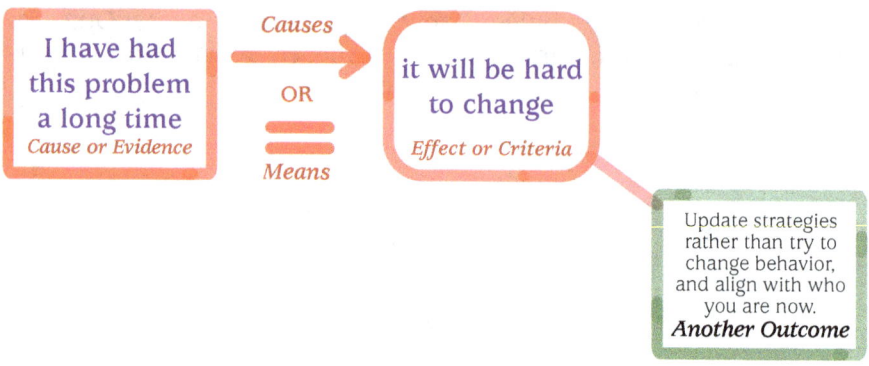

Again, a problem frame has been transformed into an outcome frame and the issue has been shifted from one of environment (time) and trying to change behavior to the levels of capability (updating strategies), which would naturally lead to a change in behavior, and identity (aligning with who you are now). The implication is that the person has already evolved at the identity level, which would bring a natural adjustment of capabilities and behaviors without the need for effort.

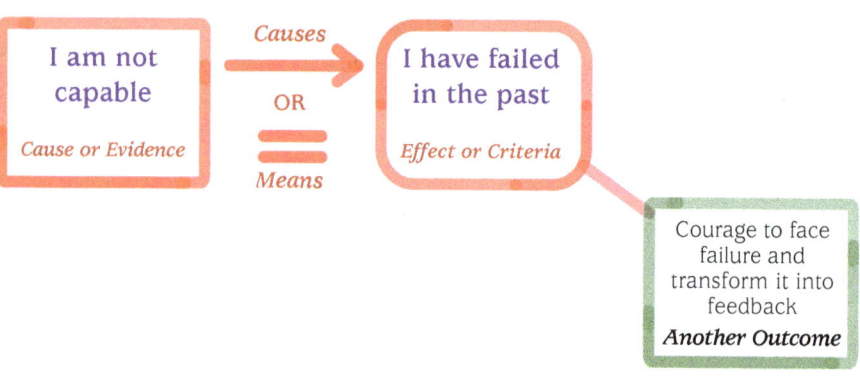

In addition to shifting from a problem frame to an outcome frame, this intervention suggests that, rather than try to avoid "failure," it should be embraced and can be transformed into something positive, and even necessary to become capable. It also introduces the notion of "courage" which suggests the connection to some higher level of purpose.

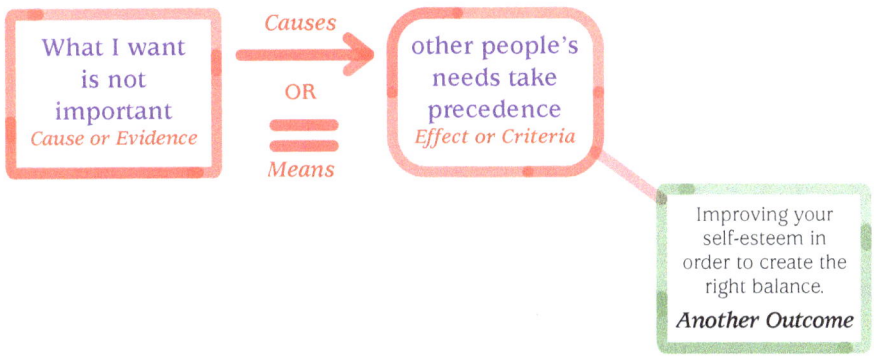

The shift from problem frame to outcome frame here involves bringing focus to the meta outcome of creating balance between self and others (ego and soul), instead of assuming it is a binary choice (one or the other). It also shifts attention from an environment and behavior level (what I want) to that of values and identity (improve your self-esteem). Again, the implication is that a shift at the belief and identity level would naturally bring about an update of the lower levels.

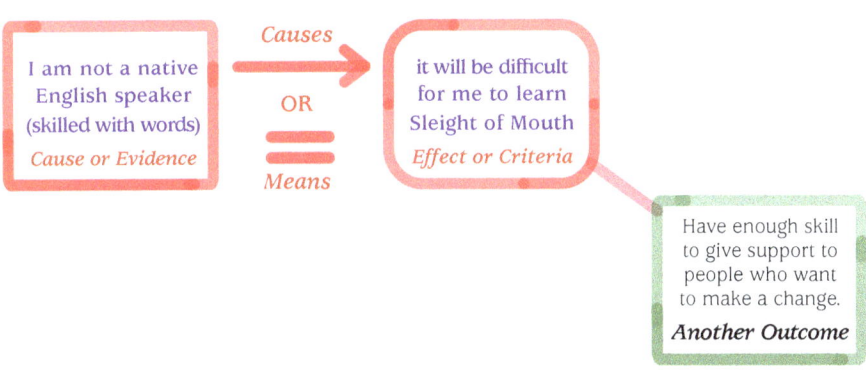

This new outcome suggests that the focus does not necessarily need to be about "learning Sleight of Mouth" completely but rather to "acquire enough skill" to give support to people who want to make a change. Those skills associated with Sleight of Mouth, as we have seen, are not necessarily verbal or specific to a particular language.

Summary and Reflections

As with the examples in previous sections, the success of any of these interventions will depend on the degree of resonance they have with the listener, which is a function of the level of rapport and second position the speaker has with the listener. It is important to be sure that there has been enough verbal and non-verbal *pacing* in order to *lead* effectively.

Outcomes and intentions are distinct but intimately linked. Shifting an intention will naturally bring changes to the actions and outcomes expected to fulfill the intention. Similarly, shifting an outcome implies a shift in intention. Thus, switching focus to another outcome can also influence the deeper intention of a belief.

The main strategies to find other relevant outcomes are (1) switching from an *away from* problem frame to a *toward* outcome frame and (2) exploring meta outcomes (the anticipated outcomes of other outcomes). The most effective applications of Another Outcome frequently involve a positive shift to a more profound Level of Change, as these will naturally promote alterations and adjustments on the lower levels.

Chapter 8
Chunk Down

Chunk Down

A "chunk" is a part or a piece of something. The term "chunking" refers to reorganizing or breaking down some object or experience into bigger or smaller pieces. *Chunking Down* involves dissecting or dividing something into its component pieces. For example, a "car" may be chunked down into "tires," "engine," "brake system," "transmission," etc. Each of those "chunks" may in turn be chunked down into their component parts, and so on. Similarly, sentences can be chunked down into clauses, which can be chunked down into phrases, which can be chunked down into words, which can be chunked down into syllables, which can be chunked down into letters. Chunking down thus involves bringing focus to successively smaller parts of a holarchy.

Chunking something down can often make it seem simpler. A problem that appears overwhelming, for instance, may be chunked down into a series of smaller more manageable problems. There is an old riddle which asks, "How do you eat a whole watermelon?" The answer is an example of chunking down: "One bite at a time." This same principle can be applied to any type of situation or experience. A very imposing goal, such as "starting a new business," may be chunked into sub-goals, such as "developing a product," "identifying potential clients," "selecting team members," "creating a business plan," "seeking investment," etc. As the saying goes, "The journey of a thousand miles starts with the first step."

Chunking down can also change the meaning or impact of something in the sense that *what is true for the whole is not necessarily true for its parts*. The human brain as a whole has different properties from the individual nerve cells of which it is made. Water has different properties from the hydrogen and oxygen atoms that create it. Groups have different properties from the individuals that form them. The fact that a person comes from a wealthy country does not necessarily mean that they are a wealthy person. A person who works for a prestigious company may not have that same prestige as an individual. A very heavy object may be made of parts that are not at all hard to lift individually. Similarly, generalizations can have an impact that is different than the various experiences it is representing when they are examined individually.

The Sleight of Mouth pattern of *Chunk Down* involves breaking the elements making up a belief statement into smaller pieces such that it changes their meaning or impact, creating a different or enriched perception of the generalization expressed by the belief.

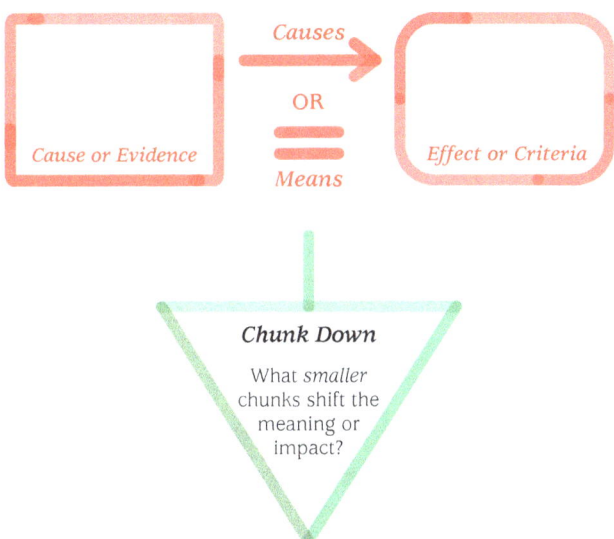

Examples of Applying Chunk Down

Milton Erickson demonstrated a good example of this pattern when working with a man who was convinced that he was "unhypnotizable." He said to Erickson, "You will never put me into a trance." Erickson's response was, "You are right. I cannot put YOU into trance... just your arm." Erickson then reached out and lifted the arm of the slightly confused man and held it up while looking meaningfully into the man's eyes. When he released the arm it remained suspended without the man intentionally trying to keep it raised. Erickson then suggested to the arm that *it* "continue floating upward" which, to the man's surprise, it did. This was the beginning of a productive series of sessions where the man did eventually learn to experience other types of hypnotic phenomena that were very helpful for some of the personal challenges he was facing.

By chunking down from the identity level ("YOU") to a part of the body (the arm) and a behavior (lifting/floating) Erickson was able to bypass resistance coming from a belief about what "hypnosis" was supposed be and be like. Erickson no doubt also realized that at least some part of the person was actually interested in having the experience since the man had come there to begin with. Erickson's Chunk Down gave him the opportunity to create resonance and rapport with that part without threatening the parts affected by the limiting belief. His use of pacing and leading then allowed him to encourage that part of the man to safely express itself.

Another interesting example of using Chunk Down is provided in *Matthew* (22:15-22) which describes the following incident.

> *Then went the Pharisees, and took counsel how they might entangle him in his talk.*
>
> *And they sent out unto him their disciples with the Herodians, saying, Master we know that thou art true, and teachest the way of God in truth, neither carest thou for any man: for thou regardest not the person of men. Tell us therefore, What thinkest thou? Is it lawful to give tribute unto Caesar, or not?*
>
> *But Jesus perceived their wickedness, and said, Why tempt me ye hypocrites? Shew me the tribute money. And they brought unto him a penny. And he saith unto them, Whose is this image and subscription. They say unto him, Caesar's. Then saith he unto them, Render therefore unto Caesar the things which are Caesar's; and unto God the things that are God's. When they had heard these words, they marveled, and left him, and went their way.*

Jesus' opponents were clearly attempting to put him in a "double bind" (entangle him in his talk) with the question, "Is it lawful to give tribute to Caesar, or not?" Jesus lived in an occupied territory and tribute is "a payment made to a ruler as a sign of dependence." The use of the term *lawful* is intentionally ambiguous. Whose law? Roman law? Jewish law? God's law? If Jesus had simply answered "yes" that it was lawful, he would have been accused of being hypocritical and inconsistent with his professed belief in an "almighty God," and putting Caesar first. On the other hand, had he answered "no" he would put himself in danger of promoting insurrection.

Instead, Jesus Chunked Down by saying, "Show me the tribute money," and then asking whose image was on it. This gave him an opportunity to reframe the issue. The money is at the level of environment and is necessary to conduct what I have called the "ego" part of our lives. It is on a different level than that of "soul" and purpose. Jesus statement, "Render therefore unto Caesar the things which are Caesar's; and unto God the things that are God's," makes a clear demarcation between those levels and yet acknowledges the complementary relationship between "ego" and "soul."

George Washington and the Cherry Tree – A Retelling

There is a well-known legend about the boyhood of American president George Washington. It is said that one day, as a young boy, he went out and cut down his father's cherry tree. When his father confronted him about the tree, Washington supposedly responded, "I cannot tell a lie. I cut down the tree with my little hatchet." Little George told the truth, even though he knew it would get him in trouble. The following is a humorous retelling of what might have happened if little George had known about the Sleight of Mouth pattern of Chunk Down and taken it to an extreme.

George?

Yes, Father.

George, I have a very serious question to ask you and I want you to promise you will answer truthfully. Will you?

Yes, father.

Good. Now here is the question. Did you cut down my cherry tree?

NO, father.

You're quite sure!

Yes, father.

Well, I'm afraid I'm very disappointed in you, George.

Why, father?

Because 12 people saw you cut down the cherry tree with your little hatchet.

Oh.

In view of that, would you like to change your previous answer, George?

No, father. I believe the answer I gave you was legally accurate.

You still insist you were telling me the truth?

In my own mind I was telling you the truth, yes father.

What is that supposed to mean?

Well, you asked me if I had "cut" down the tree. In my own mind, it seemed to me that "cutting" is something one does with a knife or a sickle. In my own mind it seemed that, since I used my little hatchet, the relationship I had with the tree, while perhaps inappropriate, was not a "cutting" relationship. I would call it a chopping relationship.

Very well. I'll give you another chance, George. Listen very carefully. Did you chop down my cherry tree?

No, father.

No? No? Why do you still say no?

Because, father, I cannot tell a lie. And in my own mind, I did not "chop down" your cherry tree.

Well, what did you do, then?

I chopped it into two pieces and one piece fell to the ground.

So you chopped it down.

No, father, I merely chopped it. I did not cause that piece to fall down. The force of gravity caused it to fall down. Were it not for the force of gravity, over which I have absolutely no control, the tree, though segmented, would presumably still be up, not down.

George, I'm losing patience with you. But I'm going to give you one last chance to tell the truth. Did you take your little hatchet and chop my cherry tree, which action on your part, combined with the force of gravity, caused the tree to fall down?

No, father.

NO? NO? IT'S STILL NO? HOW CAN YOU STILL SAY NO?

I still say no because of my legendary regard for the truth, father. What is that object at which I am pointing with my childish little finger?

It's the stump of the cherry tree you cut down.

It sure is. In fact, isn't the stump the most important part of the tree, father, since, without a stump there would be no tree?

I guess so.

Yet the stump is still standing. So when you asked me if I had chopped down the tree, my own mind said to me, "George, you must tell the truth. And the truthful answer is no. You chopped, gravity caused part of the tree to fall down yet the most important part of the tree is still standing."

I see.

All I can suppose father, is that those 12 people whose exaggerated claims allege they saw me "cut down" the entire "tree" were motivated not by a search for truth but by some personal vendetta against me, perhaps because I am from Virginia.

George, you're very crafty.

Thank you father.

Have you thought about what you want to be when you grow up?

Yes, father. If they ever build a White House I would like to occupy it as the first White House lawyer.

The reference to little George becoming a lawyer relates to the assumption that it is a lawyer's job to use Sleight of Mouth patterns like Chunk Down in order to establish and defend a particular position and the beliefs that support that position. He also questioned the Intent of his accusers, which is another common legal move.

Applying the Sleight of Mouth Pattern of Chunk Down

Of course, the examples of Jesus and little George are instances of using Sleight of Mouth as a type of self-defense. When supporting others to grow or change, the mindset associated with the pattern of Chunk Down involves exploring, *what sub-elements or smaller chunks of the words or labels used in the belief statement could produce a more resourceful or productive meaning or impact?*

For example, let's say someone has been diagnosed as "learning disabled" (an obvious problem frame label). One could take the word "learning" and chunk it down into words which reflect various components of the process to which the term "learning" refers; such as: "inputting," "representing," "storing," and "retrieving" information. One can then ask, "Does learning disabled mean someone is also 'inputting' disabled? That is, is the problem that the person unable to input information?. Likewise, does being learning disabled mean a person is "representing disabled," "storing disabled," or "retrieving disabled?"

The same thing can be done with a label like "attention deficit." You can explore different types of attention – visual, auditory or kinesthetic, for instance – or attention to goals, oneself, context, past, internal state, etc.

Verbs and process words can be *chunked* into the sequence of sub-processes which make them up (as in the example of "learning" above). A term like "failure," for example, could be chunked into the series of steps making up the "failure" experience, such as: setting (or not setting) a goal; establishing (or neglecting) a plan; taking (or avoiding) action; attending to (or ignoring) feedback; responding in a flexible (or rigid) way; etc.

Nouns and objects can also be *chunked* into the smaller components which make them up. If someone says, "This car is too expensive," for instance, one could *Chunk Down* by responding, "Well, actually the tires, windshield, exhaust pipe, gasoline and oil are as inexpensive as any other car. It is only the brakes and engine that cost a bit more in order to ensure performance and safety."

In a statement such as, "I am unattractive," even the word "I" can be chunked down (as in the Erickson example with the "unhypnotizable" man), by questioning, "Are your eyebrows, forearm, little toes, voice tone, hair color, elbows, ankles, etc., all equally unattractive?"

The purpose of all of these reframes is to open up new possibilities. Again, what may be true for the whole is not necessarily true for the parts.

The following examples show how the pattern of Chunk Down can be applied to the group of limiting beliefs we have been exploring in the previous sections.

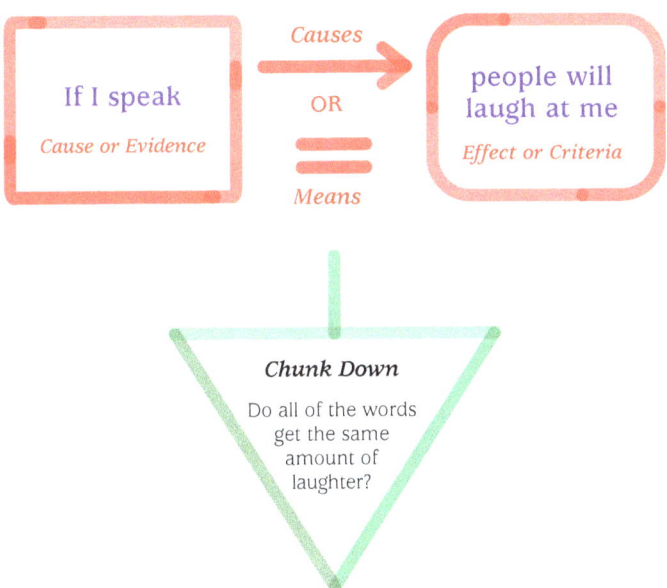

In this example, *speak* has been chunked down into "words." This places the focus clearly at the behavior level and implicates the words as the cause of the laughter rather than the person's identity. *Laugh* has been chunked down into "amounts of laughter." Considering whether different words get different amounts of laughter could lead to a potentially fruitful exploration. It is likely, however, that the person's response to this question will shift back to the identity level and reveal some type of negative identity judgment that is assumed by the belief but not explicitly stated. In that case, attention can be productively refocused to addressing that belief directly.

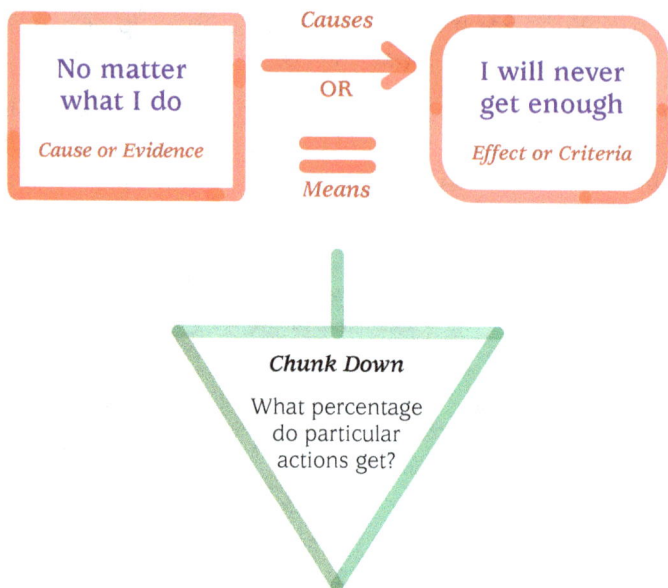

This example involves Chunking Down *doing* into "particular actions" and *enough* into an issue of "percentage." Since the determination of what is "enough" is a relative evaluation, this Chunk Down brings up the question of what percentage is *enough* – e.g., 70%, 80%, 90% – and which actions are most effective for achieving which percentages? Again, this could be a potentially useful exploration. Like the previous example, however, it could also bring out a deeper negative identity judgment about "deserving" enough.

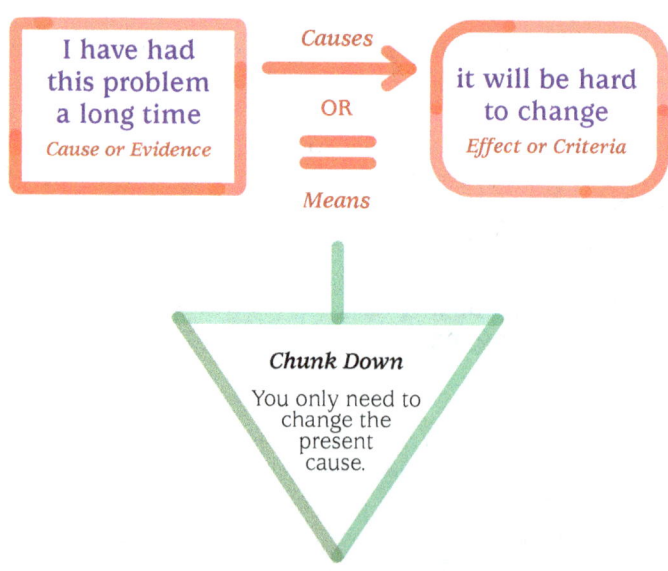

Here, both "problem" and "time" have been chunked down. *Problems* are made up of symptoms and their causes, the context in which they occur, and the history of the consequences the symptoms have brought up in the person's life. *Time* can be divided into past, present and future. The implication of the statement, "You only need to change the present cause," is that the past history is not the relevant factor in producing change. If the cause is transformed or is no longer present, the symptom will not persist.

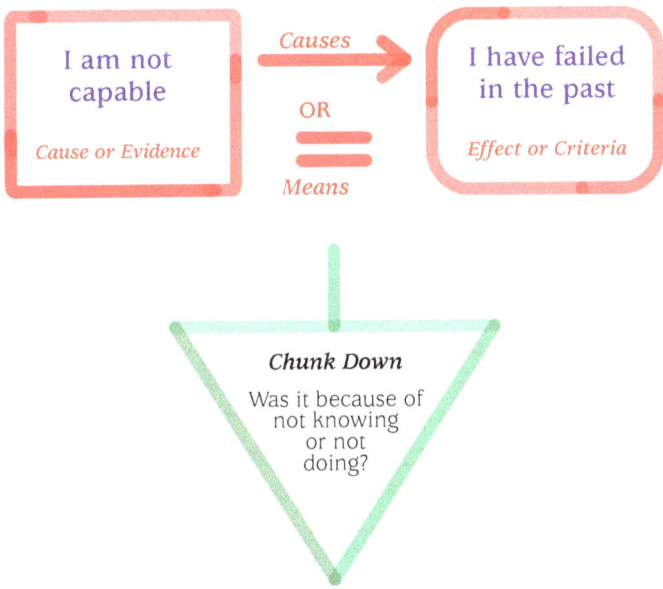

As I mentioned earlier, terms like "fail" can be usefully chunked down. So can "capable." In this case, *capable* has been chunked into "knowing" and "doing." The "failure" could have occurred because the person did not have adequate knowledge, information or training to know what to do. Another possibility is that the person knew what to do but was not able to act effectively on that knowledge. In either case, this reframe shifts the focus of the belief statement from the level of identity as a deficient person to that of capability and behavior, which are not fixed and can be learned and corrected.

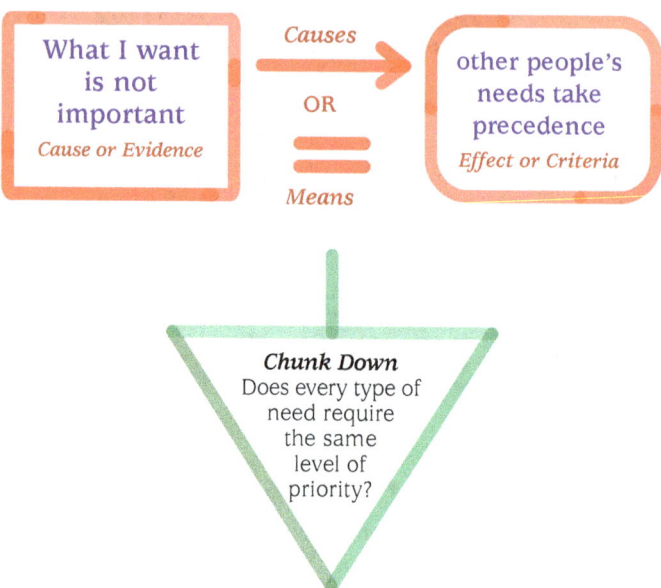

This reframe Chunks Down *precedence* into different "levels of priority" and *needs* into different "types." There are many types of needs: emotional, social, financial, physical, imagined, etc. There are "ego" needs and "soul" needs. The need for someone to have their back scratched or to have a certain kind of entertainment may not have the same urgency and importance as the need to rest and recover from a challenging life event. Such an exploration could open up other possibilities for the person holding the belief. On the other hand, as in with some of the previous examples, it could also bring up or reveal a negative identity judgment that affects the person's sense of self-esteem.

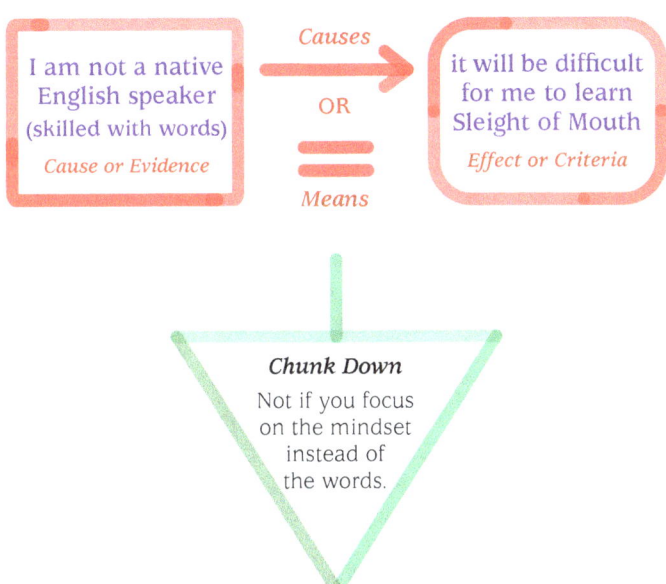

In this reframe, *learn* has been chunked down into a focus on "mindset" (the deeper structures of the Sleight of Mouth patterns) versus the "words" (the surface level product of the mindset). As we have seen in several of our examples so far, Sleight of Mouth is not about verbal formulas. It is about viewing reality through different types of filters, which are not specific to any particular language. Getting expertise with certain verbal formulations is not truly learning the essence of Sleight of Mouth.

Reflections on Chunking Down

Applying the Sleight of Mouth pattern of Chunk Down is like shining a spotlight on particular aspects of a belief statement in order to bring more clarity to the generalization being asserted. The effect of chunking down a belief is frequently to reframe it from a generalization at the identity level to an issue relating to behavior, environment or capabilities. One way to look at Chunk Down is that it transforms an "equivalence" into an "equation." An *equivalence* is a static state between phenomena that has a fixed meaning. An *equation* is a statement of relationships between variables that can have different outcomes depending on the state of the variables.

In the above examples, for instance, "If I speak (X), people will laugh (Y)," is a fixed equivalence (X = Y). Looking at which *words* (x) elicit which *amounts of laughter* (y) is more like an equation that can produce different results: $f(x) = y$. Similarly, "No matter what I do (X) I will not get enough (Y)" is transformed into "What *percentage* (y) do *particular actions* (x) get?" $f(x) = y$.

Doing this with a belief can either lead to a more productive exploration of the situation or bring clarity to a deeper identity judgment that is implied but not explicitly stated by the belief.

Chapter 9
Chunk Up

Sleight of Mouth

Chunk Up

Chunking Up involves moving to a larger, more general, or abstract level of generalization. For example, cars, trains, boats, or airplanes could all be Chunked Up to "forms of transportation," which could be chunked up even further to "types of movement." Processes can also be chunked up. Jogging, swimming, rowing, or biking could be chunked up to "types of exercise," which can be chunked up to "healthy activities," etc.

The Sleight of Mouth pattern of *Chunk Up* involves, generalizing an element of a belief statement to a larger classification or grouping that shifts the impact or implications of the belief.

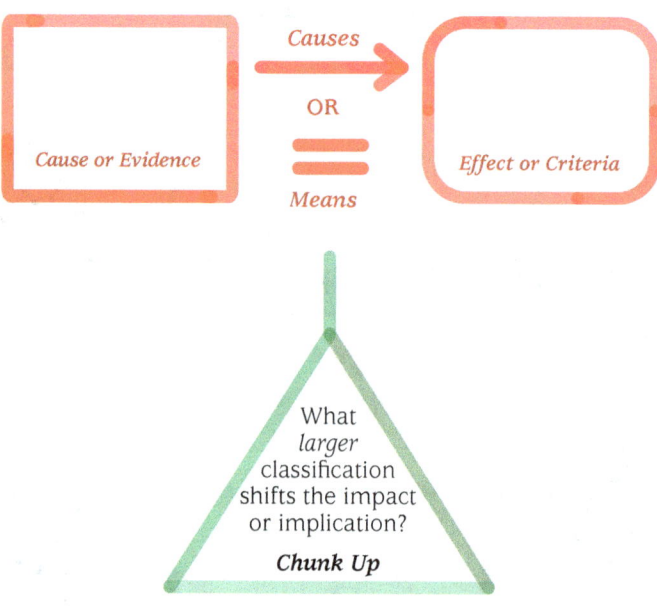

Failure, for instance, could be chunked up to the class of "behavioral consequences," or "forms of feedback." Being *unattractive* could be chunked up to "varying from the norm." *Expense* could be Chunked Up to "cash flow considerations." And so on.

Sometimes chunking up involves going to a deeper organizing principle that generates or unites a group of smaller chunks. *Matthew* (22:41-42) provides a good example of Jesus using Chunk Up to shift attention to a deeper organizing principle.

> *But when the Pharisees had heard that he had put the Sadducees to silence, they were gathered together. Then one of them, which was a lawyer, asked him a question, tempting him, and saying, Master, which is the great commandment in the law?*
>
> *Jesus said unto him, Thou shalt love the Lord thy God with all thy heart, and with all thy soul, and with all thy mind. This is the first and great commandment. And the second is like unto it, Thou shalt love thy neighbor as thyself. On these two commandments hang all the law and the prophets.*

The lawyer in this example is clearly referring to one of the classical "Ten Commandments," hoping to trap Jesus in some inconsistency or contradiction with his other teachings. Instead of answering the question at the level it was asked, Jesus Chunks Up to the deeper organizing principles upon which "hang" all the other commandments. It is an interesting side note to observe that Jesus' statement "Thou shalt love the Lord thy God with all thy heart, and with all thy soul, and with all thy mind," implies a type of alignment of the higher Levels of Change: *love the Lord thy God* (purpose), *heart* (beliefs and values), *soul* (identity) and *mind* (capabilities). Also, the statement "love they neighbor as thyself" is an interesting form of what is called *Apply to Self* in Sleight of Mouth, which we will be examining in a future section.

Chunking Up in this way can shift the way a situation is perceived and understood, leading us to reconsider its implications and open up other possibilities, as is illustrated by the following joke.

> *Mr. Smith was brought to St. Joseph's Hospital and taken quickly in for coronary surgery. The operation went well and, as the groggy man regained consciousness, he was attended by Sister Margaret, who was waiting by his bed.*
>
> *"Mr. Smith, you're going to be just fine," she said, gently patting his hand.*

"That is a relief," the man said smiling weakly.

"We do need to know, however," she continued, "how you intend to pay for your stay here. Are you covered by insurance?"

"No, I'm not," the man whispered hoarsely.

"Can you pay in cash?" persisted Sister Margaret.

"I'm afraid I cannot, Sister," he responded.

"Well, do you have any close relatives?" she inquired.

"Just my sister in New Mexico," he volunteered. "But she's a humble spinster nun."

"Oh, I must correct you, Mr. Smith. Nuns are not 'spinsters;' they are all married to God."

"WONDERFUL," said Smith. "In that case, send the bill to my brother-in-law."

Sister Margaret's Chunk Up that "Nuns are all married to God," has a humorous, if unintended, consequence. If Mr. Smith's sister is a nun and all nuns are married to God, then, by definition, God is the man's "brother-in-law" and thus a *close relative* who can be responsible for the hospital bill.

The Danger of Overgeneralizing

Sometimes Chunking Up can lead to unuseful overgeneralizations, especially if it is done within a problem frame. Divisive judgments, for instance, are frequently stated in terms of fairly large chunks or generalizations, such as: "The government is always spying on you," "The conservative/liberal media never tell the truth," "You cannot ever trust politicians" or "Healthcare administrators only care about money." Words like "always," "never," "ever," and "only," are known as *universals* or *universal quantifiers* in NLP. This type of language results from "chunking up" to a point that it may no longer be accurate or useful and, instead, becomes a rigid barrier or limitation.

Terms like "the government," "conservative/liberal media," "politicians" and "healthcare workers" are highly generalized identity labels that can be easily used to make unsubstantiated negative identity judgments. These types of overgeneralizations are other indicators to pay attention to when evaluating a belief as a potential thought virus.

Applying the Sleight of Mouth Pattern of Chunk Up

Effectively using the Sleight of Mouth pattern of Chunk Up involves generalizing an element of a statement or judgment to a larger classification or group to create a new or enriched perception of the generalization being expressed. One assumption of this pattern is that *what is true for the part is not necessarily true for the whole*, or for the other parts of that same whole. If a particular spelling is inaccurate, for instance, it does not mean that the idea expressed by that spelling is also inaccurate. If a tire is flat on a car, it does not mean the steering wheel also has a problem.

"Learning," for example, is a member of a larger class of processes which may be referred to as various forms of "adaptation"—which also includes processes such as "conditioning," "instinct," "evolution," etc. If a person has been termed "learning disabled," does that mean that the person is also to some degree "adaptation disabled?. If so, why doesn't the person also have a "conditioning disability," "instinct disability," or "evolution disability?. Some of these terms sound almost comical, and yet they are a possible logical extension of such labels.

Again, applying this type of reframing to a judgment or generalization leads us to reconsider its meaning and assumptions from a new perspective, and move it out of a problem frame.

The process of Chunking Up involves choosing one of the key words or concepts (X) in a belief statement and identifying some larger classification into which that word or concept could fit. This can be done by exploring the following questions:

- *X is a member of what larger class or group?*
- *X is the result or example of which more fundamental process or organizing principle?*

The following are examples of applying the Sleight of Mouth pattern of Chunk Up to the group of limiting beliefs we have explored in the previous sections.

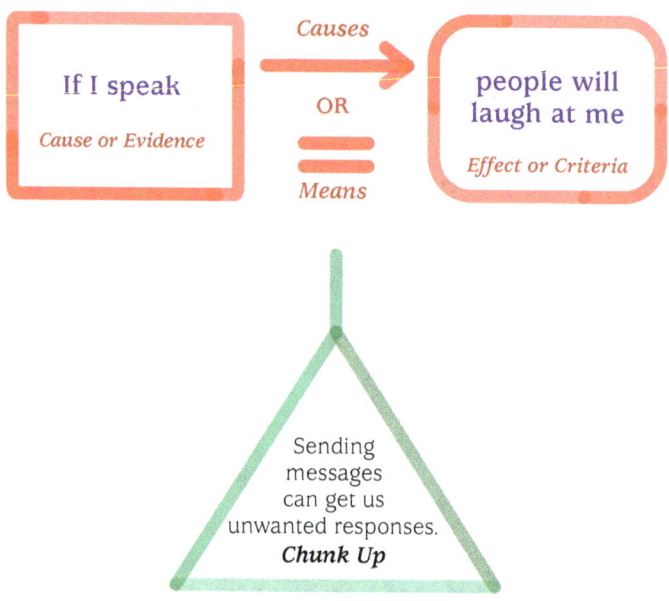

In this first example, *speak* has been chunked up to "sending messages," *laugh* has been chunked up to an "unwanted response" and "I" has been chunked up to we or "us." The Chunk Up from *I* to *we/us* is simple but potentially quite impactful. The implication is that we (as humans) all share certain archetypal issues that are reflected in such belief statements. Connecting the broader issue to the particular belief statement means the speaker is not alone in that deeper issue and that there are many potential responses to it. This reframes the situation to be less one of personal humiliation and more of a general issue to be collectively addressed. Shifting from "I speak" to "sending messages" also places the issue clearly at the level behavior and separates it from the person's identity.

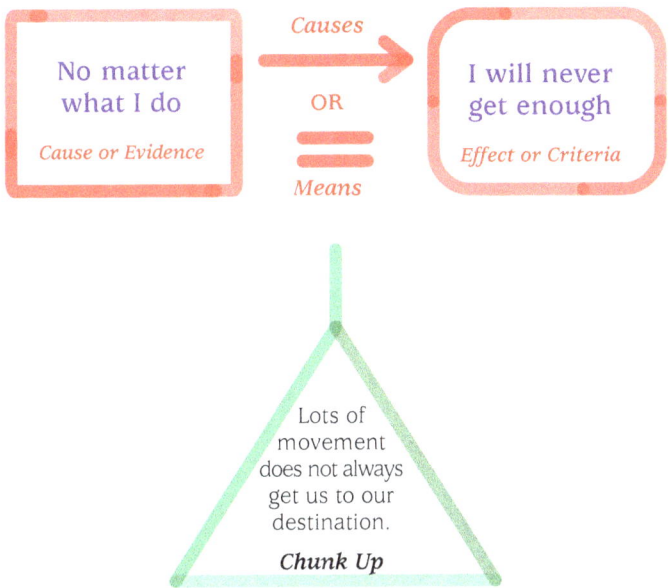

For this example, *doing* has been chunked up to a form of "movement" and *getting enough* has been chunked up to getting to a "destination." Again, *I* has been chunked up to *us*. In this reframe, the part of the statement *no matter what I do* is assumed to refer to a number of actions, which Chunks Up to "lots of movement." *Never get enough* has been reframed as "not always getting to our destination." Once more, the implication is that this is not a purely personal issue on the identity level but rather a collective experience on a behavior and environmental level shared by others, and that there are other perspectives and possibilities that can be explored.

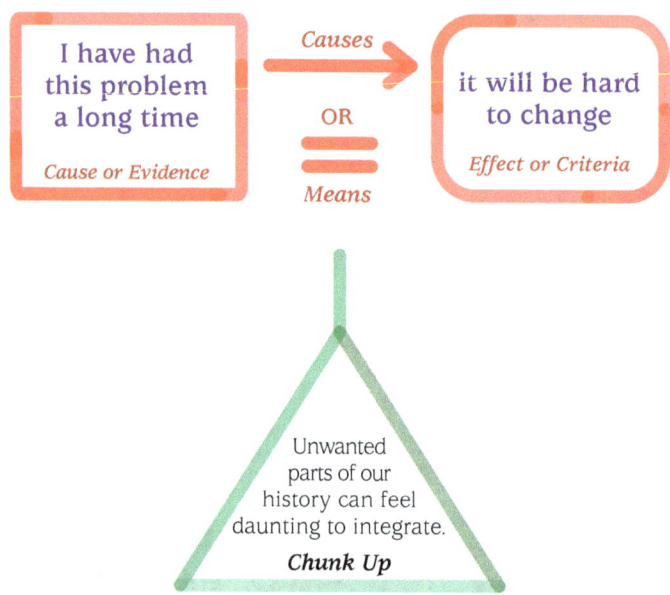

In this instance, in addition to chunking up *I* to "our," *problem* has been chunked up to being something "unwanted." The notion of *having it a long time* has been chunked up to the bigger category being a "part of our history." The experience of it *being hard* is chunked up to a type of daunting "feeling" (as opposed to a fact) and *change* is chunked up to being a way to "integrate" some experience. This shifts the implication of *change* from moving away from (getting rid of the problem) to towards (integrating it). The perception of something as part of our history also filters out the dependence on how long it has been there. It is a "part" of our history like any other part.

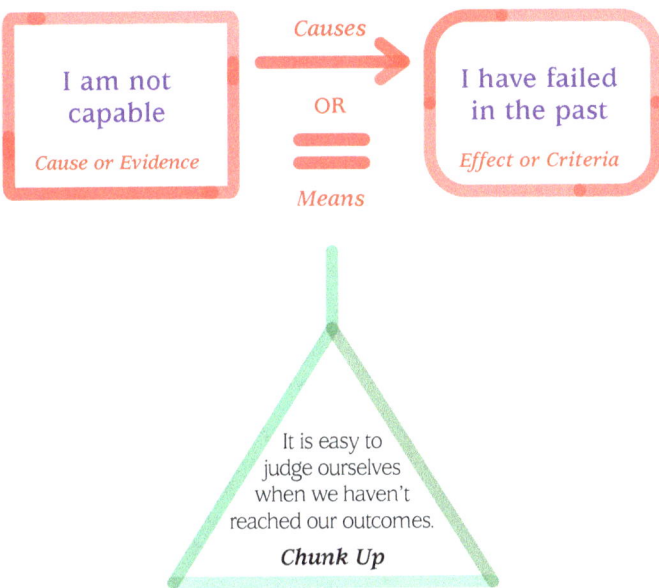

For this statement, *I am not capable* has been chunked up to a type of "self-judgment." *Failed* has been chunked up to an example of "not reaching an outcome." *I* has again been chunked up to "us." By introducing the notion of "self-judgment," the issue of incapability is shifted from being a "fact" to a personal evaluation that may or may not be accurate. Shifting the issue from being one of *failure* to being the result of trying to "reach an outcome" brings the focus back to the level of behavior and environment rather than to a defect of identity. It also begins to subtly shift attention to an outcome frame. Again, the implication is that, rather than being a rigid truth, the belief statement is referring to a shared experience that can be viewed from different perspectives and can still be updated.

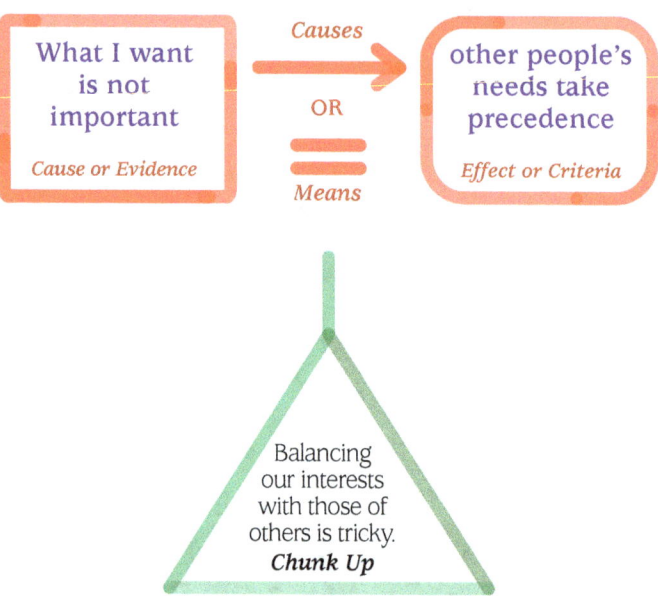

In this reframe, both *wanting* and *needs* are chunked up to be types of "interests," as well as chunking up *I* to "our." The notion of "balancing" ours versus other's interests has been brought in. This puts "what we want" and "other's needs" on the same level – both are interests. The chunking up from *I* to "our" is also helpful here in that, instead of being about what a single individual wants versus many "other people's" needs, it defines the issue as one of an archetypal "self-other" dynamic that is shared by everybody. Finding balance is not a binary choice (self or other) but rather an ongoing process.

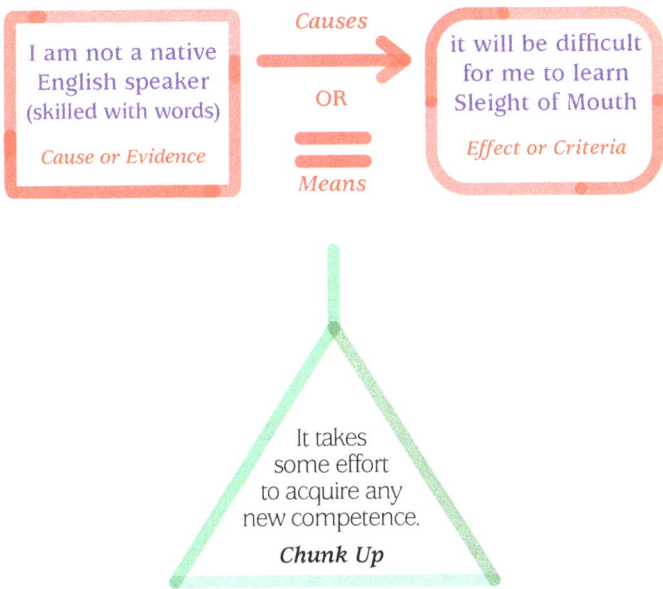

In this final example, *learning* has been chunked up to "acquiring" something; *difficult* has been chunked up to requiring "effort"; and *Sleight of Mouth* has been chunked up to a "new competence." Chunking up in this way shifts the issue from being dependent on the speaker's current level of skill with the English language (or with words in general) and focuses attention on the outcome frame of acquiring "any new competence." *Taking effort* also has a different implication than "being difficult." *Effort* is simply an exertion of energy. *Difficult* implies that something will be problematic or involve some level of hardship.

Like the pattern of Redefine, these examples of Chunk Up have been presented in the form of a type of active listening, in which the speaker's belief statement is being fed back using different words which hopefully produce some degree of resonance. When it does, this becomes a subtle form of pacing and leading. One effect of this type of chunking up is that it transforms what starts as a limiting belief into a bit of practical wisdom.

Creatively Applying the Sleight of Mouth Pattern of Chunk Up

When we take on the pattern of Chunk Up as a mindset, it opens the door other creative uses beyond active listening. The mindset that drives Chunk Up is the exploration of *what larger classification of the elements making up the belief can lead to a richer or more productive result?*

As usual, Milton Erickson provides a good example of how this mindset can help bring about a profound and positive transformation. In *Uncommon Therapy* (pp. 115-119) he describes the case of an obese 21-year-old woman who came to his office and said, "My father is dead, my mother is dead, my sister is dead, and that is all that's left for me." The woman's parents had been severe alcoholics and were quite cruel to her and her sister. Her sister had a birth defect and died of kidney disease. After the death of all her family members she had taken a job scrubbing floors, living alone in an old shack. She felt hideous and ugly, claiming, "I am four feet ten inches. I weigh between two hundred and fifty and two hundred and sixty pounds. I am just a plain, fat slob. Nobody would ever look at me except with disgust."

As part of her treatment, Erickson instructed her to go the library and look through anthropology books to find out about the "hideous kinds of women men will marry," and to read about the way people intentionally disfigure themselves with scars, tattoos, piercings, etc. He then told her to spend the next week sitting in the busiest section of the city looking at the "peculiar shapes and faces of the things men will marry" as well as those that women marry. According to Erickson, after that assignment, "She stated with simple wonderment that she had actually seen women almost as homely as she was who wore wedding rings. She had seen men and women who seemed to be man and wife, both of whom were hideously fat and clumsy." He told her that she was "beginning to learn something."

Her next assignment was to go to the library and read all the books she could on the history of cosmetology and to "discover what constituted desirable beauty to the human eye." Erickson then told her to return to the library and "look through books dealing with human customs, dress, and appearance – to find something depicted that was at least five hundred years old and still looked pretty."

After she had completed these assignments, Erickson told her that for two weeks she was to go into one women's clothing store after another and ask the clerks for advice about what she ought to wear and to "become curious about what she might look like if she weighed 150 lbs." At the next session, the woman asked Erickson if she could be permitted to "see what she could do about herself."

Within one year she weighed 150 lbs. In time she enrolled in and graduated from the university, got a job as a fashion artist, got her teeth fixed and got engaged. According to Erickson, fifteen years later she was still married with three children.

Reflections on Chunking Up

The woman's statement, "I am just a plain, fat slob. Nobody would ever look at me except with disgust," is clearly negative identity judgment couched within a problem frame. Erickson's assignments were all about *Chunking Up* in some way – to kinds of "women" and "men," "shapes and faces," criteria for "desirable beauty" and "human customs, dress and appearance." The purpose Erickson's instruction to "find something depicted that was at least five hundred years old and still looked pretty," for instance, was clearly to bring attention to deeper, archetypal organizing principles that functioned within these larger classifications. This and the other assignments created a shift from a problem frame to an outcome frame and helped neutralize the woman's negative identity judgments.

The result was that the woman began to view herself within the context of the great diversity and possibilities of a system much bigger than that of the confines of her dysfunctional and destructive family. When we learn more about what is possible within the whole, we discover more about what is possible for the individual parts. This can be one of the positive effects of chunking up. When we are part of a bigger whole, more possibilities become available to us.

Chapter 10
Analogy

Analogy

Analogies can be defined as, "the transference of the relation between one set of objects to another set for the purpose of brief explanation." (Such as, "the coordination of the people in the team was as smooth as a well orchestrated symphony.") Analogies are intimately related to metaphors, which are defined as, "a figure of speech in which a word or phrase literally denoting one kind of object or idea is used in place of another to suggest a likeness or similarity between them (as in 'drowning in money')." Analogies and metaphors involve thinking about one situation or phenomena in terms of something else, as is often done in stories, fairy tales and parables.

The Sleight of Mouth pattern of *Analogy* involves finding a metaphor or analogy for a particular belief or generalization that reinforces, shifts, or enriches its implications.

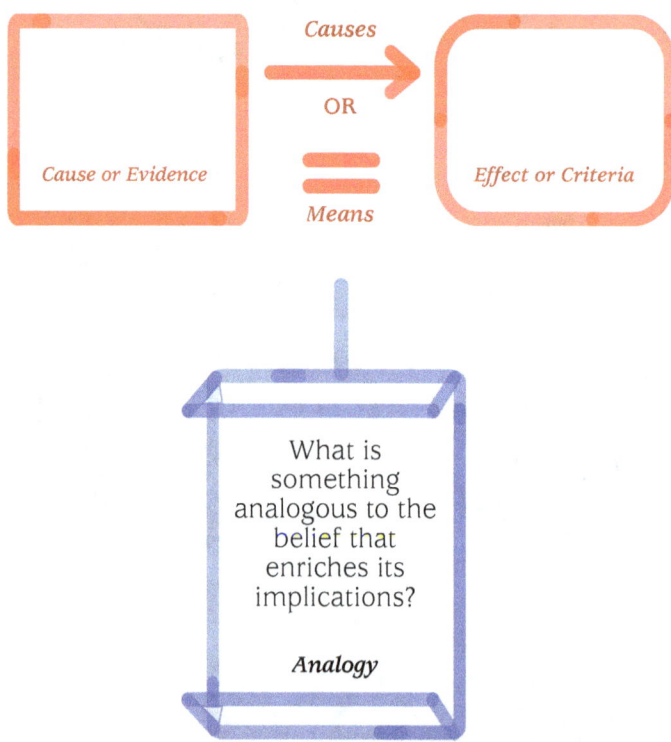

Jesus, for example, is reported to have frequently used metaphors and analogies in his teachings and other interactions. *Matthew* 6:26 quotes him as saying to his disciples, "Look at the birds of the air; they do not sow or reap or store away in barns, and yet your heavenly Father feeds them. Are you not much more valuable than they?" Here, he is using the pattern of Analogy with his disciples to imply that, as similar creatures to birds, their creator (heavenly Father) will provide for their fundamental needs.

In another instance, *Matthew* 9:11-12 recounts:

> *And it came to pass, as Jesus sat at meat* [at dinner – RD] *in the house, behold, many publicans and sinners came and sat down with him and his disciples. And when the Pharisees saw it, they said unto his disciples, Why eateth your Master with publicans and sinners? But when Jesus heard that, he said unto them, They that be whole need not a physician, but they that are sick.*

Here, Jesus makes the analogy of the publicans (tax collectors) and sinners as people who are "sick" and in need of a "physician" and that he himself is the physician.

In yet another situation, Jesus' own analogy was turned back on him with a positive result for him and the other person. *Matthew* 15:25-28 describes an event where a woman who was a Gentile (non-Jewish) of Syrophoenician descent approaches Jesus and asks for his help to heal her daughter.

> *Then came she and worshiped him, saying, Lord, help me. But he answered and said, It is not meet to take the children's bread, and cast it to dogs. And she said, Truth, Lord: yet the dogs eat of the crumbs which fall from their masters' table.*
>
> *Then Jesus answered and said unto her, O woman, great is thy faith: be it unto thee even as thou wilt. And her daughter was made whole from that very hour.*

In this description, Jesus initially uses the analogy of "dogs" to characterize the woman and other Gentiles, saying that his healing mission (the "bread") is exclusively for the "children" (of Israel). The woman's ensuing reframe paces and leads the analogy to a broader outcome frame when she responds "Truth, Lord: yet the dogs eat of the crumbs which fall from their masters' table." Jesus is clearly impressed by her wit and commitment to her daughter and agrees to support the daughter's healing. It is also interesting to note that biblical accounts represent this incident as a turning point for the expansion of Jesus' mission to the non-Jewish world. This illustrates the potential transformational power of the effective use of Sleight of Mouth.

Jesus' analogies of his disciples as "birds of the air," of the publicans and sinners as people in need of a "physician," of the Israelites as his "children," Gentiles as "dogs" and healing as "bread" are all examples of chunking "laterally."

Chunking Laterally and "Abductive" Thinking

"*Chunking laterally*" involves identifying phenomena, at a similar level, that share common features; for instance, "driving a car" could be likened to "riding a horse," "peddling a bicycle" or "sailing a boat." According to anthropologist, communication specialist and systems theory pioneer Gregory Bateson, "*Everything is a metaphor for everything else.*" Metaphorical thinking is one of our most important forms of intelligence and is responsible for much or our creativity. We generate these metaphors and analogies by chunking laterally to find similarities between one system and another. This is a function of what Bateson termed *abductive thinking*. "Abductive" thinking can be contrasted with "inductive" and "deductive" processes.

- *Inductive* processing involves classifying particular objects or phenomena according to common features that they share – noticing that all birds have feathers for example. Inductive reasoning is essentially the process of *chunking up*.

- *Deductive* processing involves making predictions about a particular object or phenomenon based on its classification; i.e., *if-then* type logic – deducing that if something has feathers, it must be a bird. Deduction involves *chunking down*.

- *Abductive* processing involves looking for the similarities between objects and phenomena – i.e., X is like Y – observing that birds and airplanes both have wings. Abduction involves *chunking laterally*.

Bateson illustrated the difference between deductive logic and abductive thinking by contrasting the following statements:

Deductive Thinking
- Men die
- Socrates is a man
- Socrates will die

Abductive Thinking
- Men die
- Grass dies
- Men are grass

Comparison of Deductive and Abductive Thinking Processes

The essence of abductive thinking is looking for some type of quality, pattern or relationship (e.g., dying) that some *X* (men) shares with some *Y* (grass). A child struggling with a new life situation such as learning to ride a bicycle, for instance, can be likened to a baby bird struggling to learn to fly.

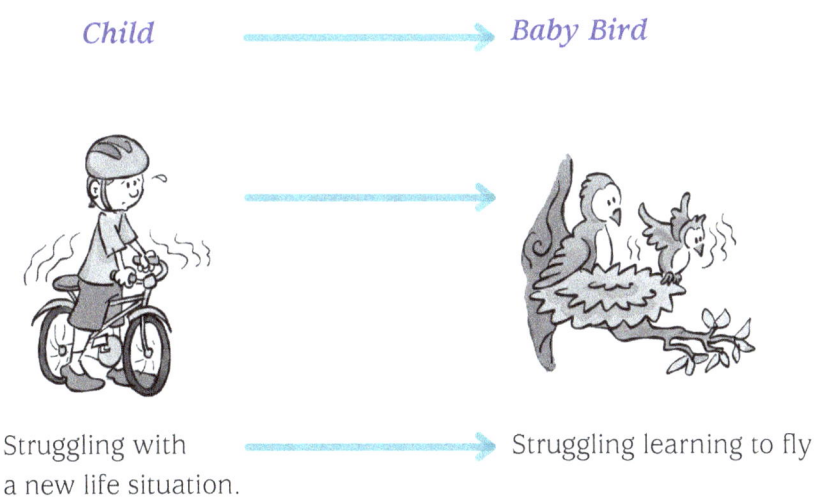

Child → *Baby Bird*

Struggling with a new life situation. → Struggling learning to fly

Martin Luther King, Jr. used analogies and abductive thinking in his "I Have a Dream" speech mentioned earlier in this book. His reference to "the sons of former slaves and sons of former slave-owners" sitting down together at "*the table of brotherhood*" is one example. Another is his assertion that "even the state of Mississippi, *a desert state sweltering with heat of injustice and oppression,* will be transformed into *an oasis of freedom and justice.*" Powerful public speakers have used analogies throughout history as a way to appeal to what Aristotle called *pathos* and our emotions.

Milton Erickson was constantly applying this type of thinking process with his patients. As an example, if Erickson was dealing with a married couple who had a conflict over sexual relations, he might approach the problem metaphorically. He would choose some aspect of their lives that was analogous to sexual relations and change that as a way of influencing their sexual behavior. He might, for example, talk to them about having dinner together and ask them about their preferences. He might learn that the wife liked appetizers before dinner, while the husband preferred to dive right into the main course. Or the wife might prefer a quiet and leisurely dinner, while the husband wanted the finish the meal quickly and move on to other things. Erickson would then end the conversation with the instruction that the couple discuss and co-arrange a series of dinners that were satisfactory to both of them. When successful, the more satisfying dinners would spontaneously lead the couple to more mutually satisfying sexual relations.

"And to finish we will have the chocolate cake..."

128   Analogy

Like all Sleight of Mouth patterns, Analogy and the process of abductive thinking can be taken too far in some instances. A good example is the following humorous tale.

> *Many years back, Patty, a Protestant lad from Northern Ireland, fell in love with Mary, a Catholic lass from Southern Ireland. In order to wed, Mary told Patty that it would be necessary for him to convert to Catholicism. Patty decided that his love for Mary was more important than his religious beliefs and agreed to become a Catholic.*
>
> *Sometime after the wedding, Father Murphy, the parish priest, decided to visit the new couple to see how they were doing. Now, this was back in the days when Catholics were not allowed to heat meat on Fridays. It just so happened that the good priest came by on a Friday evening. As he enters the house, Father Murphy is aghast to smell the odor of meat permeating the house. Walking into the kitchen he sees Patty cooking up a steak in the frying pan.*
>
> *"Patty," exclaims the priest, "You're a Catholic now. You can't be eating meat on Friday!"*
>
> *"Oh, I'm sorry Father," replies the embarrassed Patty. "But it's difficult to change my old habits. I've been a Protestant all my life."*
>
> *"Come on Patty. It isn't so hard," admonishes Father Murphy. "All you have to do is keep reminding yourself that you are a Catholic, not a Protestant. Repeat after me, 'I'm a Catholic, not a Protestant. I'm a Catholic, not a Protestant.'"*
>
> *Dutifully, Patty repeats again and again, "I'm a Catholic, not a Protestant. I'm a Catholic, not a Protestant." After many repetitions, he says, "OK, Father, I think I've got it now." The pleased priest heads back to the rectory, satisfied with a good day's work.*
>
> *A few weeks later, he decides to check in on the new couple. Again, it just so happens to be a Friday evening. Father Murphy is shocked to once more smell the odor of meat being cooked in the house. He goes charging into the kitchen, and to his surprise, sees Patty flipping a steak in the pan, saying over and over again, "You're a fish not a steak. You're a fish not a steak."*

Apparently Patty had figured that, if speaking words were enough to change his own identity (Protestant to Catholic), by analogy, saying those same types of words should be enough to change the identity of his food (steak to fish). This brings up an important principle about the limitations of analogy and abductive thinking. Since not all systems are 100% similar, metaphors and analogies will break down at some point. The brain, for instance, is like a computer in many ways, but is completely different in others. If we begin to take the analogy literally, we will eventually run into trouble. This is especially important with analogies at the identity level.

Hitler, for instance, also used analogies to appeal to emotions, but in quite a different way than Jesus Martin Luther King or Milton Erickson. In *Mein Kampf*, he characterized the effect of the Jewish presence in the world as a "race-tuberculosis of the peoples" and a "parasite upon the nations." Unlike the other examples, these analogies are overgeneralized negative identity judgments, stated in an "away from" problem frame. [The one exception was Jesus' initial rejection of the Gentile woman's request to heal her daughter. Her reframe back to positive outcome frame, however, clearly had a profound affect on Jesus.] As with the other Sleight of Mouth patterns, these are strong indications of potential thought viruses.

Applying the Sleight of Mouth Pattern of Analogy

The effective application of the Sleight of Mouth pattern of *Analogy* engages abductive thinking and chunking laterally to find a metaphor or analogy for some aspect of a belief statement which opens a new perspective or shifts the implications of the belief to something more productive. The mindset associated with the patterns of Analogy explores *what is some other relationship which is analogous to that defined by the belief statement (a metaphor for some aspect of the belief), but which has more positive or productive implications or can stimulate new possibilities*?

We might say, for example, that a "learning disability" *is like* a "malfunctioning computer program." This would lead us naturally to ask questions such as, "Where is the malfunction?" "What is its cause and how can it be corrected?" "Does the problem come from a particular line of code? Is it in the whole program? The computer media. Perhaps the source of the problem is with the programmer?"

Analogies such as this stimulate us to enrich our perspective of a particular generalization or judgment, and to discover and evaluate our assumptions. They also help us to shift from a problem frame to an outcome frame.

Examples of the Sleight of Mouth Pattern of Analogy

Returning to the six examples of limiting beliefs that we have used in the previous sections; we can apply the processes of chunking laterally and abductive thinking to find analogies that can open up new possibilities with respect to those beliefs.

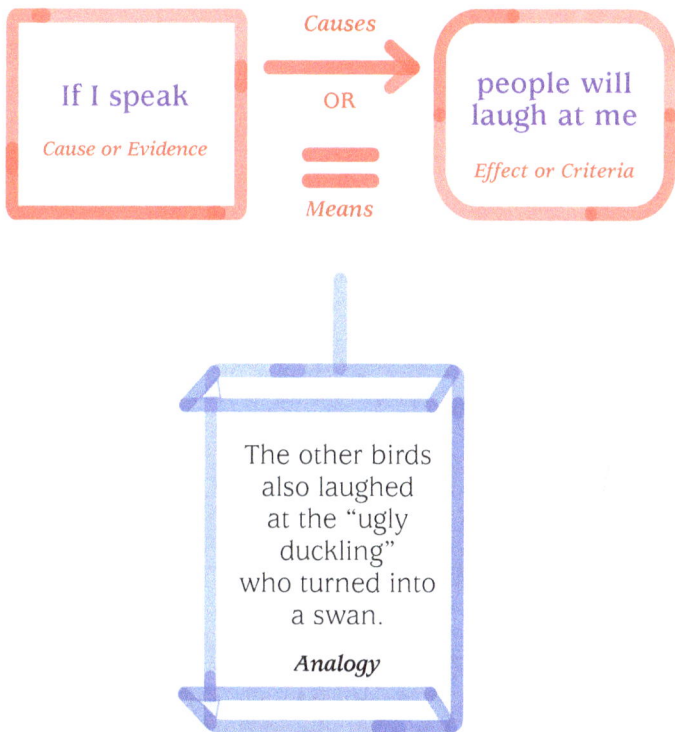

This first reframe makes an analogy to the classic tale of the "ugly duckling" who turned into a swan and was then admired and sought after by those who had laughed at it earlier. The implication is that the speaker is also a type of "ugly duckling" – someone with a beautiful and noble identity who has been misperceived by others. It is not necessary for the speaker to change anything, as their true nature will eventually emerge with time. What is most important is for them to stay congruent to who they are and not withdraw.

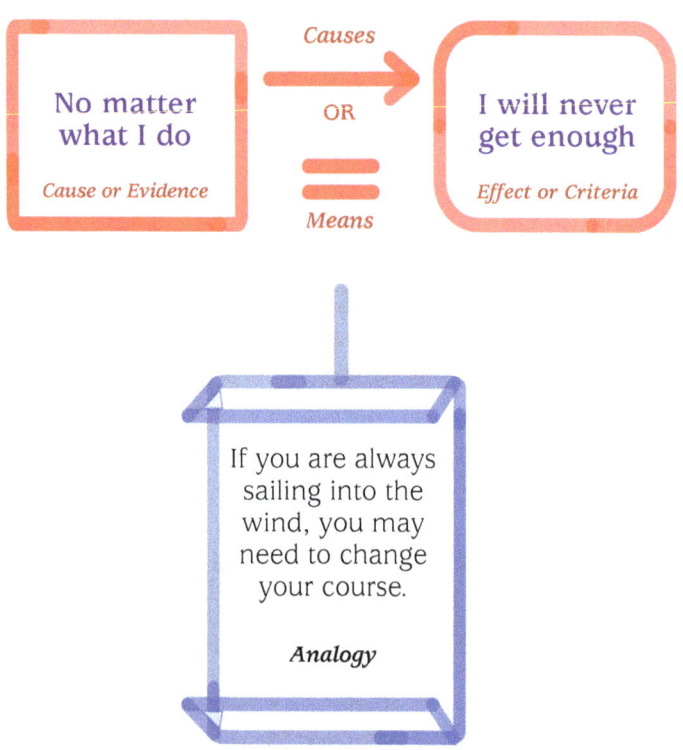

In this instance, an analogy has been made with sailing. Trying different things and not getting enough is like "sailing into the wind." Rather than keeping trying and ending up frustrated because one is not making progress, the implication is to become aware of the wind and the direction it is blowing and to change course accordingly. Like the Erickson example cited earlier about the couple struggling with their sexual relations, the metaphor of sailing can be used as the beginning of a discussion with the speaker about what is the wind and what course are they on? Interestingly, this intervention would reframe the issue from being one at the behavior and environment level (doing and not getting enough) to issues related to higher levels of change (values, identity, and purpose).

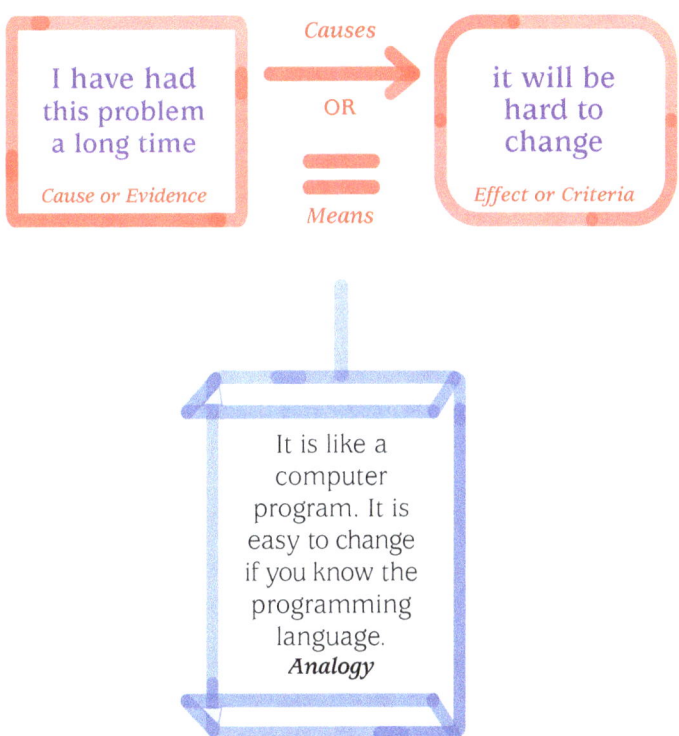

An analogy to programming a computer is made in this example. The implication is that once the program is changed, the problem is solved. The key is to know the programming language in which the "problem" has been coded. Thus, the issue is not so much one of time, but rather one of knowledge with respect to "programming." This can open up a very interesting conversation (at the levels of capability, values and belief) about *how* the problem started to begin with and what makes it continue in the present.

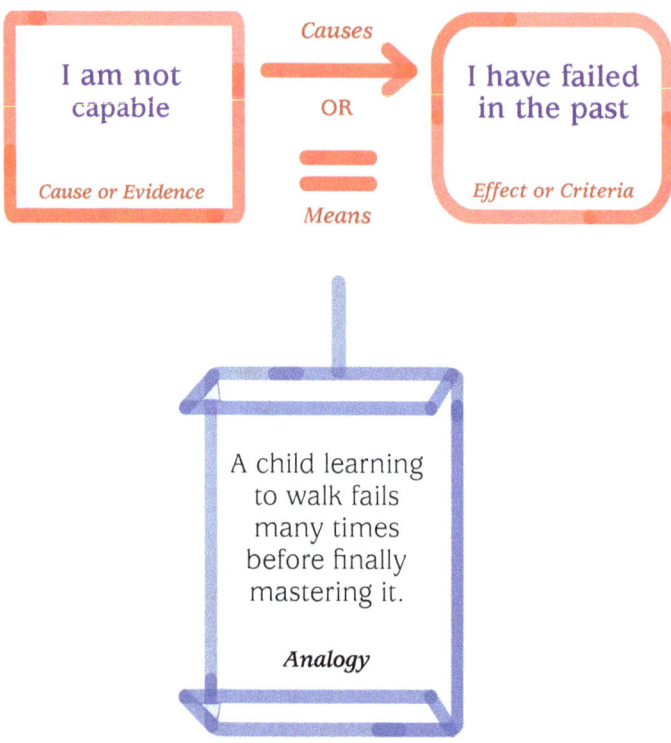

For this belief, an analogy has been made between trying and "failing" and a child learning to walk. The implication of this metaphor is that a child "fails" to walk many times (by falling down) before being able to truly master the ability. This means that the child is "capable" of walking (potentially even from the time it is conceived) because it is human and that is what human's do. The issue is one of turning each failure into feedback and to keep trying in order to fulfill that inborn capacity. This analogy could lead to a fruitful discussion about what, specifically, the "capability" and "failure" refer to and whether the past "failure" can be turned into "feedback."

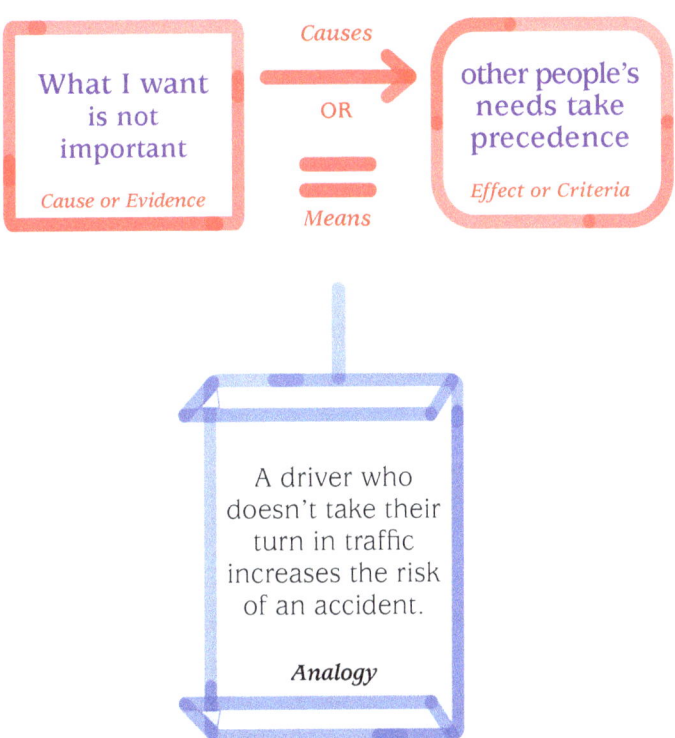

In this case, an analogy has been made to a driver in traffic who is not appropriately taking their turn. A driver who never proceeds and constantly lets others go in front of them becomes a risk to other drivers. The implication is that, if the speaker truly values the needs of others, they will need to take their place and take action to get to their desired destination. If not, they are actually endangering others rather than supporting those needs. Such an analogy could lead to an interesting discussion about the speaker's destination (as a "driver") and what they are assuming are the destinations of the "other people."

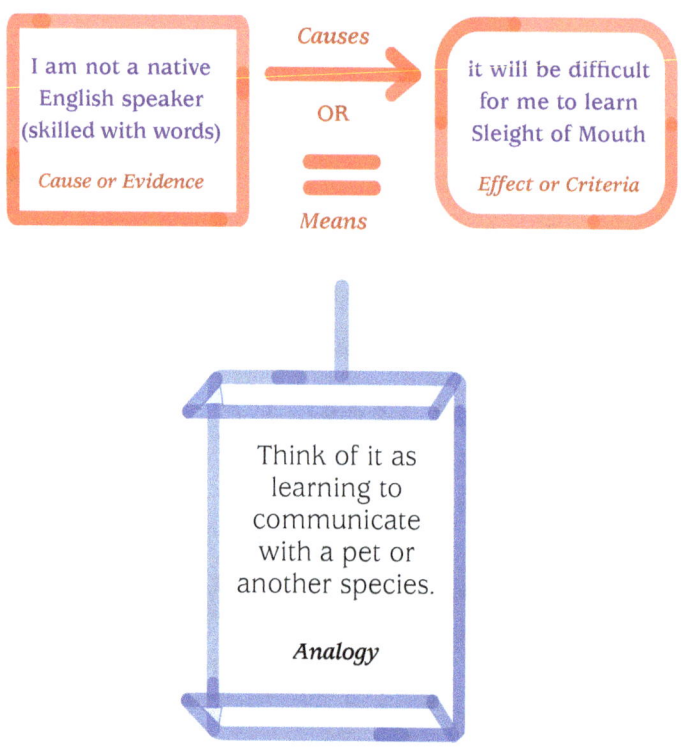

For having difficulty learning Sleight of Mouth, the analogy of communicating with a pet or another species has been used. This would mean not comparing it to other typical learning experiences (such as at school in the classroom). Learning to communicate with a pet is not about getting some abstract formulation "right" but about interacting effectively with that pet (whatever species it may be). This, of course, places a strong emphasis on an outcome frame and takes attention away from the details of verbal language.

The Creative Use of Analogy

The examples of Analogy provided thus far are, hopefully, fairly obvious and direct. Analogies and metaphors that are less obvious can also be quite useful, when applied with the appropriate skill. A fascinating example is described by Milton Erickson (*Uncommon Therapy*, pp. 301-306) in which a man who was a florist developed a growth on the side of his face that turned out to be a malignancy. After being told he had a month to live, the man became distressed and developed severe pain. Narcotics were giving him little relief and he had developed toxic reactions to the excessive medication given as treatment. The man had also had a tracheotomy because of the damage to his face and could only communicate through writing. A relative asked Erickson to do hypnosis with him for the pain. The man was very skeptical and disliked even the mention of the word "hypnosis." Knowing that he was a florist, Erickson, used an analogy to a tomato plant and began talking to the man about the joys of watching tomato plants grow:

> *Speaking of the tomato plant, it grows so slowly. You cannot see it grow, you cannot hear it grow, but grow it does – the first little leaflike things on the stalk, the fine little hairs on the stem. Those hairs are on the leaves too, like the cilia on the roots; they must make the tomato plant feel very good, very comfortable if you can think of a plant as feeling, and then, you can't see it growing, you can't feel it growing, but another leaf appears on that little tomato stalk and then another. Maybe the tomato plant does feel comfortable and peaceful as it grows. Each day it grows and grows and grows, it's so comfortable to watch a plant grow and not see its growth, not feel it, but just know that all is getting better for that little tomato plant that is adding yet another leaf and still another and a branch, and it is growing comfortably in all directions.*

Erickson went on in this fashion for a while. Following the session, the florist's mental and physical condition improved markedly.

Analogies, metaphors, chunking laterally and abductive thinking constitute a whole area of intelligence in and of themselves. They help us to find patterns and generate possibilities that other types of intelligence are unable to do. In this example, Erickson never explicitly says, "You are like the tomato plant." The analogy is made more subtly and, as with the effective use of all Sleight of Mouth patterns, involves a shift from a problem frame (away from illness and pain) to an outcome frame (toward growing peace and comfort). Of course, its effectiveness is also dependent on the degree of resonance it creates with the listener, which depends a great deal on the listener's level of rapport with the speaker. Had Erickson used the same analogy with a jeweler or a carpenter, it would most likely not have had the same positive effect.

Chapter 11

Counter Example

Counter Example

A *Counter Example* is an example, experience or piece of information which challenges the universality of a particular belief or generalization about the world. Counter Examples are essentially exceptions to a rule, i.e., an example or experience that does not fit the generalization defined by a belief statement. The consequence of many Sleight of Mouth patterns, in fact, is to find or bring up Counter Examples.

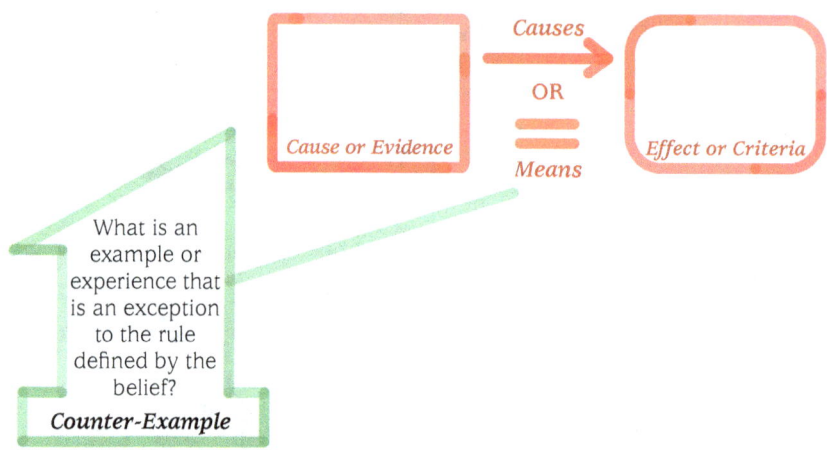

Like all the Sleight of Mouth patterns, eliciting or finding counter examples has been used for thousands of years. The great ancient Greek philosophers, such as Socrates, Plato, and Aristotle, used counter examples as a key mechanism to appeal to reason or *logos*.

In fact, in his book on *Logic*, Aristotle claimed that the evaluation of the strength of a particular generalization or "premise" essentially involved looking for counter examples which challenged its "universality." For a generalization to be truly definitive, we should find no counter examples. If we say, "All birds have wings," for instance, then we should not find any birds that do not have wings. This does not necessarily mean, however, that all animals with wings are birds – insects, bats and some dinosaurs also have or had wings. But if we say that "all animals with wings and beaks are birds," it is likely that we will find fewer counter examples, i.e., animals that are not birds that have both wings and beaks. The fewer counter examples there are, the more "universal" the generalization.

Adding Nuance and Flexibility to a Generalization through Counter Examples

As the above example about birds and wings illustrates, finding a counter example does not necessarily mean that a generalization is "wrong"; it often means that the situation or phenomenon that it refers to is more complex than it has been perceived to be, and that there are other factors involved that have not yet been identified. This is especially true when generalizations have to do with phenomena that are more abstract and less directly observable. A good example is this excerpt from Plato's *Republic* in which Socrates is dialoging with one of his students, Polemarcus, about the nature of "doing right."

Socrates: *Well then as heir to this argument, tell me, what is this saying of Simonides that you think tells us the truth about doing right?*

Polemarcus: *That it is right to give every man his due, in that, I think, he puts the matter fairly enough.*

S: *It is indeed difficult to disagree with Simonides, he had the poet's wisdom and inspiration; but though you may know what he meant by what he said, I'm afraid I don't. For he clearly does not mean... that we should return weapons entrusted to us even though the person asking for it has gone mad. Yet what one has entrusted to another is due to one, isn't it?*

P: *Yes.*

S: *Yet in no circumstances should one return (weapons) to a madman.*

P: *"True."*

S: *So Simonides must mean something different from this when he says that it is right to give every man his due.*

P: *He certainly must, for his thought is that one friend owes it as a due to another to do him good, not harm.*

S: *I see. Then as between two friends one is not giving the other his due when he returns a sum of money the other has entrusted to him if the return is going to cause harm – is this what Simonides means?*

P: *Certainly.*

S: *Well then, ought we to give our enemies too whatever is due to them?*

P: *Certainly, what is due to them; and that is, I assume, what is appropriate between enemies, an injury of some sort.*

S: *It looks as if Simonides was talking about what is right with a poet's ambiguity. For it appears that he meant that it is right to give everyone what is appropriate to him, but he called this his "due."*

In this exchange, Socrates elicits several counter examples that shift the discussion from what is "right" to what is "due" to what is "good" to what is "appropriate." While still relatively abstract, the terms take on progressively more nuance. This is typically the goal of applying the Sleight of Mouth pattern of *Counter Example*; to bring more nuance and flexibility to a potentially rigid generalization.

Challenging the Validity of a Generalization with Counter Examples

Of course, sometimes a Counter Example can cast doubt on the underlying validity of a generalization. This is humorously illustrated in the following joke, related to a quite serious situation.

> *Years ago, during a period of political and religious unrest in Northern Ireland, a reporter was interviewing one of the locals about a recent outbreak of violence. "Oh, the media is blowing it all out of proportion," claimed the local. "It isn't nearly as bad as they make it out to be. They're just exaggerating the situation to get a story." "Are you sure?" asks the reporter. "Absolutely," responds the local, "Things are pretty much normal around here." "OK," says the reporter, turning to leave, "And, just for the record, what is your occupation, sir?" "Oh, I ride shotgun on the bread truck."*

The local's comment that he is "riding shotgun on the bread truck" is a seemingly stark Counter Example to his claim that "things are pretty much normal around here." The whole purpose of "riding shotgun" is to protect the driver from violence, which would presumably not be necessary if the situation were being exaggerated and "blown out of proportion." Of course, the other implication could be that the local being interviewed has become so accustomed to a certain level of unrest and violence that he perceives it as "normal."

This brings up a point that beliefs and generalizations are often used to "spin" the perception of a situation, for better or for worse. Counter Examples can help to keep the situation from being perceived too naively or one-sidedly. They can also, at times, help to change a limiting generalization completely.

Milton Erickson presents a good example of this (*Uncommon Therapy*, pp. 197-198) in his intervention with a fourteen-year-old girl who had developed the belief that her feet were much too large. For three months the girl had been becoming more and more obsessed with her feet and progressively more withdrawn, not wanting to go to school or to church or to be seen on the street. The girl would not allow the subject of her feet to be discussed, and she would not go to see a doctor. No amount of reassurance by her mother had any influence, and the girl was becoming increasingly reclusive. Erickson reports:

> *I arranged with the mother to visit the home on the following day under false pretenses. The girl would be told that I was coming to examine the mother to see if she had the flu... When I arrived at the home, the mother was in bed. I did a careful physical examination of her, listening to her chest, examining her throat, and so on. The girl was present. I sent her for a towel, and I asked that she stand beside me in case I needed something... As I finished my examination of the mother, I maneuvered the girl into a position directly behind me. I was sitting on the bed talking to the mother, and I got up slowly and carefully and then stepped back awkwardly. I put my heel down squarely on the girl's toes. The girl, of course, squawked with pain. I turned on her and in a tone of absolute fury said, "If you would grow those things large enough for a man to see, I wouldn't be in this sort of situation." The girl looked at me, puzzled, while I wrote out a prescription and called the drugstore. That day the girl asked her mother if she could go out to a show, which she hadn't done in months. She went to school and church, and that was the end of a pattern of three months' reclusiveness.*

Erickson's admonishment that, "If you would grow those things large enough for a man to see, I wouldn't be in this sort of situation," created a direct counter example to the girl's belief that her feet were "too big." That, combined with the fact that he had stepped on her toes because her feet weren't "large enough," was enough to effectively challenge her limiting belief. As Erickson points out, there was no further trouble about the feet.

Eliciting Resources by Identifying Counter Examples

Sometimes *Counter Examples* to a generalization can be used to identify and elicit inner resources. Let's say a person states, "I always get anxious when I speak in front of big groups." We can ask whether there has ever been a time when the person spoke in front of a big group and was not anxious. If so, what was the difference? What inner resource was present in that instance that made it different. What if it was a big group of friends/children/animals, would the person still feel as anxious? What would be different?

Finding resources through *Counter Examples* has a double advantage in that a counter example can have an influence both on the level of behavior or capability and on the level of belief. That is, as an exception to the rule, a counter example provides us with alternative options and pathways within the context that the generalization is addressing (differences that make a difference). A *Counter Example* also loosens the universality or rigidity of certain limiting beliefs. For instance, the statement, "I always get anxious when I speak in front of big groups," is a belief as much as it is a statement about the reality of the person's experience. Thus, finding *Counter Examples* can not only bring out resources but can open up the possibility for new and more empowering beliefs.

Given the deep connection between beliefs and our nervous system, Counter Examples can even influence physical health. For instance, the NLP Allergy Technique (*Beliefs, Pathways to Health and Well-Being*, Dilts, Hallbom, and Smith, 1990) uses the counter example process to help people achieve relief from allergic reactions.

Applying the Sleight of Mouth Pattern of Counter Example Using Questions

When applying the Sleight of Mouth pattern of Counter Example, we take on the mindset, *what is an example or experience that is an exception to the premise or rule defined by the belief/generalization that can bring more nuance and flexibility?*

Finding counter examples involves checking the universality of the equivalence or cause-effect asserted or implied by the belief statement to see if there are any exceptions to that rule. A typical belief statement has the structure:

(A)_____ *equals/or causes* **(B)** _____

Seeking potential counter examples can be done using the following formats:

- *Are there any examples of **A** that are not accompanied by **B**? Or, Are there any examples of **A** that do not cause/mean **B**?*
- *Are there any examples of **B** that are not accompanied by or caused by **A**?*

One of the most direct ways to find counter examples is to ask these types of questions of the person making the belief statement. The following are examples of how we might apply the above formulas to the group of limiting beliefs we have been examining in the previous chapters.

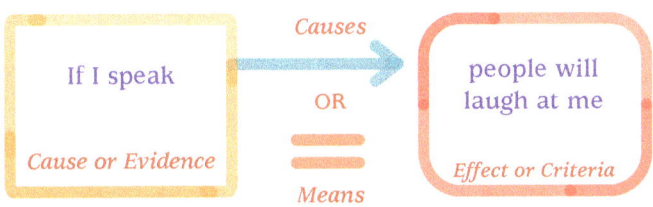

Has there ever been a time that you spoke, and people did not laugh at you?

Have people ever laughed at you even though you did not speak?

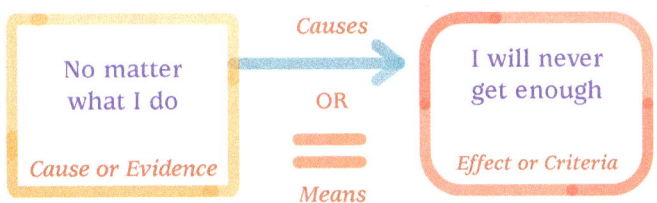

Has there ever been a time that you did something and felt that you did get enough?

Are there instances where you felt like you would not get enough even though you had not yet taken any action?

Sleight of Mouth 145

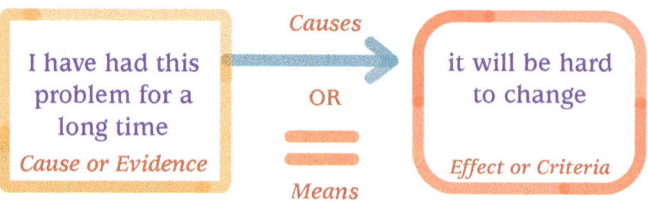

Have you ever had a problem for a long time that was easy to change?

Have you had a problem that has been hard to change even though you only had it a short time?

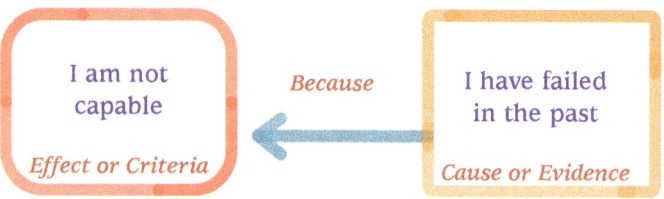

Is there something you feel capable to do even though you failed at it in the past?

Is there anything you believe you are not capable of even though you succeeded at it in your past?

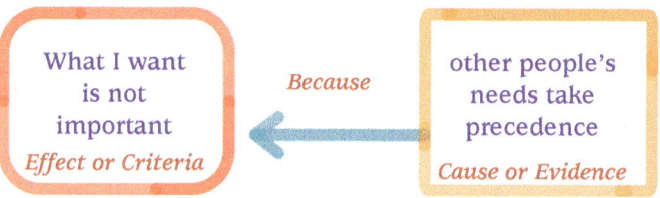

Has there been a time when other people's needs did not take precedence over what you wanted?

Has there ever been a time that you believed what you wanted was not important even when other people's needs did not take precedence?

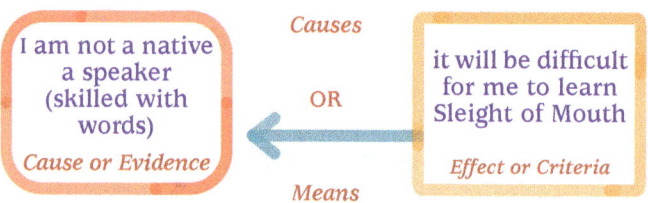

Have you ever learned something easily in English (or involving words)?

Have you ever had difficulty learning something even hough it was in your own birth language?

Some of these questions, especially the second one of the various pairs, will often result in stimulating the person who has made the belief statement to reflect more deeply about the causes they have identified. Question like, "Have people ever laughed at you even though you did not speak?" "Have you had a problem that has been hard to change even though you only had it a short time?" "Is there anything you believe you are not capable of even though you succeeded at it in your past?" and "Has there ever been a time that you believed what you wanted was not important even when other people's needs did not take precedence?" bring up the possibility that the issue addressed by the generalization could have other or deeper causes or be connected to other limiting beliefs that have not yet been identified and examined.

Applying the Sleight of Mouth Pattern of Counter Example Using Statements

Another way to apply the pattern of Counter Example is to generate your own exceptions to the rule and check it with the other person; like Socrates did in the excerpt at the beginning of this section. The following examples reference the same six limiting beliefs that we have been using as our primary reference.

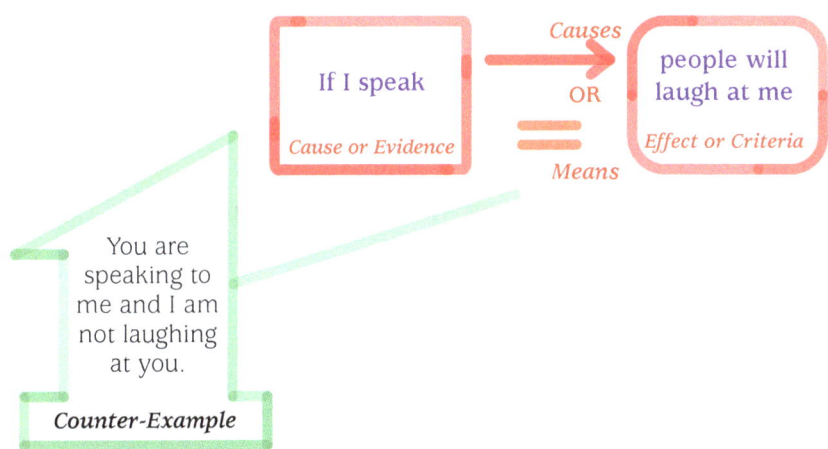

One of the most effective ways to present a counter example is by generating one in the ongoing interaction. Erickson did exactly this with the girl who thought her feet were "too big" by stepping on her toes and claiming that it was because her feet were "not big enough" for him to see. In the above example, pointing out that "You are speaking to me, and I am not laughing at you," creates an irrefutable ongoing exception to the belief statement. The person who made the belief statement must reflect and come up with some reason or explanation for what is the difference that is making the difference. This will most likely lead to a more nuanced or contextualized interpretation of the generalization.

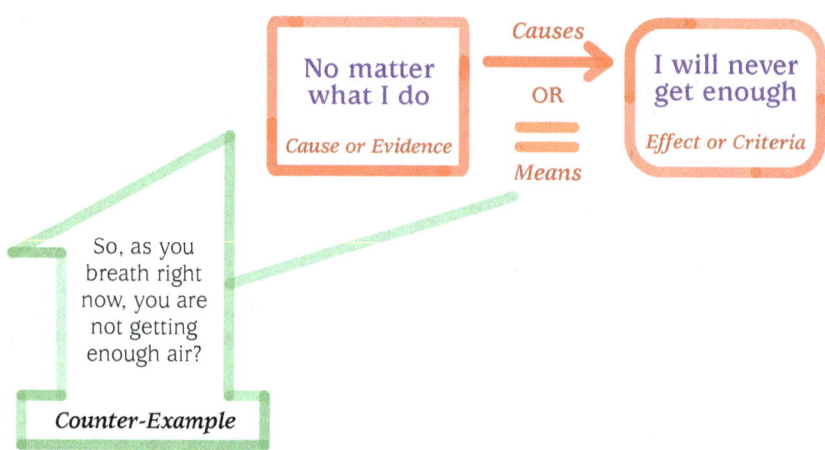

This counter example is also one that is part of the ongoing interaction, though from a very different perspective. If the person expressing the belief never gets enough of anything, no matter what they do, then that should be true for breathing as well. If that were the case, the person would never get enough air and either be constantly out of breath or suffocating, which is most likely not the case. By bringing up such an exaggerated Counter Example at the behavioral level, the person stating the belief will need to Chunk Down his or her generalization and become more aware and specific about the context or level of issues being addressed by the belief.

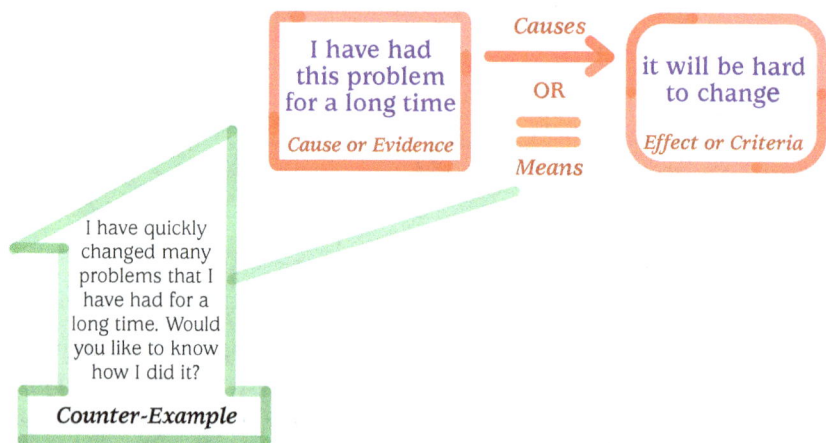

In this case, one's own personal experience is being used as the Counter Example and, in doing so, helping to shift from a problem frame to an outcome frame. One benefit of using our own experience as a Counter Example is that we can more easily identify and share the "difference that makes the difference."

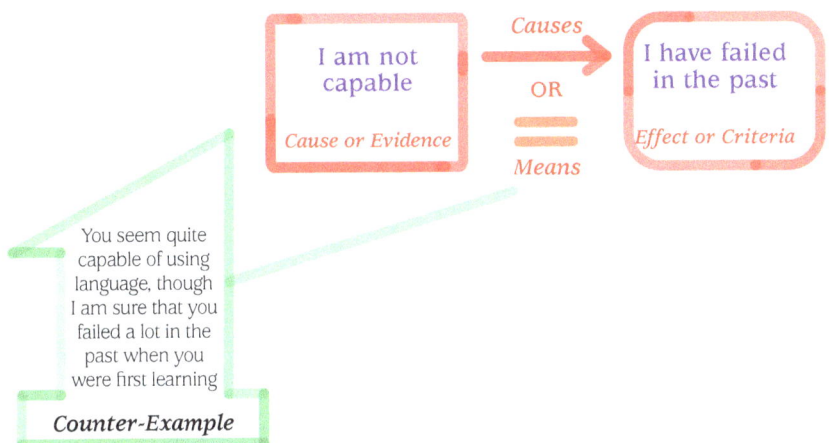

Here, the Counter Example is the person making the belief statement's ability to verbally articulate the generalization to begin with. If we are never capable of learning or doing something because we have failed at in the past, we would probably not be capable of anything! The fact that the person is capable of expressing the belief in words is an indisputable Counter Example to that. The consequence of this is to stimulate the person stating the generalization to be more specific about (Chunk Down) the particular type of capability and past failure they are referring to, which can lead to a much more productive exploration.

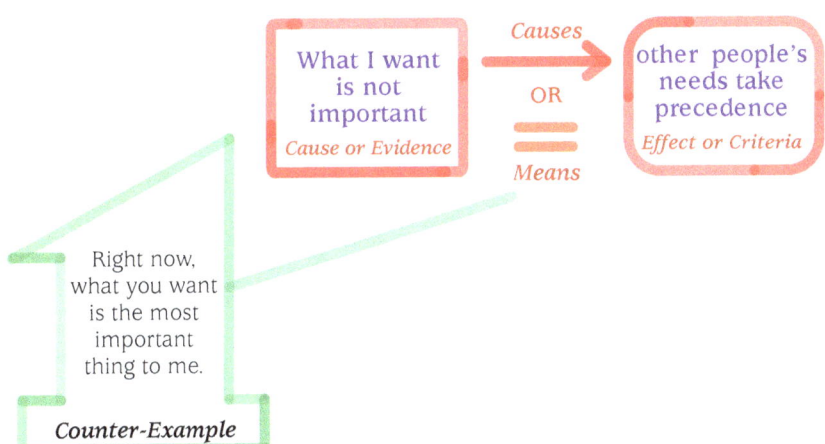

This is another Counter Example created as a result of the ongoing interaction. The individual presenting the Counter Example is an *example* of "other people," but whose own needs are *not* taking precedence over what the person making the belief statement wants in the current situation. This means that the person must reflect more deeply on the reasons for making the generalization or take advantage of the situation and focus on what they actually want.

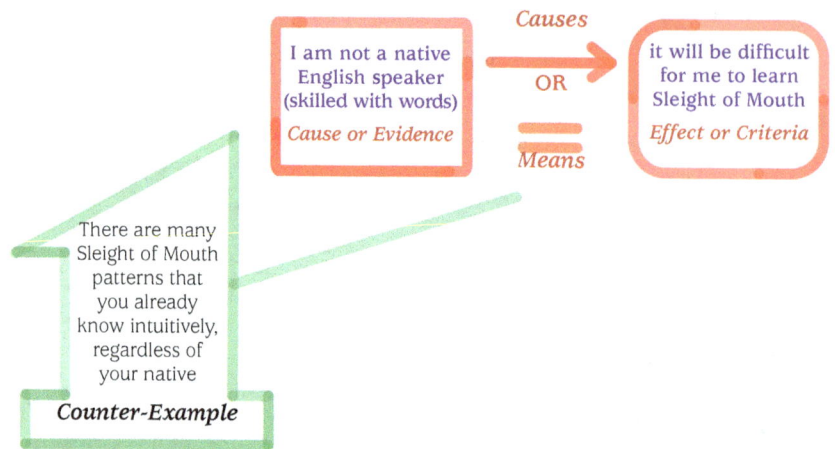

In this last illustration, the Counter Example comes from an assumption that the person making the limiting belief statement already intuitively knows many of the Sleight of Mouth patterns. The implication is that learning the Sleight of Mouth patterns is more a function of intuitions that come from our ability to speak any language that we have some facility with, i.e., that Sleight of Mouth patterns are not language specific but rather relate to deeper structures that we express through words and language.

Reflections on Counter Examples

The purpose of the Sleight of Mouth pattern of Counter Example is to find exceptions to the rule defined by a belief statement that challenge the universality of the generalization. The more Counter Examples there are, the less universal is the generalization. Counter Examples can produce several possible results. They can bring more nuance and flexibility to a generalization or challenge the underlying validity of the generalization. They can also elicit potential resources associated with the counter example by bringing out "differences that make a difference" with respect to the generalization that can lead to other options and possibilities.

Counter Examples can be found or elicited by asking questions related to the verbal equivalence or cause-effect statement made in or implied by the belief statement, or by generating our own equivalences or cause-effect statements and checking them with the person who has made the generalization. Like all Sleight of Mouth patterns, the effectiveness of any Counter Example will be a function of the level of resonance it produces in the listener. When possible, creating exceptions in an ongoing interaction can particularly impactful.

Chapter 12
Hierarchy of Criteria

Hierarchy of Criteria

Hierarchies of Criteria relate to the degree of importance or meaning that people attach to various actions and experiences. A person's *hierarchy of criteria* is essentially the order of priorities that person applies to act in the world. An example of a Hierarchy of Criteria would be a person who values "health" more than "financial success." Such a person would tend to put his or her health "first." This person would probably structure his or her life more around activities that promote personal vitality and physical sustainability rather than professional opportunities. A person whose *Hierarchy of Criteria* placed "financial success" over "health" would have a different lifestyle. He or she might sacrifice health and physical well-being in order to "get ahead" monetarily.

There is a vivid, if somewhat gruesome, illustration of this provided by a joke that was going around some years ago about an overly materialistic "Yuppie" (Young Urban Professional).

> *The Yuppie is opening the door of his Porsche to go to work, when suddenly a car comes by and hits the door, ripping it off completely along with the Yuppie's arm.*
>
> *When the police arrive at the scene, the Yuppie is complaining bitterly about the damage to his precious vehicle. "Officer, look at what has happened to my Porsche!" he whines.*
>
> *"I can't believe that you Yuppies are so materialistic," retorts the officer. "You are so worried about your car, that you haven't even noticed what has happened to your left arm."*
>
> *Finally noticing the remaining shoulder where his arm once was, the Yuppie exclaims, "Oh nooo! My Rolex is gone, too!!"*

The message of the joke is that the individual's material possessions (his car and his watch) are more important to him than his own body. The implication is clearly that the person has a distorted Hierarchy of Criteria. Establishing an effective, ecological, and sustainable Hierarchy of Criteria is an important life skill.

The Sleight of Mouth pattern of *Hierarchy of Criteria* involves re-evaluating (or reinforcing) a belief statement according to an effect or criterion that is potentially more important and impactful than the one addressed by the belief statement.

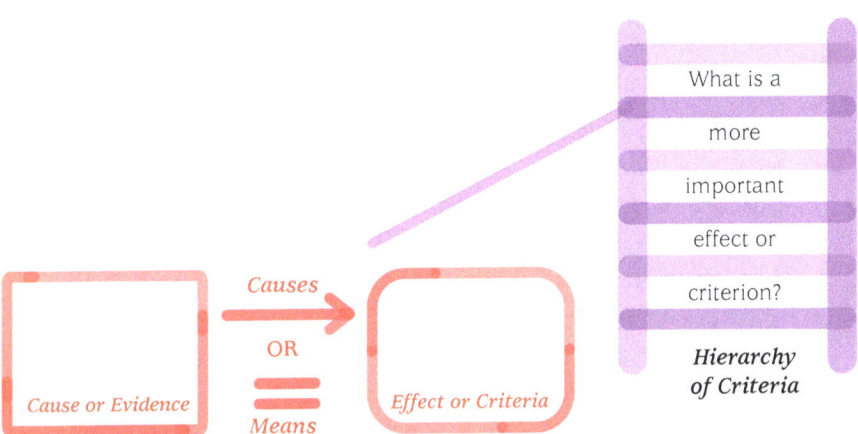

Dynamics and Dilemmas of Hierarchies of Criteria

A good example of a Hierarchy of Criteria, and how it operates, is provided by the following excerpt from Martin Luther King, Jr.'s speech at Riverside Church in New York City in 1967, in which he broke his silence and denounced the Vietnam War.

> *There is never a good time to oppose your government... on some positions, cowardice asks the question, "is it safe?" Expediency asks the question, "Is it politic (appropriate)?" And vanity comes along and asks the question, "Is it popular?" But conscience asks the question, "Is it right?" And there comes a time when one must take a position that is neither safe, nor politic, nor popular, but he must do it because conscience tells him it is right.*

In this statement King is establishing a clear Hierarchy of Criteria – safety, appropriateness, popularity and ultimately *right*, which is the highest-level criterion. As King asserts, in significant and challenging situations, it is the highest-level criterion which should take precedence over the others.

An interesting illustration of applying the Sleight of Mouth pattern of Hierarchy of Criteria comes from a speech made by the character Brutus in William Shakespeare's *Julius Caesar*. In the scene, Brutus along with some other Roman senators have just stabbed Caesar to death. Brutus is addressing the crowd that has gathered to explain his actions.

> *Romans, countrymen, and lovers! Hear me for my cause, and be silent, that you may hear: believe me for mine honor, that you may believe: censure me in your wisdom, and awake your senses, that you may the better judge. If there be any in this assembly, any dear friend of Caesar's, to him I say, that Brutus' love to Caesar was no less than his. If that friend demand why Brutus rose against Caesar, this is my answer: Not that I loved Caesar less, but that I loved Rome more. Had you rather Caesar were living and die all slaves than that Caesar were dead to live all free men? As Caesar loved me, I weep for him; as he was fortunate, I rejoice at it; as he was valiant, I honor him; but, as he was ambitious, I slew him. There is tears for his love; joy for his fortune; honor for his valor; and death for his ambition. Who here is so base that would be a bondsman? If any, speak; for him have I offended. Who here is so rude that would not be a Roman? If any speak; for him have I offended.*

Interestingly, Brutus' opening words already set a type of hierarchy: "Romans, countrymen and lovers." Being Romans is the most important characteristic and overrides being countrymen or lovers. In the speech, Brutus establishes a clear order of criteria... and their consequences. He uses this order of criteria to justify his actions, "As Caesar loved me, I weep for him; as he was fortunate, I rejoice at it; as he was valiant, I honor him; but, as he was ambitious, I slew him." Brutus' implication is that Caesar's ambition was to be a dictator, which was a serious threat to Rome, the Republic, and the freedom of the audience members. Thus, Caesar's *ambition* overrides the others and is justification for his assassination.

Brutus' comment that he killed Caesar not because he "loved Caesar less" but because he "loved Rome more," is a classic type of reframe applying the Sleight of Mouth pattern of *Hierarchy of Criteria*. He uses the same type of reframe when asks the question, "Had you rather Caesar were living and die all slaves than that Caesar were dead to live all free men?" And again, when he ends the speech with the questions, "Who here is so base that would be a bondsman?... Who here is so rude that would not be a Roman? If any speak; for him have I offended." The implication is that, if one is "a Roman" one would have the same Hierarchy of Criteria and the same belief about Caesar as Brutus, and logically would have taken the same "justifiable" action. The choice is between Caesar or the larger "holon" of Rome.

Brutus' actions and words bring up an interesting and important dilemma with respect to beliefs, Hierarchies of Criteria and Sleight of Mouth. On the one hand, as we have already established, Hierarchies of Criteria, or belief systems that put "ego" above "soul," or part of a holon above the entire holon, will create predictable and inevitable problems. This is how Brutus views Caesar's "ambition." On the other hand, by taking the law into his own hands and killing Caesar because of his own belief system, Brutus is himself deciding for the larger holon. In a way, he is doing something like what he accuses Caesar of doing.

Brutus does not offer any direct, observable "proof" for his belief that Caesar's intention is to turn all Romans into slaves and "bondsmen," yet he states it as if it were a fact. This is an example of the type of overgeneralization that should typically set off a Sleight of Mouth alarm bell. Brutus' invitation to, "believe me for mine honor; that you may believe," indicates that he is relying heavily on the influence of his "ethos" (character) in a situation where (as Aristotle put it) "exact certainty is impossible, and opinions are divided."

In the two examples of Brutus and Martin Luther King, both are taking a stand – in King's case, opposing what he perceives as an unjust war; in Brutus' case, "rising against" what he perceives to be a potentially dangerous dictator. There are, however, some "red flags" in Brutus' language. King is ultimately going "towards" what he believes is "right." Brutus' actions against Caesar's "ambition" are an attempt to move "away from" the consequences of a presumed negative intention at the level of identity and purpose (i.e., to enslave and control the people of Rome). Like Hitler's diatribes against "the Jews," beliefs and hierarchies of criteria that incite violence against others for assumed negative intentions are inherently problematic. To use physical force on others or make them suffer as a consequence of our beliefs is imposing one part of a holon upon another.

The more people learn about and master Sleight of Mouth, the more they begin to realize that, to an extent, *everything* is Sleight of Mouth – the map is never the territory. As I pointed out earlier, a good deal of our own maps and models of the world are built from *other people's* maps and models rather than from our direct experience. This is especially true in areas such as politics and social justice. The question then arises, "how do I know what action to take; especially if I believe something is wrong?"

A Hierarchy of Criteria Creates a Consistent Path to Action

Mohandas Gandhi applied an instructive alternative to Brutus' Hierarchy of Criteria during his iconic experience in a train carriage in South Africa in 1893, which led to his first act of civil disobedience and passive resistance. In this incident, the young London-trained lawyer was forcibly removed from a "whites-only" carriage for not obeying laws that unfairly segregated each carriage according to race. Gandhi was traveling to Pretoria on a first-class ticket for official purposes. While he was seated in the first-class compartment, a European man called the railway authorities and asked for the man looking like a "coolie" to be removed from the coach.

When told by the ticket inspector that he had to leave the whites only carriage or be thrown off the train, Gandhi replied, "I refuse to get out voluntarily." His choice of words is important. Had he merely said, "I refuse to get out" he could have been ejected and his statement might have seemed weak and in denial of the reality he was confronting. However, what he said was, "I refuse to get out *voluntarily*." And this would hold true no matter how much force was used to eject him – no amount of physical force could make him do it "voluntarily." His words also placed no blame on anyone else. They merely stated his own intention.

This choice to take a stand against what he perceived as unfair had the effect of connecting Gandhi to something beyond a personally uncomfortable incident. As he recalled later, "Thus, I obtained full experience of the condition of the Indians of South Africa." His realization that his personal experience was emblematic of a larger group of people connected him to a sense of greater purpose, in which "soul force" should be placed above "physical force." It is from this *Hierarchy of Criteria* that Gandhi developed his principles for passive resistance.

> *Passive resistance is a method of securing rights by personal suffering; it is the reverse of resistance by arms. When I refuse to do a thing that is repugnant to my conscience... if I do not obey the law and accept the penalty for its breach, I use soul-force. It involves sacrifice of self.*
>
> *Everybody admits that sacrifice of self is infinitely superior to sacrifice of others. Moreover, if this kind of force is used in a cause that is unjust, only the person using it suffers. He does not make others suffer for his mistakes. Men have before now done many things which were subsequently found to have been wrong. No man can claim that he is absolutely in the right and that a particular thing is "wrong" because he thinks so, but it is*

> "wrong" for him so long as that is his deliberate judgment. It is
> therefore meet that he should not do that which he knows to be
> "wrong," and suffer the consequence [of not doing it] whatever
> it may be. This is the key to the use of soul force.

Gandhi's statement that "that sacrifice of self is infinitely superior to sacrifice of others" is a clear expression of a Hierarchy of Criteria. His placement of "soul force" over "physical force" and "sacrifice of self" over "sacrifice of others," created a compelling path to action that fits a number of the key principles that have been established in this book. Gandhi's comments that "Men have before now done many things which were subsequently found to have been wrong" and "No man can claim that he is absolutely in the right and that a particular thing is 'wrong' because he thinks so," is particularly significant with respect to the use of Sleight of Mouth. How do we act with conscience and integrity in a world that is increasingly filled with "fake news," "Deep Faked" constructions of events that never happened, and conflicting media representations of the same situation? Gandhi's Hierarchy of Criteria offers one way forward.

Similar to Martin Luther King, Jr., Gandhi placed "right" versus "wrong" and "just" versus "unjust" at the top of his Hierarchy of Criteria. He talks about how, on a personal level, something "is 'wrong' for [an individual] so long as that is his deliberate judgment" and that it is appropriate to refuse "to do a thing that is repugnant to my conscience." At the same time, he makes no accusations about the negative intentions of others and does not call for violence against them. By keeping both the "deliberate judgment" that something is wrong and the consequences of refusing to do it on a strictly personal level, he does not fall into the trap of overgeneralizing in relation to others and their intentions, and thus taking violent actions "against *them*."

In Gandhi's case, not taking action is paradoxically a type of action. Passive resistance is not "passivity." In fact, he once said, "When there is only a choice between cowardice and violence, I would advise violence." However, Gandhi argued that "passive resistance" required much more courage than violence. In his words:

> *Physical-force men are strangers to the courage that is requisite in a passive resister. Do you believe that a coward can ever disobey a law that he dislikes? But a passive resister will say he will not obey a law that is against his conscience, even though he may be blown to pieces at the mouth of a cannon. What do yo. think? Wherein is courage required— in blowing others to pieces from behind a cannon, or with a smiling face to approach the cannon and be blown to pieces?*

Gandhi's question, "Wherein is courage required—in blowing others to pieces from behind a cannon, or with a smiling face to approach the cannon and be blown to pieces?" is a good example of how Sleight of Mouth, when used effectively, can produce a dramatic change in perspectives. The words visually and viscerally contrast ego motivations and physical force (blowing others to pieces from behind a cannon) to soul force that is in service of something beyond ourselves (approaching the cannon with a smiling face and facing the possibility of being blown to pieces). The imagery makes it easy to put ourselves in one or the other positions and imagine our inner experience and motivations.

Applying the Sleight of Mouth Pattern of Hierarchy of Criteria

As we can see from Gandhi's emphasis on conscience, courage, self-sacrifice and "soul force," the effective use of the Sleight of Mouth pattern of Hierarchy of Criteria is about shifting attention to more profound and impactful criteria. The mindset driving it focuses on *what is a potentially more important or impactful criterion that has not yet been considered which could bring a significant change in perceptions or priorities?* Higher-level criteria generally encompass more of a particular holon or holarchy than lower-level criteria.

Criteria at different levels of one's "Hierarchy of Criteria" often bounce back and forth between "away from" and "toward," "self" and "others," and move to successively higher Levels of Change. That is, behavioral level criteria (e.g., "to avoid doing something that disappoints others") are often overridden by those related to capabilities (e.g., "to improve my capacity to learn"). Criteria at the level of capability are overridden by those at the level of beliefs and values (e.g., "to not abandon my moral obligations"). Beliefs and values, however, will be overridden by criteria at the level of identity (e.g., "to be a certain type of person," or "to maintain personal integrity"), which will, in turn, be overridden by criteria at the level of a higher purpose beyond ourselves ("to make a positive difference in the lives of others").

The type of courage that Gandhi was talking about, for instance, comes from connecting to a purpose beyond our individual ego. As he reportedly said, "Be the change you want to see in the world."

Of course, criteria that are oriented to an outcome frame tend to be more productive and less problematic than those which are related to an "away from" problem frame.

The following are examples of how the pattern of Hierarchy of Criteria could be applied to the group of limiting beliefs we have explored in the previous sections.

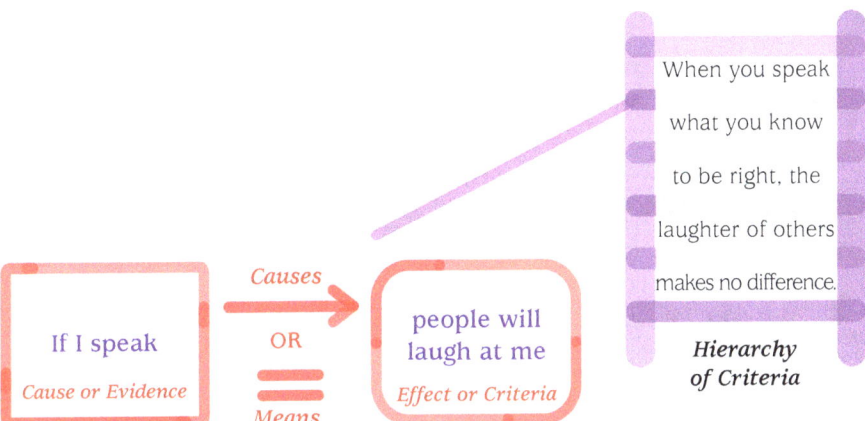

In this example, the higher-level criterion being introduced is "speak what you know to be right." This reframe brings attention to the person's purpose for speaking to begin with. The implication is that, when in service of this higher-level criterion, whether people laugh or not is not what is most relevant. People's laughter does not change whether something is right or not. It is still right independent of their response. As Martin Luther King alluded to in the quote earlier in this section, our conscience is built on standards that are not a function of other people's approval. Wanting to avoid being laughed at is most likely a criterion at the level of "ego." Speaking what is "right" shifts to "soul," a focus beyond one's individual identity to that of contributing to a greater good.

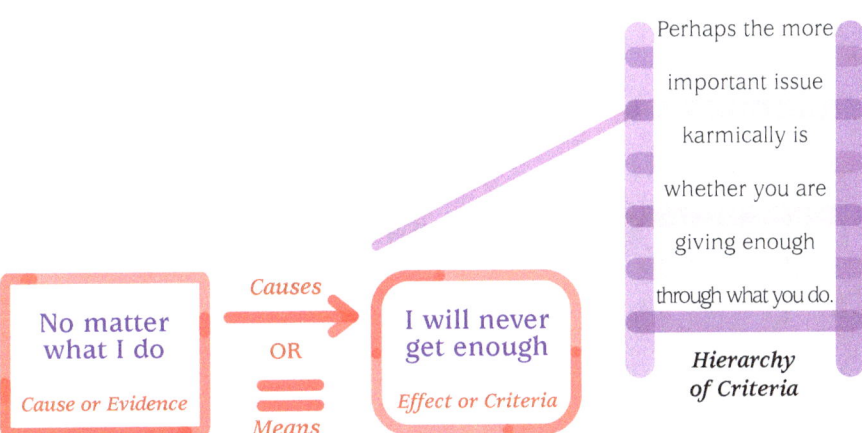

The shift of criteria in this example is to "giving enough" rather than "getting enough." Getting enough tends to be an "ego" motivation. By introducing the notion of "karma" this reframe brings in the idea that we receive in proportion to what we give. Karma is a rule relating to a bigger system than our individual egos. The implication is that, if we want to receive enough for ourselves, we need to give enough to others.

Sleight of Mouth

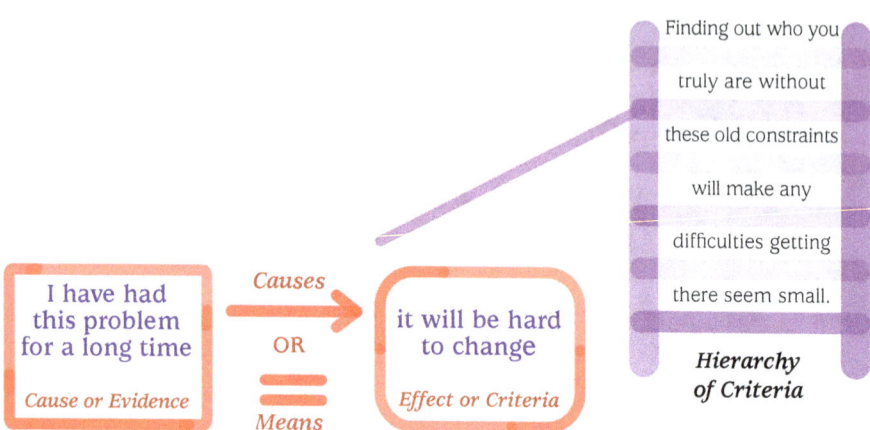

Reframing the criterion to "finding out who you truly are" shifts attention from a problem frame to an outcome frame and brings awareness to the bigger purpose of changing a long-standing problem. It moves the focus from the level of environment and behavior (i.e., time and effort) to the level of identity (who you truly are). The implication is that the "problem" is a type of constraint holding the person back from reaching his or her full potential. Focusing on the goal at the identity level will make any difficulties in achieving it seem inconsequential by comparison.

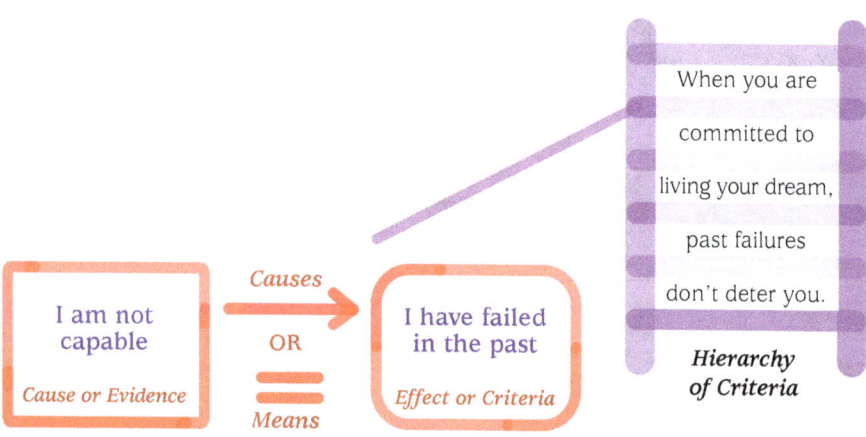

Once again, the criterion of commitment to "living your dream," moves the focus to an outcome frame on a higher level (identity) than behavior and environment (failing in the past). The issue becomes less about the development of a particular capability or set of capabilities and more about doing what is necessary to reach the ultimate destination. By doing so, it minimizes the importance and impact of previous failures and puts attention on the future.

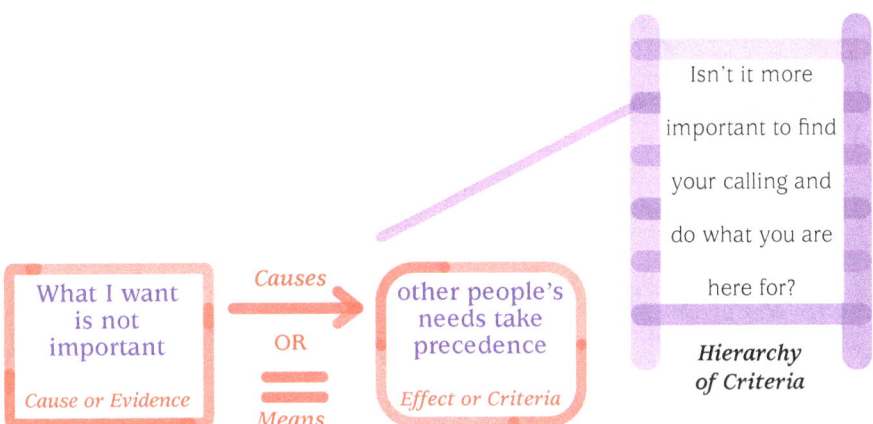

The stated challenge in this belief is that of a self-other conflict (what I want versus other people's needs). A calling is something deeper than either needs or wants, which tend to be more related to our individual ego. Our calling is more about our destiny (what we are here for) and relates to the place that we have and the contribution we make to something bigger than ourselves as a result of our identity and soul (our role and mission). When connected to such a calling, the type of dilemma stated in the belief would diminish or disappear.

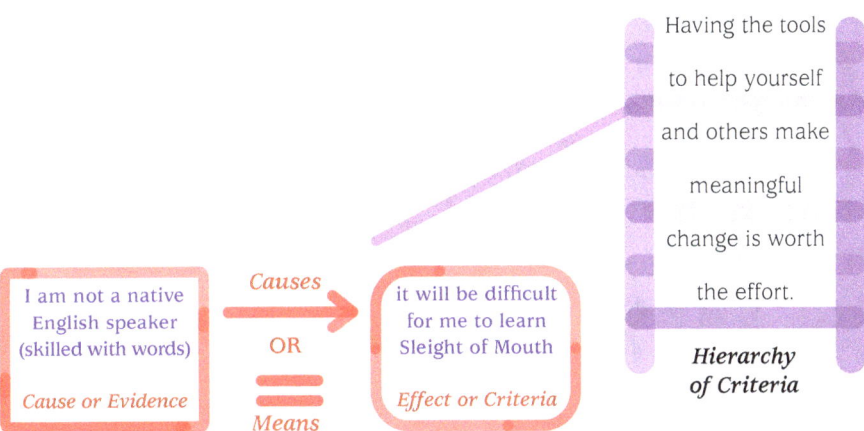

As with some of the previous examples, this reframe shifts attention to the ultimate purpose of learning Sleight of Mouth. Rather than focus on a problem frame at the level of capability (difficulty learning) it focuses on the higher-level outcome frame of helping ourselves and others make meaningful change. This shift in focus changes the relationship with potential difficulties (i.e., making it "worth the effort").

As usual, the impact and effectiveness of any of these reframes will be a function of the level of resonance they have with the listener. It is also important that they be done with the genuine desire to support the person to transcend some limitation or conflict that is creating a significant problem or barrier for the listener. This is where the skills of emotional intelligence and pacing and leading become essential.

A Creative Example of Using the Sleight of Mouth Pattern of Hierarchy of Criteria

Not surprisingly, the work of Milton Erickson provides an excellent example of how to apply these types of skills, combined with multiple intelligences, to create a significant life shift for one of his patients. In *A Teaching Seminar* (pp. 188-189) Erickson recounts the case of a 52-year-old woman who had cancer and was in great pain. Her doctor told Erickson, "I can give her a double shot of morphine and Demerol and Percodan, all at the same time, plus nine grains of sodium amytal. It doesn't even make her drowsy, she suffers so much pain." He sent her to Erickson by ambulance to see if he could do anything to help. When she entered the room, she said to Erickson (who was 70 at the time), "Sonny, do you really think that your hypnotic words will so alter my body when powerful chemicals have no effect on it?" According to Erickson:

> *I said, "Madam, as I look at your eyes, the pupils are dilating and contracting steadily, and your facial muscles are quivering. So, I know you are suffering constant pain – constant, stabbing, pulsating pain. I can see it with my eyes. Now tell me, Madam, if you saw a lean, hungry tiger in the next room, slowly walking into the room and eyeing you hungrily and licking its chops, how much pain would you feel?" She said, "I wouldn't feel any under those circumstances. Well, my goodness. I don't feel any pain now. May I take that tiger back to the hospital with me?" I said, "Certainly, but I will have to tell your doctor." She said, "But don't tell the nurses. I want to have some fun with the nurses. Every time they ask me if I am having pain, I am going to tell them, look under the bed. If the tiger is still there, I haven't got a bit of pain."*

"Can you please tell me if the tiger is still there?"

In this example, the inner state elicited by the criterion of "survival" overrode the experience of pain more than the "powerful chemicals" that had been ineffective. Erickson did not have to verbally name the deeper criterion of "survival." His question, "if you saw a lean, hungry tiger in the next room, slowly walking into the room and eyeing you hungrily and licking its chops, how much pain would you feel?" implicitly establishes a hierarchy of survival over pain. Clearly, the visual image Erickson conjured through his words was more important than the "words" themselves in creating the shift in criteria.

Erickson also "paced" the woman before "leading" by acknowledging that he could "see" how much pain she was experiencing. This serves the purpose of helping to get the necessary level of rapport for his words to have a deep enough effect.

Reflections on Hierarchy of Criteria

The Sleight of Mouth pattern of Hierarchy of Criteria can have a particularly powerful impact on our behavior. The priorities we establish with respect to our lives determine which outcomes we select, how we make decisions and what type of relationship we will have with potential obstacles and challenges.

Different criteria support different aspects of the holarchies in which we live. Some criteria are more "ego bound" and relate to our personal benefit and security. Others are more "soul" oriented and connect us to service to something beyond our individual identity. Some are more inherently "away from" what we don't want. Others direct our attention "toward" a desired state. Typically, higher-level criteria are also associated with higher Levels of Change (e.g., identity and purpose).

In this way, hierarchies of criteria are important filters on our thoughts and actions. Connecting to or shifting what is at the top of the hierarchy can produce immediate and dramatic change, as illustrated in the Erickson example.

Chapter 13
Apply to Self

Apply to Self

As I pointed out in *Sleight of Mouth I* (p. 234-235), applying a belief to itself involves evaluating the belief statement according to the generalization or criteria defined by that statement. For example, if a person expresses a belief such as, "You cannot trust words," the belief could be applied to itself by asking, "Since you cannot trust words, how can you trust the words you just said?" As another example, if a person says, "It is wrong to make generalizations," one could respond, "Then, are you sure that you are not wrong to make *that* generalization?" A good visual metaphor for Apply to Self would be that of a snake swallowing its own tail.

One purpose of applying a belief or generalization to itself is to discover whether or not the belief (or the belief holder) is a congruent example of the generalization and criteria expressed by the belief statement.

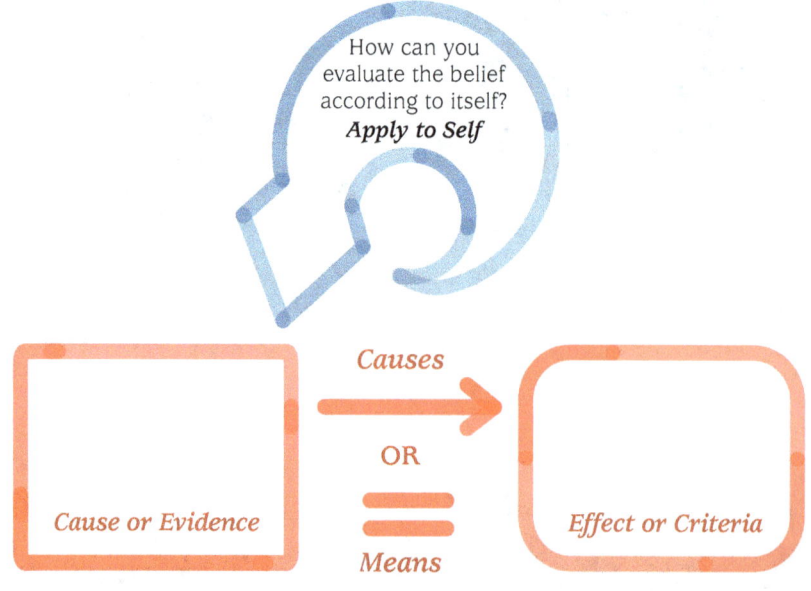

Frequently, applying a belief to itself prompts us to reconsider the validity or universality of the belief. A humorous example of the Sleight of Mouth pattern of Apply to Self and its potential consequences is illustrated in the following joke.

> *A man is strolling down the beach when he comes upon an old bottle with a cork in it. He pulls out the stopper and a large puff of blue smoke spews from the bottle, taking the form of a genie. The genie says to the man, I've been trapped in that bottle for a thousand years, and you released me. As a reward, I will grant you a wish. The condition is, however, that it must either be for great wealth or for great wisdom." The man considers the choices for a moment and finally replies nobly, "I'll take the wisdom." The genie waves his hand and zap, the man is filled with the wisdom of the ages. Suddenly, a look of great anguish appears on the man's face. Hanging his head in regret, he exclaims (with the hindsight of his newfound wisdom), "Oh darn, I should have chosen wealth."*

The humor here comes from the implication that, by applying his newly attained wisdom to his own decision, the man presumably realizes that he made the wrong the choice, and that the wealth is actually preferable to wisdom.

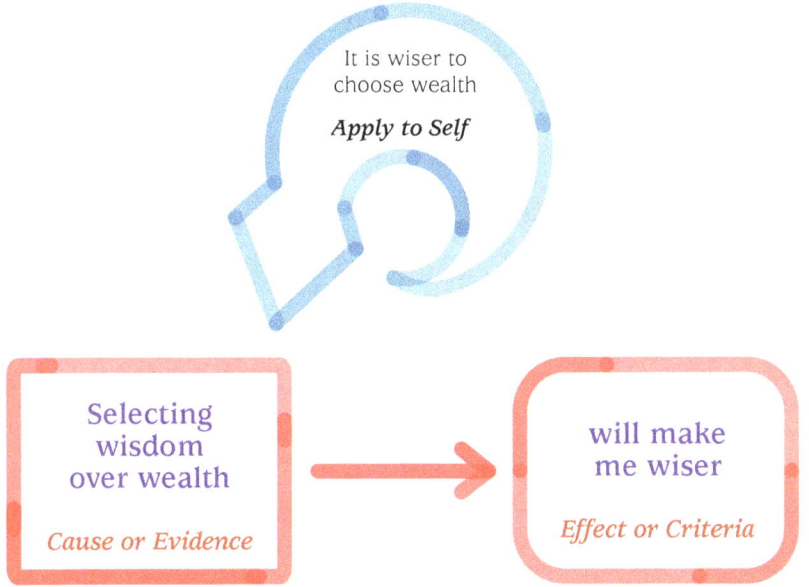

There was an interesting variation of this story (almost certainly apocryphal) going around on the Internet about Mohandas Gandhi studying law at University College in London. A white professor, whose last name was Peters, apparently disliked Gandhi intensely, which led to a spirited rivalry between the two. One day, Mr. Peters was reported to have asked, "Mr. Gandhi, if you are walking down the street and find a package, and within it there is a bag of wisdom and another bag with a lot of money; which one will you take?" Without hesitating, Gandhi responded, "the one with the money, of course." Mr. Peters, with a smile of superiority, said, "I, in your place, would have taken the wisdom, don't you think?" Also smiling, Gandhi supposedly retorted, "Each one takes what one doesn't have." The implication, of course, is that Gandhi did not need to take the wisdom because he was already plenty wise, whereas Mr. Peters was in great need of wisdom.

This anecdote moves the focus of the discourse from one of environment (money) and capability (wisdom) more to that of values and identity (our deficiencies as a person). [It is also an example of a type of Meta Frame; a Sleight of Mouth pattern we will explore later in this book.] Belief issues concerning to identity can, of course, have even bigger ramifications than those at lower levels as is humorously illustrated in the following joke.

> *Descartes is in a bistro engaged in a deep philosophical argument with his companions, asserting his famous claim, "I think, therefore I am." In the middle of a heated discussion the waitress comes by, interrupts the discussion and asks, "Do you want anything else?" Descartes considers her question for a moment and replies, "I think not," and poof, disappears into thin air.*

If "I think, therefore I am," then "If I think not, I am not!"

Another interesting example of the pattern of Apply to Self at the identity level is the story about the wife who loses her temper with her husband and shouts, "You are such a loser, if there would be a competition of losers you would get 2nd place" "Why just second?" asks the husband. "Because you are a loser," she replies. Of course, a loser could not win a competition; even a competition of losers.

Testing the Validity of a Generalization with the Sleight of Mouth Pattern of Apply to Self

Another use of Apply to Self is to test whether a generalization that we apply to others (or some other part of our bigger holon) also applies to our self (our local part of the holon), and vice versa. A number of good examples of this aspect of the pattern and principle of Apply to Self are attributed to Jesus in the Bible, such as:

> *Love thy neighbor as thyself.* (Matthew 22:41)

> *Do unto others as you would have them do unto you.* (Luke 6:31)

> *For with what judgment ye judge, ye shall be judged.* (Matthew 7:2)

> *Why beholdest thou the mote that is in thy brother's eye, but considerest not the beam that is in thine own eye? Or how wilt thou say to thy brother, Let me pull out the mote out of thine eye; and behold, a beam is in thine own eye… first cast out the beam out of thine own eye; and then shalt thou see clearly to cast out the mote out thy brother's eye.* (Matthew 7:3-5)

Each of these statements is an invitation to look beyond the filters and blind spots of one's own individual perspective and develop greater congruity and compassion with respect to one's interactions with others. One of my favorite examples of applying this pattern (that I also presented in *Sleight of Mouth I*) and how it can influence a situation is how Jesus reportedly used it to save a woman's life. The incident is described in the following account, taken from *John* (8:3-11):

> *And the scribes and Pharisees brought unto him a woman taken in adultery; and when they had set her in the midst, They said unto him, Master, this woman was taken in adultery, in the very act. Now Moses in the law commanded us, that such should be stoned: but what sayest thou?*

> *This they said, tempting him, that they might have to accuse him. But Jesus stooped down, and with his finger wrote on the ground, as though he heard them not.*

> *So when they continued asking him, he lifted up himself, and said unto them, He that is without sin among you, let him first cast a stone at her.*

And again he stooped down, and wrote on the ground.

And they which heard it, being convicted by their own conscience, went out one by one, beginning at the eldest, even unto the last: and Jesus was left alone, and the woman standing in the midst.

When Jesus had lifted himself, and saw none but the woman, he said unto her, Woman, where are those thine accusers? Hath no man condemned thee? She said, No man, Lord. And Jesus said unto her, Neither do I condemn thee: go, and sin no more.

Jesus' statement, "He that is without sin among you, let him first cast a stone at her," is a brilliant example of applying the criteria and cause-effect consequences of a belief statement to those asserting it.

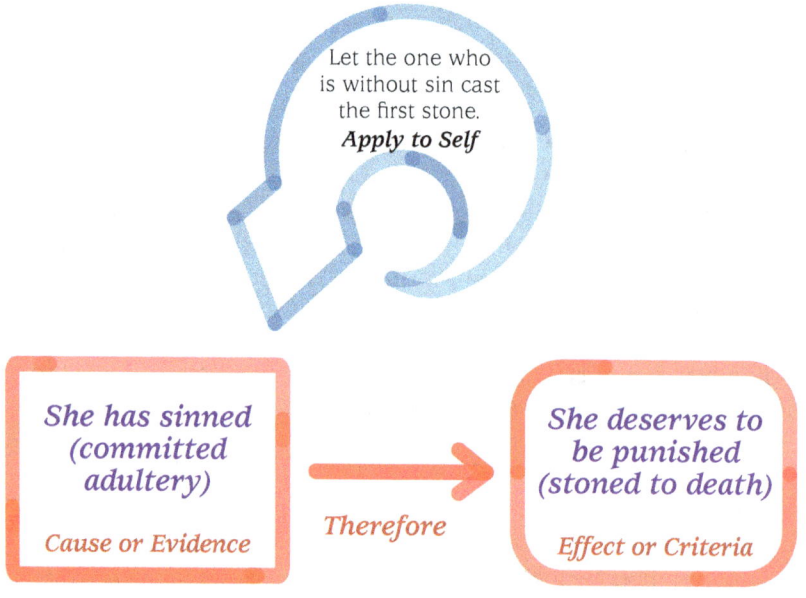

The report that "they which heard it, being convicted by their own conscience, went out one by one, beginning at the eldest" shows the potential impact of applying the generalizations that we make about others to ourselves. It creates a type of "meta" position in which we observe ourselves in the same way that we observe others. It can also potentially lead to more empathy by creating the possibility of a type of second position with others.

"Let the one who is without sin cast the first stone."

The comment, "This they said, tempting him, that they might have to accuse him," indicates that those questioning Jesus were hoping to trap him in some type of inconsistency between his teachings of forgiveness and the "laws of Moses." The report that "Jesus stooped down, and with his finger wrote on the ground, as though he heard them not," is intriguing. It could be seen as his own attempt to achieve a type of meta position and remain in a COACH state while being challenged.

Applying the Sleight of Mouth Pattern of Apply to Self

The Sleight of Mouth pattern of *Apply to Self* essentially involves applying the criteria or generalization expressed by a belief to the belief statement itself in some way, or to the individual(s) asserting the belief. As with all Sleight of Mouth patterns, the purpose of this is to prompt a new or different perspective or to introduce more flexibility.

The mindset supporting the pattern of Apply to Self involves exploring questions such as: *What happens when you view the belief statement or its consequences through the filter of belief or its criteria? Can the belief statement itself be challenged or confirmed according to the generalization or criteria defined by the belief? Is the statement (or ongoing behavior/intent of the speaker) an example of the belief or its criteria?*

The following are examples of how the pattern of Apply to Self could be applied to the group of limiting beliefs we have explored in the previous sections.

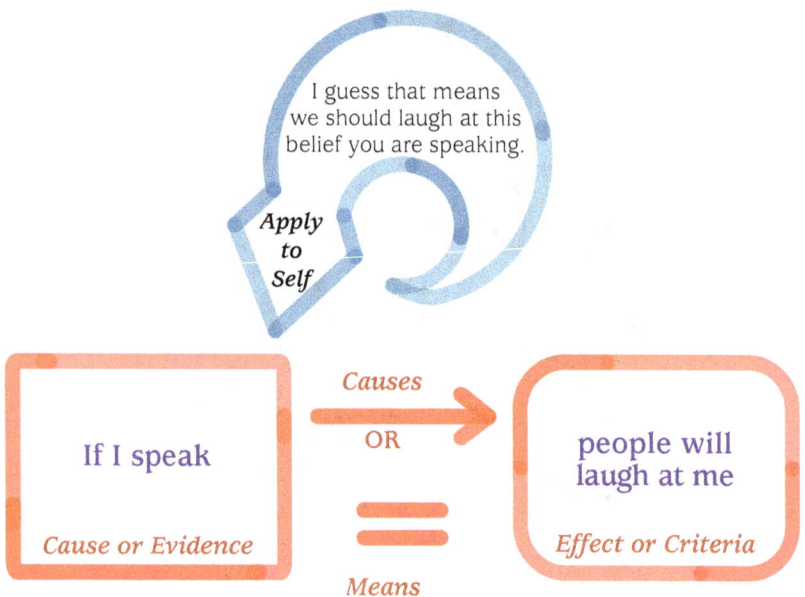

Since the person expressing the belief is presumably speaking it, the generalization being made claims that should elicit laughter from people. The use of the word "we" indicates that the person expressing the belief is also a "person" listening to what is being spoken. An important shift here is that, instead of being directed at the speaker, the laughter is directed at the belief. The implication is that perhaps the generalization could be taken more lightly and not so seriously.

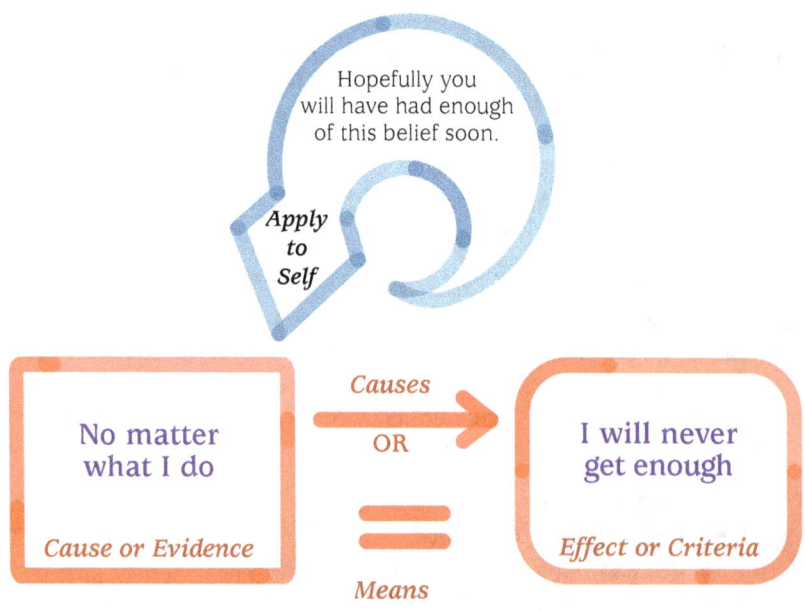

In this case, the criterion of getting "enough" is being applied to the belief. It has been switched, however, to "having" enough, which carries the implication that there can be too much of something as well as too little. Explicitly naming the generalization a "belief" also implies that it is not a "reality" or a "truth." Rather it is a perception that can be changed. The overall statement, "Hopefully you will have had enough of this belief soon," asserts that the issue is not a matter of "doing" but rather of letting go of the limiting belief. The words, "will have had enough" mean that the person making the belief statement will realize that holding onto the generalization is not serving them anymore. The addition of the word "soon" implies that the realization is inevitable and could happen quickly.

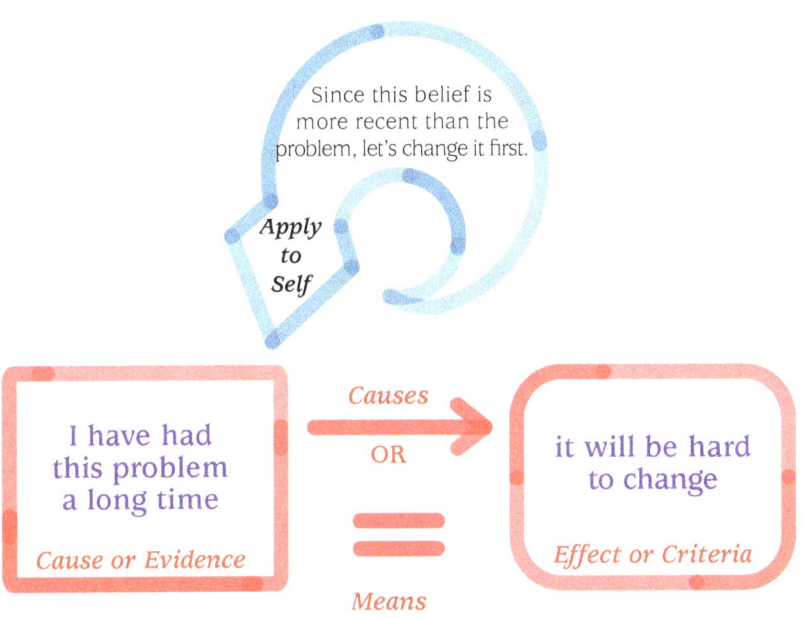

Again, in this example the generalization is explicitly named a "belief" which already creates a different relationship with it. The generalization made by the belief statement indicates that the amount of time something has existed determines the level of difficulty involved in changing it. The Apply to Self statement implies that the belief is part of what is creating the difficulty to change the problem and has probably been formed sometime after the existence of the problem being referred to. Thus, changing the generalization will be easier to do first and will consequently make the problem easier to change.

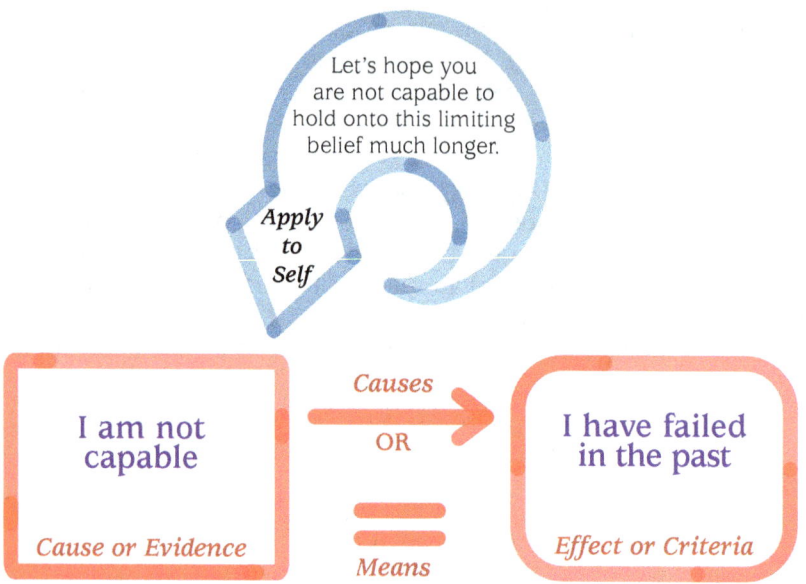

In addition to explicitly labeling the statement a "limiting belief," this example applies the criterion of being "not capable" back to the belief statement, switching it to a positive rather than negative connotation (i.e., not capable to sustain a limiting belief). The implication is that the person has formed and is holding onto a limiting belief. The words "hold onto" imply that the belief is something that the person is actively operating from and can, thus, choose to retain or let go of. The phrase "much longer" indicates that the shift to letting go of the limitation is just a matter of time and is likely to happen soon.

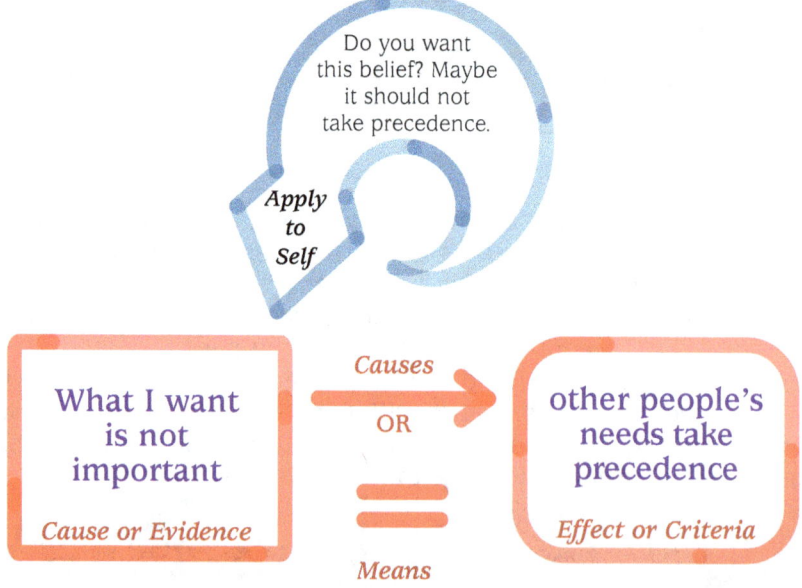

Here, two key words from the belief statement, "want" and "precedence," are used in the Apply to Self formulation. Since "wanting" is an issue, the question is posed, "Do you want this belief?" The implication is that the statement is, in fact, a belief that the person can choose to have or not. Further, since the belief itself is the person's own generalization and not someone else's "need," there is no reason for it to "take precedence" in the person's life. It can be put aside if not wanted.

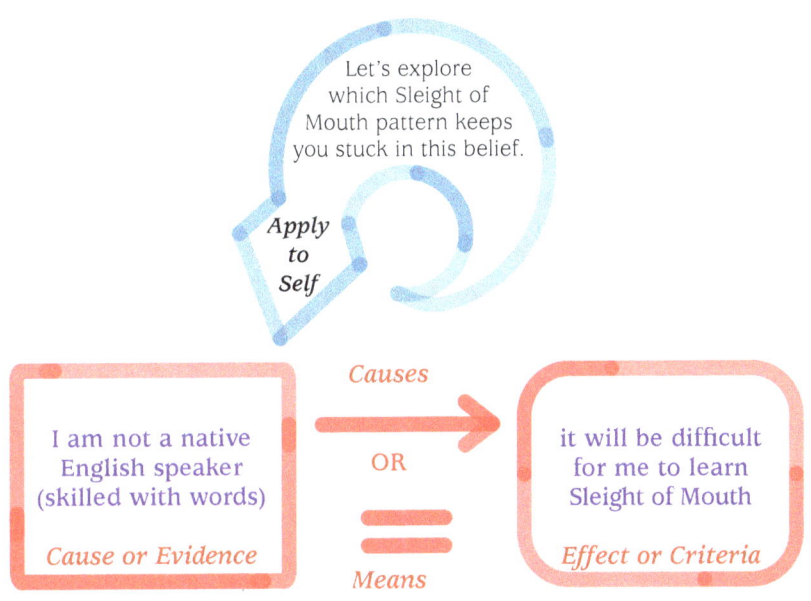

In this final example, the topic of the belief statement, "Sleight of Mouth," is used in the Apply to Self response. Once again, the assumption is that the statement itself is an expression of a limiting belief that the person could update or let go of. The implication is that the person is "stuck in" the belief due to some type of Sleight of Mouth pattern. If that pattern in discovered, new choices can be generated, and the process of learning Sleight of Mouth will become easier. Thus, the very thing (Sleight of Mouth) the person is claiming to be difficult to learn is actually what can help them to make it easier to learn.

Reflections on Apply to Self

In a majority of the above examples, the belief statement has been explicitly labeled as a "belief." This creates a type of disassociation from it, so that, instead of being experienced as some type of irrefutable truth about the territory, it can be observed for what it is – a generalization about the territory that most likely has some degree of deletion and distortion. The Apply to Self response is then directed toward the belief or belief statement and is typically done in a way that makes it a matter of choice with respect to the person expressing the belief. Sometimes the connotation of a word or phrase is shifted in the Apply to Self process, as in the cases of *not being capable* to hold on to a limiting belief and *having enough* of a limiting belief.

Depending upon the type of language used in the belief statement, the Apply to Self pattern can be done using either the whole belief statement or just parts. In some cases, the criteria used or implied by the belief statement are the focal point. Other times, it is the equivalence or cause-effect that is the focus.

As with the other Sleight of Mouth patterns, the effective use of Apply to Self is the result of a mindset where we are seeking to leverage or use the limiting belief, or some part of the belief statement, to introduce another perspective or create more flexibility. At times it is necessary to think non-linearly and non-literally in order to apply a belief statement to itself. For example, if a person says, "I cannot afford this product because it is too expensive," you might need to apply it to itself more metaphorically. This could be done by saying, "That may ultimately be an expensive belief to hold onto too tightly," or, by asking, "Are you sure you can *afford* to hold that belief so strongly, it may prevent you from taking advantage of important opportunities?"

Apply to Self can be done effectively in the form of questions as well as statements. For instance, "I guess that means we should laugh at this belief you are speaking" could formulated as, "Should we laugh at this belief that you are speaking now?" "Hopefully you will have had enough of this belief soon," can be reformulated as, "When will you have had enough of this belief?" And so on.

Leveraging a Belief to Change Itself

Apply to Self can also be used to leverage a belief or belief statement to change itself. That is, the generalization can be used to bring about change in the generalization. Milton Erickson describes a, typically, creative example of this in his work with an eight-year-old boy who had become a troublemaker after his mother, a single parent, started dating other men (*Uncommon Therapy*, pp. 218-221). He began destroying things and defying his mother and his teachers. His mother's usual disciplinary methods were ineffective and instead tended to escalate the boy's behavior. At a loss about what to do, the mother brought the boy to see Erickson. The boy boastfully declared that Erickson could not do anything to stop him, and that the boy "could do whatever he pleased" and that he would "stomp" anyone who "got in his way." Erickson responded that it was unnecessary for him to do anything to change the boy's behavior because the boy would change his behavior "all by himself."

Erickson sent the mother away for a while and challenged the boy to stomp as hard as he could, adding that he "probably could not stomp the floor hard enough to make it worth while." The boy promptly stomped his foot on the floor with all his might. Erickson responded that his effort "was really remarkably good for a little eight-year-old boy and that he could probably repeat it a number of times, but not very many." The boy angrily shouted that he could "stomp that hard fifty, a hundred, a thousand times" if he wished. Erickson replied that he was only eight years old, and no matter how angry he was he couldn't stomp a thousand times. At this, the boy furiously declared his intention of "stomping a hole in the floor even if it took a hundred million stomps." Skeptically, Erickson said to him that "such a small boy would almost certainly not be able to stomp even 50 times without getting tired and wanting to sit down." The boy started repeatedly stomping his foot as hard as he could. Erickson told the boy he was impressed with his stomping ability, but again doubted that the boy could keep it up.

After intensifying his efforts, the boy "reached a count of thirty before he realized that he had greatly overestimated his stomping ability." Erickson offered the boy the option of "just patting the floor a thousand times with his foot, since he really couldn't stand still and rest without wiggling around and wanting to sit down." The boy rejected the floor-patting and instead "declared his intention of standing still," assuming a stiff, upright position with his hands at his sides.

Erickson again expressed doubt that the boy could remain standing "without fidgeting or wanting to sit down." He showed the boy the desk clock, and commented about "the slowness of the minute hand and the even greater slowness of the hour hand despite the seeming rapidity of the ticking of the clock." Erickson then went about his business, making notes on other cases he was working with. Over the next hour and a half, the boy started to lean on the chair when he thought Erickson wasn't looking and to sit down when Erickson went out of the room, but always being sure to stand up when Erickson came back into the room.

By the time his mother returned the boy's attitude had completely changed. On the way home, the boy told his mother that Erickson was "a nice doctor," and there was no further trouble at school or in the neighborhood. When the mother decided to get married some time later, the boy wouldn't fully accept the stepfather until he found out that Erickson approved of the man.

Reflections on the Example

In this example, Erickson applied the boy's statement that he could "do whatever he pleased" and that he would "stomp" anyone who "got in his way" to the boy's own desire to rebel. By encouraging the boy to "do what he wanted" (rebelling and stomping) Erickson was able to get the boy to reevaluate whether he really wanted or could "do whatever he pleased." By challenging the boy to stomp the floor as hard as he could, the boy had to face the fact that the person who was most in his way was himself, as a result of his own overestimation of his abilities – especially when he was in a CRASH state. Ultimately, the boy realized "all by himself" that maybe he didn't really want to just "do what whatever he pleased" and that it was important to have others that he could trust that knew more than he did to help him set limits.

In Erickson's words:

> *In an undefined world where intellectual and emotional fluctuations create an enveloping state of uncertainty that varies from one mood and one moment to the next, there can be no certainty or security. [The boy] sought to learn what was really strong, secure, and safe, and he learned it in the effective way one learns not to kick a stone with a bare foot or to slap a cactus with the bare hands.*

This form of learning is one of the benefits of encouraging people to apply their judgments and generalizations to their own beliefs and to themselves. They are able to come to their conclusions on their own.

Erickson's comment about the boy's need to learn "what was really strong, secure, and safe" in "an undefined world where intellectual and emotional fluctuations create an enveloping state of uncertainty that varies from one mood and one moment to the next" is a demonstration of the importance of things like second position when employing Sleight of Mouth. This type of emotional intelligence helps to identify where and why there will be resonance with a particular approach.

Chapter 14
Change Frame Size

Change Frame Size

A *frame* is something that surrounds or encloses something else. It establishes the borders and constraints surrounding a phenomenon or interaction. Framing something creates a context in which that thing operates and is evaluated. Frames greatly influence the way that specific experiences and events are interpreted and responded to because they create reference points that direct attention to particular aspects of a phenomenon or experience.

A painful memory, for example, may loom as an all-consuming event when perceived within the short-term frame of the five minutes surrounding the event. That same painful experience may seem almost trivial when framed against the background of one's lifetime. An event that seems unbearably frustrating when we consider it with respect to our own desires and expectations, for instance, may suddenly seem unimportant when framed with respect to tragedies that can befall an entire community.

The Sleight of Mouth pattern of *Change Frame Size* involves shifting the impact or implication of a belief statement by placing it in the context of a longer (or shorter) time frame, a larger number of people (or from an individual point of view) or a bigger or smaller perspective.

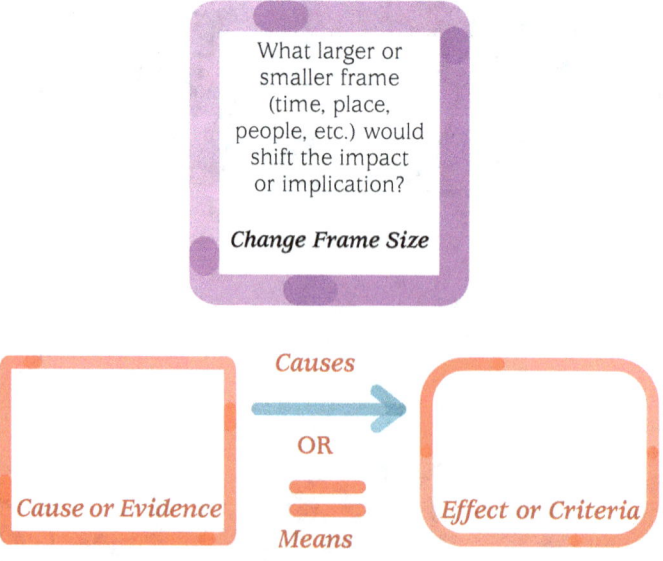

The potentially transformational effect of changing frame size is illustrated in the old Buddhist story that goes something like the following.

> *A young man came to an elderly Zen master and complained about his problems and sufferings in life. The old master listened to the man carefully and handed him a handful of salt. The master then instructed the man to put the salt in a glass of water and drink it. The man did as the master said. "How does it taste?" asked the master. "Disgusting, not good at all," said the man as he spat out the salty water.*
>
> *The master then gave the young man another handful of salt and asked him to put the salt in a nearby lake. Again, the young man did as he was told. "Now take a drink of the water from the lake," instructed the master. The young man bent down and drank the water from the lake. "How does that taste?" asked the master. The young man, who was thirsty, thoroughly enjoyed the cool water of the lake. "It is perfect. It is clear and fresh," the young man replied.*
>
> *The master then explained, "The inevitable pain in life is like the handful of salt. The amount we "taste" of that pain depends on the container we put it into. You can stay small and contracted like the glass, or expand your awareness to become like the lake. If you are a lake, then the pain and difficulties you experience in your life will not cause you suffering."*

Sometimes, Changing Frame Size can have a type of paradoxical affect. A Japanese colleague of mine grew up in Hiroshima. When he was a boy he went through a stage of being afraid of ghosts. One night before going to bed he confessed to his grandmother that he was afraid that there might be a ghost in his bedroom. "There are 60,000 skeletons under the ground in this city," she replied. "Why be afraid of just one?"

The grandmother's reference to "60,000 skeletons" is clearly about the tens of thousands of people killed within minutes when the United States dropped an atomic bomb on the unsuspecting and innocent citizens of the city at the end of the Second World War. Her Change of Frame Size to include all of those potential ghosts brings up an interesting dilemma. If there are so many ghosts around, that have been there the boy's entire life, why would one more make a difference? Her reference to all the "skeletons" also invites many questions about the nature and intentions of "ghosts."

The grandmother's question, "Why be afraid of just one?" creates an important choice for the boy. Does he amplify his fear 60,000 times and become completely overwhelmed now that he knows there are many, many potential ghosts all over the city all the time and not just in his bedroom at night? Or does he change his relationship with ghosts to something other than fear?

In the case of my colleague, it completely reframed his perception of ghosts. As soon as he thought about the possibility of one in his bedroom, he immediately became aware of the 60,000 that had been around him all of his life, and how they got there. His fear became transformed into a sense of connection with all of those souls that gave him a deep sense of profound purpose.

On a personal note, I have visited the city of Hiroshima and the Atom Bomb Museum there. As an American, whose country was responsible for the indescribable horrors that were inflicted onto its citizens because of the atom bomb, it was a touching, shocking and sobering experience to see the photographs of the destruction and listen to the recordings of the survivors describing what happened to them and their families and friends. What astonished me most, however, was that the inhabitants of the city had transformed that violence and horror into a collective commitment to "peace and creativity." All of the schools, businesses and government services were organized to support the promotion of peace and creativity as a way to ensure a future where what happened to them would never happen again. This is a future to which I hope the appropriate and effective use of Sleight of Mouth can also contribute.

The Relationship between Changing Frame Size and Chunking

Change Frame Size has similarities to Chunk Up and Chunk Down but is a fundamentally different mindset. Chunking Up and Down are about parts and wholes, and classes and members. Changing Frame Size is about widening or narrowing our frame of reference. It can be likened to zooming in or zooming out with a camera lens, or to shifting the camera angle to put something more into the foreground or background. Chunking Up or Down can certainly Change Frame Size and Changing Frame Size may lead to Chunking Up or Down, but they are not generated from the same mindset.

Chunking Up "water," for example, would be more likely to bring our attention to the bigger classification of "*liquids*" than to thinking of a lake. Chunking Down water would involve breaking it into hydrogen and oxygen atoms rather than putting it into a smaller container.

Frames can be Created by Establishing Reference Points

Changing Frame Size frequently involves establishing particular reference points relating to time, place or people that create and hold a particular mental frame of reference. As an example, Golda Mier, the first female Prime Minister of Israel during a particularly tumultuous period (1969-1974), was once asked what she did to make decisions that could significantly affect the lives of millions of people. She responded that she never made any important decision "without first consulting at least two people — my great-grandmother, who is no longer alive, and my great-granddaughter, who is not yet born." Clearly, thinking of these two individuals establishes inner reference points for a bigger, more inclusive and longer-term time frame (like the Zen master's lake).

Changing Frame Size Shifts the Context in which Something is Perceived

Shifting the size of a frame creates a different type of landscape or background against which particular phenomena or experiences are perceived and evaluated. A good example of how different frames create different interests and interpretations is humorously illustrated in the following joke.

> *An old man was rowing a boat on a lake when a frog swam up to him and yelled, "Mister. Mister. I've been put under a spell. Kiss me and I will transform into a beautiful princess and we'll live happily ever after!" The surprised old man picked up the frog, put it in his pocket and rowed to shore. The frog called out again, "Hey, mister. I'm really a gorgeous princess. Kiss me and we'll live happily ever after!" Still the man said nothing and walked down the road toward his home. The frog was getting angry at being ignored. "Why don't you kiss me? I told you I'm really a beautiful princess." "Listen, lady," the man finally replied. "I'm 90 years old and have had three wives. At this point in my life, I find a talking frog a much more fascinating companion."*

The frog/princess and the old man are clearly experiencing the situation from two different frames of reference. The bewitched princess is looking to a long-term future (live happily ever after). The old man is considering the situation with respect to a long-term past (90 years old and three wives). These different types of frames determine what is relevant and important to us.

Applying the Sleight of Mouth Pattern of Change Frame Size

The goal of Changing Frame Size is to put something into a new or different perspective. The mindset involves considering *what is a longer (or shorter) time frame, a larger number or smaller number of people, or a bigger or smaller perspective that would change the implications of the belief to be something more flexible or positive?*

The following are examples of how the pattern of Change Frame Size could be applied to the group of limiting beliefs we have explored in the previous sections.

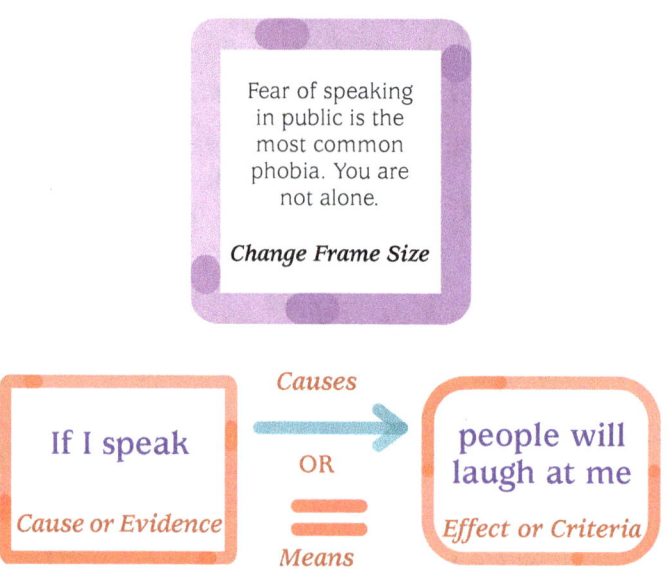

In this first example, the frame has been widened to include all of the other people who experience a similar type of fear. The statement, "You are not alone," implies that it is a communal phenomenon and that there are other "people" who feel the same way as the person stating the belief, not only those who laugh. [It is interesting to note that research on crisis and trauma demonstrates that the connection and companionship with others significantly reduces the amount of "CRASH" people experience. Recent studies show that this is even true of rattlesnakes. When two or more are together in the same stressful situation, they have lower heartbeats and rattle their tails – a sign of threat – less than when alone.] Of course, the frame size in this example could be narrowed as well by asking something like, "So, do people start laughing as soon as you say, 'Hello?'" This would involve using time as the frame instead of other people.

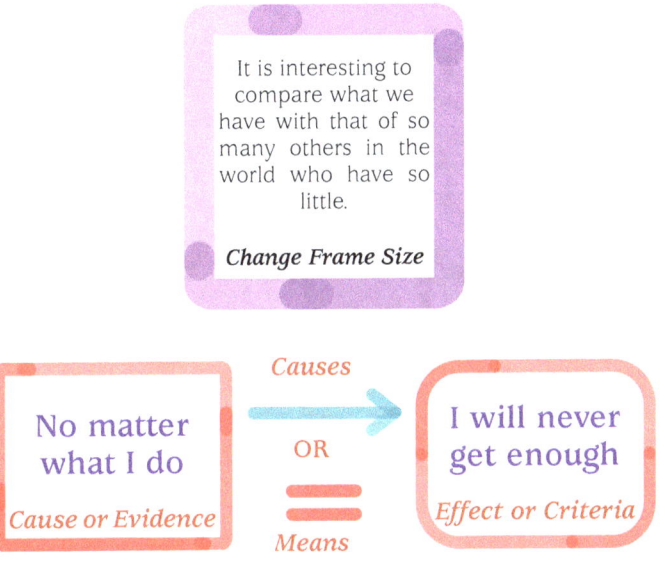

For this belief, the frame has been expanded in a different direction than the previous example. Instead of widening to include others who share the person's experience, it is enlarged to include those who are much less fortunate. This creates a very different reference point with which to compare whether one has "enough." The focus on "I" has also been widened to "we," creating a more collective perspective on the evaluation.

As with the previous example, the frame could also be narrowed along the dimension of time with a question like, "Is it that what you get is insufficient from the very beginning or is it that what you get does not last?" Something like this would help to take the comparison and evaluation out of an "all or nothing" framework and open up other potential options.

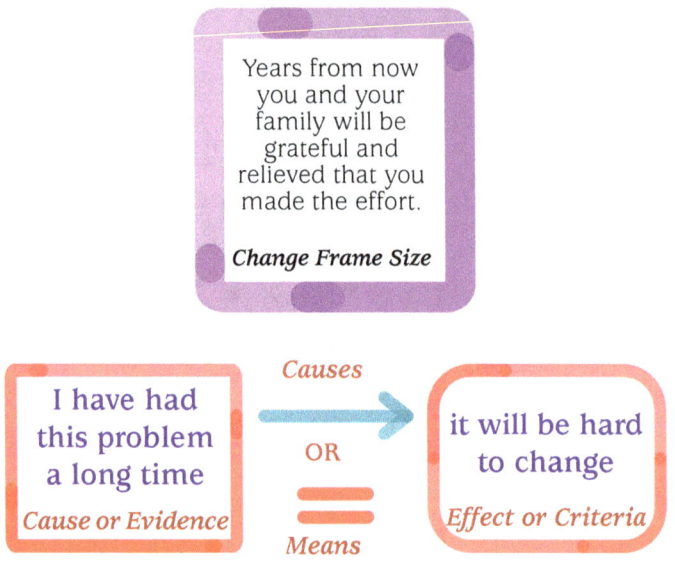

Here, a reference point has been created in the long-term future, looking back. The frame has also been widened from the person as an individual to include the bigger holon of "family." This creates a very different perspective from which to perceive the challenge of the change the person is facing in the present. Interestingly, a way to shift perspectives by narrowing the frame would be to say something like, "If you stay completely in the present moment, this change will be over before you know it."

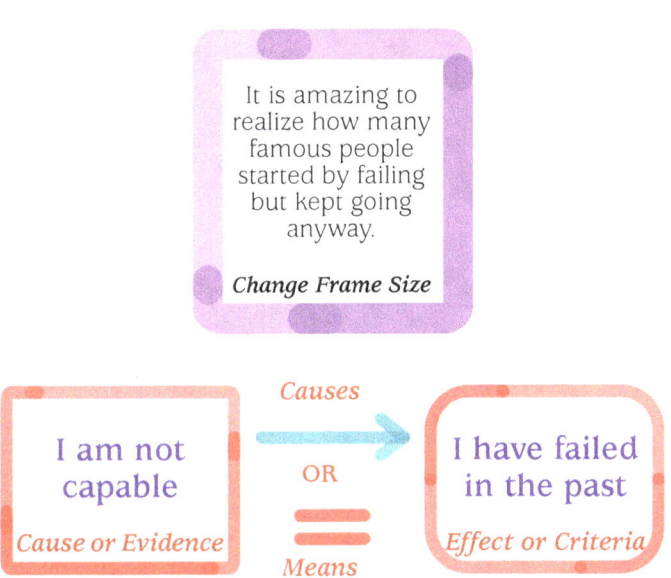

In this case, the frame size has been expanded to include well-known others who have overcome past failures and reach a level of exceptional capability at something, which also serves to create a type of counter example. From this perspective, past failures can be seen as a challenge to rise up to and overcome as opposed to a definitive evidence of insufficiency. The frame size could also be narrowed by suggesting, "Let's examine one of those past failures to see what resource you would have needed in order to succeed."

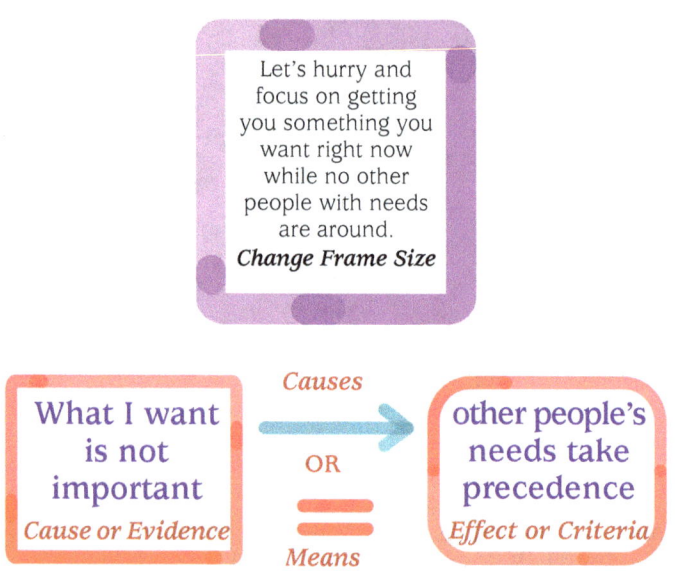

This example *narrows* the frame in time and implies that it is not an *all-or-nothing* situation, but one potentially related to the physical presence of "other people." Alternatively, the frame size could be expanded by saying something like, "I wonder how many of your family members and ancestors have struggled with this belief and how they dealt with it? Is it a belief that you want to pass on to your children (future generations)?" Enlarging the frame in this way, using family members as reference points, expands the issue from being one one relating to personal experience (what I want) to include potentially negative consequences the generalization may have with respect to significant others.

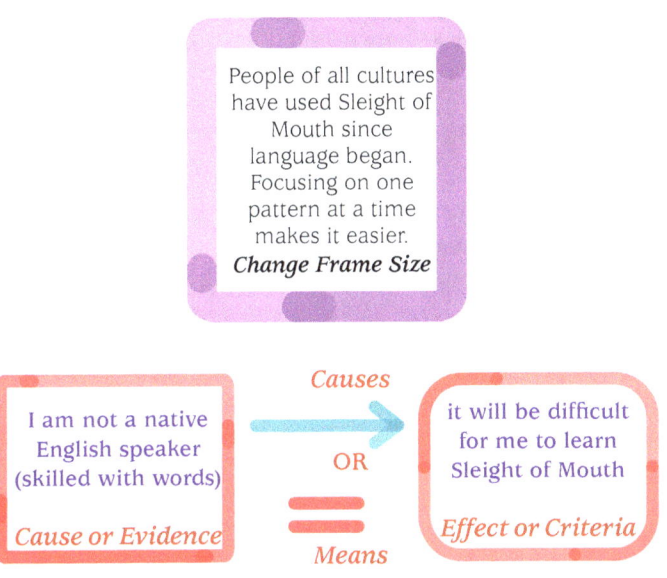

For this final belief, there is a broad expansion of the frame along two dimensions ("people of all cultures" and "since language began") followed by a narrowing of the frame on another dimension (focusing on one pattern at a time). Changing Frame Size to make it bigger in some places and smaller in others can be a particularly effective way to generate new options.

A Creative Example of Applying the Sleight of Mouth Pattern of Changing Frame Size

As usual, there is a fascinating and instructive example from the work of Milton Erickson demonstrating how the Sleight of Mouth pattern of Change Frame Size can be used in a creative way; both narrowing and widening the frame related to a particular situation. In this instance it involved one of his children. The following is excerpted from Erickson's account in *Uncommon Therapy* (pp. 128-130).

> *Three-year-old Robert fell down the back stairs, split his lip, and knocked an upper tooth back into the maxilla. He was bleeding profusely and screaming loudly with pain and fright. His mother and I went to his aid.*
>
> *No effort was made to pick him up. Instead, as he paused for breath for fresh screaming, I told him quickly, simply, sympathetically and emphatically, "That hurts awful, Robert. That hurts terrible."*
>
> *Then I told Robert, "And it will keep right on hurting."*
>
> *The next step for him and for me was to declare, as he took another breath, "And you really wish it would stop hurting." The suggestion was made, "Maybe it will stop hurting in a little while, in just a minute or two."*
>
> *The next comment was, "That's an awful lot of blood on the pavement. Is it good, red, strong blood? Look carefully, Mother, and see. I think it is, but I want you to be sure."*
>
> *His mother picked him up and carried him to the bathroom, where water was poured over his face to see if the blood "mixed properly with water" and gave it a "proper pink color." Then the redness was carefully checked and reconfirmed, following whirls the "pinkness" was reconfirmed by washing him adequately, to Robert's intense satisfaction, since his blood was good, red, and strong and made water rightly pink. Then came the question of whether or not his mouth was "bleeding right" and "swelling right." Close inspection, to*

Robert's complete satisfaction and relief, again disclosed that all developments were good and right and indicative of his essential and pleasing soundness in every way.

Next came the question of suturing his lip. [I stated] regretfully that, while he would have to have stitches taken in his lip, it was most doubtful if he could have as many stitches as he could count. In fact, it looked as if he could not even have ten stitches, and he could count to twenty. Regret was expressed that he could not have seventeen stitches, like his sister, Betty Alice, or twelve, like his brother, Allan; but comfort was offered in the statement that he would have more stitches than his siblings Bert, Lance, or Carol. Thus the entire situation became transformed into one in which he could share with his older siblings a common experience with a comforting sense of equality and even superiority. In this way he was enabled to face the question of surgery without fear or anxiety, but with hope of high accomplishment and the desire to do well the task assigned him, namely, to "be sure to count the stitches."

There are three different stages in this account where Erickson establishes different types and sizes of frames: the first addresses Robert's direct physical pain, the second deals with Robert's fear of his bleeding and injury; and the third prepares him for the suturing of his lip.

With respect to the pain, Erickson makes several statements that pace and lead Robert's experience to something more resourceful: "*(1) That hurts awful, Robert. That hurts terrible. (2) And it will keep right on hurting. (3) And you really wish it would stop hurting. (4) Maybe it will stop hurting in a little while, in just a minute or two.*" In addition from shifting from a problem frame (that hurts terrible) to an outcome frame (you really wish it would stop hurting), Erickson's words help narrow his son's attention from a type of "eternity of the present," where it seems like the pain will never end, to just "a minute or two."

The next intervention widened his son's perceptual frame from a fearful focus on "bleeding" to the larger frame of health and healing. Erickson's statements were: *That's an awful lot of blood on the pavement. Is it good, red, strong blood? Look carefully, Mother, and see. I think it is, but I want you to be sure.* Erickson's choice of words of "good, red, strong blood" are all attributes that indicate something positive. The fact that the blood "*mixed properly with water*" and gave it a "*proper pink color*" also place the situation squarely in a short-term positive outcome frame that Robert's mouth was "*bleeding right*" and "*swelling right*."

It is also notable, from an NLP perspective, that the emphasis on the visual attributes of "color" and "swelling" directs attention away from the physical and emotional feelings of pain and fear, and towards particular qualities ("submodalities") of visual imagery.

Erickson's last statements widen the frame size to include the "common experience" of Robert's siblings who have survived potentially worse injuries and are clearly still alive and thriving. As Erickson points out, *the entire situation became transformed into one in which he could share with his older siblings a common experience with a comforting sense of equality and even superiority.*

Once again, Erickson's skill with pacing and leading, and his ability to develop second position with a small boy were key to creating the resonance needed for his words to produce their transformational effect.

Chapter 15
Model of the World

Model of the World

A *model of the world* represents an entire frame of mind. It constitutes much more than just another point of view; it is a complete world view. A model of the world includes all aspects of the Levels of Change pyramid: role, mission, values, beliefs, skills, capabilities, behaviors and environment. Shifting to another model of the world essentially involves shifting attention to completely different role or identity.

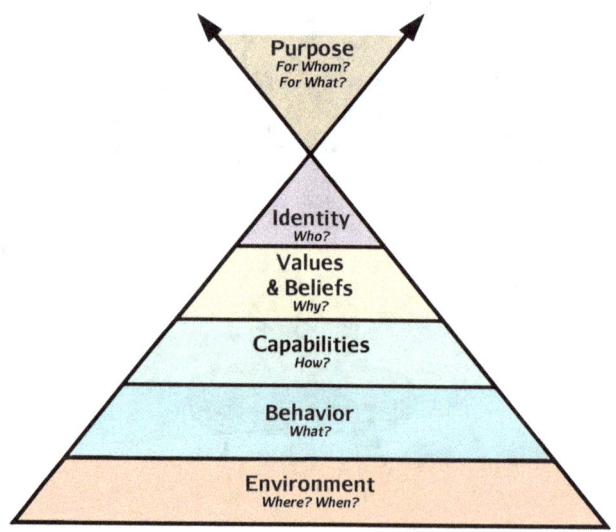

A Model of the World Includes All of the Levels of Change

The Sleight of Mouth pattern of *Model of the World* is about *evaluating a belief statement or generalization from the framework of a different model of the world that would have a totally different perspective*. This stimulates a natural and spontaneous shift to "second position" with another point of view.

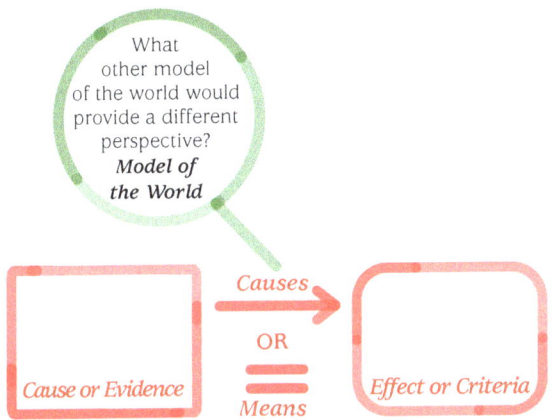

An engineer, an artist, a salesperson, doctor, an athlete, a shaman, a billionaire, an orphan and a physicist would likely have different models of the world with different priorities, different perceptions and different interpretations of the same events or situations. Switching from one model of the world to another will most likely bring about a significant shift in the way a person would perceive and respond to a particular situation.

Some of these dynamics of Model of the World are humorously illustrated in a joke that was going around the United States during the presidential race between Reagan and Carter in the late 1970's (though it could related to any presidential election). The joke refers to a man who had a special way of getting free drinks. He would walk into a bar and determine which candidate he thought the majority of people at the bar supported. If he determined that the group was for Ronald Reagan, he would then stand up and say aloud, "Jimmy Carter is a horse's a**," to which there would be a round of applause, and he would get free drinks from the Reagan supporters. If he determined that he was in "Carter country," the man would state instead that "Ronald Reagan is a horse's a**," thereby getting the applause and free drinks.

> *Entering a bar in a rural part of the U.S., having determined it was "Reagan country," the man blurted out, "Jimmy Carter is a horse's a**. To his surprise, he was picked up by the belt and thrown out into the street. After brushing himself off, he thought he must have misread the group and made a mistake. Walking back into the bar, deciding that it must be "Carter*

country," he yelled out, "Ronald Reagan is a horse's a**." Once again, he was grabbed by the belt and tossed into the street. Brushing himself off, dazed and confused, he was determined to discover what was happening. Returning to the bar, he quietly approached one of the locals and asked, "What's the deal here? Is this 'Carter country' or 'Reagan country'? The local promptly replied, "Son, this is 'horse country'."

The implication is that comparing any politician to even that part of a horse's anatomy was demeaning to the horse, if you are a horse lover.

Applying the Sleight of Mouth Pattern of Model of the World

Effectively considering other models of the world is, of course, a mindset more than simply a verbal formula. It involves exploring *what is a different model of the world (i.e., role or identity) that would provide a very different perspective on the belief that could open up other more productive or resourceful possibilities or choices*?

The following are examples of how the Sleight of Mouth pattern of Model of the World could be applied to the group of limiting beliefs we have explored so far in this book.

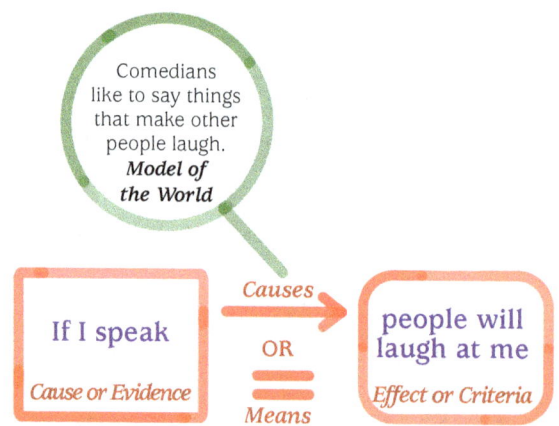

This example references comedians who, of course, make their living by saying things that are intended to make people laugh at them. The implication is that laughter can mean that what a person says can be funny and not just humiliating. The reframe is suggesting that laughter may not always be something negative.

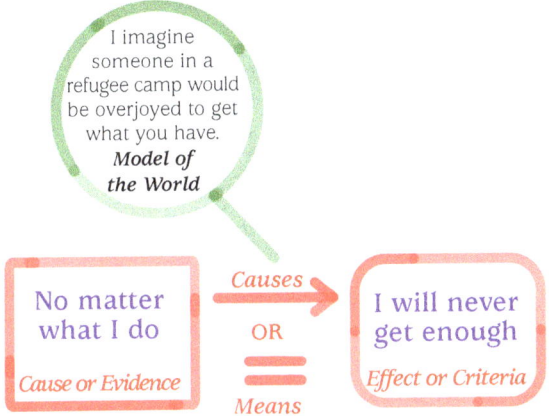

Since the evaluation of whether someone has "enough" of something is always a function of some type of comparison, the reference to a person in a "refugee camp" creates a stark contrast. The purpose of such a comparison is not to shame or demean the person's experience, but rather to help them make a more realistic and less pessimistic conclusion.

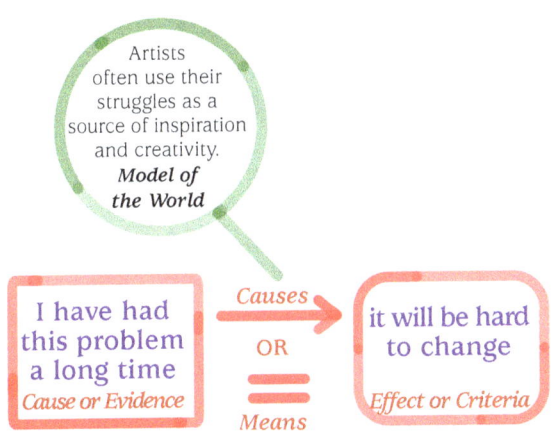

In this example, the model of the world of an artist has been brought up, which introduces the possibility of viewing a long-term problem in a different way. The idea of *transforming* the "struggle" with the problem into some type of creative expression rather than getting rid of it opens up other avenues for dealing with the situation. It reframes the "problem" from being something that is only negative and needs to be changed, to a potentially positive source of creativity and insight that can be shared with others.

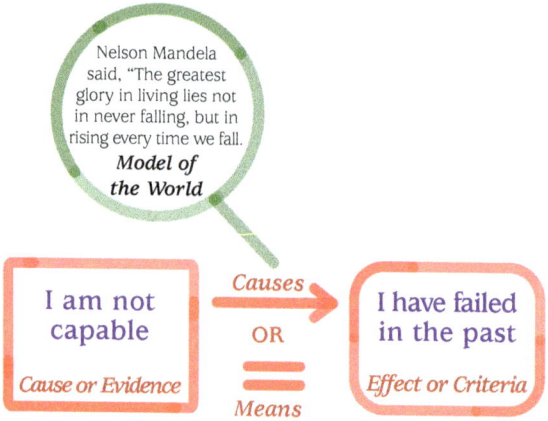

This reframe shifts the person's attention to the Model of the World of a particular iconic individual. Nelson Mandela is known for having brought major transformation to apartheid South Africa after having been imprisoned for almost 30 years (and narrowly avoiding the death penalty). In spite of many years of what could easily be considered "failure" in his anti-apartheid mission, Mandela eventually became president of South Africa and won the Nobel Peace Prize for his work. The implication is that capability cannot be judged by past success or failure alone, but rather by commitment and resilience with respect to one's ultimate goals – especially those related to "soul" issues.

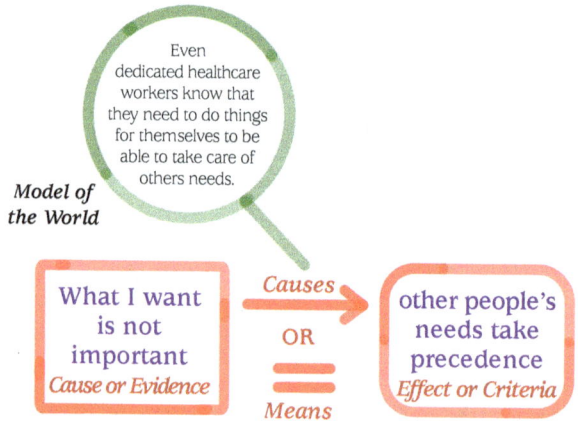

Here, reference is made to the Model of the World of dedicated healthcare workers, whose job is to clearly attend to other people's needs. If they always put the needs of those they are committed to care for above their own, however, they would eventually burn out. So doing things for themselves (things that they want) is an essential part of fulfilling their purpose.

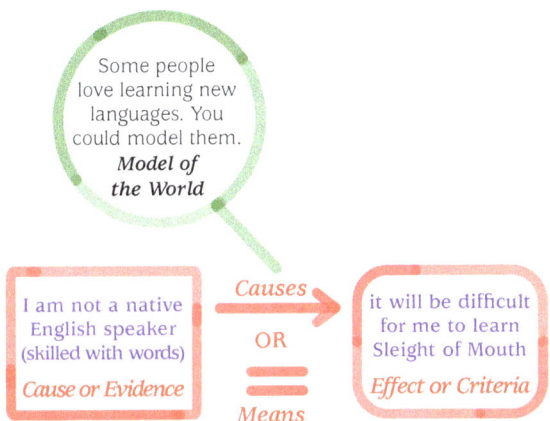

In this example, it is pointed out that there are people in the world who actually enjoy the challenge of leaning languages that are not their native tongue. The suggestion to "model them" indicates that their interest and enjoyment is a potentially acquirable attribute, which could shift the person's experience.

A Creative Example of Applying the Sleight of Mouth Pattern of Model of the World

A medical technician who had a particularly large rear end (buttocks) was working at the same hospital as Milton Erickson. One day the woman developed a severe case of hiccups that the medical doctors could not cure. They all recommended psychiatric consultation, which meant seeing Erickson. She refused to see him at first, but after her boss threatened to discontinue her free medical care she gave in. Erickson, who was always a keen observer, had noticed that on visiting days the woman would stand outside the hospital and offer to babysit the visitors' children. When she entered the consultation room, Erickson told the woman to stay quiet until she heard what he had to say. He then told her, "I know you like children. And you think because you've got such a great big fanny, no man will ever look at you. You would know better if you had read the *Song of Solomon*. The pelvis is mentioned as the *cradle of children*. The man who will want to marry you, the man who will fall in love with you, will look at that great big, fat fanny of yours and see only a cradle for children. He will be a man who wants to father a lot of children. And he will see a beautiful cradle for children."

The woman's hiccups went away later that day and a few months later she came to Erickson's office and showed him her engagement ring. A few more months after that, she brought in her fiancée who told Erickson about the plans they had for building a home that was going to have a lot of bedrooms and "a great, big nursery" for a lot of children. (From *Phoenix,* pp. 67-69.)

Reflections on the Example

Erickson was able to show the woman that what she saw as a serious flaw in her body (her large rear end) had a very different meaning from another Model of the World (a cradle for children). This shifted her perspective of herself and transformed the flaw into an asset. Again, it is important to note that Erickson begins by pacing the woman's limiting belief before leading to his reference to a different Model of the World. This helps to establish rapport, which is key for his words to have the necessary level of resonance, especially given the woman's resistance to come to see Erickson. His reference to a passage from the Bible also lent a type of credibility to his reframe, as he inferred that the woman likely came from a religious background.

Chapter 16
Reality Strategy

Reality Strategy

In *Sleight of Mouth I* (p. 89-97) I point out that a *Reality Strategy* involves the sequence of mental tests and internal criteria an individual applies in order to evaluate whether or not a particular experience or event is "real" or "really happened." It is essentially the strategy by which we distinguish "fantasy" from "reality."

From the perspective of Sleight of Mouth, we will never know exactly what reality is, because our brain doesn't really know the difference between imagined experience and remembered experience. The fact is, the same brain cells are used to represent both. There is no specific part of the brain that has been designated for "fantasy" and "reality." As I mentioned earlier, there are also many fundamental aspects of reality that are not directly perceivable through our five senses, so we must extrapolate through assumption, interpretation and inference.

The Sleight of Mouth pattern of *Reality Strategy* involves identifying, examining and evaluating the particular cognitive perceptions upon which a belief has been built. It is essentially scrutinizing different aspects of a belief statement and exploring the question, "How, specifically, do you know that?"

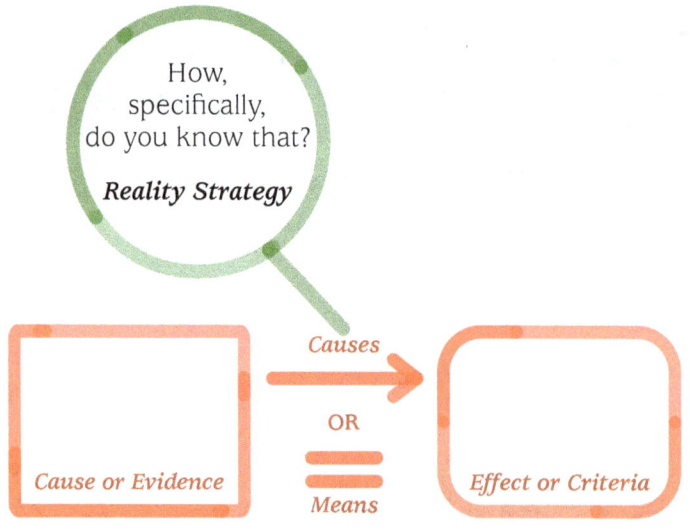

In many ways, Reality Strategy is a form of Chunk Down. You are chunking down, however, in very directed way. You are examining how, specifically, someone has determined that the data from which they have built the belief is *real* and valid. Reality Strategies are especially important when dealing with the type of "groundless reality" identified in the introduction to this book.

Different Reality Strategies can lead to interpreting the same situation in completely different ways. Depending on what someone pays attention to, and what inferences they draw from their observations, that person could end up with a completely different conclusion than someone else, as is illustrated in the following joke.

> *Saint Peter has been checking people in at the gates to heaven for many years and is getting a bit tired and bored. Jesus decides that Saint Peter needs a vacation, so Jesus sends him away for a few weeks and takes over his check-in duties. As Jesus is checking people in one-by-one, he notices someone in line who looks vaguely familiar. It is a gentle old man with white hair. Jesus can't shake the feeling that he knows this person from somewhere. Finally, the old man gets to the front of the line and Jesus asks, "Well, sir, what did you do in life?. "I was a carpenter," the old man replies. "A carpenter?" says Jesus, becoming very curious. "Did you have a son?" he asks, as a look of recognition begins to come over his face. "Ah, my son," says the old man sadly. "Yes, I had a son. He was very special. Everyone said he was a miracle, but he was still my little boy to me. He was taken from me at an early age by people who didn't understand him. I can still remember the nails in his hands and feet the last time I saw him." As tears begin to stream down his face, Jesus throws his arms open to embrace the old man, calling, "Father? Father? Is that you?. Shaking with emotion the old man grabs Jesus, saying, "Pinocchio? Pinocchio? I have finally found you."*

The humor in this unexpected encounter comes from the inferences we begin to make (as do the characters in the joke) from the data we are given. Jesus' father was a carpenter; but so was Geppetto (the maker of Pinocchio). As we see words like "he was very special" and "everyone said he was a miracle," we begin to confirm to ourselves that the carpenter is the father of Jesus. The carpenter's comment that his son was taken by "people who didn't understand him," also seems to fit with the life of Jesus. The "nails in his hands and feet" remind us of Jesus' crucifixion. However, all of these same comments could conceivably be said about Pinocchio as well. He was a puppet made of wood, presumably fastened by nails, that supposedly miraculously came to life and was kidnapped by scoundrels.

Reality Strategies and Confirmation Bias

Confirmation bias is defined as "the tendency to search for, interpret, favor, and recall information in a way that confirms or supports one's prior beliefs or values." People display this bias when they select information that supports their views, ignoring contrary information, or when they interpret ambiguous evidence as supporting their existing attitudes. The effect is strongest for desired outcomes, emotionally charged issues, and for deeply entrenched beliefs. The lighthearted account of Jesus and Geppetto is an example of how this bias can quickly and unconsciously function.

Confirmation bias shows up in three main ways when we are forming or validating beliefs.

- *Biased attention:* This is, when we selectively seek and focus on information that confirms our views while ignoring or discounting data that doesn't.

- *Biased interpretation:* This is when we interpret information in a way that confirms our perspectives. Two people could read the same news item, for instance, and their bias shapes how they make sense of the specific data and details.

- *Biased memory:* This is when we selectively remember information that supports our views while forgetting or discounting information that doesn't.

These types of biases are responsible for flawed decisions in a wide range of political, organizational, financial and scientific as well as personal contexts. Such biases contribute to overconfidence in shared beliefs and can maintain or strengthen beliefs in the face of contrary evidence. Social media tends to amplify confirmation bias by the use of filter bubbles, or "algorithmic editing," which display to individuals only information they have shown interest in and are likely to agree with, while excluding opposing views.

Confirmation bias can also be triggered and amplified by the way information is represented. Making an image of a potential negative consequence bigger, brighter and closer than the image of a potential positive consequence brings attention to the negative consequence and makes it easier to remember. The same types of distortions can happen with other modes of representation (i.e., vocal and somatic) as well. Exploring and checking reality strategies serves to help people chunk

Our reality strategies can bias our interpretation of "reality".

down to discover the (frequently unconscious) representational distortions and assumptions upon which they have built a particular belief or generalization. Evaluating reality strategies can be particularly useful as a way to counteract confirmation bias.

Applying the Sleight of Mouth Pattern of Reality Strategy

The Sleight of Mouth pattern of *Reality Strategy* engages a mindset that involves examining: *What cognitive perceptions of the world are necessary to have built this belief? How would one need to perceive the world in order for this belief to be true? What are the specific perceptions (and qualities of perception) and assumptions upon which this belief has been built and which continue to hold it in place?*

Exploring reality strategies is typically done through questions; in particular, the question, "How do you know that?" This is what is known as an "epistemological" question, which explores "how do we know what we know?" This type of question can lead to some very fruitful insights. The following are examples of how the Sleight of Mouth pattern of Reality Strategy could be applied to the group of limiting beliefs we have explored in the previous sections.

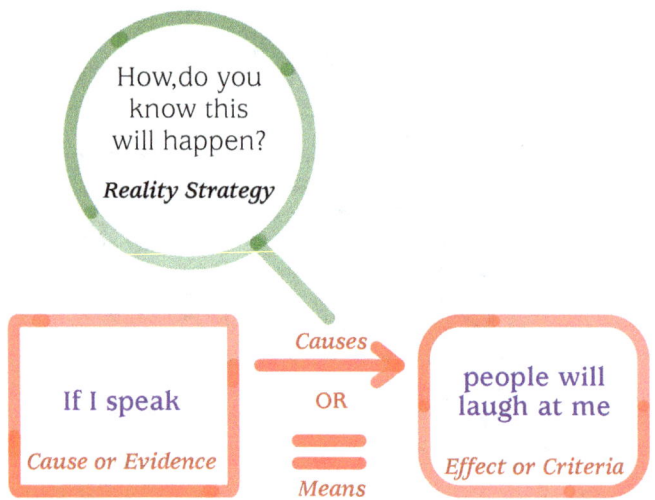

The question, "How do you know this will happen?" brings attention to the cause-effect relationship asserted by the generalization. Let's say the person answers, "Because it has happened to me many times." Applying the Reality Strategy mindset, we would ask, "How do you know that it has happened many times?" The person might answer, "I remember the incidents." We could explore further and ask, "How do you remember them? Is it a set of images? How close/distant are they? Are they clear/moving/in color? Do you see them as if you are reliving them or are you outside watching them as if viewing a video of the incidents?" Such a line of questioning can bring awareness to potential biases of attention, interpretation and memory and introduce other possible conclusions.

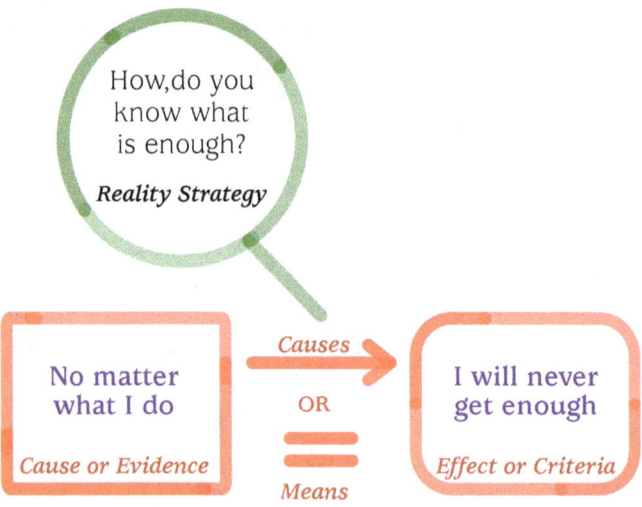

Here, the question, "How do you what is enough?" is not bringing focus the cause-effect generalization but rather the key criterion of *enough*. In addition to shifting to an outcome frame, the question can lead to new insights and the uncovering of potential confirmation biases. It can be interesting to explore whether the determination that the person has gotten "enough" is made based on a feeling, a mental calculation or by comparison with someone else. Is it a function of the presence of something (e.g., the feeling of fullness) or the absence of something (e.g., the feeling of emptiness)? Is the generalization based on past experiences or an imagined future expectation? Again, such an exploration can suggest other possible options and nuances with respect to the generalization.

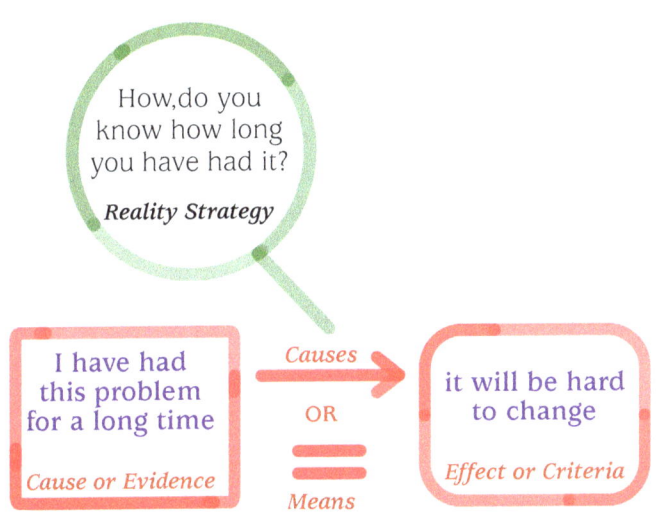

This question takes the exploration in a different direction than the first two examples. The query, "How do you know how long you have had it?" puts the focus of attention on the perception of time. Evaluations related to "length of time" can be particularly relative and subjective. Once again, the form of time representation (types of image, feelings, etc.) can introduce distortions and biases that can be examined and potentially reevaluated. There are also likely to be comparisons to other behavioral patterns that could offer new insights or perspectives that have not been considered in the forming of the generalization.

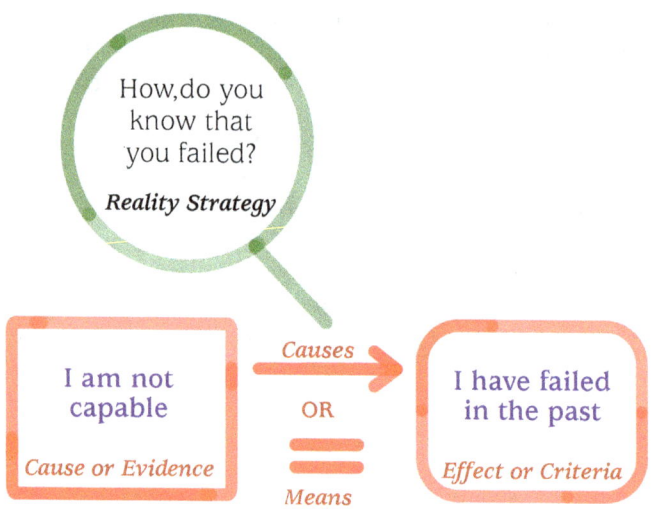

In this example, the *Reality Strategy* question is not directed toward time perception (the past) but rather the judgment about "failure." The exploration here would involve further questions such as, "How is failure evaluated? How is it represented? How many incidents of failure determine whether a person is actually truly *incapable* of doing or achieving something versus still on a learning curve?" Such evaluations are also a function of perception and subjective interpretation. The famous industrialist Henry Ford, for instance, claimed, "Success is 99% failure" and pointed out that "failure is only the opportunity to more intelligently begin again."

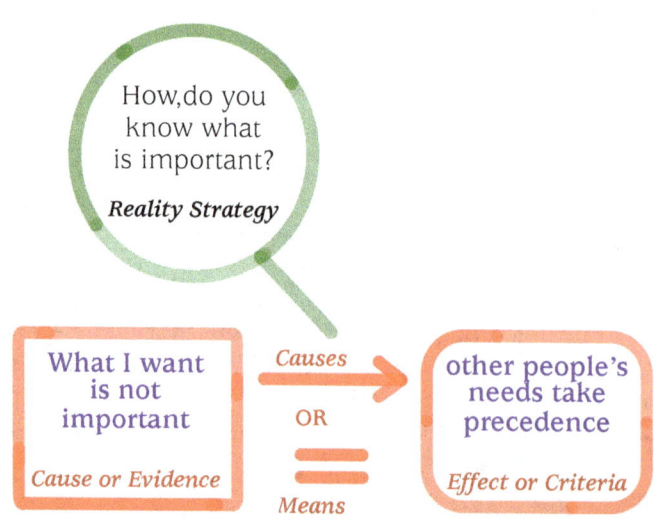

Bringing attention to the inner processes related to "How do you know what is important?" can, like the other explorations, lead to some very interesting insights about the subjective foundations and potential perceptual biases that produced the generalization. "How do you know what other people *need*?" would be another interesting *Reality Strategy* question. Comparing the two modes of evaluation (how I know what is *important* and how I know what other people *need*) can also bring out new awareness that could bring about more nuance and flexibility with respect to the belief.

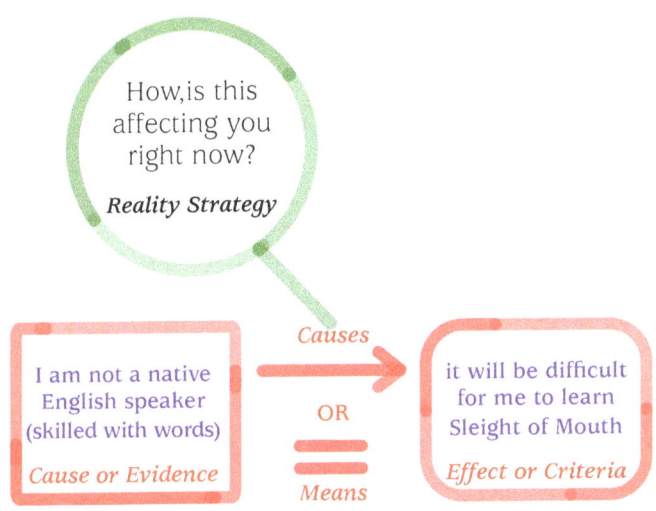

The question "How is this affecting you right now?" brings attention to another aspect of "reality" – the ongoing reality of the present. It can be further explored with questions such as, "Is this belief creating more of a CRASH state or a COACH state? How is it doing that?" This type of questioning helps the person to "taste the poison." That is, to reflect on the affect that their belief produces in them and which representational qualities or assumptions produce that affect. The implication is that the person ultimately has a choice about the belief and its mode of representation. This can lead to a reevaluation and/or reformulation of the belief that produces a more resourceful response.

Of course, it is important to ask all these types questions from a state of rapport and with genuine curiosity. As with the effective use of all Sleight of Mouth patterns, the goal is not to disprove the belief or make the person "wrong," but rather to gain deeper insight into how the generalization was formed and is experienced in order to give the person more flexibility and choice.

A Creative Application of Reality Strategy

When working with reality strategies with Sleight of Mouth, we are not always trying to bring a belief into question. Particular reality strategies can also be leveraged to create new beliefs or substitute one belief for another. A fascinating example of how reality strategies can be creatively used to shift a belief is the case of a woman who came to Milton Erickson because she had an airplane phobia. Her boss had told her that she had to fly to Dallas (from Phoenix) for a business trip or else she would lose her job. Ten years previously she had been on an airplane that crashed. Nobody on the plane was hurt but over the next five years she began to feel more and more fearful whenever she flew. She was fine when she entered the plane and when the plane was taxiing, but the moment the plane took off she was gripped with fear. Once the plane touched down she was able to relax again. Erickson used a version of Reality Strategy to help the woman get over her phobia. According to him (*Teaching Seminar*, pp. 64-70):

> I said, "Go into a trance and hallucinate being 35,000 feet up in the air, traveling 650 miles per hour ground speed." She was shuddering frightfully, bent over, her forehead touching her knees. I said, "And now, I want you to have the plane descend and by the time it reaches the ground all your fears and phobias, anxiety and devils of torture will slide off your body and into the seat beside you." And so she hallucinated landing the plane, awakened from the trance and suddenly leapt out of the chair with a scream and came rushing to the other side of room saying, "They are there. They are there!"

Erickson then called his wife in and asked her to sit in the chair. According to him, the woman said, "Please Mrs. Erickson, don't sit in that chair." Mrs. Erickson continued walking toward the chair and the patient rushed forward and physically prevented her from sitting in the chair.

At this point, Erickson told her, "Your therapy is complete. Have a good time flying to Dallas and flying back to Phoenix, and call me from the airport and tell me how much you enjoyed the plane trips." The following Saturday Erickson got an excited phone call from the woman, who had just landed at the airport, exclaiming, "It was magnificent. It was utterly wonderful, the most beautiful experience of my life!"

Erickson's use of trance allowed him to work a lot with reality strategies and the overlap between what happened in "trance" – which frequently includes a lot of imagination and "hallucination" – and the person's "waking reality." In this example, Erickson paces the woman's fear by first having her imagine that she is "35,000 feet up in the air, traveling 650 miles per hour ground speed." He then leads by having "the plane descend and by the time it reaches the ground all your fears and phobias, anxiety and devils of torture will slide off your body and into the seat beside you." This is not something that would be able to happen in normal "waking reality" but could be done in the context of a hypnotic trance hallucination. Erickson reports that she "awakened from the trance and suddenly leapt out of the chair with a scream and came rushing to the other side of room saying, 'They are there. They are there!'" Thus, the imaginary incident that took place in a trance state had transferred to her waking state.

Erickson took advantage of this overlap between the "trance hallucination" and "waking reality" to say, "Your therapy is complete. Have a good time flying to Dallas and flying back to Phoenix, and call me from the airport and tell me how much you enjoyed the plane trips." This validated that what had happened in the imaginary scenario was somehow now "real." By leaving her "fears and phobias, anxiety and devils of torture" there in the chair, the woman was able to travel comfortably without them.

Reflections on Reality Strategies

Reality strategies can be used to either reevaluate the foundations of existing beliefs or to help build new beliefs. One important application of the Sleight of Mouth pattern of Reality Strategy is to expose potential confirmation biases and other distortions at the foundation of limiting beliefs. Exploring and checking reality strategies helps to counteract confirmation biases by helping people discover the (frequently unconscious) representations and assumptions upon which they have built a particular belief or generalization.

Another use of reality strategies is to enhance the potentially positive consequences of imaginary scenarios. Something similar to what Erickson did with the woman who had the phobia of flying could be done with each of the six limiting beliefs we have been using as examples. For instance, the person who believes, "If I speak people will laugh at me" could be asked to "Imagine you are speaking and people are listening with attention and applauding." The question could then be asked, "How do you know which scenario is real?" The person will likely respond be describing differences in various details of the two representations. Maybe the imagery involved in the one that is "real" is bigger, closer, brighter and moving. The person could then be invited to make those adjustments to their imaginary scenario: "Make it bigger, brighter and moving." The exploration of which one is the "real" scenario can then be repeated, adding other visual, auditory and somatic qualities, until the representations of the two scenarios are essentially equal. Interestingly, even if I still know that one is "real" and the other "imagined" the impact of the two may be the same, giving me the choice to select which one I give my attention to.

The same type of exploration could be done for the other five belief statements we have been examining:

- *No matter what I do I will never get enough.* ⇨ "Imagine you are able to get enough from something that you have done. What is it like?"

- *I have had this problem a long time, it will be hard to change.* ⇨ "Imagine that you are able to change this problem easily. What is that like?"

- *I am not capable because I have failed in the past.* ⇨ "Imagine that you succeeded in the past. What would that be like?"

- *What I want is not important because other people's needs take precedence.* ⇨ "Imagine that you have given priority to what you want. What is that like?"

- *I am not a native English speaker (skilled with words) so it will be difficult for me to learn Sleight of Mouth.* ⇨ "Imagine that you have been able to learn Sleight of Mouth quickly and effortlessly anyway. What would that be like?"

The conversation following any of these questions might involve the suggestion, "Really put yourself into that imagination. How, specifically, do you experience it?" The next step would be to compare the imagined scenarios to the memories associated with the related generalizations and explore, "How do you know which one is real?" Adjusting the qualities of the imagined representation to match those of the remembered experiences not only produces a more robust outcome frame but can also trigger or reawaken memories that have been ignored or rejected as a result of previous confirmation bias.

Of course, making these adjustments can also serve to bring up possible positive intentions or secondary gains of the limiting belief that would be important to acknowledge and address.

The qualities of the memories and representations associated with the limiting belief can also be altered, reducing their potential impact and significance.

Chapter 17
Meta Frame

Meta Frame

Constructing a Meta Frame involves reflecting on a belief statement from a larger frame of reference that brings a different perspective or understanding to the belief or how it was formed. As I pointed out earlier, the term *meta* is a Greek word meaning "over," "between" or "above." A *Meta Frame* is, in essence, a belief *about* a belief that changes or enriches the perception of that belief. Meta Framing frequently diffuses the impact of a limiting belief by shifting a person's perspective of the belief to an observer of his or her own mental processes. Taking a meta perspective with respect to a belief helps a person to recognize that it is indeed a "belief" and not necessarily the only interpretation of reality.

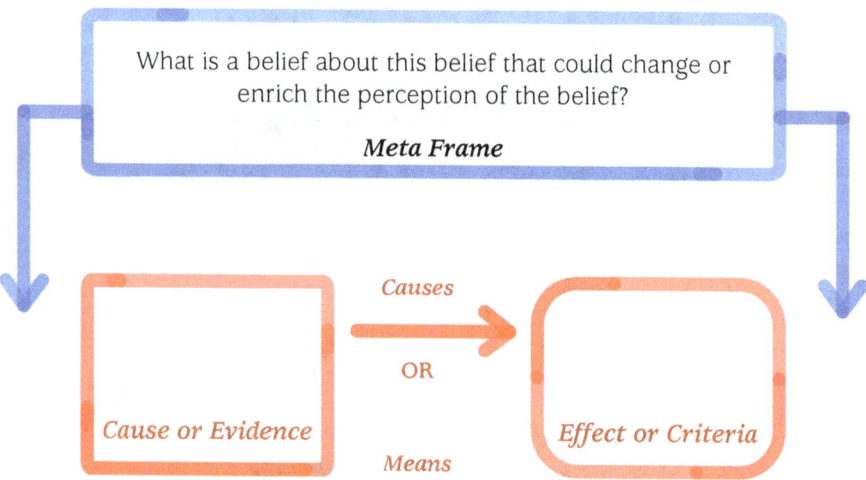

A good example of a Meta Frame is the comical statement often attributed to Mark Twain that "I have suffered a great many catastrophes in my life; most of which never happened." The belief "I have suffered a great many catastrophes in my life" is Meta Framed by the statement, "most of which never happened." The implication is that the "catastrophes" were either imagined or were events that were magnified as a result of worry or mental exaggeration.

Another good, and humorous, example of a Meta Frame is illustrated in the following anecdote about the famous physicist Nils Bohr.

> *A woman goes to visit Nils Bohr and, as she enters the house, she notices a horseshoe nailed above the front door as a good luck charm. "I'm a bit surprised you have something like that over your door," she says to the physicist. "I didn't think a scientist like you would believe in that type of thing." "Oh, I don't believe in it at all," replied Bohr with a smile, "But I understand that it works whether you believe it or not."*

The Meta Frame, and the source of the humor, is the remark "I understand that it works whether you believe it or not." The implication is that whether the good luck charm "works" is independent of belief in it.

Sleight of Mouth 215

In a similar, but more serious vein, Bohr also described "Two sorts of truth: profound truths recognized by the fact that the opposite is also a profound truth, in contrast to trivialities where opposites are obviously absurd." This creates a very interesting Meta Frame around beliefs of all types. If they are a "profound truth" then their opposite is also a profound truth. Only if they are "trivial" is their opposite clearly false. As a physicist, Bohr, who was a key figure in the development of quantum mechanics, was primarily referring to perceptions of physical reality. For instance, if it is true that light is a "wave of energy," then its opposite, that light is a "stream of particles," should be false. Instead, depending on how they are observed and measured, both have validity. In fact, quantum theory considers light to be both energy and matter, depending upon how you observe and measure it.

Applying Bohr's Meta Frame to limiting beliefs can also be quite powerful. For instance, if the belief that "I am *not* capable because I have failed in the past" is not trivial, then the opposite must also contain some profound truth – i.e., "I am capable because I have failed in the past." Similarly for a belief like, "No matter what I do I will never get enough," its opposite – "No matter what I do I will always get enough" – would also contain some degree of profound truth.

The Difference between Meta Frame, Apply to Self and Change Frame Size

There are similarities and potential overlaps between Meta Frame and the Sleight of Mouth patterns of Apply to Self and Change Frame Size. The difference between applying the belief to itself and meta framing it is that, when a belief is applied to itself, the content of the belief (i.e., the values and generalization which the belief expresses) is used to evaluate the belief. Similarly, changing frame size is also an operation that is done with respect to the content of the belief statement. In Meta Framing, the belief about the other belief involves a switch to some other belief entirely.

For example, let's consider the generalization, "You have to be strong to survive." Applying the generalization to itself would involve saying something like, "It will be interesting to see if that belief is strong enough to continue to survive much longer." It is done with respect to the content of the statement ("strong" and "survive"). Changing Frame Size would also be done with respect to the content of the belief statement, such as, "If that were true for all creatures, then it shouldn't be possible for weaker creatures, like butterflies, to have survived until now." In this case, the frame has been expanded to include "all creatures." To Meta Frame the belief, on the other hand, someone might say, "That belief most likely came from a relatively narrow view of life that fails to recognize the importance of cooperation and flexibility with respect to survival." This statement shifts to a different belief *about* the belief statement, bringing attention to how and why the belief may have initially been formed.

In the earlier section on Apply to Self (p. 167), I presented two humorous examples of the choice between wisdom and wealth and the belief that it was "wiser to choose wisdom" (or wealth, depending upon which one you already have enough of). Applying the belief to itself was essentially about questioning the wisdom of whether the belief that "it was wiser to choose wisdom" was in fact the wisest choice. The Gandhi example addressed the same belief with the Meta Frame that "Each one takes what one doesn't have." This does not question the wisdom of the belief itself, but rather frames the choice as one of acquiring what one needs. It is only wiser to choose wisdom when one does not already have it.

A Meta Frame Determines How a Particular Experience is Perceived, Interpreted, and Evaluated

Meta Frames generally establish a higher-level point of reference from which the content of some experience or phenomenon is interpreted or evaluated. A good example of this is in *Matthew* (21:23-27).

> *And when Jesus was come to the temple, the chief priests and the elders of the people came unto him as he was teaching, and said, "By what authority doest thou these things and who gave thee this authority?"*
>
> *And Jesus answered and said unto them, I also will ask you one thing, which if ye tell me, I in like wise will tell you by what authority I do these things. The baptism of John, whence was it? from heaven, or of men?*
>
> *And they reasoned with themselves, saying, If we shall say From heaven; he will say unto us, Why did ye not then believe him? But if we shall say, Of men; we fear the people; for all hold John as a prophet.*
>
> *And they answered Jesus, and said, We cannot tell. And he said unto them, Neither tell I you by what authority I do these things.*

The purpose of Jesus' question, "The baptism of John, whence was it? from heaven, or of men?" is to establish a Meta Frame around the issue of the "authority" of John's teachings and other works. Jesus is clearly drawing a parallel between his own work and teaching and that of John the Baptist (who had acknowledged and endorsed Jesus as his successor). As the incident illustrates, the Meta Frame regarding the "source" of John the Baptist's and Jesus' teaching establishes a reference to the deeper dynamics – i.e., from heaven (soul) or of men (ego) – from which they are derived. This determines how they will be perceived and interpreted.

Meta Framing is a common strategy for working with symptoms in psychotherapy and counseling; in which they are placed in the Meta Frame of the client's personal history or other social influences. Sigmund Freud's technique of psychoanalysis is a classic example of the application of Meta Framing. Freud was constantly explaining and "framing" the complaints of his patients by placing them within the framework of his theories about the unconscious. Consider the quotation below, taken from Freud's account of his work with a patient who was obsessed with fantasies about rats (the case of the so called "Ratman"):

> *I pointed out to him that he ought logically to consider himself as in no way responsible for any of these traits in his character; for all of these reprehensible impulses originated from his infancy, and were only derivatives of his infantile character surviving in his unconscious; and he must know that moral responsibility could not be applied to children.*

Freud Meta Framed the man's thoughts and "reprehensible impulses" as being the product of his "infantile character surviving in his unconscious." Freud then implied that, because "moral responsibility could not be applied to children," the man should not blame himself for his compulsions.

Applying the Sleight of Mouth Pattern of Meta Frame

When applying the Sleight of Mouth pattern of Meta Frame to limiting beliefs, the focus of our mindset is on the question, *"What is a belief about this belief that could change or enrich the perception or implication of the belief?"*

The following are examples of how the pattern of Meta Frame could be applied to the group of limiting beliefs we have explored in the previous sections.

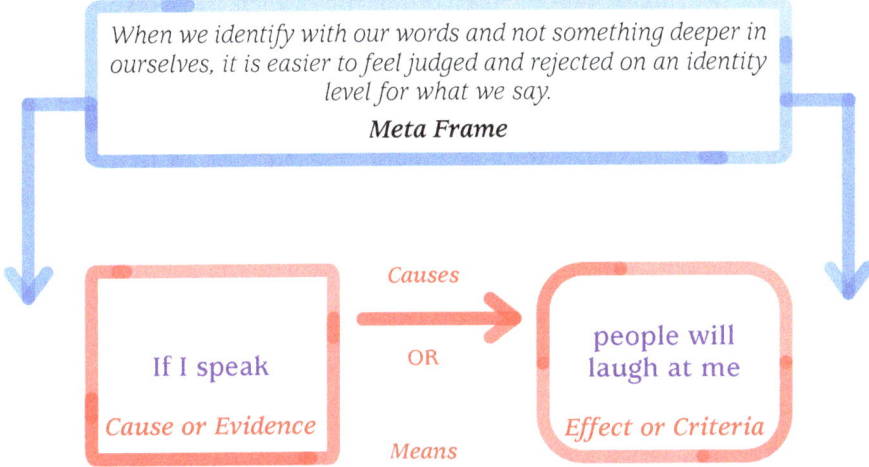

This first Meta Frame puts the belief inside of the higher-level frame of identity and identification, with "our words" in this example. It suggests that it is possible to identify with "something deeper" than words. This shifts the issue from being one related to the reactions and behaviors of others (laughter) to something that the person could modify within him/herself. The use of the word "we" implies that it is a collective matter shared by others as well.

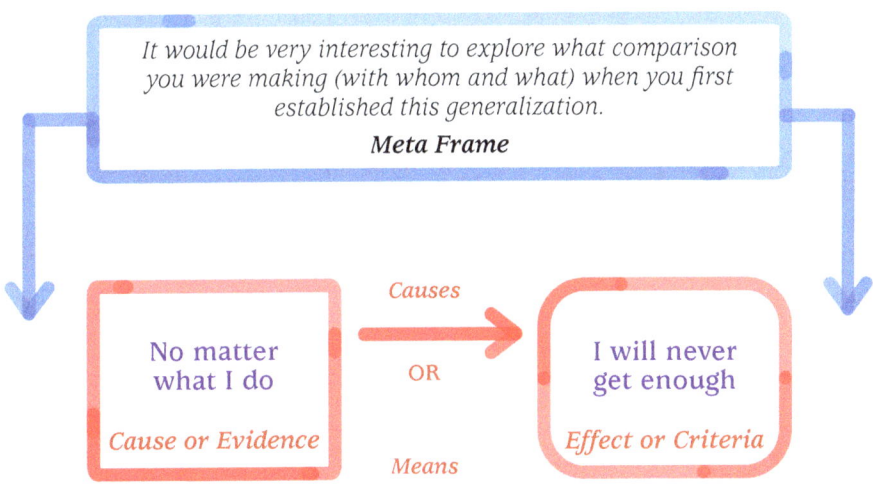

This next Meta Frame interprets the belief as a response to particular past circumstances. It is suggesting that the generalization about "never getting enough" is a result of a comparison made at an earlier age, and that reflecting on that from an updated perspective in the present might lead to a different conclusion. The implication is that the evaluation of getting "enough" is a perception that could be shifted by making a different comparison or by reevaluating the earlier comparison and conclusion from a more current point of view.

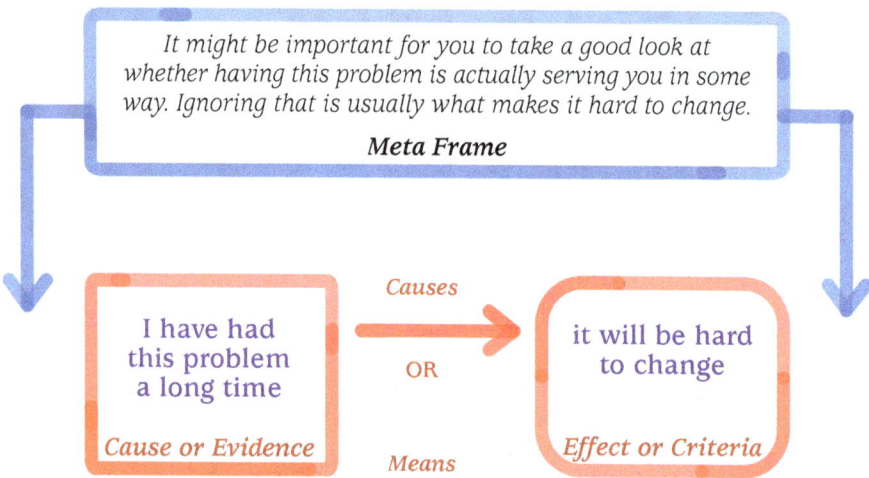

The Meta Frame in this example involves considering the issue expressed by the belief within the context of its potential benefits to the person making the statement. The implication is that, if the person has had the problem "a long time" then it must be serving some purpose, and that ignoring the positive benefits of the problem is what makes it difficult to change, as opposed to the amount of time the person has had the problem. This provides a whole new avenue of exploration that may be quite revealing and more productive than simply trying to get rid of the problem.

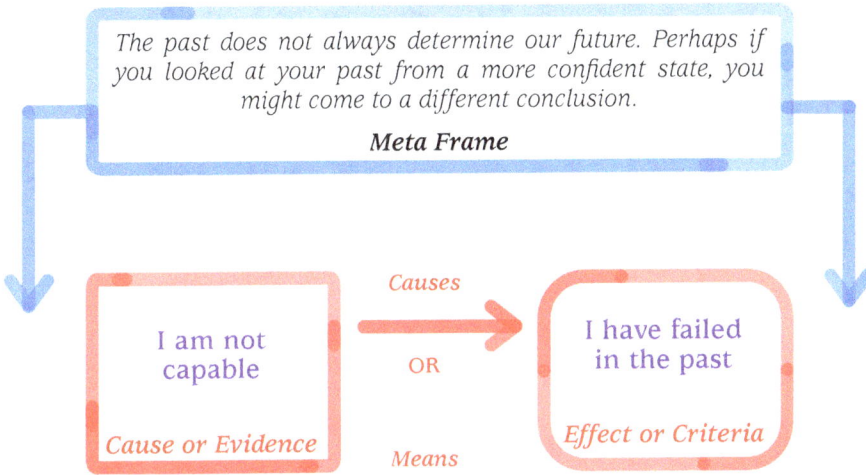

The first part of this Meta Frame, "The past does not always determine our future," brings attention to the future as part of the evaluation being made. It suggests that we cannot always accurately know or assess reality by only looking back to the past. As we have already established, a person's internal state will greatly affect the impact a particular belief statement will have on them. The implication of this Meta Frame is that the person's evaluation of their capability is more a function of their state than of the actual reality of their ability. A more confident state might put a different filter on their perception of past events.

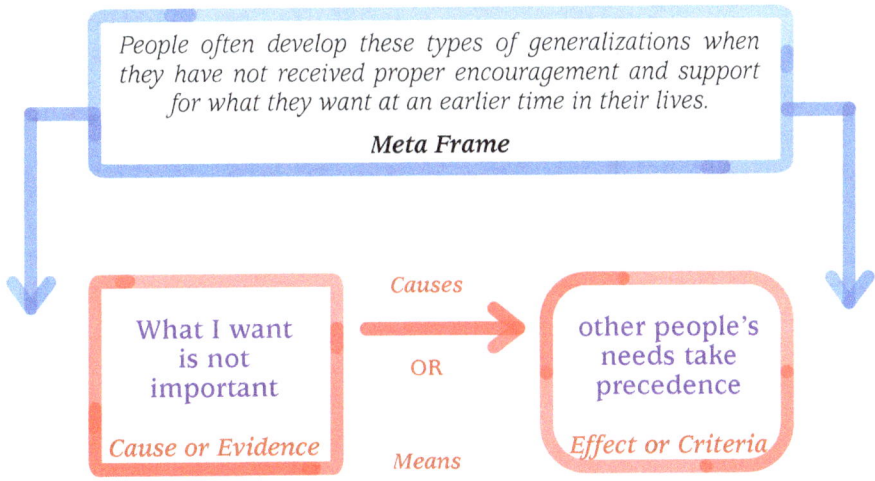

Viewing a belief or generalization within the context of the person's personal history (like Freud did with the Ratman) is a common form of Meta Frame. While the belief statement is being made about a present situation, it is likely a pattern of thinking and acting that has its roots in a much earlier period in the person's life. This Meta Frame is suggesting that, rather than being a truth about the person's life, it is a habit of thinking created by a lack of "proper encouragement and support" at some earlier time. The implication is that, with the proper assistance, the generalization could be updated to something more balanced and appropriate.

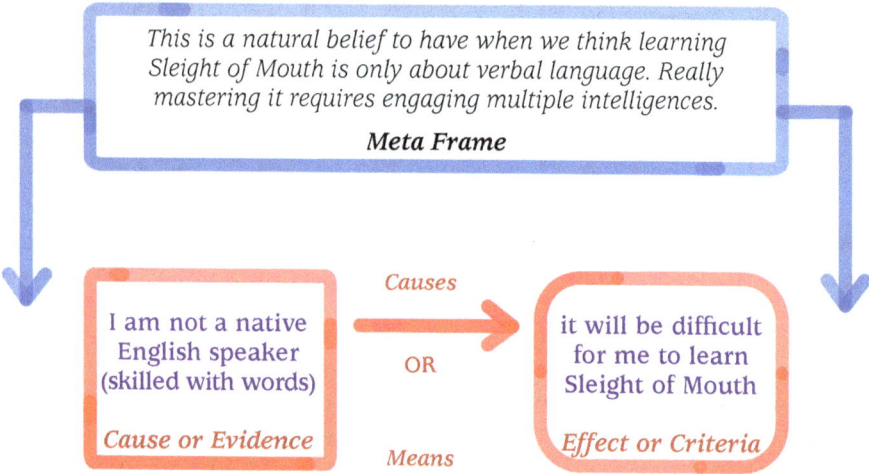

Identifying and commenting on the assumptions that underlie a particular belief statement is another type of Meta Frame. In this example, the assumption is that "learning Sleight of Mouth" is exclusively about verbal language. The implication is that engaging other intelligences that are not linguistically based is key to effective learning, and will make the process of learning Sleight of Mouth more efficiently and easily.

A Creative Example of Meta Framing

As the previous examples illustrate, there are a number of ways to establish and apply a Meta Frame. Milton Erickson utilized another type of Meta Frame (*Collected Papers II*, pp. 189-190) with a 19-year-old dental assistant who fainted or became extremely nauseated and distressed every time she saw blood. The dentist who employed her referred her to Erickson. She insisted that he treat her in one session and not psychiatrically, but only with hypnosis. Erickson induced a trance and then asked her if she would mind if he smoked while she was in trance. She assented. He then told her that, during the time it took him to smoke the cigarette, she would "review all the traumatic incidents in her life and anything connected with blood or fear or fainting."

He finished the cigarette and she awakened. They then just chatted about various things unrelated to the problem for the remainder of the time. As Erickson was about to conclude the session, the young woman protested that he "should have really done something for her problem if he was to charge her a fee." Erickson picked up on her statement and agreed with her, repeatedly emphasizing the idea that he "should have really done something" for her problem. The young woman left perplexed but was surprised to find that the next day and thereafter she no longer fainted at the sight of blood. Her employer called Erickson and reported the dramatic change he witnessed the next day. He said that she had observed and handled bloody teeth and dental procedures all day without the slightest sign of discomfort. In fact, she did not seem to even notice the change.

Erickson turned the woman's constraint that "he treat her in one session and not psychiatrically, but only with hypnosis" into an advantage. By having the woman briefly "review all the traumatic incidents in her life and anything connected with blood or fear or fainting" in a trance state, as opposed to a CRASH state, Erickson was having her unconsciously shift her inner relationship to those incidents. Then, instead of doing anything "psychiatrically," he chatted about things unrelated to the problem. Erickson's repeated emphasis of the woman's seeming complaint that he "should have really done something" for her problem to charge her a fee, turned the statement into a subtle and powerful type of Meta Frame. The frame, in this case, was the belief that Erickson should have, indeed, "done something" for her problem and that *something really should have happened*.

This type of Meta Frame is similar to Nils Bohr's statement that his lucky horseshoe "works whether you believe it or not." The implication of Erickson's Meta Frame was that he did, in fact, do something for her problem during the session and that something really *did happen* that the woman was not yet aware of. That is, that something had happened whether she knew it and believed in it or not. Like the placebo effect, this can engage unconscious, self-organizing changes. In fact, the placebo effect itself is a result of a type of Meta Frame regarding a medication or procedure

Reflections on Meta Frames

Meta Frames create a higher-level point of reference from which the content of some experience or phenomenon is interpreted or evaluated. They are not directly related to the content of an experience or generalization, but they influence its impact and how that content is given meaning.

Meta Frames are most effectively created by shifting perspective to that of an observer of the experience or generalization rather than being directly engaged in or with it. This meta perspective makes it clear that any interpretation or generalization is just that – an interpretation or generalization subject to distortion and fallibility. From this perspective it is possible to consider the potential influence of things like:

- the source of the experience or generalization
- past circumstances that may have shaped it
- potential benefits
- what comparisons have been or are being made
- the impact of the person's internal state
- assumptions upon which the experience or generalization is based

Bringing attention to any of these influences can shift the implication or meaning of the experience or generalization to something that is potentially more flexible or resourceful.

Chapter 18

Strategies for Using Sleight of Mouth

Strategies for Using Sleight of Mouth

In actual interactions, Sleight of Mouth patterns are rarely used in isolation (i.e., just one at a time). They are most frequently and effectively applied either repetitively or in combination with other Sleight of Mouth patterns. In this chapter, I will present some common strategies for applying the patterns to either strengthen a belief or to question its validity or universality.

In *Sleight of Mouth 1*, I described several strategies that could be used for applying combinations of Sleight of Mouth patterns, such as: the *Belief Change Cycle* (pp. 192-196), *Belief Chaining* (pp. 197-201) and *Changing Logical Levels* (pp. 250-251). I strongly suggest that you review these processes in light of what has been presented in this book.

In the following pages, I will go over several other strategies for using Sleight of Mouth patterns to either reinforce, cast doubt upon, or shift perspectives with respect to a particular generalization or belief.

Chains of Meaning

A *Chain of Meaning* is a type of Belief Chain which can be used to link a limiting belief to more empowering possibilities through the Sleight of Mouth pattern of *Redefining*. Chains of meaning use the structure:

$$\text{If } A\text{-} = B = C = D\text{+ Then } A\text{-} = D\text{+}$$

In a Chain of Meaning, a negative label or evaluation (**A-**) is linked to a more positive conclusion (**D+**) by creating a chain of "equivalences" (**B** and **C**), which each redefine the limiting judgment in a more positive direction. In the following example, the negative label "learning disabled" is linked to being "a thorough learner" through a simple chain of meaning.

> If being *learning disabled* (**A-**) <u>means</u> that one is a *slow learner* (**B**), <u>and</u> being a slow learner <u>means</u> that it *takes longer to learn* (**C**), <u>and</u> taking longer to learn something <u>means</u> one is a more *thorough learner* (**D+**), <u>then</u> being *learning disabled* (**A-**) <u>means</u> one is a *more thorough learner* (**D+**).

As a practice, fill in the blank spaces below to create a chain of meaning with respect to some limiting belief or generalization.

a. **A-** (a negative quality, situation or experience)
_____ (e.g., *failure*)

b. *means* **B** (a neutral or not so negative quality or characteristic)
_____ (e.g., *what I tried did not work*)

c. *which means* **C** (another neutral or slightly positive quality or characteristic) _____
(e.g., *I have more experience about what is and is not effective*)

d. *which means* **D+** (a positive quality, characteristic or experience) _____
(e.g., *it will be easier to find a successful solution*)

Therefore _____ (**A-**: *failure*) means

_____ (**D+**: *it will be easier to find a successful solution*).

Of course, a chain of meaning could also be applied to make something that appears neutral or positive seem more negative. Lincoln, for instance, made use of a chain of meaning (see p. 69) when he equated "inferior" with being "needy" and "slavery" with "taking something away." He then applied this chain to conclude that "slavery" *means* taking from the needy."

Chains of Causes

A *Chain of Causes* is another type of belief chaining method which links a particular belief to a more enriched map of the world through a series of *Consequences*. Establishing a Chain of Causes involves connecting a particular phenomenon to other behaviors and experiences through "cause-and-effect" statements. Chains of Causes use the structure:

If A B C D   Then changing A will automatically change D.

This structure is illustrated in the following example:

"*If visualizing oneself as a healthy person* (**A**) makes *a person more hopeful* (**B**), and *hope reduces stress* (**C**), and *reducing stress reduces the chance of illness* (**D**), then *visualizing oneself as a healthy person* (**A**) *reduces the chances of illness* (**D**)."

In this case, the reduction of a problem state ("illness") is connected to the process of visualization by establishing a series of consequences stemming from visualization as the root cause.

Defining a Chain of Causes can be done by answering the following questions:

a. What is a negative quality, characteristic or experience (**D-**) that you would like to change? (e.g., *anger*)
  _____

b. What process, situation or occurrence (**C**) causes that negative quality, characteristic or experience? (e.g., *disappointment*)
  _____

c. What process, situation or occurrence (**B**) causes **C**? (e.g., *expectations*) _____

d. What process, situation or occurrence (**A**) causes **B**? (e.g., *focusing on a particular path or outcome*)
  _____

Since **A** causes **B**, **B** causes **C**, and **C** causes **D**; *then adjusting* **A** _____ (e.g., *the path or outcome one is focusing on*) will shift **D** _____ (e.g., *anger*).

This is essentially the pattern used in the quote from Lao Tsu presented at the beginning of this book that: thoughts become words, which become actions, which become habits, which become our character, which become our destiny. Thus our thoughts and words can ultimately influence our destiny,.

Chains of Causes can also be used to enhance a positive belief or generalization by linking a desired state or conclusion to other behaviors and activities, which give a person a greater sense of participation and influence. Again, this is done by establishing a series of consequences, as is demonstrated in the following exercise.

    a. What is a positive quality, characteristic or experience (**D+**) that you would like to have more of?
    _____ (e.g., *patience*)

    b. What process, situation or occurrence (**C**) causes that positive quality, characteristic or experience?
    _____ (e.g., *acceptance*)

    c. What process, situation or occurrence (**B**) causes **C**?
    _____ (e.g., *trust that things will turn out OK*)

    d. What process, situation or occurrence (**A**) causes **B**?
    _____ (e.g., *shifting to a longer-term perspective*)

    Since **A** causes **B**, **B** causes **C**, and **C** causes **D**; then enhancing **A**

    _____ (*shifting to a longer-term perspective*)

    will enhance **D+** _____ (*patience*).

Another method of using chains of causes to "reframe" limiting beliefs and generalizations is to create a chain of consequences that "frames" the problem experience as the consequence of some positive cause (such as a positive intention), and as leading to some positive end, as in the following example:

    Fear (**B-**) is caused by the *desire to protect oneself* (**A+**). Fear also *prevents people from rushing into something* (**C**), which helps them to *act more ecologically* (**D+**). Therefore fear isn't such a bad thing because its positive intention is protection and it causes people to act more ecologically.

This process can be summarized using the following structure:

If A+ B- C D+   Then B comes from a positive and ends in a positive so it is not so negative in context.

The following questions can be used to create this type of belief "reframe":

a. What is the problematic quality, characteristic or experience (**B**)?
_____ (e.g., *self doubt*)

b. What is the positive intention (**A**) behind the problematic quality, characteristic or experience?
_____ (e.g., *desire to improve*)

c. What is a neutral, or slightly positive consequence (**C**) resulting from the problematic quality, characteristic or experience?
_____ (e.g., *self-doubt* makes a person *more aware of his or her own limitations*)

d. What is a positive consequence (**D+**) that results from this first consequence? _____
(e.g., *being more humble and careful*)

Therefore, *self-doubt* (**B-**) <u>comes from</u> the *desire to improve* (**A+**). Self doubt also <u>makes</u> people more *aware of their own limitations* (**C**), which helps them to *be more humble and careful* (**D+**). Therefore, self-doubt isn't such a bad thing because its <u>positive intention</u> is *improvement* and it <u>causes</u> people to have *more humility* and to be *more careful*."

Of course, Chains of Causes (or Consequences) can also be used to invalidate a generalization or belief. A good example is that presented earlier in this book on page 76, in which a driver, pulled over by a police officer for speeding, makes a series of increasingly disturbing statements (his driver's license has been revoked for driving under the influence of alcohol or drugs, he has stolen the vehicle, there is a gun in the glove compartment that he has used to kill the owner of the car whose body is in the trunk). Believing it is a serious and dangerous situation, the police officer calls in his commander and other reinforcements. The driver then refutes each statement (he has a valid license and vehicle registration card. There is no gun in the glove box and no body in the trunk. Using this Chain of Consequences, the driver attempts to convince the officer's superior that he was not speeding either.

Comparisons

Another strategy for shifting perceptions related to limiting beliefs and generalizations is by making comparisons. A particular experience may seem either more positive or more negative depending on what you compare it with. In general, if you compare **A+** to **B** to **C-**, then **B** is negative compared to **A+**, but positive compared to **C-**.

> e.g., "Compared to Gandhi/Jesus (**A+**) I'm a sinner. Compared to Hitler (**C-**), I'm a saint."

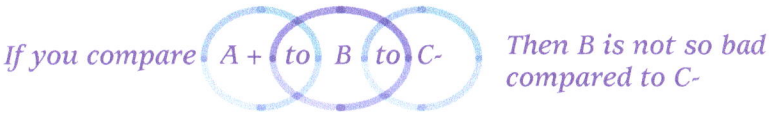

If you compare A+ to B to C-   Then B is not so bad compared to C-

Polya Patterns

Polya Patterns are named after mathematician George Polya. In his book *Patterns of Plausible Inference* (1954), Polya presents some of the strategies by which we go about drawing conclusions and making decisions with respect situations for which we have only partial data. Polya's "patterns of plausible inference" are essentially "belief strategies" – cognitive structures defining the ways in which we establish beliefs and test conclusions. Polya Patterns focus on the ways in which we build credibility and strengthen the plausibility of a particular belief, generalization, or assertion.

Polya pointed out that in many circumstances, such as attempting to prove a mathematical theorem, or attempting to prove the guilt or innocence of a person accused of a crime, we must make decisions based on incomplete data. In mathematics, for example, since there is an infinite amount of numbers, we can never actually test a theorem for every single possible number. Thus, we can never know for certain that any particular mathematical theorem is "true" for every number. We must generalize at a certain point. Polya shows how certain seemingly solid mathematical formulas (computing prime numbers, for example) fail after being tested for larger and larger numbers. Similarly, many judicial proceedings must operate on only partial information pieced together from a few witnesses and from sparse facts gathered at "the scene of the crime." There have been many cases of false conviction from "circumstantial evidence."

In many other situations as well, we must accept it as a "fact of life" that we need to build beliefs and make decisions without the benefit of having all of the information or knowing the "whole truth." In such situations, we act from very deeply ingrained, and often unconscious, patterns by which we form and test inferences. Polya formalized these intuitions into the following patterns of "plausible inference."

Polya's Patterns of Plausible Inference

1. **Meta Pattern**: <u>Probability</u> – Our perception of the likelihood that something will occur is typically based on its past performance (measured by *occurrences ÷ opportunities*).

    The most common argument that something will happen again is that it has happened before. The sun will rise tomorrow because it has risen every day so far; If dinner at a hotel has been served precisely at 7 PM for 10 days in a row, it is likely that it will be served precisely at 7 PM on day 11 as well; If a person has spelled a word correctly a number of times, it is likely that he or she will spell it correctly again the next time. According to basic probability theory, if a person has spelled a word correctly 8 out of 10 times, the probability that he or she will spell the word correctly the next time is 8 ÷ 10 or 80%.

    a. The more something occurs, the more we believe it will occur again.

    e.g., Let's say we want to explore the validity of the belief that "an integrated treatment approach (i.e., medical, nutritional, emotional, psychological) is most effective for serious illness." The larger the number of clinical trials with many patients that show a high percentage of positive outcomes for patients with serious illness as a result of integrated treatment, the more confident we are that same or greater percentage will continue to occur.

    b. If something which is not very probable occurs, it tends to validate the cause-effect belief which predicted it.

    e.g., The belief that "an integrated treatment approach is most effective for serious illness" would develop even more credibility if a person with an advanced illness unresponsive to other individual treatments has a remarkable recovery using an integrated approach.

2. **Verification of a Consequence** – If a particular **belief** (**B**) predicts a particular **consequence** (**C**) and we verify that consequence, then it makes the belief more plausible (it does not prove it, however). The degree of plausibility will be stronger if there is a lack of other probable causes.

   IF **B implies C** *AND* **C is verified** *THEN* **B is more credible**.

   e.g., A consequence of the belief that "an integrated treatment approach is most effective for serious illness" a particular consequence of this would be that it would be a preferred approach for patients and healthcare providers. Thus, positive testimonials for integrated treatment make the generalization more credible (though, again, they are not proof).

   a. Successive Verification of **Several Consequences**.

   e.g., Other consequences of the belief "an integrated treatment approach is most effective for serious illness" might include: (1) the approach is incorporated by more and more healthcare institutions (2) articles about it show up in medical journals and other media, and (3) physicians and institutions that have used other modalities would switch to a more integrated approach. The more of these consequences that can be observed, the more credible the belief becomes.

   b. Verification of an **Improbable Consequence** (**Extremes**).

   e.g., An extreme or improbable (under normal circumstances) consequence of the belief that "an integrated treatment approach is most effective for serious illness" might be that a person with a type of illness that has, until the present, been considered "untreatable" by normal modalities is completely cured by an integrated treatment approach. Such extreme or dramatic examples (that seem to be "miraculous") often make a particular belief appear more credible than many consequences in average circumstances.

3. **Verification of a Contingency** – If a **belief** (**B**) presupposes (or requires as a pre-condition) some event or phenomenon and we verify this **contingent event** (**C**) then it makes the belief more plausible. The degree of plausibility will be stronger if the contingent phenomenon would not probably occur in and of itself.

[Polya uses the example that having explosives, or the means to make explosives, is a pre-condition of blowing something up. If it can be shown that an accused bomber has purchased explosives, or materials to make them, it strengthens the charge against the person. If the person had no other reason to be purchasing such explosive materials, the accusation is even stronger.]

IF **B presupposes C** *AND* **C is verified** *THEN* **B is more credible**.

e.g., The belief that "an integrated treatment approach is most effective for serious illness" presupposes that there is not a single organic cause for illness and that there are other contributing causes that must be addressed. If other factors, such as psychological stress, diet, behavioral habits, etc., can be shown to increase symptoms of serious illness, it adds credibility to the belief.

4. **Inference from Analogy** – A **belief** (**B**) is more plausible if an **analogous conjecture** (**A**) is proven true. If the analogy (**A**) cannot be shown to be true but can be shown to be credible, then it still increases the plausibility of the belief (**B**) to which it is analogous.

IF **B is analogous to A** *AND* **A is credible** *THEN* **B is more credible**.

e.g., An analogous conjecture to the belief that "an integrated treatment approach is most effective for serious illness" might be that "a person with a serious illness is like any other complex system in a major crisis, and that treating the symptoms is not enough to bring the system back to a functioning and sustainable state. For example, a company about to go bankrupt cannot be saved by simply cutting expenses or getting financial investment. There will likely need to be multiple interventions that may involve changes in management, marketing, product development and quality, customer loyalty, strategic priorities, etc." While such analogies don't prove anything directly about integrated treatment for physical illness, they can make the assertion more plausible.

5. **Disprove the Converse** – The plausibility of a **belief** (**B**) increases if a **rival conjecture** (**C**) is disproven.

   IF B is competing with C *AND* C is disproved *THEN* B is more credible.

   e.g., A rival conjecture to the belief that "an integrated treatment approach is most effective for serious illness" might be that: "This generalization is a result of 'sampling error' and confirmation bias, because the people who seek and provide integrated treatment are already convinced it will work." If it can be demonstrated that people who are skeptical about the approach or unfamiliar with it have equally good results as those who are proponents then the plausibility of the initial belief is increased. As we have seen, the potential to introduce doubt about the validity or universality of a limiting belief is a common use of Sleight of Mouth.

6. **Comparison with Random** – If a belief can be shown to predict a particular result with better than random accuracy, and that it is not "by chance," then it is more credible.

   e.g., If the results of a study showing benefits of an integrated treatment intervention are highly unlikely to have occurred by chance, it is easier accept that the findings reflect a real treatment effect. It is, of course, possible that a study result showing benefits of an intervention is because of chance, particularly if the study has a small size. Confidence in the generalization is increased if it is confirmed in several studies. The larger the sample size showing a positive result, the less likely it is to be a random occurrence.

Using Polya Patterns to Introduce Doubt

Of course, all of the Polya Patterns can be applied to introduce doubt about the validity or universality of a belief or generalization as well. Staying in the area of health, let's take a common example of a potential thought virus such as, "If I get X illness (AIDS, breast cancer, Covid etc.), I will die."

The lower the **probability** of the generalization described by the belief has of occurring, the more it calls the universality of the generalization into question. If one can show, for instance, that the average 5–10-year mortality rate for the illness is relatively low (e.g.,

AIDS = 15%, breast cancer = 2.5%, Covid = 1%,), it reduces the certainty of the belief. Improbable examples of people who have had the illness living healthy and symptom free for decades would cast even more doubt on the accuracy of the generalization.

Similarly, if there are other likely **consequences** of the belief or generalization that one can demonstrate have not occurred, it will also cast doubt on the belief. For example, if getting X illness were essentially a death sentence, a consequence would be that it would have wiped out or significantly reduced certain demographic groups. If it can be shown that this has not happened, the generalization appears less valid.

Other consequences, on an individual level, would express as an increase in symptoms and deterioration of health. If these do not occur, the certainty of the generalization diminishes.

If one can show the lack or absence of some presupposition or **contingency** upon which the belief is based, then it will diminish the validity of the belief. One presupposition of the belief "If I get X illness, I will die," is that "getting" the illness is essentially binary; i.e., that as soon as one "gets" the illness it is already at the threshold necessary to lead to the outcome of dying. If it can be shown that there are different stages of the illness or degrees of "viral load" that do not reach that threshold, it reduces the universality of the generalization.

Analogies can also be made which question the validity or universality of a belief. In the case of the belief "If I get X illness, I will die," one could say, "An infestation of weeds or other invasive species does not necessarily mean the destruction of a garden or orchard. If the weeds are removed and the soil is fertilized, the garden or orchard can grow back stronger than ever."

Finding support for a **rival conjecture** will challenge the plausibility of a particular belief or generalization. A rival conjecture to the belief "If I get X illness, I will die," for instance, could be "It is not the presence of the (virus, infection, tumor) that determines life or death. It is the vitality and functioning of the immune system and other physiological defense mechanisms. Getting an illness can actually make you more immune." If it can be shown that a particular illness progresses differently depending on the state of a person's immune system, the rival conjecture begins to seem more plausible than the original belief.

Demonstrating that a generalization is no more accurate than a **random** prediction will also reduce its perceived validity and impact. For instance, if one compares the average 5–10-year mortality rate for the illness with the overall average mortality rate for any (presumably random) cause it may give a surprising result. As an example, according to a number of sources (as of the time of this writing), the chance that an average 60-year-old male would die of any cause (including swimming, jogging, cycling, etc.) within 10 years is 14.8% (and 9.45% for women). This is much less than many illnesses (such as Covid or breast cancer) or approximately equal to AIDS for men. Comparisons such as this can put generalizations about specific illnesses into a different perspective.

Polya's patterns have important implications for both establishing and changing beliefs. The following worksheet provides a series of questions, derived from Polya's patterns of plausible inference, that can be considered in order to assess the plausibility of particular beliefs or generalizations.

Polya Pattern Worksheet

What is the generalization or belief you want to explore?

1. What is the **probability** or frequency with which this pattern, or the phenomenon associated with the belief, occurs? How many occurrences of the pattern or phenomenon associated with the belief have been observed when there has been the appropriate opportunity?

    Occurrences: _____ Opportunities:_____

    Occurrences ÷ Opportunities: _____

2. What is an obvious **consequence** of this pattern or belief?

    What are some other consequences of this pattern or belief?

    What would be an extreme or exaggerated example of a consequence of this pattern or belief?

    What is a consequence that would be likely to occur *only* if this belief or pattern were valid?

    How many of these consequences can you observe, demonstrate or validate?

3. What conditions or contingencies are required or presupposed by this pattern or belief? What has to have happened already in order for this pattern or belief to be valid?

Are there any conditions or contingencies that would be unlikely or would serve no purpose if they were not followed by the pattern or phenomenon associated with the belief?

How many of these contingencies or pre-conditions can you demonstrate or validate?

4. What is an **analogy** for this belief or pattern?

5. What **rival conjectures** (other beliefs or patterns) might explain some of the same consequences you have listed above?

Can you show that any of these rival conjectures are not valid?

6. If the phenomena to which this pattern or belief relate were merely **random**, what would you expect to observe? How is what you actually observe different from this prediction related to random behavior?

It should be kept in mind that the Polya Patterns are not "proofs." Polya himself points out that these patterns only help to determine or strengthen the plausibility of a pattern or assertion, not its "truth.. Pattern verification procedures, such as seeking counter examples and perceiving causal relationships from a more systemic perspective, are important to combine with the Polya Patterns in order to continually seek other points of view and broaden our models of the world.

In the next chapter, I will go over examples of how the types of strategies presented in this chapter have been applied. By reflecting on speeches and writings of some of the well-known models that I have mentioned previously, we can explore how Sleight of Mouth can influence perceptions and bring about change in a variety of socio-political contexts.

Chapter 19
Examples of Applying Sleight of Mouth

Examples of Applying Sleight of Mouth

In the previous chapter, I presented a number of possible strategies for using Sleight of Mouth to either strengthen or question the credibility of a belief or generalization. In this chapter, I will provide a number of examples of how these strategies, or combinations of them, have been applied to shape our world by some of the role models from which the various Sleight of Mouth patterns have been modeled.

Sleight of Mouth and "The Socratic Method"
– Unpacking Beliefs and Assumptions

We begin almost 2,500 years ago with the ancient Greek philosopher Socrates. Condemned to death in 399 BC and having left no written works, most of what is known about Socrates comes from the writings of his protégé Plato, who recorded numerous "dialogues" between Socrates and his pupils. These dialogues form the basis of the so-called "Socratic Method" of philosophical inquiry, whose purpose is to examine and question the validity of a belief from many vantage points.

The *Socratic Method* is defined as "a dialectical method of inquiry that uses questions to clarify and unpack one's beliefs, to understand the assumptions, evidence and reasons used to support them, and to expose any contradictions, inconsistencies and fallacies in one's thinking." This is clearly also one of the main purposes of Sleight of Mouth. And, as it turns out, Socrates used quite a lot of Sleight of Mouth as part of his method. In fact, examining Socrates' dialogues when I was studying Political Philosophy at the University of California at Santa Cruz in 1976 was responsible for planting many of the seeds of what was to develop into Sleight of Mouth.

As I have established, Sleight of Mouth patterns are a function of specific mindsets, which can just as easily be expressed in the form of questions as they can be as statements. In fact, every Sleight of Mouth pattern can be defined and expressed as a key question. In the earlier section of this book on *Counter Example*, I referenced the dialog between Socrates and Polemarchus on "Justice" from *Book I* of Plato's *Republic* as an illustration of the pattern. The following is a continuation of that dialogue.

Socrates: *It looks as if Simonides was talking about what is right with a poet's ambiguity. For it appears that he meant that it is right to give everyone what is appropriate to him, but he called this his "due."*

Polemarchus: *Of course.*

S: *Yes, but look here, suppose someone asked him "How then does medicine get its name, Simonides? What does it supply that is due and appropriate and to whom?" How do you suppose he would reply?*

P: *Obviously that it is the science that supplies the body with remedies and with food and drink.*

S: *And if he were asked the same question about cookery?*

P: *That it supplies the flavor to our food.*

S: *Then what about justice? What does it supply?*

P: *If we are to be consistent, Socrates, it must be the ability to do good and evil to one's friends and enemies.*

S: *So, Simonides says that justice is to benefit one's friends and harm one's enemies?*

P: *I think so.*

Socrates begins by establishing the belief to be explored as the equivalence that "doing right" means "to give everyone what is appropriate to him." He then *Chunks Down* the criterion of "giving what is appropriate" to "supplying" and uses *Analogies* to *Chunk Down* "everyone" to the professions of medicine and cooking. Socrates also uses an interesting version of *Model of the World* by having Polemarchus answer as if he were Simonides.

Next, Socrates *Redefines* "doing right" as "justice" and treats it as if it were also a profession, like medicine and cooking, as opposed to a quality that he just applied to the professions of medicine and cooking (i.e., what does "doing right" and "giving what is appropriate" mean with respect to medicine and cooking?). Socrates' proceeds to apply the belief statement to itself, asking, "What does justice (i.e., doing right) supply (i.e., give that is appropriate)?"

What Socrates is essentially asking is "what does giving someone what is appropriate to them give them that is appropriate?" This would seem a complex and very abstract and confusing question if Socrates had not done the *Chunking Down* and *Redefining*. Seemingly unaware of the sophisticated maneuver Socrates has just made, Polemarchus answers the question as if it were somehow obvious. Socrates goes on to *Redefine* Polemarchus' reply that justice "is to do good and evil to one's friends and enemies" to the statement that justice means to "benefit one's friends and harm one's enemies." This leads to a completely new belief statement.

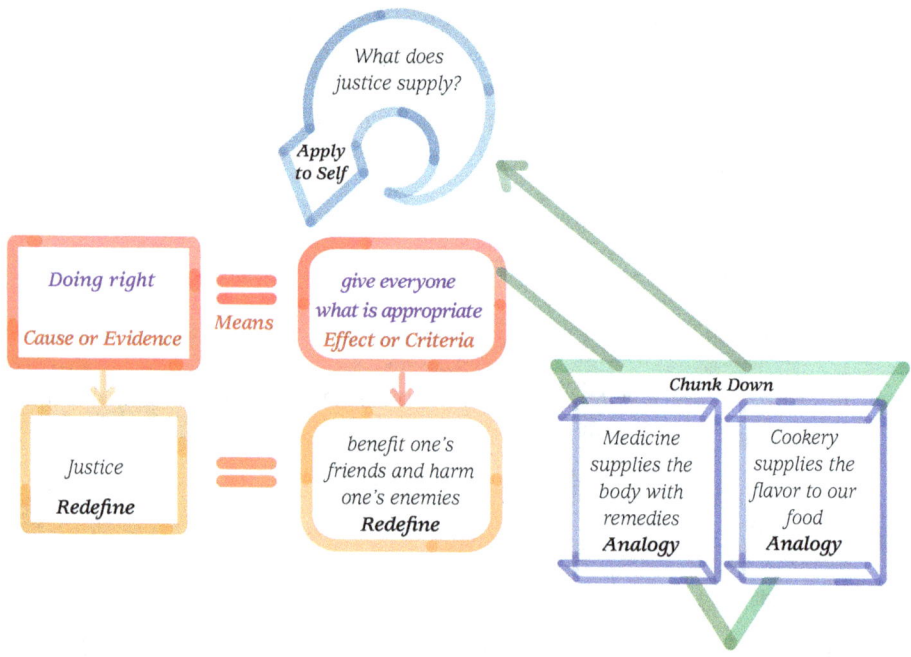

Socrates approaches the revised belief statement with a Sleight of Mouth strategy similar to the one he used for the previous one.

S: *Who then is best able to benefit his friends and harm his enemies in matters of health?*

P: *A doctor.*

S: *And on a risky sea voyage?*

P: *A navigator.*

S: *And what about the just man? When and where will he best be able to help his friends and harm his enemies?*

P: *In war: he will fight against his enemies and for his friends.*

S: *Good. Yet people who are healthy have no use for a physician, have they, Polemarchus?*

P: *True.*

S: *Nor those that stay on land of a navigator?*

P: *No.*

S: *Do you then maintain that those who are not at war have no use for a just man?*

P: *Certainly not.*

Socrates *Chunks Down* the criterion of "benefiting friends and harming enemies" using analogies to "matters of health" and a "risky sea voyage." However, instead of focusing on the quality of "justice," Socrates switches to the level of role identity, asking "*who* is best able to benefit his friends and harm his enemies" in these more concrete contexts.

Socrates then *Redefines* "justice" as the "just man," shifting from a quality (justice) to a professional role (the just man) similar to a doctor or a navigator. He asks, "*When* and *where* will he best be able to help his friends and harm his enemies?" (shifting now to the level of environment). Following Socrates' lead, Polemarchus responds, "In war."

Socrates next *Changes Frame Size* to point out that people who are healthy have no use for a physician and those who stay on land don't need a navigator. He then wonders whether the *Consequence* is that those not at war then have no use for a just man.

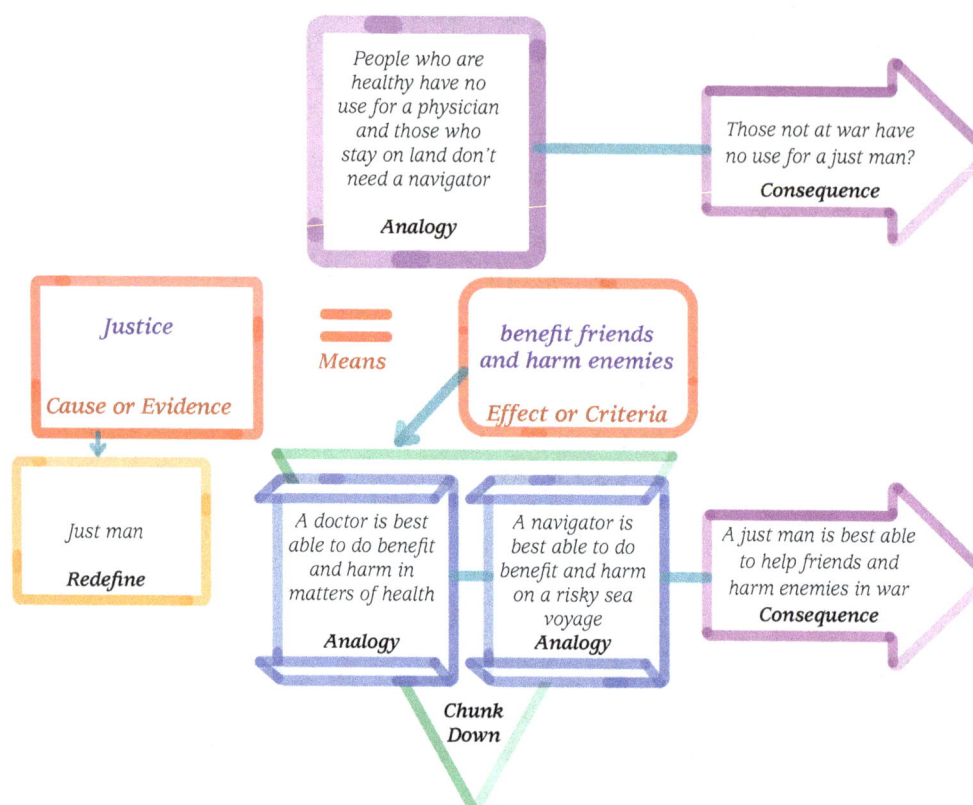

Polemarchus contends that justice is also useful in peacetime. And Socrates continues with his Sleight of Mouth strategy.

S: *So, justice is useful in peacetime?*

P: *It is.*

S: *So too is agriculture, for producing crops; and shoemaking for producing shoes.*

P: *Yes.*

S: *Well then, what is the use of justice in peacetime, and what do we get out of it?*

P: *Its useful in business.*

S: *And by that you mean some form of transaction between people?*

P: *Yes.*

S: *Well, if our transaction is a game of chess, is a just man a good and useful partner, or a chess player?*

P: *A chess player.*

S: *And if it's a matter of bricks and mortar, is the just man a better and more useful partner than a bricklayer?*

P: *No.*

S: *Well, for what kind of transaction is the just man a better partner than the bricklayer? Where does he excel the musician as the musician excels him in music?*

P: *Where money is involved, I suppose.*

Socrates *Redefines* "just man" back to "justice" and questions its usefulness in peacetime. Returning to his strategy of *Chunking Down* through *Analogy*, Socrates mentions the professions of agriculture and shoemaking and asks what we get out of justice, as if it were a similar profession. As a *Consequence* of the Analogies, Polemarchus responds that justice is "useful in business," which Socrates immediately *Redefines* as "a form of transaction between people." Continuing his strategy of using *Analogy* to *Chunk Down*, Socrates makes a series of *Analogies* to activities such as chess, bricklaying and music. At the same time, he *Redefines* "justice" back to the "just man" and compares the usefulness of a just man to a chess player, bricklayer or musician. *Chunking Down* "transaction," Socrates asks, "for what kind of transaction is the just man a better partner than the bricklayer?" This leads Polemarchus to respond that it is "where money is involved."

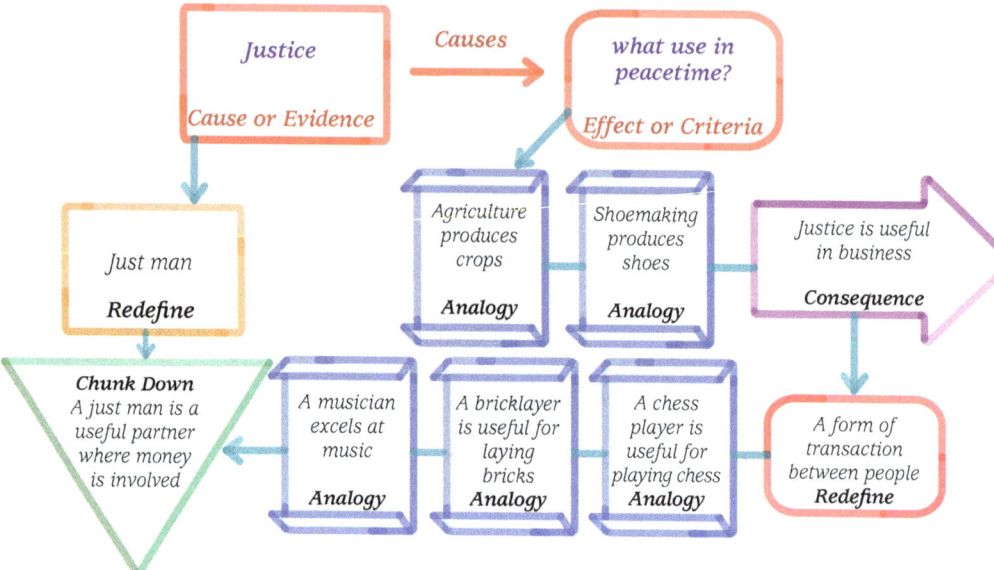

The interaction has now evolved the belief statement under examination to "a just man is a useful partner where money is involved" and Socrates continues his Sleight of Mouth strategy.

S: *Except perhaps when it's a question of buying or selling; if, for example, we are buying or selling a horse, a trainer would be a better partner, would he not? Or if it's a ship, a shipbuilder or sailor?*

P: *I suppose so.*

S: *Then in what financial transactions is the just man a better partner than others?*

P: *When we want to bank our money, Socrates.*

S: *In fact, when we don't want to make use of it at all, but lay it by?*

P: *Yes.*

S: *So, when we aren't making any use of our money, we find justice useful?*

P: *It looks rather like it.*

S: *And so, when you want to store a pruning-knife, justice is useful both to community and to individual; but if you want to use it then you turn to the vine dresser. And if you want to keep your shield or your lyre safe you look to the just man, but if you want to use it to the soldier or musician?*

P: *That seems to follow.*

S: *And so, in all spheres, justice is useless when you are using things, and useful when you are not?*

P: *Maybe.*

Socrates *Chunks Down* Polemarchus' response that a just man is useful partner "where money is involved" to the activity of "buying or selling." He then makes the *Analogy* to buying or selling a horse or a ship in order to create the *Counter Examples* that a trainer or a sailor would make a better partner for those activities. As with Socrates' previous *Analogies*, these create a type of mixing of levels, in that ships and horses are physical objects whereas "justice" is not. Rather, it is an evaluation made *about* an action or individual. For instance, it is possible to have a "just" or "unjust" sale of a horse or a ship, or to be a "just" or "unjust" trainer or sailor.

Staying within the frame of Socrates' *Analogies*, however, Polemarchus *Redefines* his original statement by responding that a just man is a useful partner when we want to "bank our money." Socrates quickly *Redefines* Polemarchus' statement further, saying that it means that "when we aren't making any use of our money, we find justice useful." In doing so, he also *Redefines* "a just man" back to "justice," as if they meant the same thing and are completely interchangeable (like saying that "death" and "a dead man" refer to the same thing).

Socrates then proceeds to make another series of *Analogies*, this time with respect to "money" – using the examples of a pruning-knife, a shield and lyre. He claims that justice is useful if you want to store these objects, but would turn to a vine-dresser, soldier or musician if you want to use them rather than to a just man. From this, Socrates *Chunks Up* and asserts the *Consequence* that "in all spheres justice is useless when you are using things, and useful when you are not."

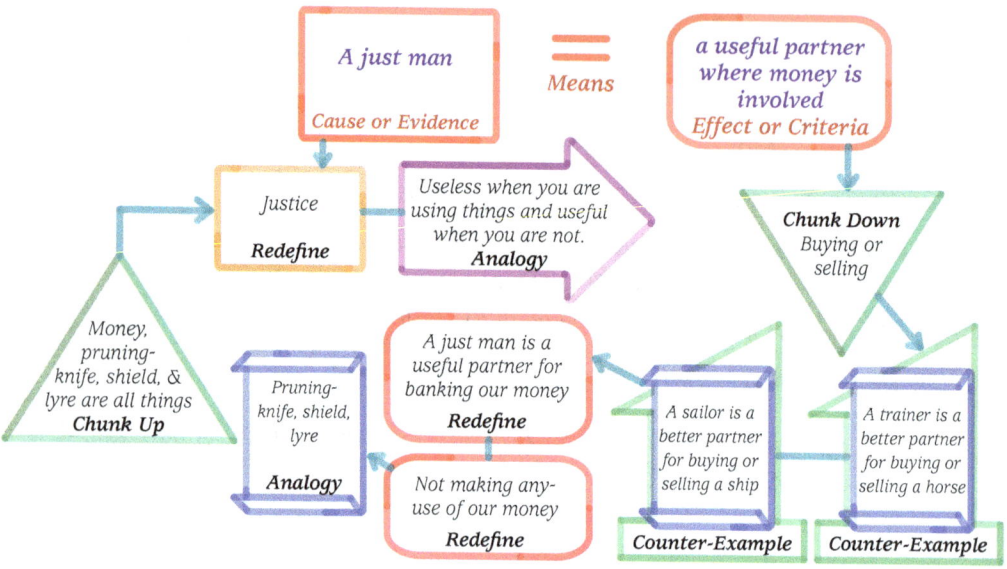

While Polemarchus is not quite certain about this conclusion, Socrates continues with his Sleight of Mouth strategy.

S: *Justice, then, can't be a very serious thing, if that is all the use it is. But there's a further point. In boxing and other kinds of fighting, skill in attack goes with skill in defense, does it not?*

P: *Of course.*

S: *So, too, the ability to save from disease implies the ability to produce it undetected, while ability to bring an army safely through a campaign goes with ability to rob the enemy of his secrets and steal a march on him in action.*

P: *I certainly think so.*

S: *So, a man who's good at keeping a thing will be good at stealing it?*

P: *I suppose so.*

S: *So, if the just man is good at keeping money safe he will be good at stealing it too.*

P: *That at any rate is the conclusion the argument leads to.*

S: *So, the just man turns out to be a kind of thief, a view you have perhaps learned from Homer. For he approves of Odysseus' grandfather Autolycus who, he says, surpassed all men in stealing and lying. Justice, in fact, according to you and Homer and Simonides, is a kind of stealing, though it must be done to help a friend or harm an enemy. Is that your meaning?*

P: *It certainly isn't, but I don't really know what I did mean.*

Keeping with his strategy of using *Analogies* to *Chunk Down* and introduce different perspectives, Socrates bring up the examples of martial arts, treatment of disease and military prowess. He makes the assertion that skill in each activity involves the ability to produce complementary or opposite actions and outcomes: i.e., attacking and defending, saving from illness and producing illness, conducting a military campaign and stealing secrets from an opponent. This leads him to *Chunk Up* to the conclusion that "a man who's good at keeping a thing will be good at stealing it."

From this, (*Redefining* "justice" back to "a just man") Socrates asserts the *Consequence* that "if the just man is good at keeping money safe, he will be good at stealing it too." As a result of this, he *Redefines* the *just man* as "a kind of thief" and *justice* as "a kind of stealing." Socrates also employs the Sleight of Mouth pattern of *Model of the World* when he makes the comment that Homer "approves of Odysseus' grandfather Autolycus who, he says, surpassed all men in stealing and lying," implying that in some models of the world stealing and lying may be seen as positive assets.

It is not surprising that, after all of Socrates' verbal gymnastics with Sleight of Mouth, when he asks Polemarchus if this conclusion is what he meant by his original definition, Polemarchus admits to being no longer sure of what he did mean.

Reflections on Socrates' Dialogue with Polemarchus and the Socratic Method

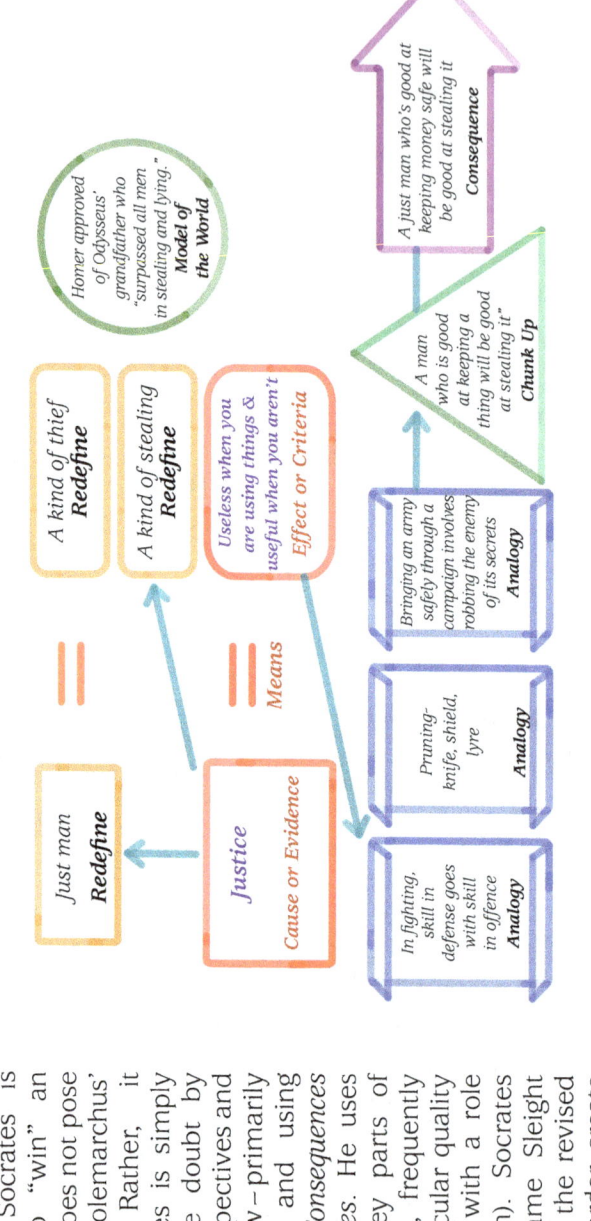

It seems clear that, in his dialogue with Polemarchus, Socrates is not really trying to "win" an argument, since he does not pose any alternative to Polemarchus' belief statement. Rather, it appears that Socrates is simply attempting to create doubt by introducing new perspectives and different points of view – primarily by *Chunking Down* and using *Analogies* to pose *Consequences* and *Counter Examples*. He uses these to *Redefine* key parts of the belief statement, frequently interchanging a particular quality or criterion (justice) with a role identity (a just man). Socrates then applies the same Sleight of Mouth strategy to the revised belief statement in order create further doubt.

250   Examples of Applying Sleight of Mouth

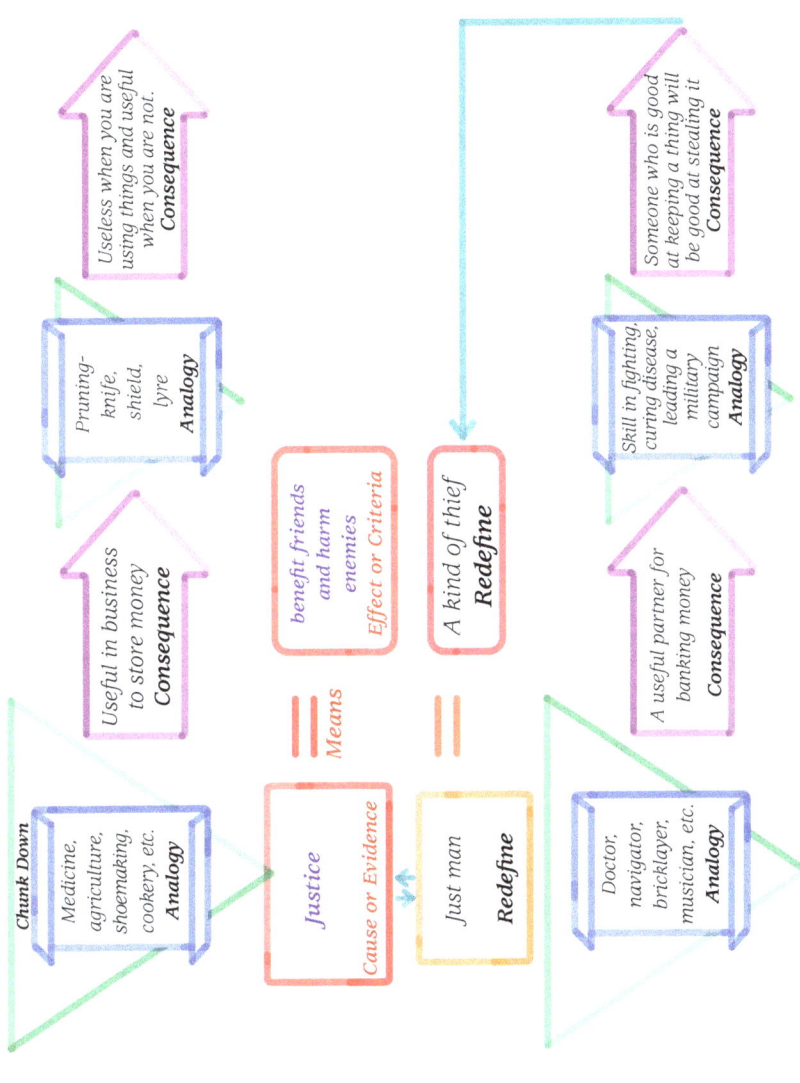

Claiming that "the highest form of human excellence is to question oneself and others," Socrates actually applies Sleight of Mouth to his own ideas and conclusions as much as to those of Polemarchus. In fact, at times, it is almost as if Socrates is having a conversation with himself through Polemarchus by posing *Consequences* or *Redefinitions* and asking whether Polemarchus agrees with them. In this way, the dialogue is more of an open intellectual exploration than an attempt to succeed in a debate.

Sleight of Mouth 251

From this perspective, Socrates' goal is essentially to get Polemarchus to question his own assumptions and conclusions about the important, though abstract, quality of "justice" and what it means to be "a just man." In fact, Socrates' use of Sleight of Mouth in his Socratic Method typically had the ultimate aim to produce a state of doubt and puzzlement known as "aporia" in philosophy – a state of uncertainty and "not knowing." A good illustration of this is Polemarchus' closing statement that he no longer really knows what he did mean when he began the exchange.

Apparently, Socrates developed his method after he heard that the Oracle of Delphi (who was considered to be infallible) had said no man in Greece was wiser than Socrates. Socrates saw this as a paradox since, as he put it, "I was fully aware that I knew absolutely nothing." So, he embarked on a quest to speak with other wise men in Athens to find out what they knew and if he could disprove the Oracle by finding someone wiser.

Am I the only one to know that we know nothing?

As Socrates questioned these supposed wise men, he quickly discovered that they didn't know what they thought they knew, and yet they were unwilling to admit it. Socrates concluded that, paradoxically, what made him wiser than other men was his willingness to acknowledge the extent of his ignorance. As he put it, "There is this difference between us: although these people know nothing, they all believe they know something; whereas, I, if I know nothing, at least have no doubts about it." (This statement itself, of course, is a type of Sleight of Mouth – i.e., knowing nothing on one level and being certain about that on another level – a type of Meta Frame.)

Applying Socrates' Sleight of Mouth Strategy

The Socratic Method is often described as the cornerstone of approaches like Cognitive Behavioral Therapy (CBT), which involves asking a series of questions that encourage reflection. By surfacing knowledge and assumptions that were previously outside of awareness, the technique can produce insightful perspectives and helps to identify more resourceful alternatives.

As I pointed out earlier, Socrates' Sleight of Mouth strategy has the basic structure of using *Analogies* to *Chunk Down* some part of the belief statement to draw a particular *Consequence*, which is then used to *Redefine* some part of the belief statement or to provide a *Counter Example*. It can be summarized in the following structure.

1. Stating the belief to be explored.

2. Identifying some concrete *Analogies* for the causes or evidence that could enrich its implications

3. Identifying the corresponding *Analogies* for the effects or criteria stated or implied by the belief.

4. Examining the *Consequences* or effects of these *Analogies*.

5. Drawing from these *Consequences* or effects, restating some part of the belief that has different implications, or using it to present a *Counter Example*.

As an illustration, let's apply this strategy to some of the examples of limiting beliefs we have been exploring throughout this book.

1. Belief Statement: e.g., *If I speak people will laugh at me.*

2. *Analogies* for cause or evidence part of the belief statement that *Chunk it Down* to something more concrete: e.g., *Speaking = cooking, music, medicine.*

3. Corresponding *Analogies* for effect or criteria part of the belief statement: e.g., *Being laughed at = If a cook prepares a meal, diners won't like the food; If a musician plays a piece of music, the audience won't appreciate the performance; If a doctor proposes a treatment, patients will not comply.*

4. *Consequence of the Analogies*: e.g., *The cook, musician and doctor need to know more about the tastes and needs of those receiving their offerings.*

5. Resulting *Counter Example* or *Redefine* when applied back to the original belief statement: e.g., *Before I speak, it is important to know the needs and tastes of my audience.*

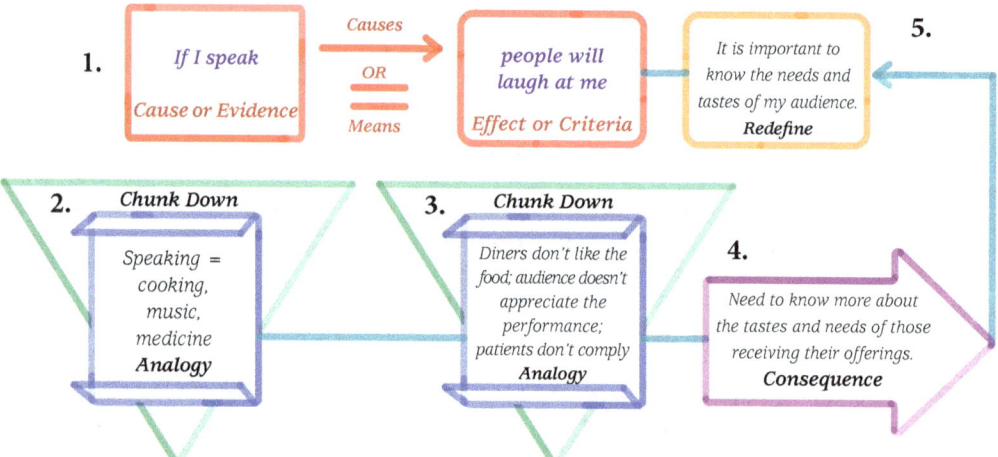

1. Belief Statement: e.g., *No matter what I do I will never get enough.*

2. *Analogies* for cause or evidence part of the belief statement that *Chunk it Down* to something more concrete: e.g., *Doing = bricklaying, agriculture, shoemaking.*

3. Corresponding *Analogies* for effect or criteria part of the belief statement: e.g., *Not getting enough = Constantly running out of bricks, seeds, or leather to successfully do their jobs.*

4. *Consequence* of the *Analogies*: *The bricklayer, farmer and shoemaker need to know the scope of their work and plan ahead appropriately.*

5. Resulting *Counter Example* or *Redefine*: *No matter what I do, I need to be sure that I have planned ahead appropriately.*

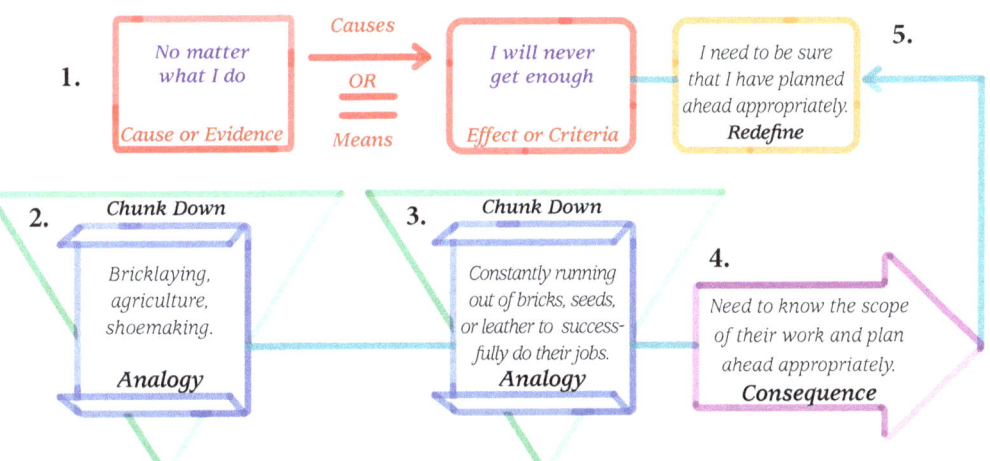

Sleight of Mouth 255

1. Belief Statement: e.g., *I have had this problem for a long time, it will be hard to change.*

2. *Analogies* for some key part of the statement that *Chunk it Down* to something more concrete: e.g., *I = military commander, ship navigator, horse trainer.*

3. Corresponding *Analogies* for effect or criteria part of the belief statement: e.g., *Long-term problem = a stalled military campaign, being lost at sea, having to work with inexperienced and anxious horses.*

4. *Consequence* of the *Analogies*: *Resolving the problem successfully requires patience, creativity, and courage.*

5. Resulting *Counter Example* or *Redefine*: *I have had this problem a long time, I will need patience, creativity, and courage.*

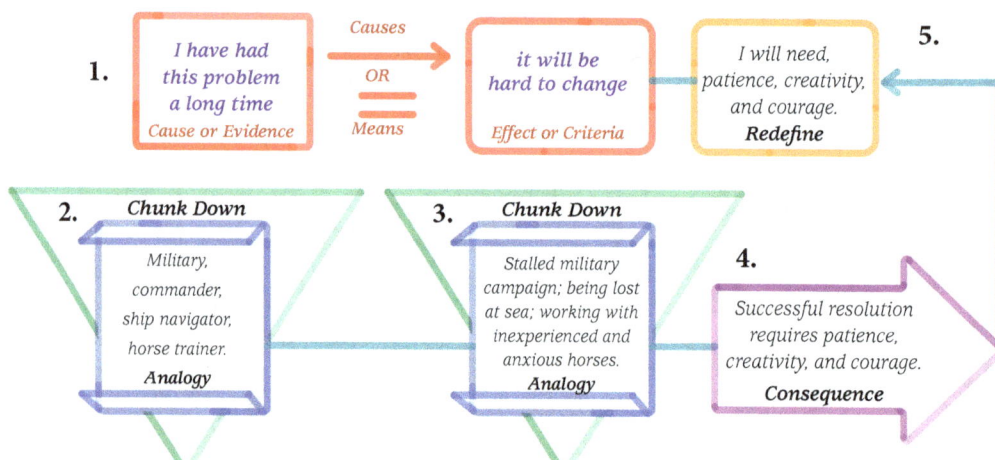

1. Belief Statement: e.g., *I am not a native English speaker (skilled with words), it will be difficult for me to learn Sleight of Mouth.*

2. *Analogies* for cause or evidence part of the belief statement that *Chunk it Down* to something more concrete: e.g., *Sleight of Mouth = cooking, shoemaking, farming.*

3. Corresponding *Analogies* for effect or criteria part of the belief statement: e.g., *Non-native speaker (not skilled with words) = a child taking a cooking class, a shoemaker's apprentice, a new farmhand.*

4. *Consequence* of the *Analogies*: *Acquiring a skill is a natural step-by-step process that comes from practice.*

5. Resulting *Counter Example* or *Redefine*: *For non-native speakers (or people not skilled with words) learning Sleight of Mouth is a natural step-by-step process that comes from practice.*

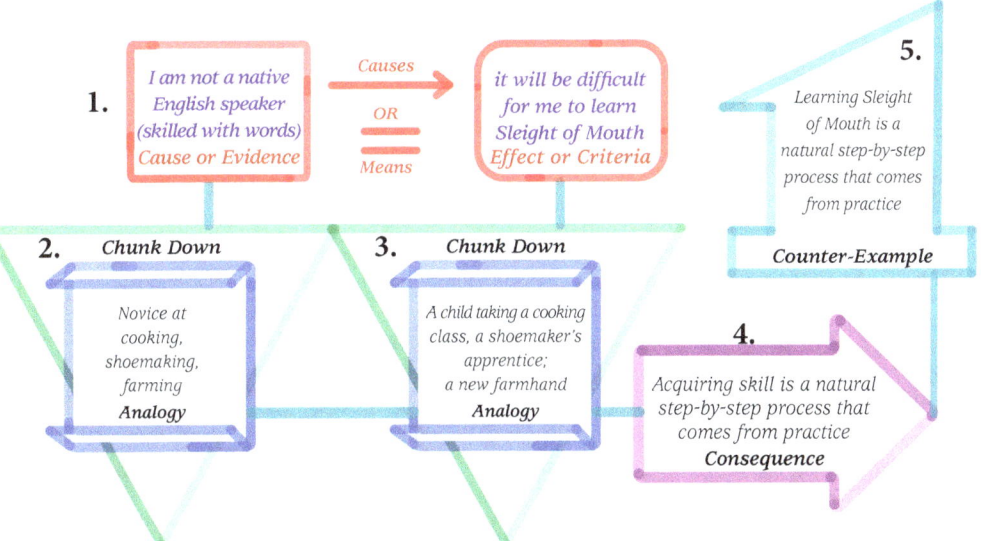

Sleight of Mouth 257

Try this strategy yourself with a belief you would like to explore. Fill in the diagram below by answering the following questions:

1. *What is the belief statement to be explored?*

2. *What are some concrete analogies for the causes or evidence that could enrich its implications?*

3. *What are the corresponding analogies for the effects or criteria stated or implied by the belief?*

4. *What are the consequences or effects of these analogies?*

5. *Drawing from these consequences or effects, how could you restate some part of the belief that has different implications?*

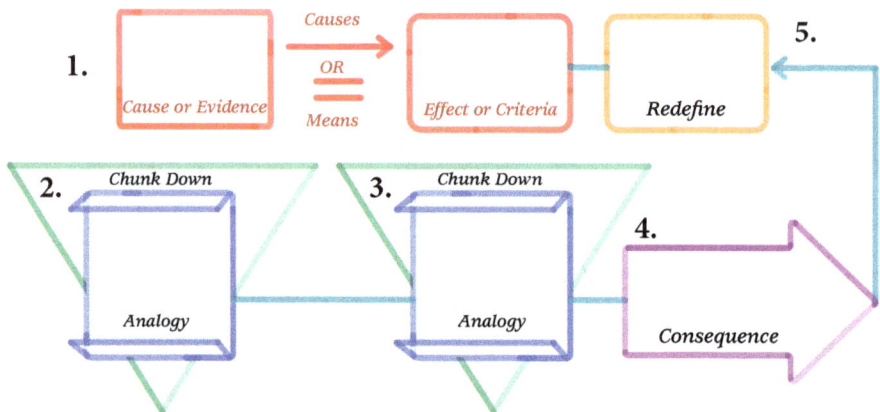

Using Sleight of Mouth to Challenge and Transform "Thought Viruses"

Sleight of Mouth patterns are sometimes effective in situations where other belief change techniques and interventions are difficult to apply or are ineffective. Sleight of Mouth is often necessary in order to deal with "thought viruses," for example. As I pointed out in the introduction to this book, a thought virus is a special class of limiting belief. A typical limiting belief is a generalization drawn from experience. Consequently, it can be updated or corrected as a result of experience. New data or "counter examples" that do not fit with the generalization will lead the person to reconsider the validity of his or her belief.

Thought viruses, on the other hand, are based on other limiting beliefs rather than on direct experiences. They are usually generalizations, drawn from other beliefs or assumptions; frequently beliefs that are not even our own, but that have been installed by others. Thus, thought viruses are not naturally corrected or updated by experience. Rather, the beliefs upon which they are based (and which hold them in place) must be identified and transformed.

This is probably no more evident than in situations involving political, philosophical, and theological debate. Many of the individuals who served as models for the Sleight of Mouth patterns had missions in the area of social change, and used Sleight of Mouth in order to transform limiting cultural beliefs through oratory and debate.

Within the framework of Sleight of Mouth, the goal of all speeches, oratory, debate, etc., is to create, reinforce, challenge, outframe, or recode a particular belief or belief system. To effectively install a new belief system, it is also sometimes necessary to first create doubt with respect to the existing belief system. One cannot simply assert alternative beliefs and expect them to be considered or accepted based on their own merit. Belief change often requires destabilizing current beliefs by introducing doubt. This sometimes includes refuting a number of "rival conjectures" which may challenge the new belief.

Abraham Lincoln's Use of Sleight of Mouth to Invalidate Pro-Slavery Theology

The following excerpt from a speech by Abraham Lincoln challenging pro-slavery theology (October 1, 1858) is a classic example of how Sleight of Mouth patterns can be used to refute existing limiting beliefs and create a wider map of the world.

> *The sum of pro-slavery theology seems to be this: "Slavery is not universally right, nor yet universally wrong; it is better for some people to be slaves; and, in such cases, it is the Will of God that they be such.*
>
> *Certainly, there is no contending against the Will of God; but still there is some difficulty in ascertaining, and applying it, to particular cases. For instance, we will suppose the Rev. Dr. Ross has a slave named Sambo, and the question is "Is it the Will of God that Sambo shall remain a slave, or be set free?" The Almighty gives no audible answer to the question, and his revelation—the Bible—gives none, or, at most, none but such as admits of a squabble, as to its meaning. No one thinks of asking Sambo's opinion on it. So, at last, it comes to this, that Dr. Ross is to decide the question. And while he considers it, he sits in the shade, with gloves on his hand, and subsists on the bread that Sambo is earning in the burning sun. If he decides that God wills Sambo to continue a slave, he thereby retains his own comfortable position; but if he decides that God wills Sambo to be free, he thereby must walk out of the shade, throw off his gloves, and delve for his own bread. Will Dr. Ross be actuated by that perfect impartiality, which has ever been considered most favorable to correct decisions?*
>
> *But slavery is good for some people!!! As a good thing, slavery is strikingly peculiar, in this, that it is the only good thing which no man ever seeks the good of, for himself.*
>
> *Nonsense! Wolves devouring lambs, not because it is good for their own greedy maws, but because it is good for the lambs!!!*

As with all effective change processes, Lincoln's primary approach is one of *Pacing and Leading*. Lincoln systematically begins by first acknowledging or "pacing" the existing belief or belief statement. He then applies several different Sleight of Mouth strategies within his speech to begin to "lead" his listeners into doubt about the validity of the belief.

He first "paces" by summarizing "pro-slavery theology" as the belief that, "Slavery is not universally right, nor yet universally wrong; it is better for some people to be slaves; and, in such cases, it is the Will of God that they be such." Lincoln does not challenge the belief directly, claiming that "there is no contending against the Will of God." Instead, he uses the Sleight of Mouth pattern of *Chunking Down*; attempting to apply the belief to the "particular case" of "Dr. Ross and Sambo." The question is, "Is it the Will of God that Sambo shall remain a slave, or be set free?" Lincoln quickly establishes the *Meta Frame* that "Dr. Ross is to decide the question," pointing out that "while he considers it, he sits in the shade, with gloves on his hand, and subsists on the bread that Sambo is earning in the burning sun." (This level of detail is clearly indicative of much more "sensory based" chunking than the abstract language originally used to state the belief).

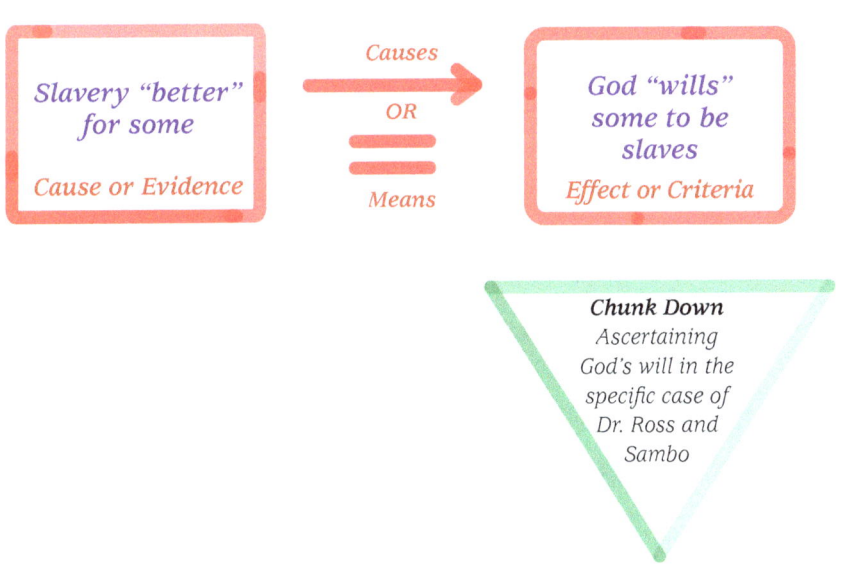

Lincoln points out the *Consequences* that, if Dr. Ross decides that "God" wills Sambo to continue to be a slave, "he thereby retains his own comfortable position" and does not have to "walk out of the shade, throw off his gloves, and delve for his own bread." This leads to the *Meta Frame* that it will not be possible for Dr. Ross to make an impartial decision related to "God's will" for Sambo, introducing doubt about the validity of the belief.

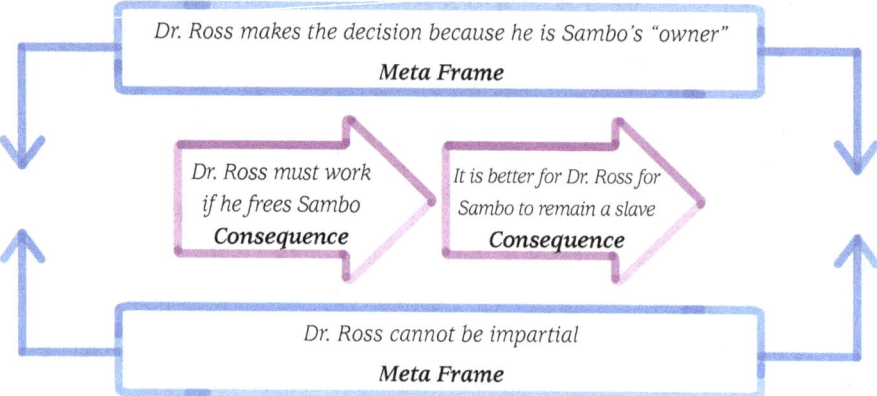

Lincoln then shifts to using *Counter Example* and *Analogy* to challenge the notion that "slavery is 'better' for some people." He first redefines "better" to "good," and then points out that "as a good thing, slavery is strikingly peculiar" in that "it is the only good thing which no man ever seeks the good of, for himself." He draws out the power of the *Counter Example* even more by making the *Analogy* to "wolves devouring lambs because it is good for the lambs."

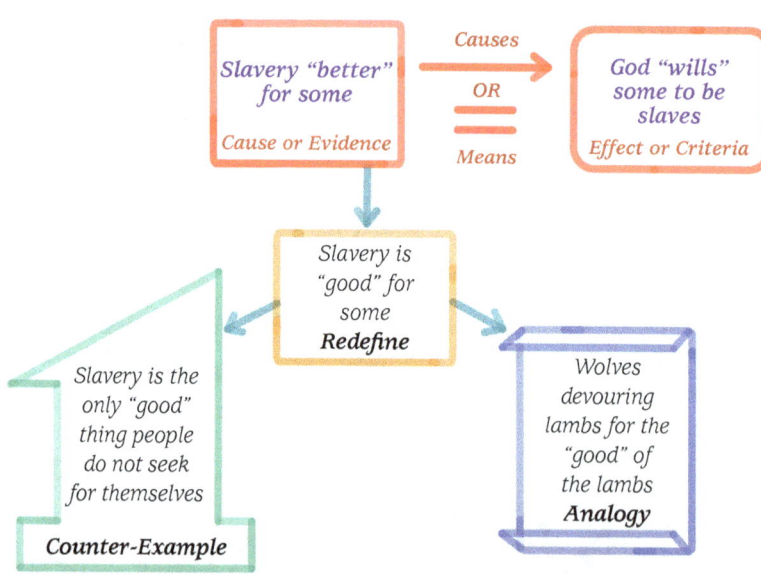

Reflections on Lincoln's Sleight of Mouth Strategy

Similar in some ways to Socrates, Lincoln uses the Sleight of Mouth patterns of *Chunking Down* and *Analogy* to produce *Consequences* and *Counter Examples* that question the validity of the thought virus that "slavery is better for some people and, in those cases, God wills them to be slaves." Rather than using *Analogy* first, Lincoln *Chunks Down* to a specific, concrete example (Dr. Ross and Sambo) and identifies *Consequences* (Dr. Ross has to do Sambo's work if Sambo is no longer his slave so it is better for him if Sambo stays his slave) that lead to a *Meta Frame* that highlights the inconsistency of a key premise of the belief statement (God does not will Sambo to be a slave; Dr. Ross does).

Unlike Socrates, Lincoln does not use *Analogy* in order to *Chunk Down*. Rather, he uses the *Analogy* of "wolves devouring lambs for the good of the lambs" to enhance and amplify his *Counter Example* to the assertion that slavery was better for some people – i.e., that if it was truly "better" or "good" for them, people would seek it for themselves. Wolves clearly don't eat lambs because it is good for or better for the lambs, and lambs don't seek to be eaten by wolves. The graphic *Analogy* is also a not so subtle identity level reference to the character of slave owners as "greedy wolves" while slaves are innocent and helpless "lambs."

Filtering out some of the specific references related to the particular content and context of Lincoln's remarks, we can summarize the essence of Lincoln's strategy for transforming thought viruses with the following structure:

1. State the limiting belief to be transformed

2. Restate (*Redefine*) the cause or evidence using words that have different implications.

3. Restate (*Redefine*) the effect or criteria using words that have different implications.

4. Identify a more positive *Consequence* or effect of these *Redefinitions*.

5. Use the *Redefinitions* find a *Counter Example*.

6. Make an *Analogy* that enhances the *Counter Example* and transforms the meaning of the limiting belief.

This approach can be applied to any limiting belief. As an example, we can apply it to one of the limiting belief examples we have been exploring throughout this book.

1. Limiting belief to be transformed: *If I speak people will laugh at me.*

2. Another way to say the cause or evidence that has different implications: *"speak" = express myself*

3. Another way to say the effect or criteria that has different implications: *"laugh at" = find humorous*

4. A more positive Consequence or effect of these redefinitions: *Give you appreciation for people who dare to express themselves.*

5. A Counter Example these redefinitions could lead to: *I find what you are expressing to be quite serious.*

6. An Analogy that enhances the Counter Example and transforms the meaning of the limiting belief: *Other birds found the "ugly duckling" humorous until it became a swan.*

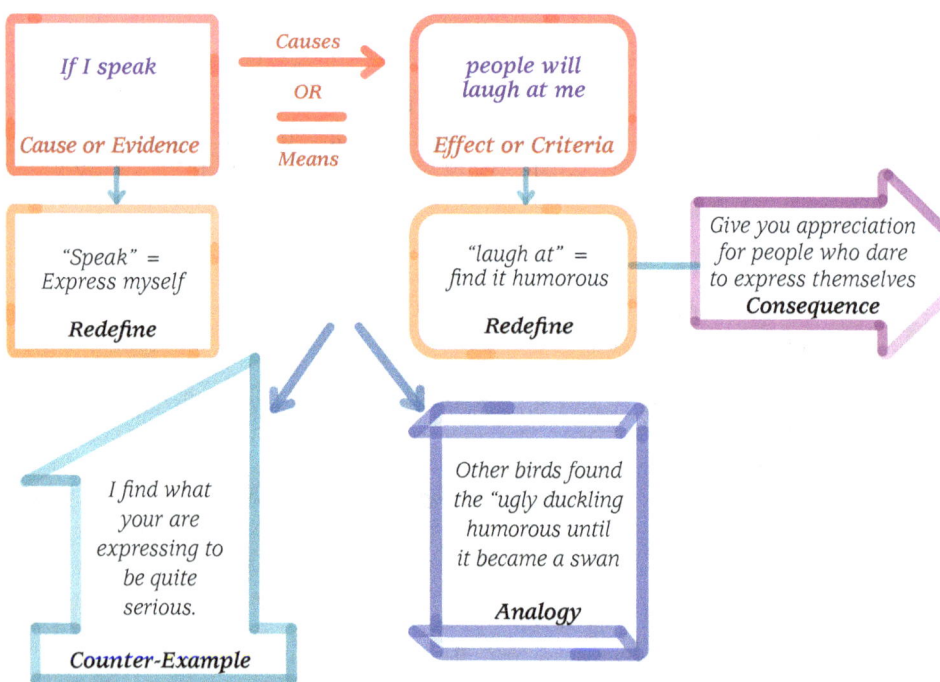

As with the Socratic Method, practice this strategy by applying to a limiting belief you would like to transform. Fill in the diagram below by answering the following questions:

1. *What is the limiting belief to be transformed?*
2. *What is another way to say the cause or evidence that has different implications?*
3. *What is another way to say the effect or criteria that has different implications?*
4. *What is a more positive consequence or effect of these redefinitions?*
5. *What counter example could these redefinitions lead to?*
6. *What is an analogy for that counter example?*

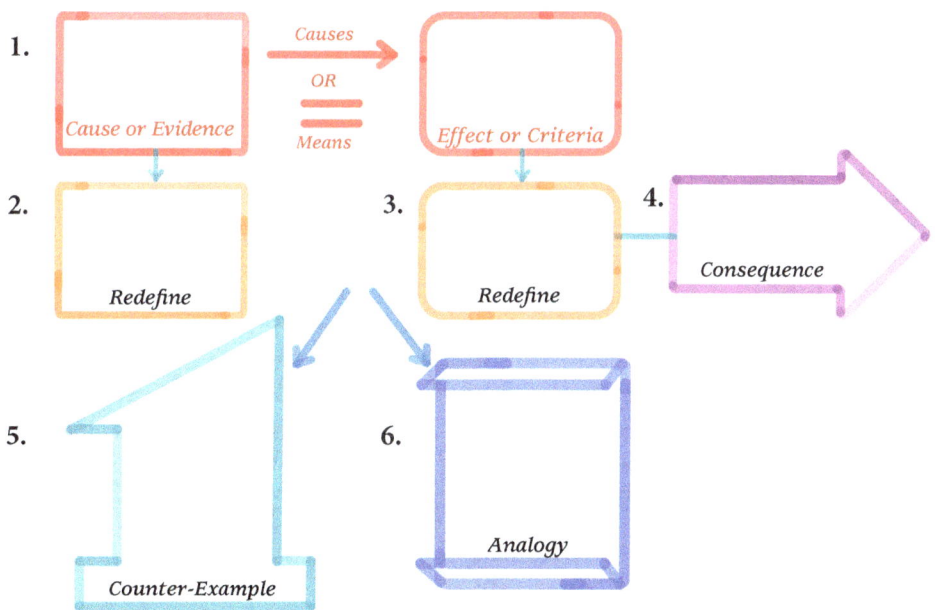

William Shakespeare's Mark Antony – Using Sleight of Mouth to Flip Perceptions of Reality

Plato's Socrates used Sleight of Mouth to create a state of uncertainty and "not-knowing" with his students. Lincoln applied Sleight of Mouth to refute beliefs and thought viruses used to justify slavery. Shakespeare's Mark Antony used Sleight of Mouth for another purpose in his rebuttal to Brutus in the play *Julius Caesar*. In earlier sections (*Another Outcome* and *Hierarchy of Criteria*), I have referred to a famous scene in Shakespeare's play in which Brutus, with a group of other Roman senators, has just stabbed Caesar to death. Imploring the crowd that has gathered to "believe me for mine honor," Brutus claims that Caesar was an ambitious dictator who intended to enslave the people of Rome and therefor deserved to be killed. The members of the crowd are satisfied with Brutus' explanation and support Caesar's assassination saying, "We are blest that Rome is rid of him."

It is significant to note that Brutus is basing his argument on what Aristotle referred to as "ethos" (his character). His justification is based on his claim that he is believable because he is an honorable man, and that Caesar was an ambitious dictator. As Aristotle pointed out, reference to character is crucial when "exact certainty is impossible, and opinions are divided." In the play, Brutus is successful in persuading the crowd whose members call out to "Bring him (Brutus) with triumph home unto his house," "Give him a statue with his ancestors" and "Let him be Caesar."

Mark Antony, who is an acknowledged friend of Caesar, has been given permission by Brutus and his co-conspirators to speak at Caesar's funeral, so long as he does not blame or denounce them for Caesar's death. Antony finds himself in somewhat of a double bind. If he speaks without denouncing Caesar's killers, he is tacitly condoning their actions. If he does not speak, he is abandoning his friend and letting the killers get away with their actions. In Shakespeare's account, Antony is able to talk his way out of this predicament. While clearly a fictitious account, Anthony's speech is an iconic illustration of effective persuasion. According to Wikipedia, "The speech is a famous example of the use of emotionally charged rhetoric. Comparisons have been drawn between this speech and political speeches throughout history in terms of the rhetorical devices employed to win over a crowd."

As I have already noted (p. 89), Antony begins his address to the potentially hostile crowd using the Sleight of Mouth pattern of *Another Outcome* by stating, "I have come to bury Caesar not to praise him" in order to reduce suspicions about his intentions in speaking. The following is an excerpt of the rest of Antony's opening remarks.

Friends, Romans, countrymen, lend me your ears; I have come to bury Caesar, not to praise him. The evil that men do lives after them; the good is oft interred with their bones; So let it be with Caesar. The noble Brutus Hath told you Caesar was ambitious: If it were so, it was a grievous fault, And grievously hath Caesar answered it. Here, under the leave of Brutus and the rest – For Brutus is an honorable man; So are they all, all honorable men – come I to speak at Caesar's funeral. He was my friend, faithful and just to me: But Brutus says he was ambitious; and Brutus is an honorable man. He hath brought many captives home to Rome, whose ransoms did the general coffers fill: Did this in Caesar seem ambitious? When that the poor have cried, Caesar hath wept: Ambition should be made of sterner stuff: Yet Brutus says he was ambitious; and Brutus is an honorable man. You all did see that on the Lupercal I thrice presented him a kingly crown, which he did thrice refuse: was this ambition? Yet Brutus says he was ambitious; and, sure, he is an honorable man.

In contrast to Brutus, who has addressed the crowd as "Romans, countrymen, and lovers" (see p. 159), Antony starts his speech by saying "Friends, Romans, countrymen." This is already establishing a different *Hierarchy of Criteria*. Brutus puts Romans first and lovers last, and claims that, though he loved Caesar, he killed him for the good of Rome. Antony puts friends ahead of Romans and emphasizes Caesar's qualities as a good friend.

Antony opens his remarks by immediately *Changing Frame Size* – expanding it to the future by pointing out that "the evil that men do lives after them; the good is oft interred with their bones." This serves to bring attention to the fact that Caesar did "good" things as well and was not all bad. Antony acknowledges that "*if* it were so" that Caesar was ambitious "it was a grievous fault." The use of the word "if" subtly creates the possibility for doubt that Caesar was in fact ambitious. He then uses the pattern of *Consequence* to point out that being stabbed to death as a penalty for such a fault is also is exceptionally severe ("grievous").

Antony then proceeds to cite a number of *Counter Examples* to Brutus' claim that Caesar was "ambitious," pointing out that 1) Caesar was a faithful and loyal friend, 2) he won victories and used his efforts to promote the good of Rome by filling the country's treasury with ransoms, 3) he was attuned to the needs of his people and "cried" when "the poor wept" and 4) he refused to be crowned king when offered a crown.

Claiming that "ambition should be made of sterner stuff," Anthony uses these *Counter Examples* to significantly undermine Brutus' argument that Caesar's killing was justified by his ambition and to support the *Meta Frame* that Brutus may not be as "honorable" as he says he is, drawing is character into question.

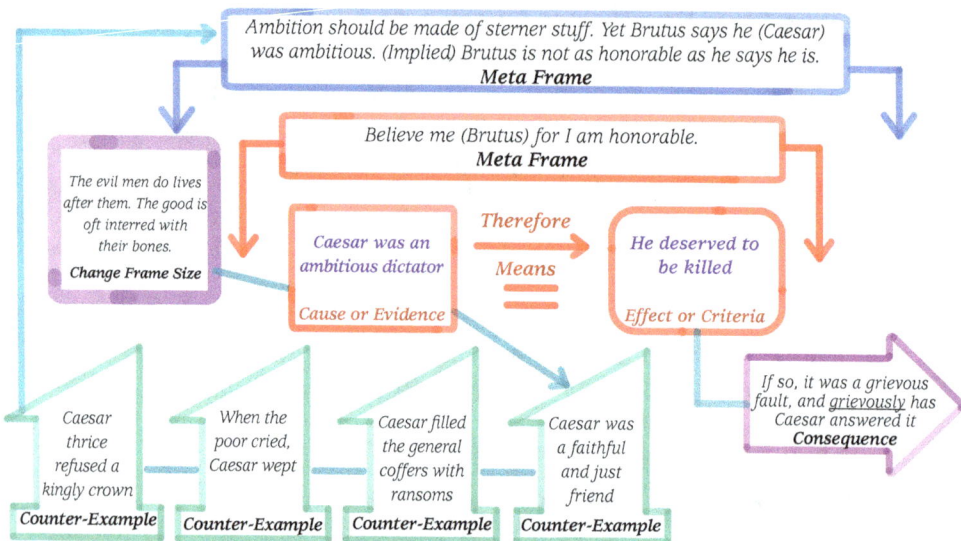

Antony continues his oration with the following words.

> *I speak not to disprove what Brutus spoke, but I am here to speak what I do know. You all did love him once, not without cause: What cause withholds you then to mourn for him? O judgment! thou art fled to brutish beasts, and men have lost their reason. Bear with me; My heart is in the coffin there with Caesar, And I must pause till it come back to me.*

With these words, Antony brings more pathos (emotion) into his speech. He once again uses the pattern of *Another Outcome* when he says, "I speak not to disprove what Brutus spoke, but I am here to speak what I do know" in order to deflect what would be natural skepticism regarding his intent. Antony then *Changes Frame Size*, this time to include a longer-term past. This brings up another *Counter Example* to Brutus' claim about Caesar's character. He points out, "You all did love him once, not without cause." As a *Consequence* of this, he then asks, "What cause stops you from mourning for him?"

In an apparent emotional outburst, Antony next *Chunks Up* and sets a type of *Meta Frame* claiming, "O judgment! thou art fled to brutish beasts, and men have lost their reason." While Antony does not explicitly name Brutus and his co-conspirators, he is clearly implying that Caesar has been treated unjustly. As Antony reflects on Caesar's death and the injustice that nobody will be blamed for it, he seemingly becomes overwhelmed with emotion and deliberately pauses and *Changes Frame Size* back to the immediate moment ("My heart is in the coffin there with Caesar, And I must pause till it come back to me").

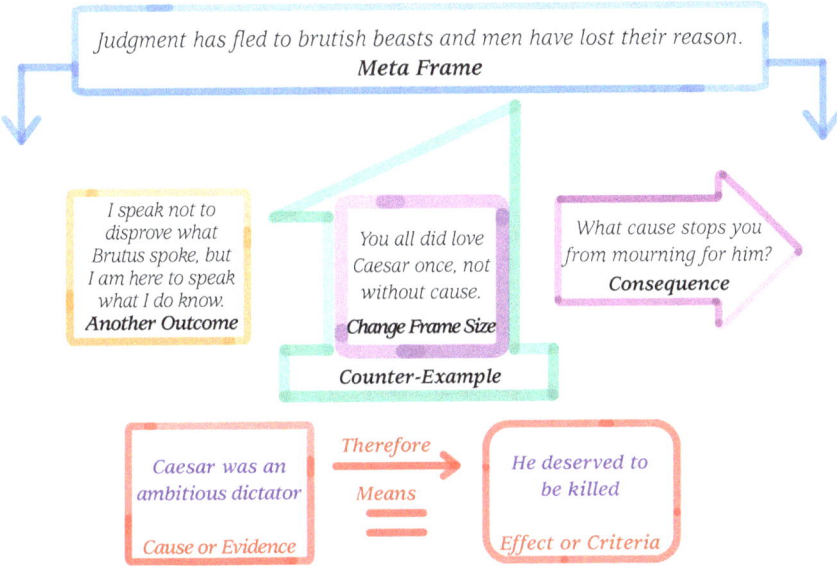

By this time, there has been a shift in the emotions and mood of the crowd, and they begin to question the motives of the conspirators. Antony then continues in the following way.

> But yesterday the word of Caesar might have stood against the world; now he lies there. O masters, if I were disposed to stir your hearts and minds to mutiny and rage, I should do Brutus wrong, and Cassius wrong, who, you all know are honorable men: I will not do them wrong; I rather choose to wrong the dead, to wrong myself and you, than I will wrong such honorable men.

Antony again *Changes Frame Size* to the past to bring up a *Counter Example* to Brutus' claim about Caesar's character, asserting that "but yesterday the word of Caesar might have stood against the world." In his next statements, Antony makes a creative use of *Intention*, *Consequence* and *Another Outcome*. He claims that if he had the *Intent* to stir the crowd's "hearts and minds to mutiny and rage" it would have the *Consequence* of doing Brutus and the others who killed Caesar "wrong." He then, however, uses *Another Outcome* to claim that he will instead wrong "the dead" (an interesting *Chunk Up* from Caesar as an individual), himself and the crowd.

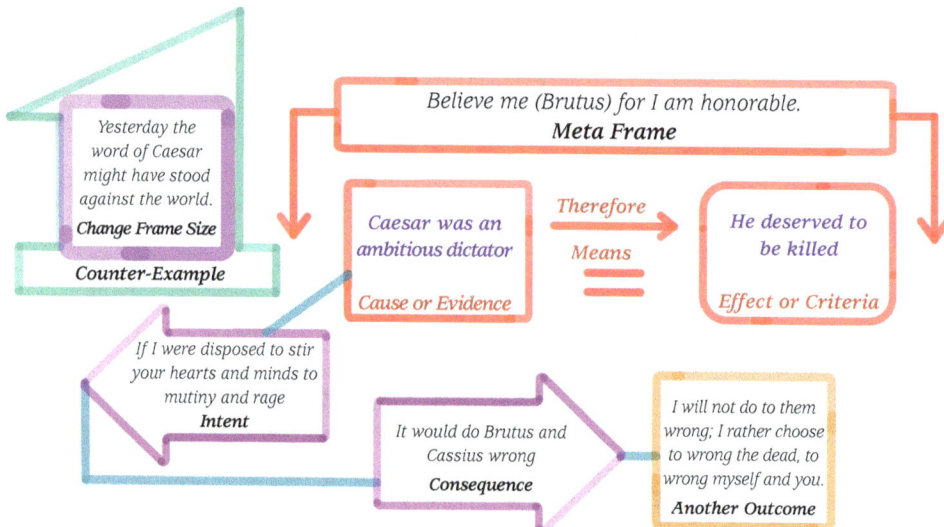

Despite his claim that his Intent is not to "stir up" the crowd, Antony proceeds in the following way.

> But here's a parchment with the seal of Caesar; I found it in his closet, 'tis his will: Let but the commons hear this testament – which, pardon me, I do not mean to read – and they would go and kiss dead Caesar's wounds and dip their napkins in his sacred blood, Yea, beg a hair of him for memory, and, dying, mention it in their wills, bequeathing it as rich legacy unto their issue.

Antony claims to have found Caesar's will, hinting that it is a major *Counter Example* to Brutus' assertion that Caesar was an ambitious dictator. Following the strategy, he has established with his previous comments, Antony claims he has no *Intent* to read the will, but says the *Consequence* would be that the crowd would not only mourn for Caesar but feel deeply grateful for him. He *Chunks Down* the *Consequence* down saying that they would "kiss dead Caesar's wounds and dip their napkins in his sacred blood." He then *Changes Frame Size* to the future, talking about how people would "beg a hair of him for memory, and, dying, mention it in their wills, bequeathing it as rich legacy unto their issue."

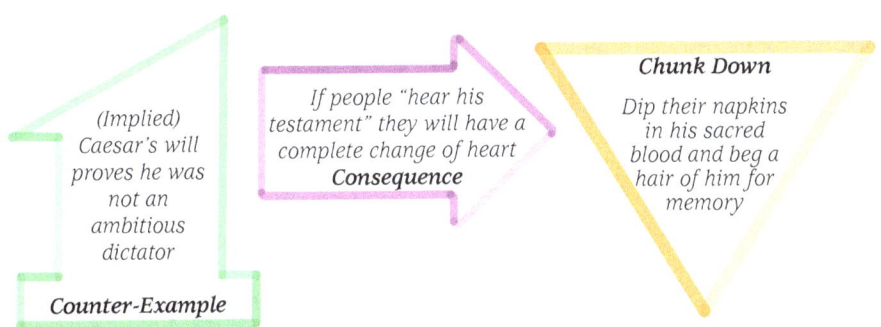

It is important to note that shifting to such a level of concrete detail and using words such as "kissing Caesar's wounds," "dipping napkins in his sacred blood," "begging a hair of him for memory," etc., activate a whole different part of the nervous system than relatively abstract and vague terms such as "ambition." Antony has brought the situation to a much more immediate and personal level. The crowd, of course, begs Antony to read the will, but he refuses.

> *Have patience, gentle friends; I must not read it. It is not meet you know how Caesar loved you. You are not wood, you are not stones, but men; and, being men, hearing the will of Caesar, it will inflame you, it will make you mad. 'Tis good you know not that you are his heirs; for, if you should, O, what would come of it?*

Antony tells the crowd to "have patience," addressing them as "friends" (the Hierarchy he established at the beginning of his speech). He expresses the *Consequence* that "hearing the will of Caesar, it will inflame you, it will make you mad." He then sets a type of contradictory *Meta Frame*, claiming that it is "good you know not that you are his heirs." In doing so, he reveals that the people of Rome are, in fact, Caesar's heirs.

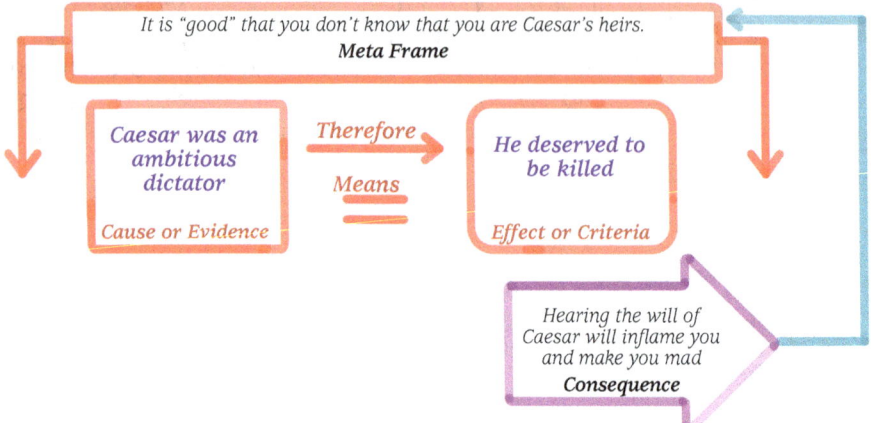

The crowd, increasingly agitated, calls the conspirators "traitors" and demands that Antony read out the will.

> *You will compel me, then, to read the will? Then make a ring about the corpse of Caesar, And let me show you him that made the will… Look, in this place ran Cassius' dagger through: See what a rent the envious Casca made: Through this the well-beloved Brutus stabbed; And as he plucked his cursed steel away, mark how the blood of Caesar followed it …*

Antony's question, "You will compel me, then, to read the will?" is a sophisticated way of validating his *Intent* to simply "bury Caesar" and not "disprove what Brutus spoke." The implication is that the crowd is compelling him to do it against his will (though this, of course, is precisely what he has been inciting them to demand). Instead of reading the will immediately, however, Antony *Chunks Down* again and focuses the crowd's attention on Caesar's body, pointing out his wounds, stressing the conspirators' betrayal of a man who trusted them, in particular the betrayal of Brutus (again challenging Brutus' claim of being an "honorable man"). He then continues.

I come not, friends, to steal away your hearts: I am no orator, as Brutus is; But, as you know me all, a plain blunt man, that love my friend; and that they know full well that gave me public leave to speak of him: For I have neither wit, nor words, nor worth, action, nor utterance, nor the power of speech, to stir men's blood: I only speak right on; I tell you that which you yourselves do know; show you sweet Caesar's wounds, poor poor dumb mouths, and bid them speak for me: But were I Brutus, and Brutus Antony, there were an Antony would ruffle up your spirits and put a tongue in every wound of Caesar that should move the stones of Rome to rise and mutiny.

Antony once again uses *Another Outcome/Intent* to deny that he is trying to agitate the crowd ("I come not, friends, to steal away your hearts"). He then sets another *Meta Frame*, claiming that he is "no orator, as Brutus is" but is rather "a plain, blunt man" that loves his friend, and that Caesar's killers knew this when they let him speak at the funeral. He makes an *Analogy* that Caesar's wounds are "poor dumb mouths" and dramatically asserts the *Consequence* that, if he were as eloquent as Brutus and to give a voice to each of those wounds, it would "move the stones of Rome to rise and mutiny."

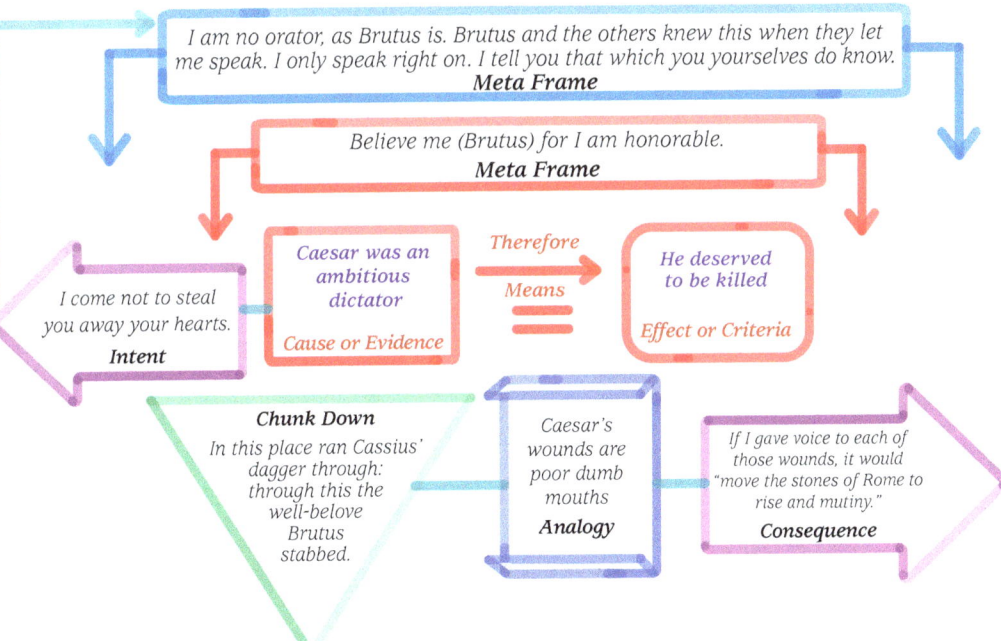

Sleight of Mouth

Antony then reveals Caesar's will.

> *Here is the will, and under Caesar's seal. To every Roman citizen he gives, to every several man, seventy-five drachmas... Moreover, he hath left you all his walks, his private arbors and new-planted orchards, on this side Tiber; he hath left them you, and to your heirs for ever, common pleasures, to walk abroad, and recreate yourselves. Here was a Caesar, when comes such another?*

Caesar's will presents a final clear *Counter Example* to Brutus' claim that Caesar was an ambitious dictator and deserved to be killed. Antony ends his speech by *Changing Frame Size* to include the crowd and their "heirs forever," concluding, "Here was a Caesar, when comes such another?"

At this point the crowd begins to do what Antony has actually intended all along, to riot and search out the assassins with the intention of killing them as Antony says to himself, "Now let it work. Mischief, thou art afoot; take thou what course thou wilt."

Reflections on Antony's Sleight of Mouth Strategy

A key part of Antony's strategy is to use the Sleight of Mouth patterns of *Another Outcome* and *Intent* to (paradoxically) suggest particular outcomes by denying that he wants them (i.e., praising Caesar, disproving Brutus, stirring the crowd's hearts and minds to rage, wronging the conspirators, reading Caesar's will, stealing away the crowd's hearts). As I pointed out in chapter 2, using negation brings attention to something because it names it. Antony consistently uses negation (e.g., "I have come *not to*...") in order to simultaneously deny something on one level and bring attention to it at another level.

Praise Caesar and Disprove Brutus **Intent** **Another Outcome**	*Stir people's hearts and minds to rage* **Intent** **Another Outcome**	*Read Caesar's will* **Intent** **Another Outcome**	*Steal away people's hearts* **Intent** **Another Outcome**

Antony then frequently *Changes Frame Size* in order to introduce some type of *Counter Example* to Brutus' claim that Caesar was an ambitious dictator who deserved to be killed (i.e., Caesar did many good things; people loved him; what he said was respected throughout the world).

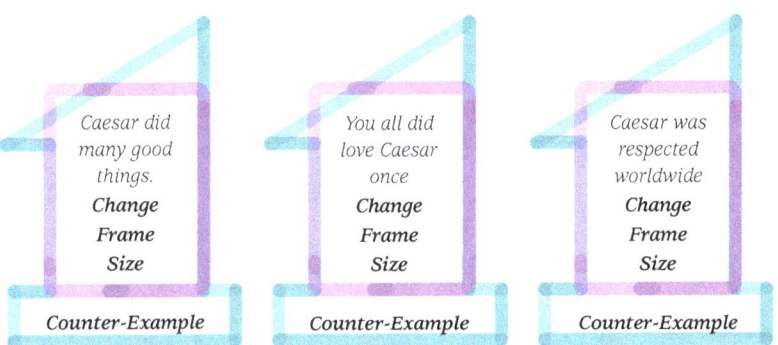

Antony uses these *Counter Examples* to build a series of *Meta Frames* (i.e., Brutus is not as honorable as he said he was; people have lost their reason; they don't know they are Caesar's heirs; unlike Brutus, Antony is no "orator" and is simply speaking straight and telling people what they already know).

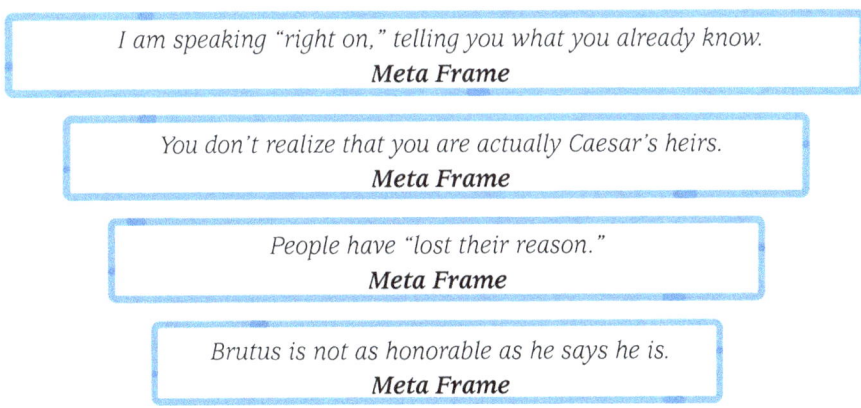

Antony uses the *Counter Examples* and *Meta Frames* to suggest and foster an escalating sequence of *Consequences* (i.e., "wronging" the co-conspirators; mourning and appreciating Caesar; inflaming and making people mad); the ultimate *Consequence* being to incite people to rise up and mutiny.

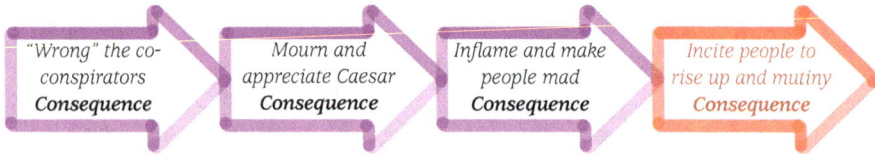

Antony periodically uses *Chunk Down* to bring attention to specifics in order to create a more personal and emotional connection to what is happening. A first instance is when he claims that, were he to read Caesar's will, people would "kiss dead Caesar's wounds," "dip their napkins in his sacred blood," "beg a hair of him for memory" and "dying, mention it in their wills, bequeathing it as rich legacy unto their issue." Later, before he reads Caesar's will, he has people stand in a circle around his body and examine the wounds made by the assassins, calling them "poor dumb mouths" that need to be spoken for.

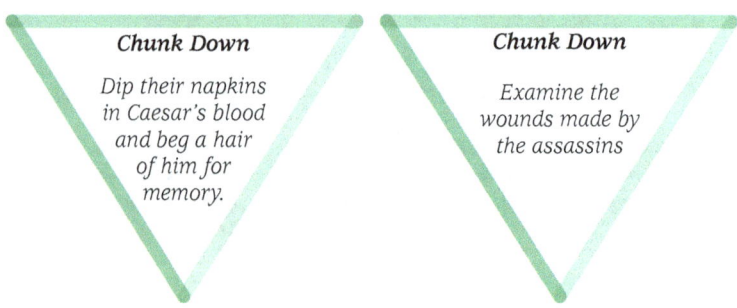

Such language stands in contrast to Brutus' more impersonal, abstract and intellectually based *Hierarchy of Criteria*.

Summary of Antony's Sleight of Mouth Strategy

We can map out Antony's overall Sleight of Mouth strategy with the following diagram.

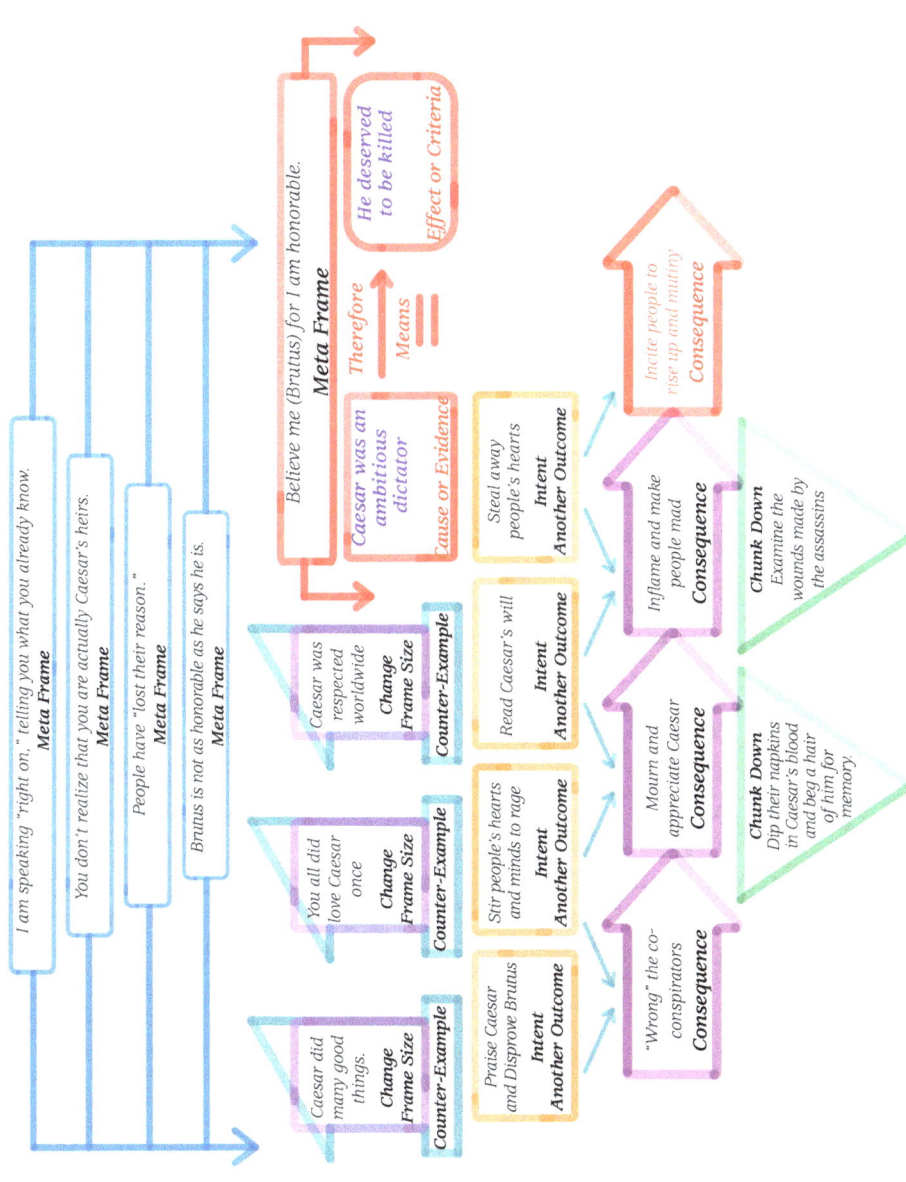

Antony applies a complex mix of "Sleight of Mouth" patterns to change the perception of reality for his Roman audience. He Chunks Down to show Caesar's wounds and uses Analogy to compare them to mouths crying for justice. He uses several Counter Examples to demonstrate that Caesar was not an ambitious dictator... and he evokes the Consequence of rage and mutiny, even though he says that is not what he wants.

By applying this Sleight of Mouth strategy, Antony completely flips his audience's perception of reality. Similar to the way a skilled card magician can use sleight of hand to transform a king into a jester and the two of spades into the ace of hearts, Antony has, through his words, transformed his audience's perception of Brutus from being an "honorable man" into a being a traitor, and their perception of Caesar has shifted from being an "ambitious dictator" into a generous benefactor.

Applying Antony's Sleight of Mouth Strategy to Flip Perceptions of Reality

Similar to the example of Lincoln, we can filter out a number of the specific references related to the particular content and context of Antony's remarks and summarize the essence of Antony's strategy for flipping perceptions of reality with the following structure:

1. State the limiting belief to be "flipped."
2. Clarify the belief about the source of the limiting belief and what makes it credible.
3. Shifting to a larger or smaller frame (time, place, people, etc.), find three potential Counter Examples to the limiting belief.
4. Use the *Counter Examples* to suggest a belief that challenges the validity/universality of the source of the limiting belief and its credibility.
5. Identify a consequence of that challenge that calls the limiting belief into question.
6. Bring up a specific example of that consequence.
7. Use that to suggest a further consequence that is the opposite of ("flips") what the limiting belief claims.

Once again, this is a strategy can be applied to practically any limiting belief. The following are examples of how it can be applied it to a couple of the limiting belief examples we have used earlier in this book.

1. Limiting belief to be "flipped": *If I speak, people will laugh at me.*

2. Belief about the source of the limiting belief and what makes it credible: *I believe this because I have experienced it many times.*

3. Three potential *Counter Examples* to the limiting belief: *(a) Your parents were excited when you first spoke, (b) The waiter does not laugh when you order, (c) Caring people would not laugh.*

4. A belief, based on the *Counter Examples* that challenges the validity/universality of the source of the limiting belief and its credibility: *This belief is likely a result of your own cognitive bias.*

5. A consequence of that challenge that calls the limiting belief into question: *A distorted perception is limiting you.*

6. Bring up a specific example of that consequence: *I am not laughing right now. I am listening.*

7. A further consequence that is the opposite of ("flips") what the limiting belief claims: *There are probably many people interested in what you have to say.*

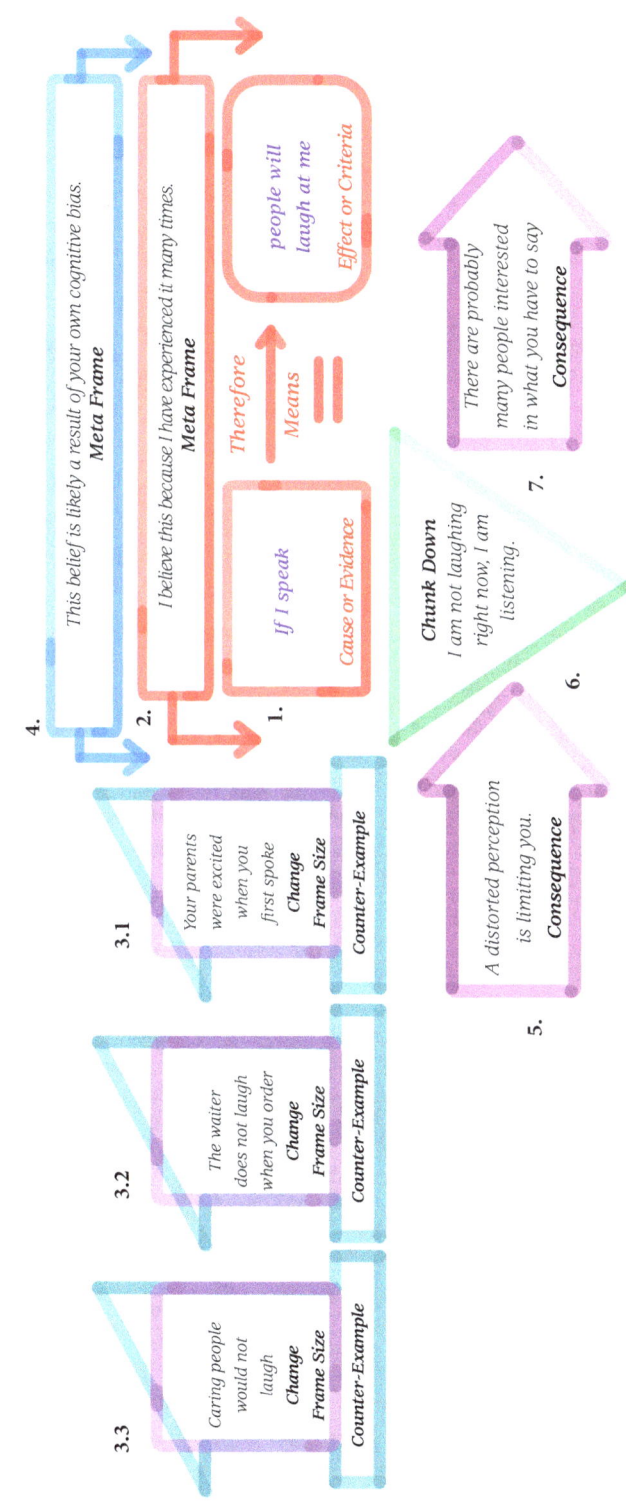

1. Limiting belief to be "flipped": *No matter what I do I will never get enough.*

2. Belief about the source of the limiting belief and what makes it credible: *I believe this because I feel dissatisfied much of the time.*

3. Three potential *Counter Examples* to the limiting belief: *(a) You breathe enough air to live, (b) You have learned enough language to communicate, (c) You have taken good enough care of yourself to survive.*

4. A belief, based on the *Counter Examples* that challenges the validity/universality of the source of the limiting belief and its credibility: *This belief is focused on a small part of your existence.*

5. A consequence of that challenge that calls the limiting belief into question: *There are many places where you have enough or more than others.*

6. Bring up a specific example of that consequence: *The fact that you have any X is probably more than most.*

7. A further consequence that is the opposite of ("flips") what the limiting belief claims: *You have a lot to feel grateful for.*

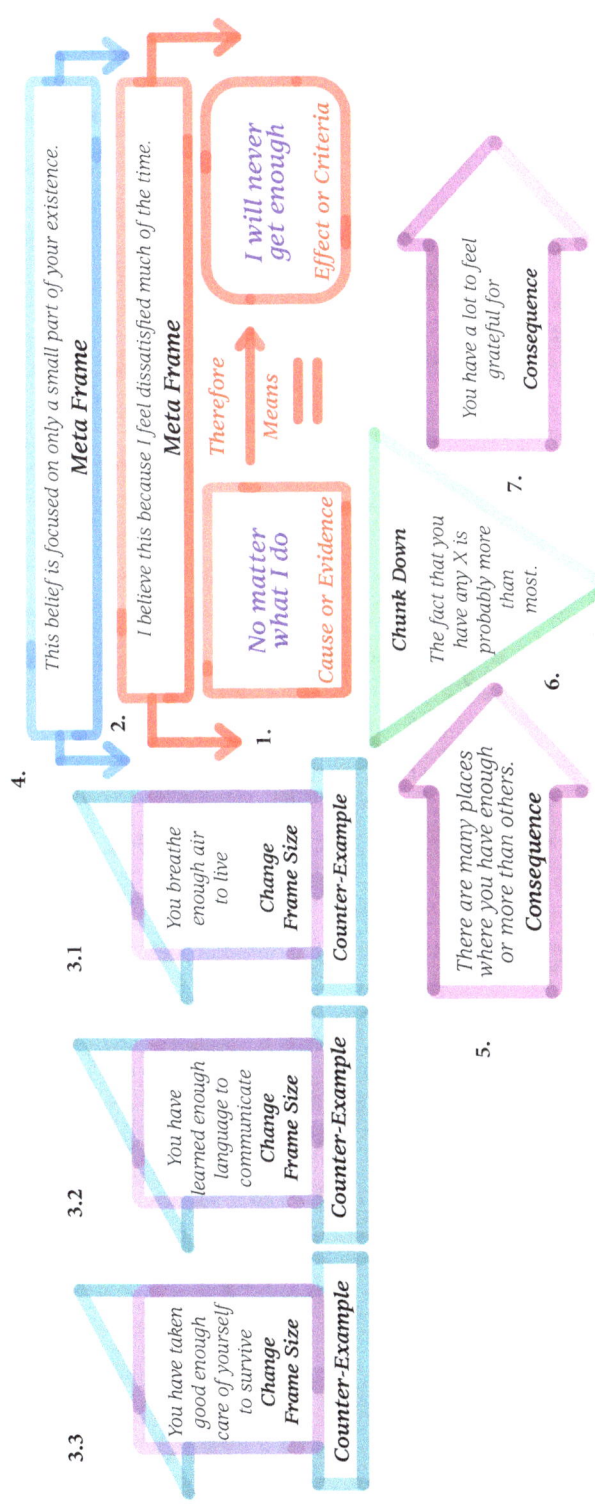

As with the previous examples, practice this strategy by exploring how you could flip the perception of a limiting belief by answering the following questions and filling in the diagram below:

1. *What is the limiting belief to be "flipped?"*

2. *What is the belief about the source of the limiting belief and what makes it credible?*

3. *Shifting to a larger or smaller frame (time, place, people, etc.), what are three potential counterexamples to the limiting belief?*

4. *What belief do these counterexamples suggest that challenges the validity/universality of the source of the limiting belief and its credibility?*

5. *What is a consequence of that challenge that calls the limiting belief into question?*

6. *What is a specific example of that consequence?*

7. *What is a further consequence that is the opposite of ("flips") what the limiting belief suggests?*

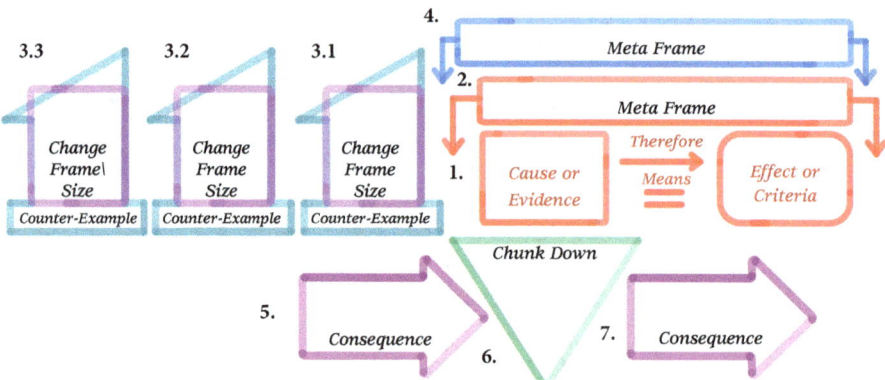

William Shakespeare's Henry V – The Power of "Outframing" with Sleight of Mouth to Inspire Fervent Motivation

Still another application of Sleight of Mouth is illustrated by William Shakespeare in his play *Henry V*. The scene in question is set at the beginning of the *Battle of Agincourt*, which took place in northern France on October 25th, 1415 (the feast day of the Christian saint Crispin). The English soldiers, led by Henry V, are fatigued, depleted, and significantly outnumbered by their French opponents. While Henry's forces consist of around 6,000 men, the size of the French army is estimated at around 30,000. This means that the English are essentially outnumbered five to one. They are essentially in a double bind. They will be defeated if they fight, and they will also suffer defeat and potentially death if they surrender.

In the play, the dire situation prompts one of Henry's commanding officers (the Earl of Westmoreland) to wish that they had the support of some of their English countrymen who are at home celebrating the holiday. He exclaims, "O that we now had here but one ten thousand of those men in England that do no work today!" The underlying belief expressed by this comment and the reactions of the other soldiers contemplating their fate in the dire situation is that "because we are outnumbered five to one, we will be defeated and killed."

Like Mark Antony's speech in *Julius Caesar*, Shakespeare's depiction of Henry V's response to his troop's legitimate concerns is fictional yet captures another iconic use of Sleight of Mouth. As a military leader, Henry needs to motivate his men to risk their lives and face "fearful odds" that will mean certain death for some of them. This is not an abstract intellectual issue. It is probably the biggest and most intense life decision that most of them have experienced. Henry begins his remarks in the following manner, speaking loudly enough that all around him can hear.

> *What's he that wishes so? My cousin Westmoreland? No, my fair cousin; if we are marked to die, we are enough to do our country loss; and if to live, the fewer men, the greater share of honor. God's will! I pray thee, wish not one man more. Rather proclaim it, Westmoreland, through my host, that he which hath no stomach to this fight, let him depart; his passport shall be made, and crowns for convoy put into his purse. We would not die in that man's company that fears his fellowship to die with us.*

Henry begins by setting the *Meta Frame* that "if we are marked to die, we are enough to do our country loss." The implication of being "marked to die" is that there is some larger power/influence that is at work in the situation that is independent of the "fearful odds." If one is not marked to die, then he will somehow survive no matter how fierce the fighting. If he is marked to die, then that is his fate regardless of the circumstances. The implication of the *Consequence* that "if to live, the fewer men, the greater share of honor" is that, rather than being problem, their smaller number is actually potentially something positive. Henry also invokes the value of "honor," which shifts attention from individual safety and survival to the acknowledgment of service and contribution to a larger collective.

Henry also does a very creative and powerful type of *Apply to Self* when he proclaims that any of the soldiers that "hath no stomach to this fight" can freely leave – asserting that those who are willing to risk their lives in service of the their larger collective do not want to "die in that man's company" who is not willing to "die with us." Not only will those persons who are unwilling to share their fate with others be given permission to return to England (their passport shall be made), their travel expenses will be paid (crowns for convey put into their purse). Combined with his statement to "wish not one man more," Henry is moving focus to a powerful felt sense of collective identity ("We" and "Us").

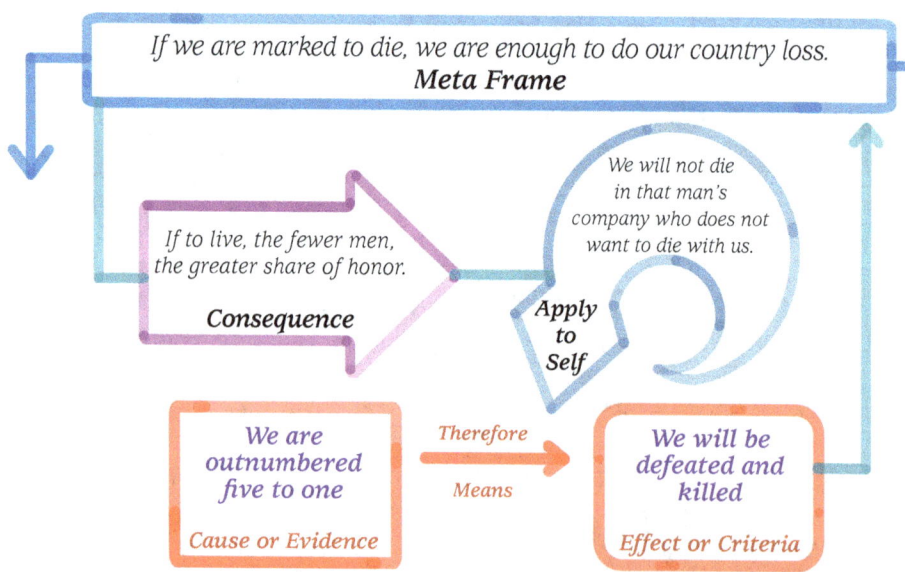

Henry then proceeds to make a case for why staying and taking the risk to die is actually deeply desirable.

> *This day is called the feast of Crispian. He that outlives this day, and comes safe home, will stand a tip-toe when this day is named, and rouse him at the name of Crispian. He that shall live this day, and see old age, will yearly on the vigil feast his neighbors, and say "Tomorrow is Saint Crispian." Then will he strip his sleeve and show his scars, and say "These wounds I had on Crispian's day." Old men forget; yet all shall be forgot, but he'll remember, with advantages, what feats he did that day. Then shall our names, familiar in his mouth as household words – Harry the King, Bedford and Exeter, Warwick and Talbot, Salisbury and Gloucester – be in their flowing cups freshly remembered. This story shall the good man teach his son; and Crispin Crispian shall never go by, from this day to the ending of the world, but we in it shall be remembered – we few, we happy few, we band of brothers. For he today that sheds his blood with me shall be my brother; be he never so vile, this day shall gentle his condition. And gentlemen in England now-a-bed shall think themselves accursed they were not here, and hold their manhoods cheap whiles any speaks that fought with us upon Saint Crispian's day.*

Henry makes a dramatic shift from a "problem frame" to an "outcome frame" by *Changing Frame Size* along the dimension of time to far beyond the immanent battle, saying, "He that outlives this day, and comes safe home, will stand a tip-toe when this day is named." The implication is that all men who fight in the battle that day, survive and return safely home afterwards, will feel proud or walk tall ("stand a-tiptoe") whenever St. Crispian's day is mentioned, because it will remind them of their courage and heroism. Henry then *Chunks Down* and puts the listeners into the future frame saying, "He that shall live this day, and see old age, will yearly on the vigil feast his neighbors,… strip his sleeve and show his scars, and say 'These wounds I had on Crispian's day.'" Bringing in this level of detail makes the possibility of not only survival but also of pride and admiration seem more plausible and real.

Henry goes on to point out that, as men grow old, they become more and more forgetful, but that, even if a survivor of the battle remembers nothing else, he'll "remember what feats he did that day," implying that this day and this battle will be special beyond all others in that person's life. He also asserts the *Consequence* that the names of the participants in the battle (whether or not they survive) will be remembered, as familiar as the most common items in every home. The implication is that all participants in the battle will become famous and that "a good man" will "teach his son" their story, passing it down from generation to generation.

Henry then *Changes Frame Size* to expand it even further when he claims that all the participants will be remembered on the anniversary of the battle "from this day to ending of the world." So, that in addition to being famous, all of the participants will become immortal in a way. Henry follows this by *Redefining* all the participants as brothers, saying, "We few, we happy few, we band of brothers." He makes the Analogy explicit when he states, "For he today that sheds his blood with me shall be my brother." He next asserts the *Consequence* of that being that, no matter how lowly that person is, his participation in the battle with Henry will elevate his status (to that of a type of hero along with the others).

He claims that the ultimate *Consequence* is that, rather than being in a horrible and hopeless situation, what they are doing together is so special, important, and momentous that, instead of being content and happy to be home and safe, those who did not have the opportunity to be with them will "think themselves accursed they were not here."

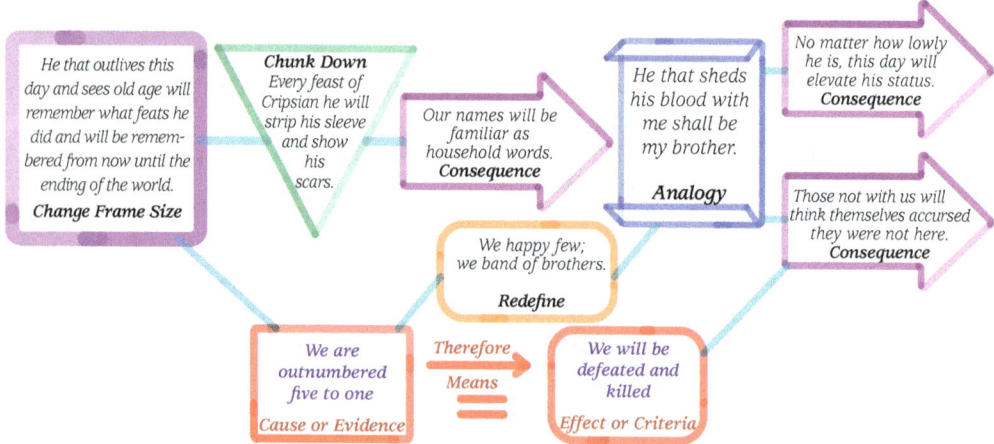

In Shakespeare's play, Henry's speech completely shifts the attitude of his men, and they begin to cheer loudly, not a one deciding to take up the offer to go back home. At that moment, one of Henry's nobles rides up with the news that the French troops are preparing to start their attack and that the English forces need to get ready for battle. Henry replies with the *Meta Frame* that "All things are ready if our minds be so." This reflects the Sleight of Mouth principle that it is our internal map and perception of a situation or event that determines what it means to us and, therefor, our corresponding level of performance. That is, it is our minds, and especially our beliefs, that ultimately determine our actions and their outcomes rather than the outward reality of the situation.

The Earl of Westmoreland, whose lamentation and wish for more men triggered Henry's speech, says to Henry, "Perish the man whose mind is backward now!" A smiling Henry asks, "Thou dost not wish more help from England, coz?" to which Westmoreland passionately cries, "Would you and I alone, without more help, could fight this royal battle!" This clearly reflects a complete change of attitude about the situation. And, both in the play and historically, the English army goes on to achieve a surprising and decisive victory in spite of the numerical superiority of its opponent.

Reflections on Henry's St. Crispian's Day Speech

Shakespeare's depiction of Henry's St. Crispian's day speech is another prime example of why I named the group of patterns presented in this book "Sleight of Mouth." Through the use of language, Henry transforms what initially seems to be a frightening and seemingly hopeless situation into the most valuable, important and meaningful day of his soldier's lives. And this is accomplished using just over three hundred words. That is in many respects "magical." But it also has a structure that can be identified and potentially replicated, in the same way that a card magician who performs an amazing and seemingly inexplicable card trick (i.e., sleight of hand) could describe and teach the steps of the trick to anyone willing to put in the time and effort to develop the requisite knowledge and skill.

In this instance, it is important to note that, unlike Socrates, Lincoln or Mark Antony, Henry makes no attempt to refute the belief that is creating the anxiety and fear. Rather he "outframes" the belief by connecting people to a bigger frame of reference and turns what seems to be something one would want to avoid at all costs into something deeply desirable.

I have long pointed out that courage is not the absence of fear. In fact, if a person doesn't feel any fear, they don't need courage. Courage, then, is the connection to something bigger than fear. This is often the result of *Changing Frame Size*. Henry's use of *Change Frame Size* connects his men to a much bigger and long-term future than their immediate dire circumstances: i.e., their safe return home, their old age and even to "the ending of the world." Instead of staying their comfort zone like the "gentlemen now abed in England," they are being given the opportunity to cross the threshold to a type of hero's journey, where their actions will make a difference and they will be remembered far beyond their own lifespan.

Henry is essentially saying that those who stay and fight with him will have the possibility of honor, heroism, pride, fame, status, intimate camaraderie, and immortality regardless of whether they win or lose, or even whether they live or die. This is quite a compelling *Consequence*. So compelling, that those who are not with them will consider themselves cursed.

It is important and intriguing to note that not once did Henry say anything negative or disparaging about their French opponents in order to accomplish the remarkable turnabout of attitude. His focus is entirely toward longer-term future positives, while still acknowledging the real danger of the immediate situation. This is power of *outframing*.

Once again, by filtering out the details related to the particular situation and its contents, we can outline the deeper structure of Henry's Sleight of Mouth strategy with the following steps.

1. Identify the limiting belief to be outframed.

2. State a belief about the limiting belief that brings out something potentially positive.

3. Bring up a bigger frame of reference than the one indicated by the limiting belief statement that could greatly enhance the potential positive.

4. Describe a specific instance/example of that enhanced positive.

5. Point out a beneficial Consequence of that enhanced positive.

6. Assert an adverse Consequence of not having the enhanced positive.

The following is an example of how this outframing strategy can be applied to one of the limiting beliefs we have been using as a reference throughout the book.

1. Limiting belief to be outframed: *If I speak people will laugh at me.*

2. A belief about the limiting belief that brings out something potentially positive: *Most of the world's greatest leaders and innovators were laughed at when they first spoke out.*

3. A bigger frame of reference than the one indicated by the limiting belief statement that could greatly enhance the potential positive: *Looking back from the future, being honored for having spoken out and remembering being laughed at in the past.*

4. A specific instance/example of that enhanced positive: *Feeling proud and vindicated. Getting the "last laugh."*

5. A beneficial Consequence of that enhanced positive: *Having been laughed at for speaking is a prerequisite for success.*

6. An adverse Consequence of not having the enhanced positive: *Those who have never been laughed at for speaking have missed a key growth opportunity.*

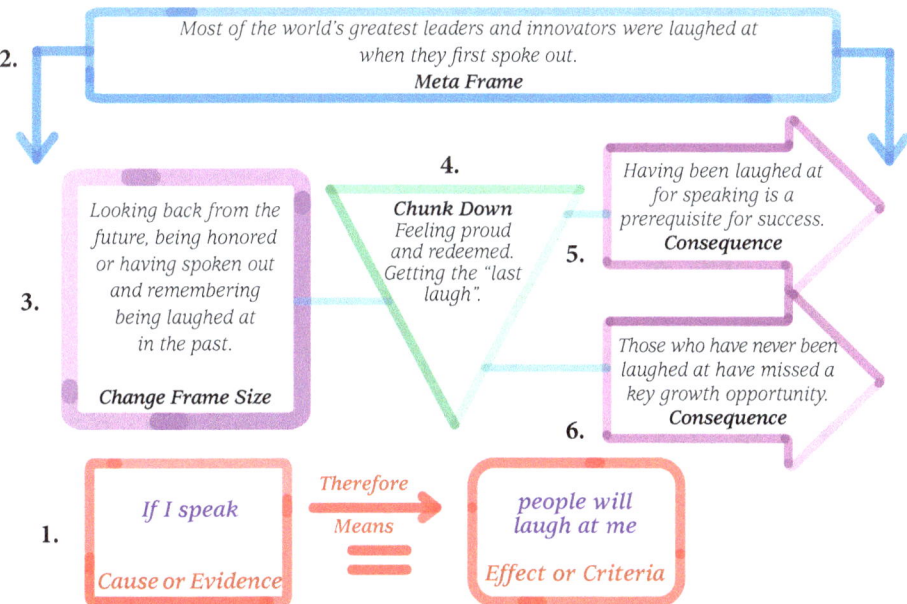

Try outframing a limiting belief yourself using Henry V's strategy. Fill in the diagram below by answering the questions:

1. *What is the limiting belief to be outframed?*
2. *What is a belief about the limiting belief that brings out something potentially positive?*
3. *What is a bigger frame of reference than that indicated by the belief statement that could greatly enhance the potential positive?*
4. *What would be a specific instance/example of that enhanced positive?*
5. *What is a beneficial consequence of that enhanced positive?*
6. *What is an adverse consequence of not having the enhanced positive?*

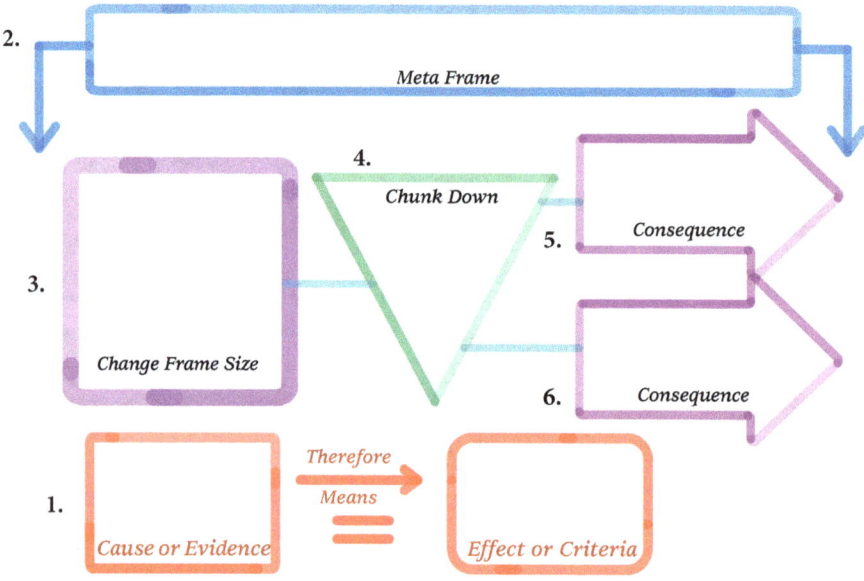

Dwight Eisenhower's D-Day Message to his Troops on June 6, 1944 – Pre-Framing a Deeper Connection to Create Confidence

While Shakespeare's account of Henry V's Saint Crispian's day speech is clearly fictional, we can also feel that it is entirely plausible. In fact, it is interesting to compare the structure of the speech to General Dwight Eisenhower's message to the allied troops on the eve of the D-Day invasion of Normandy.

June 6, 1944, is perhaps one of the most decisive days in the last century. Known as D-Day, it is the day that the allied troops invaded the beaches of Normandy, France during the Second World War. The allied invasion force faced a 2,400-mile fortification of bunkers and landmines, plus beach and water obstacles. Storming the beaches was clearly a difficult and risky operation and many casualties were anticipated. In fact, according to some estimates, more than 4,000 Allied troops lost their lives in the D-Day invasion, with thousands more wounded or missing. In this sense, though on a different scale, the situation was not so different from the one facing Henry and his army at Agincourt.

American General Dwight Eisenhower was in charge of the allied invading forces and well aware of the risks and potential for disaster. The following message was his printed *Order of the Day* (and also a recorded speech), which was distributed to the 175,000-member allied force on the eve of the invasion of the Normandy beaches. Even though it was a situation and a world which Shakespeare could never have consciously envisioned, there are interesting parallels to Henry V's St. Crispian's day speech.

> *Soldiers, Sailors, and Airmen of the Allied Expeditionary Force!*
>
> *You are about to embark upon the Great Crusade, toward which we have striven these many months. The eyes of the world are upon you. The hopes and prayers of liberty-loving people everywhere march with you. In company with our brave Allies and brothers-in-arms on other Fronts, you will bring about the destruction of the German war machine, the elimination of Nazi tyranny over the oppressed peoples of Europe, and security for ourselves in a free world.*
>
> *Your task will not be an easy one. Your enemy is well-trained, well-equipped and battle-hardened. He will fight savagely.*
>
> *But this is the year 1944! Much has happened since the Nazi triumphs of 1940-41. The United Nations have inflicted upon the Germans great defeats, in open battle, man-to-man. Our air offensive has seriously reduced their strength in the air and their capacity to wage war on the ground. Our Home Fronts have given us an overwhelming superiority in weapons and munitions of war, and placed at our disposal great reserves of trained fighting men. The tide has turned! The free men of the world are marching together to Victory!*
>
> *I have full confidence in your courage, devotion to duty and skill in battle. We will accept nothing less than full Victory!*
>
> *Good luck! And let us all beseech the blessing of Almighty God upon this great and noble undertaking.*

As a key part of the message, Eisenhower states the belief that he knew most of the 175,000 soldiers, sailors and airmen were grappling with: "The enemy is well-trained, well-equipped and battle-hardened and will fight savagely." Therefore, the allied forces' task "will not be an easy one."

Before stating this belief directly, however, Eisenhower does what is known as "pre-framing" in Sleight of Mouth. *Pre-framing* involves "setting the stage" or establishing the context within which some other message will be interpreted. In this case, Eisenhower has already *Changed Frame Size* to a much larger scope before bringing attention to the challenging situation addressed by the belief statement. Instead of extending the frame along the dimension of time into the future as Henry V did, however, Eisenhower expands the frame to include a larger present. He uses the *Analogy* of a "Great Crusade" and claims, "The eyes of the world are upon you," and "The hopes and prayers of liberty-loving people everywhere march with you." In his pre-framing remarks, Eisenhower also *Redefines* "the Allies" as "brothers in arms" (echoing Henry V's "band of brothers") while using the *Analogy* of a "war machine" to Redefine "the enemy." This sets up an interesting contrast and contest at the identity level between caring humans (brothers in arms) versus something that is brutal and mechanical (a war machine). Eisenhower has also *Chunked Up* the "task" of the allied forces to be nothing less than the higher purpose of achieving "the elimination of Nazi tyranny over the oppressed peoples of Europe, and security for ourselves in a free world."

Immediately after stating the belief about the difficult, risky and dangerous task ahead, Eisenhower presents a series of *Counter Examples* to the superiority of the German forces: 1) The United Nations have inflicted great defeats upon the Germans; 2) the allied air offensive has seriously reduced the German's strength in the air and their capacity to wage war on the ground; 3) the allies have an overwhelming superiority in weapons and munitions, and great reserves of trained fighting men. As *Consequences* of these *Counter Examples*, Eisenhower asserts, "The tide has turned. The free men of the world are marching together to Victory!" and that "We will accept nothing less than full Victory!"

Eisenhower ends by establishing a type of *Meta Frame* around the anticipated challenges of the situation when he says, "let us all beseech the blessing of Almighty God upon this great and noble undertaking." By invoking the blessing of "Almighty God" and calling their task a "great and noble undertaking," Eisenhower is connecting people to a purpose beyond their individual identities. His references to a Crusade, the blessing of Almighty God and the notion of a great and a noble undertaking invoke the sense that it is as much of a spiritual undertaking as it is a human one.

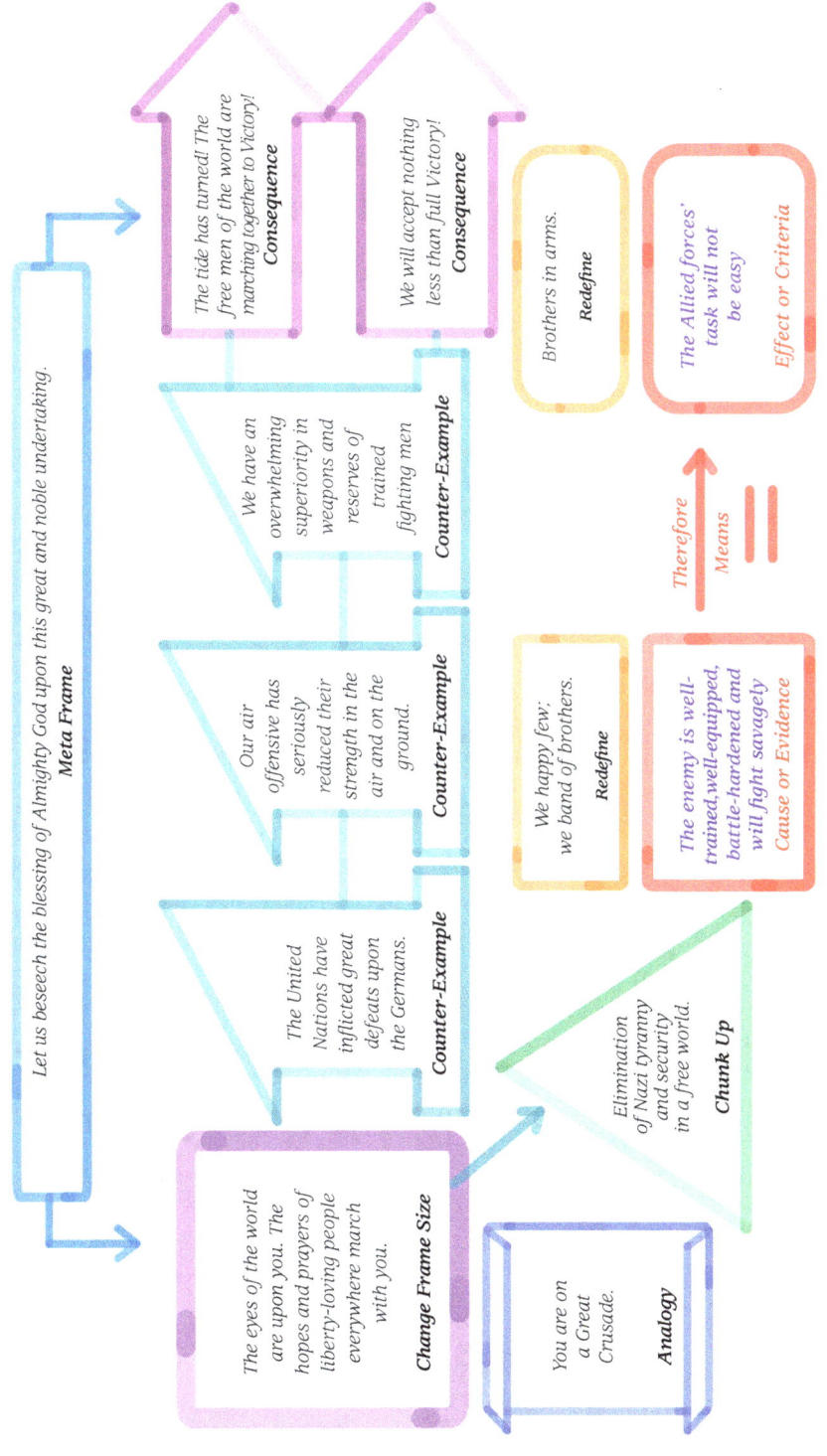

Reflections on Eisenhower's D-Day Message

The purpose of Eisenhower's message, which is just under 250 words, is to acknowledge the fears and concerns that his soldiers, sailors, and airmen would naturally feel as individuals and to connect them to a larger purpose that outframes those fears and concerns. Rather than immediately state the fears and then attempt to reframe them or outframe them, Eisenhower's pre-framing involves setting up a series of frames ahead of time that already begin to determine the way in which the belief statement and the situation it relates to will be perceived.

Obviously, both Henry V and Eisenhower seek to connect the individuals in their armies to something bigger than their fear of potential death and defeat. Henry appeals to personal ambition and collective identity (which would be more *ego* related motivations); i.e., "He will show his scars and remember the feats he did; our names will be as familiar as household words; we will be remembered from now until the ending of the world." Eisenhower does something similar when he talks about achieving "security for ourselves in a free world." However, he puts primary focus on the contribution to a higher purpose and vision (which would be more *soul* related motivations); i.e., the "elimination of Nazi tyranny over the oppressed peoples of Europe," which he calls "a Great Crusade" and a "noble undertaking."

It is interesting to note that Eisenhower uses an "away from" statement (the destruction of the German war machine and the elimination of Nazi tyranny over the oppressed peoples of Europe) followed by a "toward" one (security for ourselves in a free world). This helps to establish and support an overall "outcome frame," similar to Martin Luther King Jr.'s "I have a Dream" speech discussed in Chapter 2.

Eisenhower also brings attention to the character of the individuals of his fighting forces when he says. "I have full confidence in your courage, devotion to duty and skill in battle." (As a personal side note, one of my uncles was an infantryman with the American forces on Omaha Beach in Normandy on D-Day, and his account of what happened and what they had to do validates Eisenhower's confidence in their character and the effectiveness of his message.)

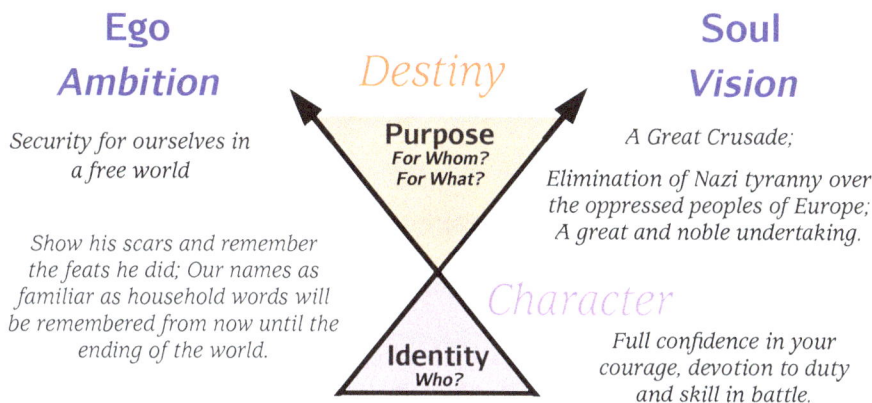

Henry appeals to personal ambition and collective identity
while Eisenhower emphasizes character and contribution to a higher purpose and vision.

As with the previous examples, we can filter out the details related to the particular situation and its contents to arrive at the deeper structure of Eisenhower's strategy for pre-framing a deeper connection.

1. Invoking a larger frame of reference that connects to something deeper than the limiting belief. Eisenhower uses the analogy of "a Great Crusade" to introduce this bigger frame, though it doesn't seem an essential part of the strategy. The crucial thing is to establish a bigger frame size.

2. Generalizing from that larger frame of reference to establish a key outcome to be achieved.

3. Explicitly acknowledging the limiting belief.

4. Identifying three Counter Examples to the limiting belief that are brought to light by the larger frame of reference.

5. Deriving a positive Consequence of these Counter Examples.

6. Expressing a belief about a bigger system that supports that positive Consequence.

The following is an example of how Eisenhower's "pre-framing" strategy can be applied to limiting belief that "*If I speak people will laugh at me,*" that we have been using to illustrate the impact of the various Sleight of Mouth patterns and strategies in this book.

1. Invoking a larger frame of reference that connects to something deeper than the limiting belief: *Our world is in desperate need of people who do not give in to the ridicule of others.*

2. Generalizing from that larger frame of reference to establish a key outcome to be achieved: *Transforming the divisiveness that unnecessarily diminishes people.*

3. Explicitly acknowledging the limiting belief: *If you speak people will laugh at you.*

4. Identifying three Counter Examples to the limiting belief that are brought to light by the larger frame of reference: (a) *I am sure you have faced down ridicule before when something is important enough*, (b) *What you have to say is as important as what anyone else has to say*, (c) *People who laugh at others are hiding their own self-doubt.*

5. Deriving a positive Consequence of these Counter Examples: *You are not alone and there are many others like you who support you.*

6. Expressing a belief about a bigger system that supports that positive Consequence: *You will get support from others that you do not know yet, because what you have to say is so important.*

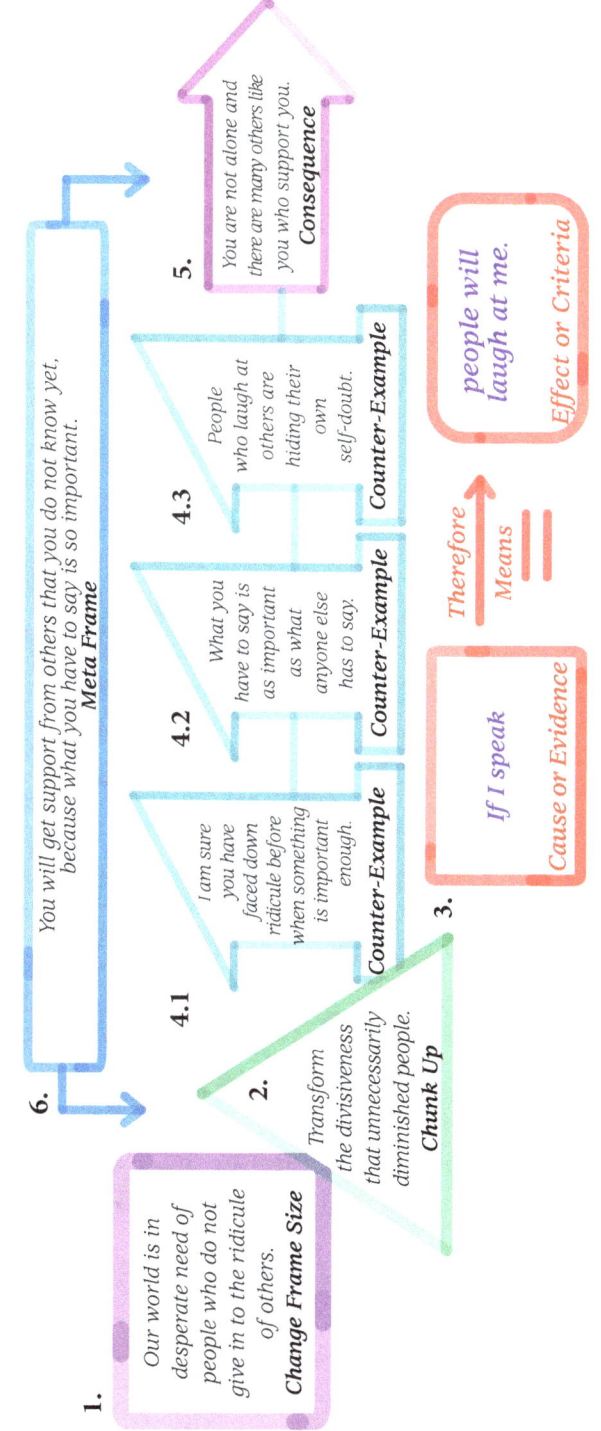

Practice "pre-framing" a particular limiting belief by answering the following questions and filling in the template below.

1. *What is a larger frame of reference that connects to something deeper than the limiting belief?*
2. *Generalizing from that larger frame of reference, what is the key outcome to be achieved?*
3. *What is the limiting belief to be acknowledged?*
4. *What are three Counter Examples to the limiting belief that are brought to light by the larger frame of reference?*
5. *What is a positive Consequence of these Counter Examples?*
6. *What is a belief about a bigger system that supports that positive Consequence?*

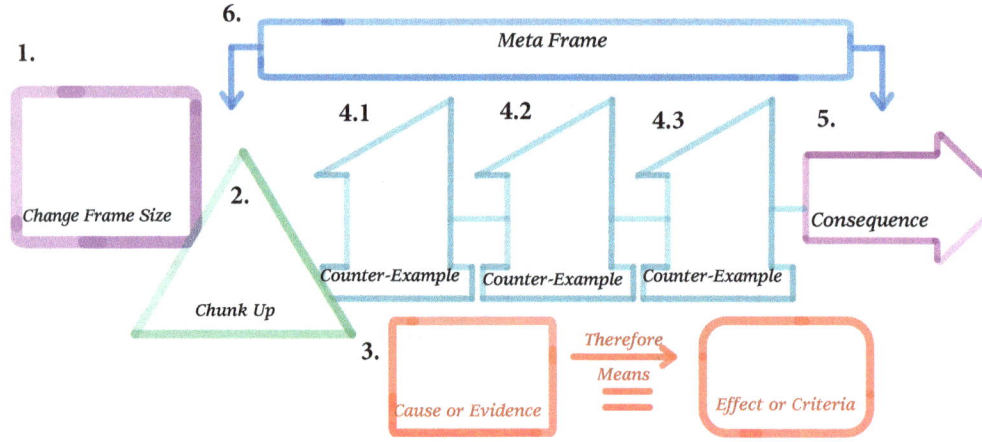

300   Examples of Applying Sleight of Mouth

Gandhi on Passive Resistance and the "Soul Force" – Connecting Beyond Individual Identity

Of course, Sleight of Mouth has not only been used to incite people to mutiny or motivate them into battle. It can also be used to avert war, support positive social change and to promote non-violence, as Martin Luther King, Jr. and Mohandas Gandhi did. In the earlier section on *Hierarchy of Criteria* (p. 158), I referenced Gandhi's awakening to a sense of higher purpose, his development of the principles of passive resistance and his notion of the "soul-force."

The following are excerpts from Gandhi's booklet *Hind Swaraj or Indian Home Rule* (1938 edition) in which he further develops his arguments in favor of passive resistance and the power of the soul-force. Gandhi uses a type of dialog between himself and a skeptic as the vehicle to introduce and refute "rival conjectures" and to reinforce his alternative belief.

> **Why should we not obtain our goal, which is good, by any means whatsoever, even by using violence?**
>
> *Your belief that there is no connection between the means and the end is a great mistake. Through that mistake even men who have been considered religious have committed grievous crimes. Your reasoning is the same as saying that we can get a rose through planting a noxious weed. If I want to cross the ocean, I can do so only by means of a vessel; if I were to use a cart for that purpose, both the cart and I would soon find the bottom… The means may be likened to a seed, the end to a tree; and there is just the same inviolable connection between the means and the end as there is between the seed and the tree. I am not likely to obtain the result flowing from the worship of God by laying myself prostrate before Satan. If, therefore, anyone were to say: "I want to worship God; it does not matter that I do so by means of Satan," it would be set down as ignorant folly. We reap exactly as we sow.*

Gandhi begins by *Meta Framing* the proposition that "it is okay to use violence obtain a goal which is good" as the *belief there is no connection between means and end*. He points out the *Consequence* that "through that mistake even men who have been considered religious have committed grievous crimes." He then uses a series of *Analogies* to graphically illustrate the connection between means and end: trying to grow a rose by planting a noxious weed; trying to cross the ocean in a cart; a seed growing into a tree; and attempting to worship God by prostrating oneself before Satan. He uses these *Analogies* to support the converse *Meta Frame* that there is an intimate connection between means and end using the *Analogy* that "we reap exactly as we sow."

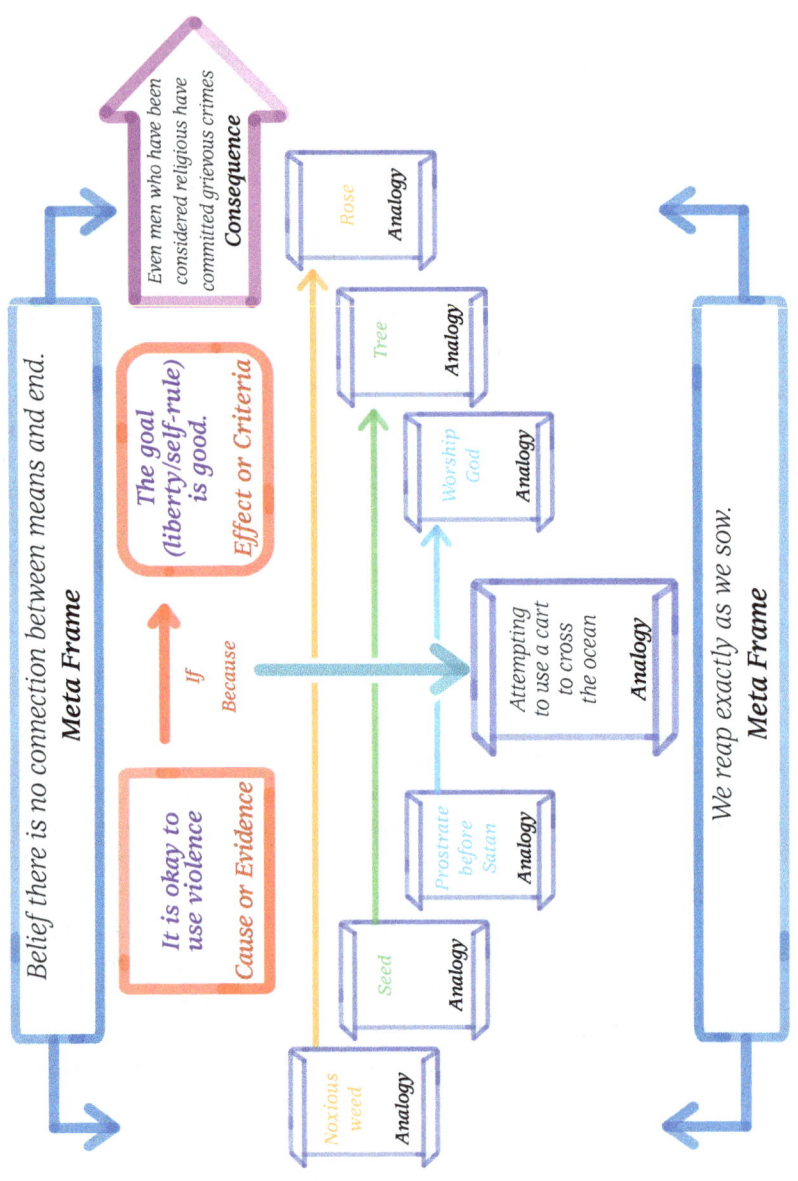

Gandhi then sets out to add credibility to his own belief that it is important to use passive resistance and the "soul-force" to attain the goal of liberty and self-rule. He begins by presenting and casting doubt on the "rival conjecture" that there is no historical evidence of success of these methods and that physical punishment is necessary to combat "evil-doers."

302　Examples of Applying Sleight of Mouth

> **Is there any historical evidence as to the success of what you have called soul-force or truth-force? No instance seems to have happened of any nation having risen through soul-force. I still think that the evil-doers will not cease doing evil without physical punishment.**
>
> *The force of love is the same as the force of soul or truth. We have evidence of its working at every step. The universe would disappear without the existence of that force. But you ask for historical evidence. It is, therefore, necessary to know what history means. The Gujarati equivalent means; "it so happened." If that is the meaning of history, it is possible to give copious evidence. But, if it means the doings of kings and emperors, there can be no evidence of soul-force or passive resistance is such history. You cannot expect silver ore in a tin mine. History, as we know it, is a record of the wars of the world… How kings played, how they became enemies of one another, how they murdered one another, is found accurately in history, and if this were all that had happened in the world, it would have ended long ago. If the history of the universe had commenced with wars, not a man would be found alive today… The fact that there are so many men still alive in the world show that it is based not on the force of arms but on the force of truth or love. Therefore, the greatest and most unimpeachable evidence of the success of the force is to be found in the fact that, in spite of the wars of the world, it still lives on.*

  Gandhi begins by bringing up the observation that, seemingly, there is no historical evidence of the success of the so-called "soul-force," and "that evil-doers will not cease doing evil without physical punishment." Gandhi begins by setting a *Meta Frame* (and consequently expanding the frame size) by stating that "the universe would disappear" without the existence of the soul-force. He then *Redefines* "history" as *the doings of kings and emperors* and *the record of the wars of the world*, making the *Analogy* that "you cannot expect silver ore in a tin mine." He equates "physical punishment" with *war* and *force of arms* and asserts the *Consequence* that, "If this were all that happened, the world would have ended long ago." Gandhi uses the fact that "so many people are alive today" as a *Counter Example* to the claim that there is no evidence of the power of soul-force.

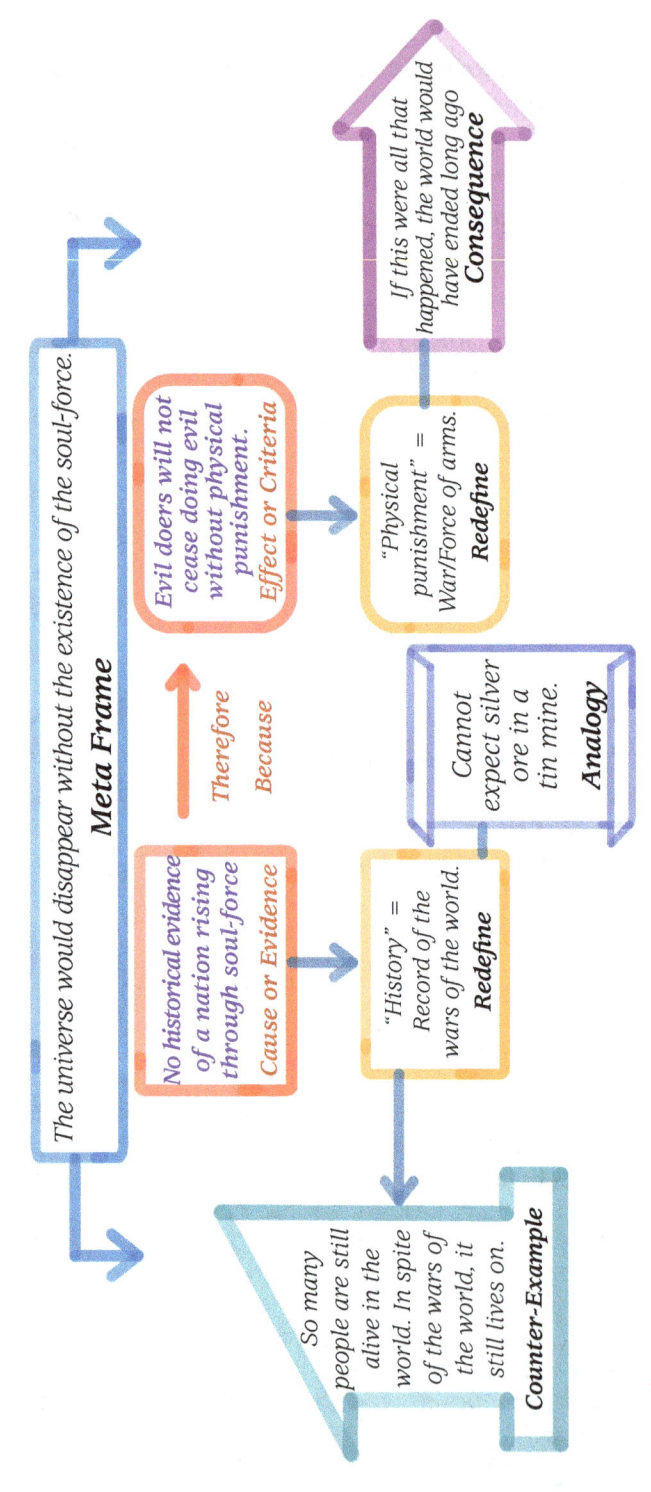

Gandhi goes on to point out:

> *Thousands, indeed tens of thousands, depend for their existence on a very active working of this force. Little quarrels of millions of families in their daily lives disappear before the exercise of this force. Hundreds of nations live at peace. History does not and cannot take note of this fact. History is really a record of every interruption of the even working of the force of true love or of the soul. Two brothers quarrel; one of them repents and re-awakens the love that was lying dormant in him; the two again begin to live in peace; nobody takes note of this. But if the two brothers, through the intervention of solicitors or some other reason, take up arms or go to law-which is another form of the exhibition of brute force-their doings would be immediately noticed in the press, they would be the talk of the neighbors and would probably go down in history. And what is true of families and communities is true of nations. There is no reason to believe that there is one law for families and another for nations. History, then, is a record of an interruption of the course of nature. Soul-force, being natural, is not noted in history.*

What is true for two brothers is also true for families, nations and the whole world thanks to the existence of the soul-force.

Sleight of Mouth

In this statement, Gandhi proceeds to *Chunk Down*, claiming, "Little quarrels of millions of families in their daily lives disappear before the exercise of this force" and "Hundreds of nations live at peace." As a *Consequence*, he says, history cannot take note of all of these ongoing natural expressions of the soul-force. Instead, he claims that it is the exceptions to the rule that stand out. *Chunking Down* further to a specific example, he makes the point that if two brothers quarrel and make up, it is normal and not newsworthy. It would only be publicly noticed if the situation escalated to violence or legal action. Gandhi then *Chunks Up* by saying "what is true for families is true for nations." He concludes with the Meta Frame that "history" is *a record of the interruption of the course of nature and the soul-force* rather than a proof that it does not exist.

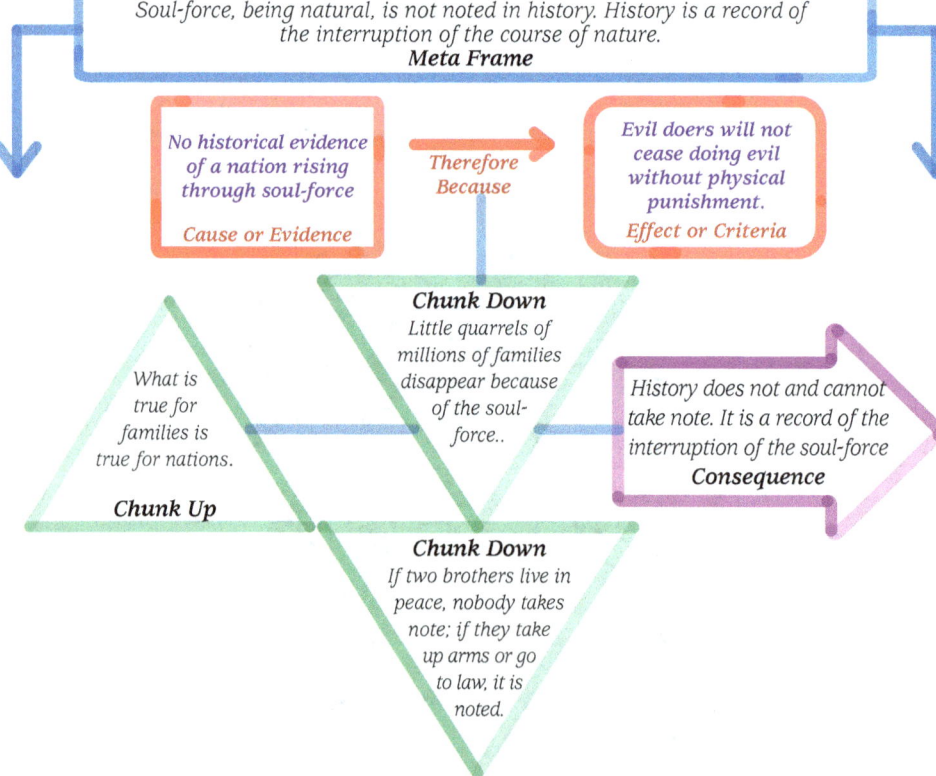

Reflections on Gandhi's Sleight of Mouth Strategy

Of all the Sleight of Mouth examples that we have been examining, Gandhi's defense of passive resistance, non-violence and the soul-force establishes the largest and widest frame of reference. He talks about "millions of families," "hundreds of nations," "all of history," "the wars of the world," the "course of nature," and how the "world would have ended long ago" and the "the universe would disappear" without the soul-force. These are big considerations. Gandhi's continual reference to the "soul-force" clearly has the purpose to connect his audience to something much bigger than the individual ego.

The objections Gandhi brings up to his principles of passive resistance are essentially related to ego issues: i.e., obtaining our goal by any means; rising as a nation; punishing "evil-doers." He continually brings the focus of attention back to a larger spiritual/soul perspective. That strategy is no doubt one of the reasons why his followers called him "Mahatma," which means *Great Soul*. At the same time, Gandhi is able to *Chunk Down* to specific examples, like that of the two brothers.

We can summarize the fundamental structure of Gandhi's Sleight of Mouth strategy in the following steps:

1. State the limiting belief to be addressed.
2. Formulate an alternative belief that challenges the cause-effect assumption behind the limiting belief by viewing it from a perspective beyond individual identity.
3. Identify a predicted consequence of the cause-effect assumption of the limiting belief that can be shown to be invalid?
4. Make Analogies that challenge the cause-effect assumption of the limiting belief or support the alternative belief.
5. Identify a Counter Example that challenges that cause-effect assumption of the limiting belief.
6. Present a specific example of the alternative belief.
7. Draw a generalization from that example that supports the alternative belief.

This leads us in a very different direction than the other examples I have presented in this chapter. Here is how it could be applied to one of the limiting beliefs we have been using as a reference.

1. Limiting belief to be addressed: *If I speak people will laugh at me.*

2. An alternative belief that challenges the cause-effect assumption behind the limiting belief by viewing it from a perspective beyond individual identity: *Your belief that your actions control other people's behavior is very narrow. We all have a larger purpose and calling.*

3. A predicted consequence of the cause-effect assumption of the limiting belief that can be shown to be invalid: *You should be able make everyone laugh every time you speak.*

4. Analogies that challenge the cause-effect assumption of the limiting belief or support the alternative belief: *(a) You are not a white billiard ball and they a red one, (b) We take care of the seeds in our own garden.*

5. A Counter Example that challenges that cause-effect assumption of the limiting belief: *There are probably many people who have appreciated something you have said.*

6. A specific example of the alternative belief: *You can choose to consider or reject what I am saying right now.*

7. A generalization from that example that supports the alternative belief: *The way you interpret an interaction will determine how it serves your calling.*

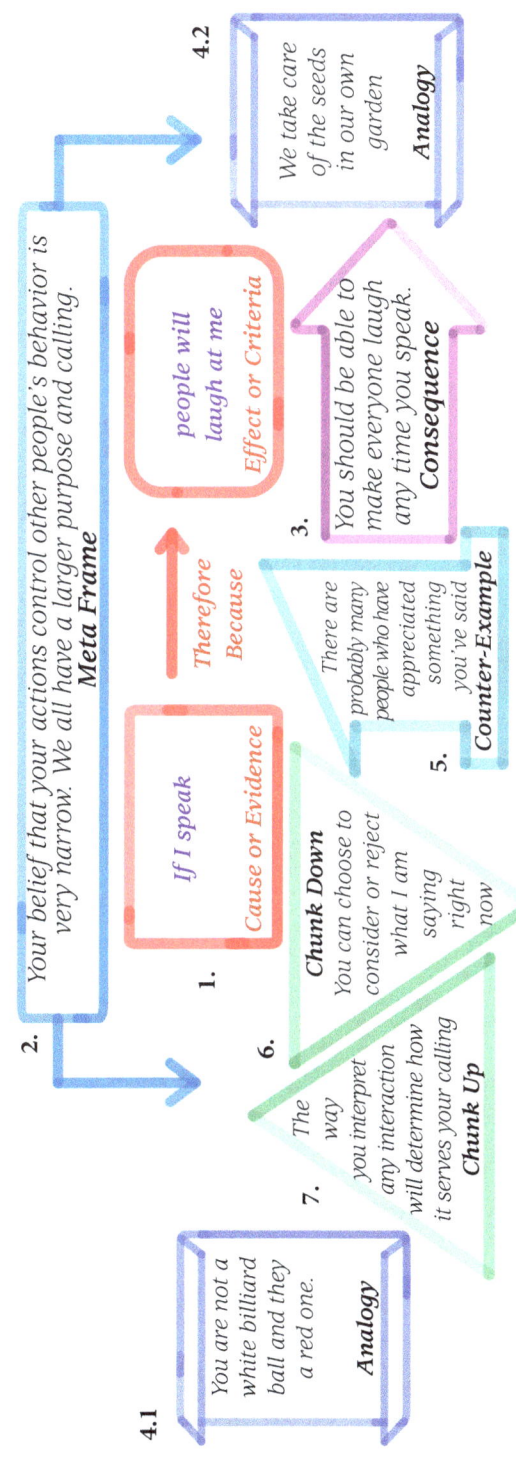

As with the previous examples you can practice using Gandhi's Sleight of Mouth strategy of connecting beyond individual identity by choosing a limiting belief and filling in the diagram below with your answers to the following questions:

1. *What is the limiting belief to be addressed?*
2. *What is an alternative belief that challenges the cause-effect assumption behind the limiting belief by viewing it from a perspective beyond individual identity?*
3. *What is a predicted consequence of the cause-effect assumption of the limiting belief that can be shown to be invalid?*
4. *What Analogies challenge the cause-effect assumption of the limiting belief or support the alternative belief?*
5. *What is a Counter Example that challenges that cause-effect assumption of the limiting belief?*
6. *What is a specific example of the alternative belief?*
7. *What generalization can be made from that example that supports the alternative belief?*

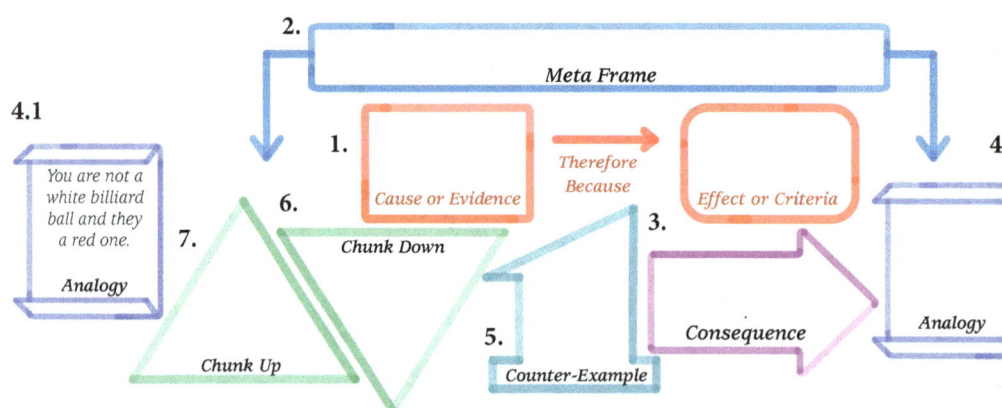

Examples of Applying Sleight of Mouth

Sleight of Mouth and Strategies of Genius

Interestingly, Gandhi's use of Sleight of Mouth demonstrates a number of the key patterns I have identified in my study of *Strategies of Genius*. One is that geniuses have a sense of connection and contribution to something beyond their individual identity. Another is their ability to move back and forth between different chunk sizes and levels of thinking; maintaining a feedback loop between the abstract and the concrete. As Gandhi once said, "Live as if you were to die tomorrow. Learn as if you were to live forever."

As I have asserted throughout this book, effectively generating the various Sleight of Mouth patterns is a function of particular qualities of mindset rather than a simplistic verbal formula. Not surprisingly then, the examples of applying the Sleight of Mouth patterns in this chapter demonstrate a number of the key Patterns of Genius that I have identified in my studies of *Strategies of Genius* (1994-1995), summarized in *Strategies of Genius Volume 3* (pp. 389-402).

1. Have a highly developed use of imagination.

Geniuses have the ability to envision possible scenarios. As Albert Einstein pointed out, "imagination is more important than knowledge." Socrates, for instance, has Polemarchus imagining a number of different scenarios. Lincoln did something similar when having his audience imagine the situation involving Dr. Ross and Sambo. Shakespeare's Antony brings the crowd into a future scenario where they are "dipping their napkins" in Caesar's blood and begging a hair from his head. Henry V takes his soldiers into a vivid future scenario where they are showing their scars and reliving their heroic feats. Gandhi invites us to imagine the world with and without the existence of the soul-force.

2. Maintain a strong orientation toward the future and a belief in what is possible.

And a key characteristic of geniuses is that they believe in their ideas and visions for the future. As Walt Disney maintained, "If you can dream it, you can do it." Martin Luther King, Jr.'s *I Have a Dream* speech is a good example of this. Much of the power of Shakespeare's Henry V's address to his troops is his ability to make the potential future scenario he is describing seem real. Similarly, Eisenhower's message to his troops expresses a strong belief in them and in the ultimate success of their mission. Mark Antony clearly believes that Caesar has been wronged and will be avenged. Gandhi has an unshakeable belief in his principles of non-violence and the power of the soul-force.

3. Use metaphors and analogies.

Geniuses are constantly using metaphors and lateral or non-linear thinking strategies. Metaphor or analogy seems to be at the core of every act of genius. In fact, every single example of Sleight of Mouth in this section involves the use of analogies or metaphors of some type. Socrates used analogies constantly as part of his method. Lincoln used the analogy of wolves devouring lambs to graphically illustrate his point. Antony used the metaphor of Caesar's wounds being "mouths" that could condemn his murderers and talks about "the stones of Rome" rising to mutiny. Both Henry V and Eisenhower invoked the metaphor of brothers. Gandhi, of course, used analogies to a weed versus a rose, a seed and a tree, trying to use a cart to cross the ocean and seeking silver in a tin mine.

"This is for your own good little lamb"

4. Use multiple intelligences and have developed numerous links between the senses.

While vision may be a central focus, geniuses tend to use all of their senses and engage multiple intelligences. A good deal of the effectiveness of some of the examples examined comes from using words to invoke other sensory modalities. Lincoln, for instance, talks about Sambo working in the "burning sun" while Dr. Ross "sits in the shade, with gloves on his hand." Antony describes Caesar "weeping," his injuries speaking, "stirring men's blood" and people "kissing" Caesar's wounds. These engage both physical sensation and emotion. Similarly, Henry V speaks of men "standing a tip toe" and their names "familiar" in people's "mouths" and "flowing cups." These also evoke rich sensory experiences.

5. Use multiple perspectives.

One of the most common characteristics of genius is to be able to entertain more perspectives of a particular subject or process than is typical, and to find the perspective(s) that no one else has taken. In addition to being able to take different points of view, geniuses have the ability to identify with different perceptual positions. Socrates invokes many different perspectives, bringing up physicians, cooks, navigators, farmers, shoemakers, musicians, bricklayers, vinedressers, soldiers, etc. Lincoln, of course, switches between the perspective of slave owners (Dr. Ross), slaves (Sambo), those attempting to justify slavery (pro-slavery theologians) and those opposed to it. Mark Antony takes the crowd through his own perspective, that of Caesar's killers, Caesar (his wounds and his will) and their own. Henry V leads his men through the point of view of their future selves, their neighbors, future generations, and all of the "other gentlemen now abed in England." Gandhi clearly cycles between his own perspective and that of a skeptic.

6. Ability to move back and forth between different chunk sizes and levels of thinking.

Geniuses are able to move easily between a broader vision and the specific actions required to manifest that bigger picture. They can work with the little pieces and yet not become caught up in all of the details. They are also able to see the big picture without losing sight of the little pieces. Geniuses seem to be uniquely able to balance both. Geniuses are also able to move between abstract models and principles and specific concrete expressions of those abstractions. They are able to find the abstract principles in the concrete examples they are working with, and to embody abstract relationships in specific examples. This forms a kind of loop that allows them to refine their theories through feedback from the concrete world, and at the same time refine their physical works through feedback from more abstract principles. Socrates, Lincoln, Antony, Henry V, Eisenhower, and Gandhi are all clearly able to do this. They chunk down to specific details in order to validate some part of their own belief statements or to identify counter examples that challenge or refute rival conjectures. I already mentioned how Gandhi was able to Chunk Up to the history of nations and Chunk back Down to the squabbles of two brothers. Socrates Chunked Up and Down between abstract qualities like "justice" and specific examples like returning a borrowed object to someone who has gone mad. Lincoln moves between "the will of God" and Dr. Ross sitting in the shade while Sambo works. Eisenhower Chunks Down to specific Counter Examples to the superiority of the "Nazi war machine" and back up to the elimination of Nazi tyranny and security in a free world.

7. *Have a mission beyond their individual identity.*

Another common characteristic of all geniuses is that they perceive their work as coming from something and serving something larger than themselves. As I already pointed out, Gandhi's soul-force is an obvious example. Lincoln's mission to eradicate slavery from the United States is another example as is Eisenhower's comments that the allied forces "great and noble undertaking" represented "the hopes and prayers of liberty-loving people everywhere." On a smaller scale, Antony was on a mission to clear Caesar's name and reverse a hostile takeover of the government. Henry V was on a mission to rally his troops through a dire situation. Even Socrates considered what he was doing to be "the highest form of human excellence."

A mission beyond individual identity : the hopes and prayers of liberty-loving people everywhere.

8. Have Determination and operate in 'feedback' as opposed to 'failure' frame.

Geniuses frequently have ideas that challenge and transform existing ways of thinking. Geniuses have the ability to stick with what they believe, even when they are getting no external acknowledgment or support. They also have a unique ability to perceive lack of success not as failure but as feedback for where to look next. This trait is unquestionably at the foundation of the mindset driving all of our examples. In fact, this is the essence of applying the Sleight of Mouth patterns. If one pattern does not work, you switch to another. As Socrates demonstrated, there is always some other perspective, time frame, level of chunking or set of filters that can be applied to any belief statement. Because Sleight of Mouth is about beliefs and meaning, and not about objective reality, there is never any ultimate end. Reframing and outframing could conceivably go on forever. This pattern is, of course, easier to observe when there is a dialogue, as with Socrates. It is also evident in the examples of Mark Antony and Gandhi where there is more interaction with others (even if imagined in Gandhi's case).

9. Think systemically and focus on "deep structure" as opposed to "surface structure."

One of the most essential patterns of genius is the ability to think systemically rather than mechanically. The mental strategies of geniuses typically allow them to track whole systems of interacting elements. Perhaps the most definitive characteristic of genius is the commitment to get to the "deep structure" beneath the "surface structure." Socrates' exploration of justice, Lincoln's exposure of the harmful hypocrisy of slavery, the skillful pacing and leading of their respective audiences done by Antony, Henry V and Eisenhower, and Gandhi's reflections on ends versus means, the biases of history and the functioning of the soul-force are all examples of the capacity to think systemically and focus on deeper structures.

These strategies of genius also are evident in the examples of Milton Erickson spread throughout the earlier sections of this book.

Clearly using these strategies of genius to apply Sleight of Mouth patterns supports a mindset that makes those patterns even more potentially powerful and effective.

Review and Examples of Some Key Strategies for Using Sleight of Mouth

In the previous chapter, I presented an overview of some other common strategies for applying Sleight of Mouth patterns to either strengthen a belief or to question its validity or universality. The various examples presented in this chapter provide some interesting illustrations of those strategies as well.

Chains of Meaning

In his dialogue with Polemarechus, Socrates sought to create chains of meaning by prompting a series of *Redefines* such as: "justice" *means* "doing right" which *means* "giving what is due" which *means* "giving everyone what is appropriate" which means "benefiting friends and harming enemies" which *means* "a just man is a useful partner where money is involved." However, he then also starts another chain of meaning when he asserts "skill in defense goes with skill in offence," the "ability to save from disease implies ability to produce it" and "bringing an army safely through a campaign involves robbing the enemy of its secrets." He concludes that this *means* "a man who is good at keeping a thing will be good at stealing it" which *means* "a just man who's good at keeping money safe will be good at stealing it" which *means* "a just man is a type of thief" and justice is "a kind of stealing." This directly contradicts the previous chain of meanings, which achieves Socrates' goal of "knowing nothing" and demonstrating that no single perspective has universal validity.

Chains of Causes

Lincoln gives a good example of applying a chain of causes in his challenge to pro-slavery theology when points out that *because* Dr. Ross makes the decision about whether it is "God's will" that Sambo remain a slave, as he is Sambo's owner, and *if* Dr. Ross decides God doesn't will Sambo to be Dr. Ross' slave, *then* Dr. Ross has to do the work. So, it is to Dr. Ross' advantage for Sambo to remain a slave. *Thus*, Dr. Ross cannot give an impartial interpretation of "God's will."

Antony makes creative use of a chain of causes when he claims that *if* he were disposed to praise Caesar and disprove Brutus, *then* it would "wrong" the co-conspirators and stir the crowd's hearts to rage and *cause* them to mourn and appreciate Caesar. In addition, *if* he were to read Caesar's will *then* it would inflame the crowd and make them mad which would *cause* them to recognize the injustice that had been done to Caesar and incite them to rise up and mutiny. Of course, Antony's chain of causes produces exactly that effect.

Comparisons

Eisenhower uses a comparison between 1940-41 and 1944 as a means to convince his troops that their current task is not as onerous as it may seem to some of them. Compared to the "Nazi triumphs" of 1940-41, the invasion would appear dire and difficult. Compared with the recent victories and increased strength of the allied forces in 1944, "the tide has turned" and their "victory is assured."

The examples in this chapter also utilize a number of Polya's *Patterns of Plausible Inference*.

Probability

Much of Gandhi's "proof" of the existence of the soul-force is based on this Polya Pattern. Gandhi emphasizes the fact that so many people are still alive in the world and that it still lives on in spite of all of the violence and wars. Gandhi's point is that it is extremely improbable that so many people would still be alive if war and violence were actually the norm instead of the peaceful influence of the soul-force.

Verification/Invalidation of Consequences

Antony uses this strategy when he provides a series of counter examples to Brutus' claim that Caesar was "ambitious." If Caesar was an ambitious despot, the consequences should be that he would be narcissistic and turn against his friends instead of being faithful and just. He would take the spoils of his victories for himself as opposed to promoting the good of Rome by filling the country's treasury with ransoms. He would not be attuned to the needs of his people and would not have "cried" when "the poor wept." He would have welcomed being crowned king when offered it instead of refusing it.

Verification/Invalidation of Contingencies

Antony applies this strategy when he presents Caesar's will. If Caesar was a despot who wanted to enslave the people of Rome and turn them into "bondsmen," he would not have planned to give them all a percentage of his money and left his property to them and their heirs. Instead, the existence of this "pre-condition" validates that Caesar was a benevolent benefactor rather than an ambitious dictator.

Inference from Analogy

Every one of the examples in this chapter makes use of Analogies in some way. As I have already pointed out, inference from analogy (cooking, music, medicine, bricklaying, horse training, navigating, etc.) is central to Socrates' method. It is also a foundational part of Gandhi's strategy (weeds and roses, seeds and trees, tin in a silver mine, etc.). Lincoln and Antony use analogies to illustrate key parts of their argument. Henry V and Eisenhower use the analogy of brothers ("band of brothers," "brothers in arms") to build and strengthen a perception of caring and camaraderie between the members of their armies.

Disproving the Converse

A majority of the examples in this chapter involve the attempt to disprove a rival conjecture to a particular stated or implied belief. Lincoln seeks to refute the belief that "it is better for some people to be slaves and that it is God's will that they be slaves." Antony aims to disprove that Caesar was an ambitious despot. Eisenhower provides counter examples to the superiority of the "Nazi war machine." Gandhi brings up a number of rival conjectures ("violence is okay if it is for a good cause," "there is no connection between means and end," "there is no evidence that soul-force is effective," "evil doers will not cease doing evil without physical punishment") and challenges their validity.

Comparison with Random

While none of the examples explicitly makes a comparison with random, there are some interesting implicit references. When Henry V says, "if we are marked to die," the implication is that it is in some way a predetermined and not random occurrence. As I pointed out earlier, the implication of being "marked to die" is that there is some larger power/influence that is at work in the situation and that, if one is not marked to die, then he will somehow survive no matter how fearful the odds. Similarly, Gandhi's reference to the fact that "there are so many people are still alive in the world, in spite of the wars of the world," implies that it is something other than random and that a larger "soul-force" is at work.

Chapter 20
Conclusion

Conclusion

In the *Introduction* to this book, I pointed out that one of the goals in writing it was to provide ways of being able to know when Sleight of Mouth patterns are being used helpfully or potentially harmfully. I pointed out that the harmful use of Sleight of Mouth can create or reinforce a type of limiting belief that I call a "thought virus." Thought viruses are limiting beliefs built as a result of other people's thoughts, words and beliefs, rather than on our own personal experiences.

Because many beliefs are based on the assumptions, inferences, or conclusions of other beliefs, they cannot be validated or refuted empirically. We need to develop a type of "virus detection" filter similar to the way our immune systems identify and remove physical viruses or to the way a computer virus protection program operates with respect to digital viruses. Throughout this book I have provided some "red flags" that indicate potential limiting beliefs and thought viruses.

We also need a way to know when beliefs have the potential to empower us and others and to support positive change and human evolution. Such guidelines can help neutralize limiting beliefs and thought viruses and guide us to reframe them into a more productive and helpful form. Applying the opposite or converse of the various red flag indicators that I have identified can also provide some effective guidelines for using Sleight of Mouth in positive and productive way.

Detecting Thought Viruses

The following is a review and summary of some of the key indicators that I have pointed out at various places in this book.

CRASH state versus COACH State

This is a type of "meta" indicator that supersedes all of the others. Any belief statement that creates contraction, reactivity, analysis paralysis, separation or hostility is likely to be or become a problem. As I have pointed out before, when we are in a CRASH state, our filters are shut down. We are in a state of "neuromuscular lock" and our main choices for responding are limited to survival strategies such as attack, escape or rigidity (fight, flight, freeze). Of course, in certain cases, like that of Mark Antony inciting his audience to "rage and mutiny," that may be the intended outcome of some Sleight of Mouth strategies, but it is risky and can eventually backfire. (As both Jesus and Gandhi maintained, "Those that take the sword shall perish by the sword.") Interestingly, in the case of Henry V, who was leading his army into a dangerous battle, his use of Sleight of Mouth was to intentionally reduce the amount of CRASH state that his soldiers were experiencing and bring them back into a COACH state. Eisenhower's message to his forces on the eve of D-Day had a similar purpose.

A major challenge in identifying this indicator is that it is not really possible to assess from the words used in a belief statement alone. We must observe the responses of others to our words and make a determination from there.

1. Problem Frame Versus Outcome Frame

A problem frame fixates attention on what is not working, why it won't work and whose fault it is. When a belief is stated in a "problem frame," it is one of the first and most important indicators that the belief statement is likely to be or become a limiting belief or thought virus. An *outcome frame* involves staying solution focused and oriented toward positive possibilities in the future. There are many examples in this book showing how various Sleight of Mouth patterns can be used to shift a belief statement from a problem frame to an outcome frame.

2. Exclusion of Part of a Holon/System

Any belief that focuses on benefiting one part of the holon (system) to which we belong at the expense of another will be inherently problematic. Limiting beliefs and thought viruses tend to, either knowingly or unwittingly, exclude or even attempt to get rid of or destroy crucial parts of the holons to which they refer. This creates predictable and unavoidable problems. Expanding the frame of reference addressed by a particular belief statement to be wider or more inclusive helps to avoid becoming overly focused on only one particular part of an interconnected system. Keeping attention on the impact of a belief on the health and harmony of the larger ecosystem it affects is also an important guideline.

3. Negative Identity Judgments

Negative identity judgments, about oneself or others, are another major source and indicator of limiting beliefs and thought viruses. As I have previously indicated, such judgments are often the result of interpreting particular behaviors, or the lack of ability to produce certain behavioral results, as a statement about a person's character or identity. Shifting a negative identity judgment to an outcome frame or back to a statement about a person's behavior or capabilities can greatly reduce the impact it has mentally and emotionally. As we have also seen in various examples in this book, asserting positive judgments about character (ethos) is a way to strengthen the credibility of a belief statement.

4. Imbalance of "Ego" and "Soul"

Some beliefs will emphasize ego needs at the sacrifice of the soul, creating isolation and narcissism. Others demean or even vilify the ego, leading to a lack of self-care and burnout. It is important to realize that neither ego inflation nor deflation is sustainable or productive. Maintaining a healthy and dynamic balance between ego and soul, and identifying beliefs that threaten that, is key to applying the Sleight of Mouth patterns properly. As we have observed in a number of examples, creating a connection to something bigger than the individual can be in important and transformational use of Sleight of Mouth patterns such as Hierarchy of Criteria, Change Frame Size and Meta Frame.

5. Assumption of Negative Intentions and "Othering"

The assumption of negative intentions is another one of the major "red flags" to pay attention to with respect to Sleight of Mouth, as it usually means that the patterns are likely to be used reactively or defensively. This is especially important when it is combined with the process of "othering" – i.e., creating binary distinctions at the identity level. Examples of this would include terms like: Jews, Negroes, Whites, Capitalists, Communists, Conservatives, Liberals, Socialists, Americans, Russians, Germans, Chinese, etc.; any type of anonymous, collective "other." Applying the NLP principle that there is ultimately a positive intention behind every thought and behavior and Chunking Down highly generalized identity statements are ways to offset or correct these types of limiting belief statements.

6. "Away From" Versus "Towards" Intentions

Another key distinction with respect to belief statements is whether they are directed "towards" or "away from" something, e.g., "toward safety" or "away from danger." *Away from* intentions often create paradoxes by focusing attention and energy on what is *not* wanted rather than on what is wanted. If we do not know what we want to go toward, we can "jump out of the frying pan and into the fire," which could be a potentially worse situation. When combined with the assumption of the negative intent of "others" at the identity level, "away from" intentions can easily precipitate reactivity and violence. The result is to trigger the fundamental survival strategies associated with CRASH state of "fight, flight or freeze." Thus, this combination of "negatively intended anonymous others" with "away from" motivation constitutes another fundamental red flag to the potentially manipulative and unecological use of Sleight of Mouth. Shifting from "problem frame" to "outcome frame" and applying the strategy of identifying "meta outcomes" help to ensure that belief statements are directed toward some positive purposes are good ways to keep intention and attention focused on the actual desired state.

7. Absence of Multiple Intelligences

While Sleight of Mouth is naturally focused on words, using it successfully requires more than words. Words themselves only gain meaning through their connection to other parts of our experience. To apply Sleight of Mouth effectively, it is important to engage *multiple intelligences*. The basic principle of multiple intelligences is that, *the more ways you have to understand something, the more you understand it*. If you only have a verbal way to express or understanding something, you are very limited, and there are many potential deletions, distortions, and generalizations. If, however, in addition to literal language you have a symbolic/metaphoric way, a somatic way and a visual way, you can express it more creatively and understand it more completely. Tracking which modalities (verbal, visual, emotional, somatic, metaphoric, etc.) are being engaged by a belief statement is a useful way of checking the potential richness (or lack thereof) of experience it is evoking.

Strategies of Genius Promote a Useful Mindset for Ecologically Applying Sleight of Mouth

Interestingly, the Strategies of Genius I presented in the previous chapter provide some good ways to ensure that the Sleight of Mouth patterns are being used in a productive and helpful manner. The following reflections show how particular patterns of genius can help to avoid, neutralize, or transform potential thought viruses.

Problem Frame Versus Outcome Frame

I pointed out that geniuses have *a highly developed use of imagination and maintain a strong orientation toward the future and a belief in what is possible*. This helps to ensure that belief statements will likely be formulated in an outcome frame and toward a positive future.

Exclusion of Part of a Holon/System

A key strategy of genius is to *think systemically and focus on "deep structure"* as opposed to "surface structure." This helps to bring attention to all of the parts of the larger ecosystem affected by a belief statement and keep it from harmfully biasing one part in favor of the others.

Negative Identity Judgments

As I indicated earlier, negative identity judgments are often the result of interpreting particular behaviors or the lack of certain behaviors as a statement about character or identity. Geniuses are *constantly moving between generalizations and specific concrete expressions*. They are able to identify the abstract principles in the concrete examples they are working with, and also to embody abstract relationships in specific examples. The ability to Chunk Down and Up and the resulting clarity about the relationship between different levels of process (i.e., behavior versus beliefs versus identity, etc.) helps to avoid confusion of levels and filter out negative identity judgments.

Imbalance of "Ego" and "Soul"

Geniuses have *a sense of a mission beyond their individual identity*. They perceive their work as coming from something and serving something larger than themselves. This helps to develop a healthy ego, that is neither inflated nor deflated. They know that, on the one hand, their personal presence and participation is needed as an important "difference that makes a difference." They are also clear that, on the other hand, they are contributing to something beyond themselves.

This helps to maintain a healthy balance between ego (I am important) and soul (there is something bigger than me that I am part of and contributing to).

Assumption of Negative Intentions and "Othering"

One of the most common characteristics of genius is to be *able to entertain more perspectives of a particular subject or process than is typical, and to find the perspective(s) that no one else has taken.*

In addition to being able to take different points of view, geniuses have the ability to identify with different perceptual positions. The capacity to take a robust "second position" (i.e., standing in another person's shoes and perceiving the world from their perspective as if you were that person) is the opposite of "othering." It promotes greater understanding and empathy. Further, holding multiple perspectives about any situation keeps it from perceived as "black and white" or entirely "negative or positive," as there are different ways to look at it.

"Away From" Versus "Towards" Intentions

Geniuses have determination and operate in a "feedback" as opposed to "failure" frame. They frequently have ideas that challenge and transform existing ways of thinking. Thus, they need the ability to stick with what they believe, even when they are getting no external acknowledgment or support. They also have a unique ability to perceive lack of success not as failure but as feedback for where to look next. This clearly creates a "toward" rather than "away from" mindset, somewhat like a guided missile.

Absence of Multiple Intelligences

Geniuses tend to use *all of their senses and engage multiple intelligences. They are also constantly using metaphors and lateral or non-linear thinking strategies*. Metaphor or analogy seems to be at the core of every act of genius. Engaging all of our intelligences is essential to keep Sleight of Mouth from simply being "a war of words." Using multiple intelligences also creates deeper understanding and insight into any situation.

It is important to point out that you don't necessarily have perceive yourself as "a genius" to use these "strategies" of genius. Anyone can apply and improve at any of these strategies. In fact, the more we use them the more we are able to release and express our own personal genius. You can find out more about them in my book series *Strategies of Genius*.

Oprah Winfrey: Sleight of Mouth and the Power of Purpose

As I have said throughout this book, Sleight of Mouth patterns are reflections of particular qualities and filters of mindset. It is ultimately the mindset, not the words, that produces change. Language is the vehicle that expresses and shapes our mindset; for better or for worse. Oprah Winfrey's journey from poverty to success provides a powerful demonstration of how the mindset created by the strategies of genius can be combined with the Sleight of Mouth patterns to shape our character and destiny for the better.

I began this book with the quote, attributed to Lao Tsu, which stated:

> *Watch your thoughts, they become words.*
> *Watch your words, they become actions.*
> *Watch your actions, they become habits.*
> *Watch your habits, they become your character.*
> *Watch your character, it becomes your destiny.*

The extraordinary success of talk show diva and media mogul Oprah Winfrey provides a compelling illustration of how this progression can function. Born into poverty in rural Mississippi to a teenage single mother and later raised in an inner-city Milwaukee neighborhood, Winfrey was molested during her childhood and early teenage years. She became pregnant at fourteen; her son was born prematurely and died in infancy. When fired from her first broadcasting job, she was told that she "wasn't fit for TV." As she puts it, "My bosses certainly made no secret of their feelings. They told me I was the wrong color, the wrong size and that I showed too much emotion."

Certainly, being born female, colored and poor in the Southern United States during the 1950s is not the most obvious or easiest start for attaining any type of success. Many people in similar circumstances could have easily and understandably given up or not even tried. Winfrey, however, persisted, boosting a third-rated local talk show to first place. She then launched her own production company, becoming a millionaire by age 32 and the first black woman billionaire in world history. As of 2022, Winfrey had a net worth in excess of 3.5 billion dollars.

In addition to her financial success, Winfrey has won 18 Emmy Awards, a Tony Award and received two Academy Award nominations. She has also been given a number of humanitarian awards for her extensive philanthropic work and, in 2013, was presented with the Presidential Medal of Freedom.

The Path

In her 2019 book *The Path Made Clear: Discovering Your Life's Direction and Purpose*, Winfrey employs the magic of Sleight of Mouth to support her belief that *"the best way to succeed is to discover what you love and then find a way to offer it to others in the form of service, working hard, and also allowing the energy of the universe to lead you."* Winfrey's focus on purpose is a clear expression of one of the fundamental patterns of genius – a felt sense of connection and contribution to something beyond one's individual identity. The book follows a path of metaphors that define the key steps of her own personal journey, supplemented by quotes of inspiring individuals that she interviewed on her show. The chapters of the book cover such topics as: *The Seeds*, *The Roots*, *The Road*, and *The Climb*.

Intuitively touching on every Sleight of Mouth Pattern, Winfrey uses these themes to share statements that both support her belief system and subtly transform the unspoken thought virus which she and many others have had to contend with throughout their lives that *"I/You can't succeed/live my/your dreams because I/you have the wrong color/gender/size/background, etc."*

The Seeds

As one of the key "seeds" that started her remarkable journey, Winfrey expresses the *Meta Frame* that *"You don't become what you want, you become what you believe."* She adds that *"The greatest discovery of all time is that a person can change his (or her) future by merely changing his (or her) attitude."* This Meta Frame both reflects and supports another important pattern of genius – maintaining a strong orientation toward the future and a belief in what is possible.

Winfrey also addresses the issue of *Intent*, claiming, *"If you want your life to be more rewarding, you have to change the way you think."* The implication is that if your intent is to have a more rewarding life, you will need to evaluate and adjust your beliefs to support that. She goes on to make it clear that, in her *Model of the World*, *"You are not your circumstances. You are your possibilities."*

These are a powerful set of generalizations that support a clear sense of individual agency in shaping one's destiny. For Winfrey, this individual agency comes from being clear about the unique contribution you can make. According to Winfrey, "Everyone has a calling. Your real job in life is to figure out as soon as possible what that is, who you are meant to be, and begin to honor your calling in the best way possible."

In her own case, it wasn't until she was "unceremoniously demoted" from her job as a television journalist to co-host of a third-rated local talk show that Winfrey's true path began to become clear. At the end of hosting her first talk show, she felt *"a sense of knowing resonating within my heart and radiating to the hairs on the back of my neck. My entire body told me this was what I was supposed to do. As a reporter, I'd been exhausted all the time. I really had to drag myself in to work. But after one day on this local talk show, I was energized in a way that fueled every cell of my being. There was no doubt that the seeds of what was to give my life meaning and purpose had been planted."* In addition to the felt sense of connection and contribution to something beyond her individual identity, Winfrey is also applying the pattern of genius of using multiple intelligences and the links between the senses when she talks about her "heart," the "hairs on the back of her neck," her "entire body" responding, her "exhaustion" and the subsequent energizing of "every cell" of her being.

The Roots

Planting the seeds is only the beginning. To become realities, beliefs need to be put into action. This is where the pattern of genius involving the ability to move back and forth between different chunk sizes and levels of thinking becomes important. Winfrey addresses this by stating a type of *Reality Strategy* in which she claims, *"(w)ith every experience, you alone are painting your own canvas, thought by thought, choice by choice."* She further stresses this through the *Chunk Down* statement that: *"Doing the best at this moment puts you in the best place for the next moment."*

Putting the beliefs that Winfrey has expressed as her "seeds" into action is not easy and there are the inevitable obstacles and setbacks on the way. Winfrey *Chunks Up* all of these interferences to the larger category of challenges and claims, *"Challenges are gifts that force us to search for a new center of gravity. Don't fight them. Just find a different way to stand."* This is a clear expression of the pattern of genius to have determination and operate in a "feedback" as opposed to "failure" frame.

The Road

The Road is another important metaphor for Winfrey. And it is certainly an archetypal symbol for a journey. Once seeds are planted and the roots are established, the growth of the plant is a bit like traveling down a road. There are straight stretches, there are curves, there are hills and mountains, there is traffic and there are likely be accidents and road closures. To best travel this road, Winfrey advises, "Find your lane. Make space for the flow to show itself. Follow the natural rhythm of your life, and you will discover a force far greater than your own."

The road that Oprah Winfrey traveled with respect to her own calling was certainly not always an easy one. In her various projects and businesses, she encountered her share of "dead ends" and "detours." At one point, when she was first starting up her own television network, the business was not performing as it should have, and Winfrey found herself struggling with a venture that seemed overwhelming. Rather than give up, she found a way to *Redefine* her "struggle." As she describes it:

> *One of my favorite lessons from Joel Osteen is, "What follows 'I am' is what we're inviting into our life." Meaning when you use phrases like, "I am exhausted," or, "I am overwhelmed," you are inviting exactly that kind of energy into your life. The moment I shifted my perspective from "I am struggling" to "I am honored," my climb was transformed from an arduous trek into a still challenging but now stimulating adventure, and my entire outlook changed. Ever since that time, whenever I've encountered a disruption, rather than allowing it to rattle me, I ask myself one of the most meaningful and productive questions there is: What is this here to teach me? ... Every day brings a new teachable moment. And I look back on each step of the journey with gratitude.*

This example demonstrates the power that language can have to transform our perception of a particular situation (and Winfrey's awareness of that power). Even simply substituting one word for another (i.e., "honored" for "struggling") can change our entire outlook. The example is also an illustration of the pattern of genius to use multiple perspectives and entertain different points of view (i.e., perceiving "disruptions" as "learning experiences").

Another challenge of a long journey along The Road is to maintain the necessary level of energy to keep going while avoiding becoming exhausted and burned out, or running out of fuel. To meet this challenge, Winfrey uses the *Analogies* of a battery and a road race. She states, *"If you neglect to recharge a battery, it dies. And if you run full speed ahead without stopping for water, you lose momentum to finish the race."* The purpose of these Analogies is clearly to bring attention to the importance of balance and self-care while in pursuit of one's calling or purpose.

She also brings up the positive *Consequences* of embracing her belief about pursuing purpose and passion when she states: *"What I know is, is that if you do work that you love, and the work fulfills you, the rest will come."* Winfrey reinforces and enriches this by using the Sleight of Mouth pattern of Another Outcome, pointing out: *"The key to realizing a dream is to focus not on success but significance – and then even the small steps and little victories along your path will take on greater meaning."* Shifting the outcome from "success" to "significance" reorients our attention and interpretation regarding the progress of our journey.

The Climb

The *Analogy* of *The Climb* indicates that we will inevitably encounter steep inclines on the path to fulfilling our calling (as Winfrey indicated when she referred to her "climb" related to the startup of her television network earlier). It can also mean climbing out of the box of our own self-imposed limitations. In this regard, Winfrey offers a *Counter Example* to the belief *"I can't succeed/live my dream because I have the wrong color/gender/size/background, etc."* She claims: *"Often we don't even realize who we're meant to be because we're so busy trying to live out someone else's ideas. But other people and their opinions hold no power in defining our destiny."* The implication is that there are many people who could be born rich, stereotypically beautiful, white, or male, etc., and still not succeed in living their dreams. There are certainly many people who have been born into those circumstances who have not found success or done great things. And, as Winfrey points out, such judgments (about "beauty," "wealth," "privilege," etc.) are simply the opinions of others and not really what fundamentally determines our destiny. Rather, our destiny is shaped by our own choices (thoughts, words, actions) with respect to our perceived calling or purpose. Her life is a testament to that.

In this regard, Winfrey employs the pattern of *Change Frame Size* to point out:

> *All of us have a limited number of years here on earth. What do you want to do with yours? How do you want to spend your precious, ever-unfolding future? There's no need to waste another day wondering if there's more to life. There is. And it's yours for the finding.*

Another implication of the metaphor of *The Climb* has to do with our own desire to attain the peak of our potential. As Winfrey puts it, "The choice to be excellent begins with aligning your thoughts and words with the intention to require more from yourself." She goes on to add, "Always continue the climb. It is possible for you to do whatever you choose, if you first get to know who you are and are willing to work with a power that is greater than yourself to do it." She brings in the Sleight of Mouth pattern of *Hierarchy of Criteria* when she claims: *"Unless you choose to do great things, it makes no difference how much you are rewarded or how much you have."* The implication of this is that "success" is not about amassing material rewards and possessions. Rather, it is about pursuing your potential and your purpose. As she goes on to clarify: "Wealth is a tool that gives you choices, but it can't compensate for a life not fully lived."

Of course, *The Climb* to excellence, purpose and greatness is never simple or straightforward. There are many challenges on the way. In the mindset of successful people, however, challenges are something to be embraced, not avoided. This is another expression of the pattern of genius to have determination and operate in a "feedback" as opposed to "failure" frame. As Winfrey asserts: "You get to know who you really are in a crisis." And, as she pointed out in a previous statement, knowing who you really are is essential to being able to "do whatever you choose." If you don't know who you are, you cannot really choose for yourself because you can't truly know what *you* want. You are much more likely to be swayed by the opinions and judgments of others or by concern about the potential risks you perceive.

Especially during a challenge or crisis, it is easy to get into an "away from" mindset – one of the "red flags" for potential thought viruses. To help address and transform this, Winfrey makes an interesting and creative use of the pattern of A*pply to Self*, saying: *"Whatever you fear most has no power – it is your fear that has the power."* The implication is that our perception of and reaction to what we experience is what ultimately determines its influence on us. This echoes one of the fundamental principles of Sleight of Mouth: the content of a particular circumstance or situation is given meaning (and thus "power") by our interpretation and relationship with it. Shifting our perception shifts our focus of attention, which, in turn, shifts the direction and quality of our energy and ultimately determines the outcome we achieve.

Winfrey summarizes this with a *Meta Frame* that encapsulates much of her belief system, "Understand that the right to choose your own path is a sacred privilege. Use it. Dwell in possibility."

Overview of Oprah Winfrey's Use of Sleight of Mouth

As I mentioned at the beginning of this example, Oprah Winfrey intuitively covers all of the Sleight of Mouth patterns in presenting and supporting a belief system that emphasizes possibilities and personal empowerment. The use of the Sleight of Mouth patterns is not random. It follows a type of path in which the various frames and reframes build upon each other. Unlike most of our previous examples, Winfrey's application of Sleight of Mouth is not tied to a particular context or circumstance. It is intended as a general belief system to guide one's life.

In fact, as you reflect on the following over of the sequence of statements, as a thought experiment, take the time to imagine taking on the beliefs as your own and notice how they shift your perceptions of your current life circumstances. This is one of the most profound lessons of Sleight of Mouth: all beliefs are ultimately a choice, and we can choose those that produce the most positive impact.

The Seeds

1. Meta Frame: *You don't become what you want. You become what you believe. The greatest discovery of all time is that a person can change his (or her) future by merely changing his (or her) attitude.*

2. Intent: *If you want your life to be more rewarding, you have to change the way you think.*

3. Model of the World: *You are not your circumstances. You are your possibilities.*

The Roots

4. Reality Strategy: *With every experience, you alone are painting your own canvas, thought by thought, choice by choice.*

5. Chunk Down: *Doing the best at this moment puts you in the best place for the next moment.*

6. Chunk Up: *Challenges are gifts that force us to search for a new center of gravity. Don't fight them. Just find a different way to stand.*

The Road

7. Redefine: *The moment I shifted my perspective from "I am struggling" to "I am honored", my climb was transformed from an arduous trek into a still challenging but now stimulating adventure, and my entire outlook changed.*

8. Analogy: *If you neglect to recharge a battery, it dies. And if you run full speed ahead without stopping for water, you lose momentum to finish the race.*

9. Consequence: *What I know is, is that if you do work that you love, and the work fulfills you, the rest will come.*

10. Another Outcome: *The key to realizing a dream is to focus not on success but significance – and then even the small steps and little victories along your path will take on greater meaning.*

The Climb

11. Counter Example: *Often we don't even realize who we're meant to be because we're so busy trying to live out someone else's ideas. But other people and their opinions hold no power in defining our destiny.*

12. Change Frame Size: *All of us have a limited number of years here on earth. What do you want to do with yours? How do you want to spend your precious, ever-unfolding future? There's no need to waste another day wondering if there's more to life. There is. And it's yours for the finding.*

13. Hierarchy of Criteria: *Unless you choose to do great things, it makes no difference how much you are rewarded or how much you have.*

14. Apply to Self: *Whatever you fear most has no power – it is your fear that has the power.*

Final Reflections

Oprah Winfrey's climb to success is an inspiring example of the impact that thoughts and words can have on our habits, character, and destiny. Her ability to express her beliefs through the patterns of Sleight of Mouth provides an invitation to others to take on a similar mindset. In doing so, she illustrates how Sleight of Mouth can be used to establish a positive and empowering belief system.

It is my hope that this book has provided readers a rich sample of the many ways that Sleight of Mouth can be used – to examine beliefs and the assumptions upon which they are built, to challenge limiting beliefs, to motivate others to action, to connect to something beyond ourselves, and to awaken a deeper sense of purpose.

It has been my wish in writing this book that readers will become better equipped to navigate the complex landscape of today's world by having a better understanding of how language can shape our beliefs and vice versa. This involves the ability to recognize and embrace those beliefs that enrich your life and the other lives that you touch, and to become more aware of those limiting beliefs and thought viruses that perpetuate unnecessary harm and suffering to ourselves and others.

In fact, a part my plan for the next volume in this series is to present a collection of fundamental empowering beliefs, modeled from great teachers, leaders, and healers, etc., that, if shared by enough people, could be both life changing and world changing. I will then identify the objections and resistance to these beliefs and explore how Sleight of Mouth could transform these objections.

Whatever you fear most has no power–it is your fear that has the power

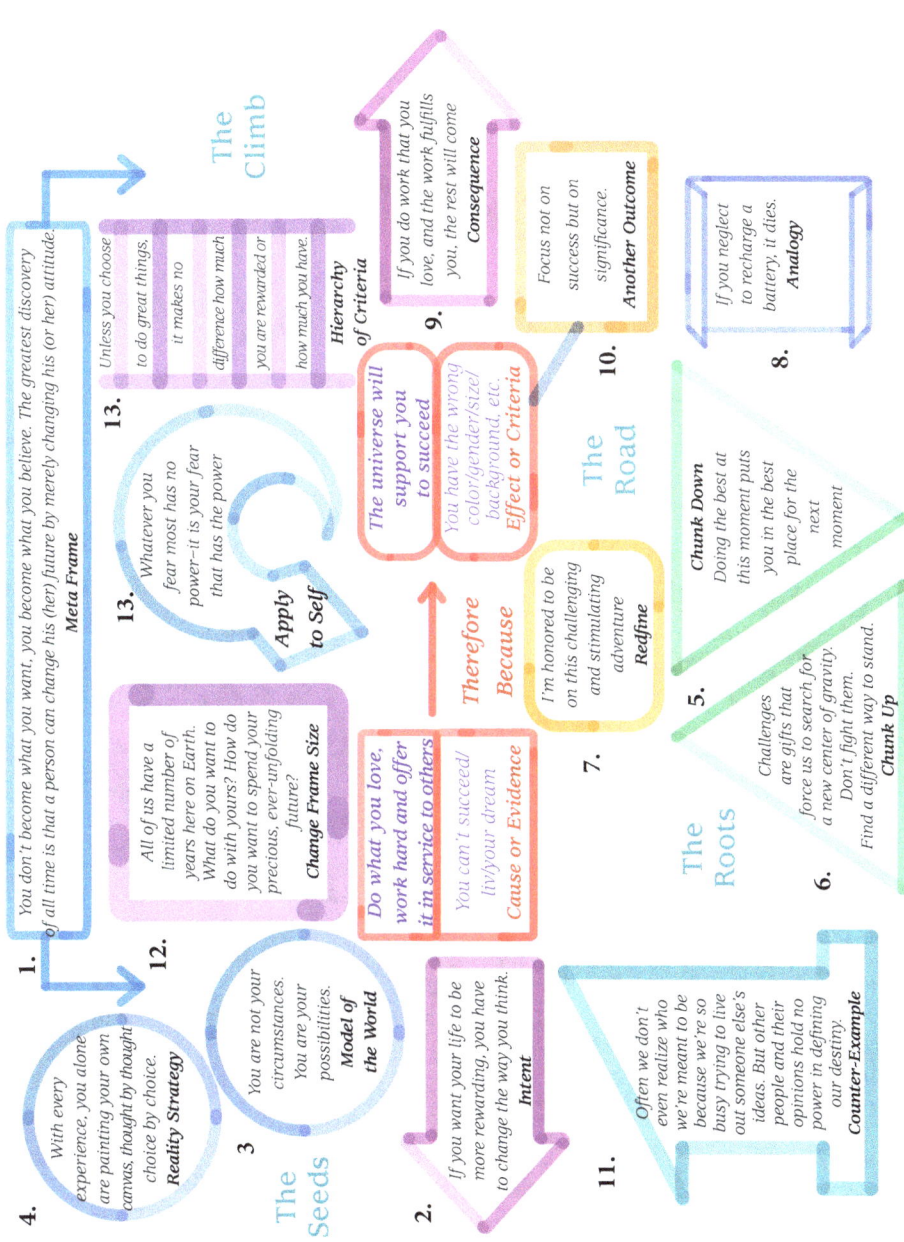

Oprah Winfrey's Path of Empowering Sleight of Mouth Patterns

Sleight of Mouth 335

Afterword

I hope you have enjoyed this exploration into Sleight of Mouth and how words can change worlds. If you are interested in finding out more about the patterns and applications of Sleight of Mouth, I have other resources, such as audio and video recordings that are available through my website:

http://www.robertdilts.com.

You can also email my office at:

rdilts@nlpu.com

In addition, I travel internationally, presenting seminars and specialty programs on a variety of topics related to Sleight of Mouth, NeuroLinguistic Programming and Success Factor Modeling. For more information you can contact:

Dilts Strategy Group
Homepage: http://www.diltsstrategygroup.com
E-Mail: diltsstrategygroup@gmail.com

NLP University
Homepage: http://www.nlpu.com
E-Mail: Teresanlp@aol.com

I have written more than 30 books on a variety of topics including beliefs, health, education, coaching, leadership, collective intelligence and strategies of genius. Many of these, as well as other products are available through:

Journey to Genius
E-Mail: info@journeytogenius.com
Homepage: http://www.journeytogenius.com

There is also a website dedicated to information on Sleight of Mouth at:

https://7007.info

Appendix A: Biographies of Key Sleight of Mouth Models

The verbal patterns of *Sleight of Mouth* were modeled from people who have in some way influenced the world with words in areas such as philosophy, politics, religion, law, psychotherapy, literature, media, etc. The following are brief biographies of some of the individuals referred to in the body of this book.

Socrates

Socrates (470–399 B.C.) was a Greek philosopher from Athens who is credited as the founder of Western philosophy and has exerted a profound influence on Western thought. Socrates authored no texts and is known mainly through the posthumous accounts of contemporary writers, particularly his students Plato and Xenophon. These accounts are written in the form dialogues, in which Socrates questions his counterparts about a particular subject. These dialogues gave rise to what is known the Socratic Method of inquiry. An enigmatic figure, Socrates was accused of "impiety and corrupting the youth" and sentenced to death by forced suicide.

Jesus

Jesus (6 to 4 B.C.–A.D. 30 or 33), also referred to as Jesus Christ, Jesus of Nazareth, and several other names and titles, was a first-century Jewish preacher and religious leader. Jesus' words and ideas have had a major influence on the thinking of Western civilization for almost two thousand years. "Christianity" of some form is the primary religion of almost every Western nation. The story of the life and deeds of Jesus of Nazareth has been translated into every major language and has been spread around the world by the various missionaries and churches that were spawned by his teachings. During his lifetime, Jesus debated with fellow Jews on how to best follow God, engaged in works of healing, taught in parables, and gathered followers. He was arrested for "heresy" and tried by the Jewish authorities, turned over to the Roman government, and crucified.

William Shakespeare

William Shakespeare (1564–1616) was an English playwright, poet and actor. He is widely regarded as the greatest writer in the English language and the world's pre-eminent dramatist. Shakespeare's plays, which range from comedies to histories to romances to tragedies, have been translated into every major living language and are performed more often than those of any other playwright. His intuitive mastery of language and human nature are considered unrivaled. Even today, Shakespeare remains arguably the most influential writer in the English language, and his works continue to be studied and reinterpreted.

Abraham Lincoln

Abraham Lincoln (1809–1865) was an American lawyer, politician, and statesman who served as the 16th president of the United States from 1861 until his assassination in 1865. Lincoln led the Union through the American Civil War and succeeded in abolishing slavery, bolstering the federal government, and modernizing the U.S. economy. Over the decades, Lincoln's words and deeds have continued to have a unique appeal. Self-taught and self-made, he rose from being born in a backwoods log cabin to become president of the United States, savior of the Union and emancipator of enslaved people. His relevance has endured and grown, especially because of his eloquence as a spokesman for democracy and self-government.

Mark Twain (Samuel Clemens)

Samuel Langhorne Clemens (1835–1910), best known by his pen name Mark Twain, was an American writer, humorist, entrepreneur, publisher, and lecturer. He has been praised as the "greatest humorist the United States has produced" and "the father of American literature." His novels include *The Adventures of Tom Sawyer* (1876) and its sequel, *Adventures of Huckleberry Finn* (1884), which has often been termed the "Great American Novel." In many of his novels and essays Twain upheld the inherent dignity of the marginalized—the slave, the impoverished—and wrote scathingly of the prejudice and exploitation of colonial powers and religious dogmatism.

Sigmund Freud

Sigmund Freud (1856–1939) is considered by many to be one of the most influential thinkers of the twentieth century. His theories of the unconscious psychodynamic forces which underlie human behavior have shaped our modern understanding of the mind. The methods he developed for his process of psychoanalysis not only formed the foundation for modern psychotherapy, but have also been applied to the understanding of social behavior, artistic creation, religion and the development of civilization. In many ways, Freud's work was responsible for bringing psychology from a laboratory curiosity to an applied science.

Mohandas Gandhi

Mohandas Gandhi (1869–1948) was an Indian lawyer, anti-colonial nationalist and political activist who employed the doctrine of nonviolent resistance (satyagraha) to achieve political and social progress. Considered the father of his country, he led the successful campaign for India's independence from British rule. Gandhi wrote copiously and his work prompted movements for civil rights and freedom across the world, inspiring people such as Martin Luther King, Jr. and Nelson Mandela. Gandhi is considered the catalyst if not the initiator of three of the major revolutions of the 20th century: the movements against colonialism, racism, and violence.

Dwight D. Eisenhower

David Dwight Eisenhower (1890–1969) was an American military officer and statesman who served as the 34th president of the United States from 1953 to 1961. During World War II, he served as Supreme Commander of the Allied Expeditionary Force in Europe and achieved the five-star rank as General of the Army. Eisenhower planned and supervised two of the most consequential military campaigns of World War II: Operation Torch in the North Africa campaign in 1942–1943 and the D-Day invasion of Normandy in 1944. Eisenhower's success is attributed to not only to his knowledge of military strategy and talent for organization but also to his ability to persuade, mediate, and get along with others.

Milton H. Erickson, M.D.

Milton H. Erickson (1902-1980) is known for his brilliant and innovative strategies for psychotherapy, hypnosis and communication. His methods have become the subject of numerous international congresses and conferences. During his lifetime, Erickson was acknowledged to be the world's leading practitioner of medical hypnosis. He was the founding president of the American Society for Clinical Hypnosis as well as the founder and editor of that society's professional journal. Erickson's clinical record is astounding in the number of different kinds of medical and psychiatric issues he was able to treat successfully—both with and without the use of hypnosis. Erickson's creativity and powers of observation are legendary, and his techniques form the foundation of a whole style of therapeutic and hypnotic procedures. Erickson's work is one of the major influences on the development of Sleight of Mouth.

Martin Luther King, Jr.

Martin Luther King, Jr. (1929-1968) was an American Baptist minister and activist who was one of the most prominent leaders in the civil rights movement in the United States from 1955 until his assassination in 1968. King advanced civil rights for people of color in the United States through nonviolence and civil disobedience. Inspired by his Christian beliefs and the nonviolent activism of Mohandas Gandhi, he led targeted, nonviolent resistance against racially prejudiced laws and other forms of discrimination in the United States which helped bring about landmark legislation such as the Civil Rights Act and the Voting Rights Act. King was awarded the Nobel Peace Prize in 1964.

Oprah Winfrey

Oprah Winfrey (b. 1954) is an American television personality, award winning actress, producer, entrepreneur, and philanthropist whose internationally syndicated daily talk show program became the highest-rated talk show in television history. Winfrey built her professional life on her ability to communicate with all types of people and excelled in the casual and personal talk-show format. Her honest and engaging style put her guests at ease, and she transcended the typical stereotypes related to race, gender, and social class. Throughout her career, Winfrey has entertained, enlightened and uplifted millions of viewers. As a result of her creativity and communication ability, she became one of the richest and most influential women in the United States

References and Bibliography

Aristotle, *The Art of Rhetoric*; translated by Bartlett, R., The University of Chicago Press, Chicago Ill. 2019.

Bacon, F., *Novum Organum,* **Britannica Great Books**; *Encyclopedia Britannica,* Chicago, IL, 1952.

Bandler, R. and Grinder, J.; *The Structure of Magic, Volumes I & II*; Science and Behavior Books, Palo Alto, CA, 1975, 1976.

Bandler, R. and Grinder, J.; *Patterns of the Hypnotic Techniques of Milton H. Erickson, M.D., Volumes I & II*; Meta Publications, Capitola, CA, 1975, 1977.

Bandler R. and Grinder, J.; *Reframing*; Real People Press, Moab, UT, 1982.

Bateson, G.; *Steps to an Ecology of Mind*; Ballantine Books, New York, NY, 1972.

Bateson, G.; *Mind and Nature*; E. P. Dutton, New York, NY, 1979.

Dilts R.; *Applications of NLP;* Dilts Strategy Group, Santa Cruz, Ca., 1990, 2018.

Dilts R.; *Changing Belief Systems with NLP;* Dilts Strategy Group, Santa Cruz, Ca., 1990, 2018.

Dilts R.; *Sleight of Mouth: The Magic of Conversational Belief Change;* Dilts Strategy Group, Santa Cruz, Ca., 1999.

Dilts R.; *Strategies of Genius, Volumes I, II & III;* Dilts Strategy Group, Santa Cruz, CA, 1994-1995.

Dilts, R., Grinder, J., Bandler, R. and DeLozier, J.; *Neuro-Linguistic Programming: The Study of the Structure of Subjective Experience, Vol. I;* Meta Publications, Capitola, CA, 1980.

Dilts, R. and DeLozier, J.; *NLP II: The Next Generation*, Dilts Strategy Group, Santa Cruz, Ca., 2010.

Dilts R., DeLozier, J. and Epstein, T.; *The Encyclopedia of Systemic NLP*; NLP University Press, Santa Cruz, CA, 1999.

Dilts, R. & Gilligan, S., *Generative Coaching Volume 1: The Journey of Creative and Sustainable Change,* International Association for Generative Change, Santa Cruz, CA, 2021.

Dilts R., Hallbom, T. and Smith, S.; *Beliefs: Pathways to Health and Well-Being; Metamorphous Press, Portland, OR, 1990; 2nd Edition:* Crown House Publishers, London, 2014.

Einstein, A. & Infeld, L., *The Evolution of Physics: The Growth of Ideas from Early Concepts to Relativity and Quanta*, Cambridge University Press, Cambridge, MA, 1938.

Erickson, M. H.; *Advanced Techniques of Hypnosis and Therapy; Selected Papers of Milton H. Erickson, M.D.*, Haley, J. [Editor], Grune & Stratton Inc., New York, NY, 1967.

Erickson, M. H., *The Collected Papers of Milton H. Erickson, Vols. I-IV,* Irvington Publishers Inc., New York, New York, 1980.

Freud, S. & Breuer, J.; *Studies in Hysteria, Britannica GREAT BOOKS, Volume 54*, Encyclopedia Britannica Inc., Chicago Ill., 1979.

Gandhi, M., *Hind Swaraj or Indian Home Rule,* Navajivan Publishing House, Gujarat, India, 1938.

Gilbert, G. M., *Nuremberg Diary,* Da Capo Press, Boston, MA, 1995.

Gilligan, S., *The Courage to Love: Principles and practices of Self Relations Psychotherapy,* Norton Professional Books, New York: 1997.

Gordon, D., *Phoenix*, Meta Publications, Cupertino, California, 1982.

Haley, J.; *Uncommon Therapy; The Psychiatric Techniques of Milton H. Erickson M.D.,* W. W. Norton & Co., Inc., New York, NY, 1973.

Hitler, A., *Mein Kampf,* translated by Ralph Manheim, Houghton Mifflin, Boston, MA, 1943.

Hume, D., *A Treatise of Human Nature,* John Noon, London, 1739.

Jaynes, J., *The Origin of Consciousness in the Breakdown of the Bicameral Mind*, Houghton Mifflin Company, Boston, MA, 1976.

Lamsa, G., *The Holy Bible: From the Ancient Eastern Manuscripts,* Harper & Row, San Francisco, CA, 1981.

Lincoln, A., *Political Writings and Speeches,* Cambridge University Press, Cambridge, MA, 2012.

O'Hanlon, W., *An Uncommon Casebook: The Complete Clinical Work of Milton H. Erickson*, Smashwords, Broken Arrow, OK, 2011.

Plato, *The Republic,* Penguin Classics, London, UK, 2007.

Polya, G., *Patterns of Plausible Inference,* Princeton University Press, Princeton, NJ, 1954.

Rosen, S., *My Voice Will Go With You: The Teaching Tales of Milton H. Erickson*, MD., W. W. Norton, New York, 1993.

Schwartz, J. & McGuinness, M., *Einstein For Beginners*, Pantheon Books, New York, 1983.

Shakespeare, W., *The Complete Works of Shakespeare, Fifth Edition*, Bevington, D., ed.; Longman, London, 2003.

Winfrey, O. *The Path Made Clear: Discovering Your Life's Direction and Purpose,* Flatiron Books, New York, 2019.

Young, R., *Young's Analytical Concordance to the Bible,* W.B. Eerdmans Publishing Company, Grand Rapids, MI, 1974.

Zeig, J.K. (ed.), *A Teaching Seminar with Milton H. Erickson, M.D.,* Brunner/Mazel, New York, 1980.

About the Author

 **Robert B. Dilts** has been a developer, author, trainer and consultant in the field of Neuro-Linguistic Programming (NLP)—a model of human behavior, learning and communication—since its creation in 1975. Robert is also co-developer (with his brother John Dilts) of Success Factor Modeling and (with Stephen Gilligan) of the process of Generative Change. A long time student and colleague of both Grinder and Bandler, Mr. Dilts also studied personally with Milton H. Erickson, M.D. and Gregory Bateson.

In addition to spearheading the applications of NLP to education, creativity, health, and leadership, his personal contributions to the field of NLP include much of the seminal work on the NLP techniques of Strategies and Belief Systems, and the development of what has become known as Systemic NLP. Some of his techniques and models include: Reimprinting, the Disney Imagineering Strategy, Integration of Conflicting Beliefs, Sleight of Mouth Patterns, The Spelling Strategy, The Allergy Technique, Neuro-Logical Levels, The Belief Change Cycle, The SFM Circle of Success and the Six Steps of Generative Coaching (with Stephen Gilligan).

Robert has authored or co-authored more than thirty books and fifty articles on a variety of topics relating to personal and professional development including *From Coach to Awakener, NLP II: The Next Generation*, *Sleight of Mouth* and, *Generative Coaching* and *The Hero's Journey: A Voyage of Self Discovery* (with Dr. Stephen Gilligan). Robert's recent book series on Success Factor Modeling identifies key characteristics and capabilities shared by successful entrepreneurs, teams and ventures. His recent book *The Power of Mindset Change* (with Mickey Feher) presents a powerful methodology for assessing and shaping key aspects of mindset to achieve greater performance and satisfaction.

For the past forty-five years, Robert has conducted trainings and workshops around the world for a range of organizations, institutes and government bodies. Past clients and sponsors include Apple Inc., Microsoft, Hewlett-Packard, IBM, Société Générale, The World Bank, Fiat, Alitalia, Telecom Italia, Lucasfilms Ltd., Ernst & Young, AT Kearney, EDHEC Business School and the State Railway of Italy.

A co-founder of Dilts Strategy Group, Robert is also co-founder of NLP University International, the Institute for Advanced Studies of Health (IASH) and the International Association for Generative Change (IAGC). Robert was also founder and CEO of Behavioral Engineering, a company that developed computer software and hardware applications emphasizing behavioral change. Robert has a degree in Behavioral Technology from the University of California at Santa Cruz.

Antonio Meza is an architect of vision, supporting entrepreneurs and leaders around the world to communicate complex ideas in a simple and fun way through illustrations, cartoons, or through structuring presentations, books, or websites.

A native of Pachuca, Mexico, Antonio is a Master Practitioner and a Trainer of Neuro-Linguistic Programming (NLP). He has a degree in Communication Sciences from Fundación Universidad de las Américas Puebla, a Masters degree in Film Studies from Université de Paris 3 –Sorbonne Nouvelle, a diploma in Cinema Scriptwriting from the General Society of Writers in Mexico (SOGEM), and a diploma in Documentary Films from France's École Nationale des Métiers de l'Image et du Son (La Fémis). He is also certified in the three levels of the SFM system.

He worked in Mexico as a freelance filmmaker and participated in animated cartoons startups before moving to France where he works as a consultant, coach, and trainer, specializing in storytelling, creative thinking and collective intelligence.

Antonio is also an experienced public speaker member of Toastmasters International. In 2015 he was awarded best speaker at the International Speech Contest of District 59, covering South-West Europe, and reached the semifinals at international level.

He has illustrated 16 books including the 3 volumes of the *Success Factor Modeling* series with Robert Dilts, and the *Generative Coaching* book series with Robert Dilts and Stephen Gilligan.

He also uses his skills as a cartoonist and trainer to collaborate in seminars, conferences and brainstorming sessions as a graphic facilitator, and to produce animated videos to explain complex information in a clear and fun way.

Antonio lives in Paris with his wife Susanne, his daughter Luz Carmen and his cats Ronja and Atreju.

For more visit:

www.antoons.net

www.linkedin.com/in/antoniomeza/

Contact Antonio: hola@antoons.net

www.ingramcontent.com/pod-product-compliance
Lightning Source LLC
Chambersburg PA
CBHW070126080526
44586CB00015B/1568